Theurgy
and the
Soul

For my parents, Norman J. Shaw and Rita G. Shaw

GREGORY SHAW

Theurgy and the Soul

The Neoplatonism of Iamblichus

SECOND EDITION

Foreword   *John Milbank*
& Aaron Riches

ANGELICO PRESS
SOPHIA PERENNIS

Second Edition, Angelico Press/Sophia Perennis, 2014
© Gregory Shaw 2014
Foreword © John Milbank & Aaron Riches, 2014
Revised edition of the work originally
published by The Pennsylvania State University Press 1995

For information, address:
Angelico Press
4709 Briar Knoll Dr.
Kettering, OH 45429
angelicopress.com

Ppr. 978-1-62138-063-4
Cloth 978-1-62138-072-6

Cover Image: Figure of Iamblichus
from the oldest manuscript *of De Mysteriis Liber;*
and a modified detail of folio 4r from the
Nuremberg Chronicles, ca. 1493.
Cover Design: Michael Schrauzer

CONTENTS

III
THE LITURGY OF THE COSMOS

IV
TOWARD A UNIVERSAL PLATONISM

Acknowledgments
for the First Edition

This book began as a doctoral dissertation under the direction of Birger Pearson of the University of California, Santa Barbara. I am grateful for his unfailing support of my work and the high standards of his scholarship. I owe thanks to other professors at the University of California, Santa Barbara. Richard Hecht introduced me to Iamblichus, asked the right questions, and infected me with his passion for the religions of Late Antiquity. Hal Drake was always generous with his time, and his pointed suggestions, encouragement, and humor were a great help. Ruth Majercik taught me a great deal about theurgy and led me, by example, into the study of later Platonism.

I owe many thanks to Peter Brown of Princeton University, whose interest in this manuscript has been a source of encouragement from the beginning. He read several versions of the work and offered strategies that brought clarity and coherence to the entire manuscript. This publication is due primarily to his generous advice. Equal thanks are owed to John Dillon of Trinity College, Dublin, who also read several versions of the manuscript; he tightened my argument and corrected numerous errors, including my translations of Iamblichus's Greek. Jay Bregman of the University of Maine, Orono, initially urged me to publish the manuscript and later read the final version, making several helpful suggestions. The time these scholars have given to this work will always be appreciated.

I am also grateful to two French scholars of Neoplatonism, H. D. Saffrey and the late Jean Trouillard, who invited me into their homes to share their ideas, books, and conversation in the winter of 1982–83. Trouillard's publications had previously allowed me to glimpse the beauty of Platonic theurgy, and the intelligence and kindness he conveyed personally confirmed for me the depth and wisdom of the tradition that he embodied. My thanks also to Erma

i

Pounds of Tempe, Arizona, and Robert Johnson of Encinitas, California, who earlier helped me recognize such depth.

Two Faculty Summer Grants from Stonehill College aided my research and provided time for revisions of the manuscript, which Thomas Hallinan graciously photocopied on several occasions. The constant support of my colleagues in the Department of Religious Studies at Stonehill has also been a great help. The late Helen Nesbitt was kind enough to give the first four chapters of the manuscript hours of careful reading, which produced clearer and more economic prose. Working with the editorial staff of Penn State Press has been a pleasure. Peter Potter has always been prompt, clear, and professional, and he made several suggestions that improved the manuscript. Betty Waterhouse did a meticulous job of copyediting, correcting numerous bibliographical errors, tightening my prose, and asking for needed clarifications. My thanks also to Cherene Holland and others at Penn State Press who have helped bring the manuscript to publication. An earlier version of this manuscript has the unique distinction of having been "bottled" by Cameron Shaw, an artist, whose *Untitled Table with Thesis on Theurgy* has been displayed in galleries in New York, Boston, and Los Angeles.

Finally, I thank my wife, Lisa, for her lighthearted patience and understanding through all phases of bringing this book to publication. She has read and listened to all the revisions and has made many suggestions to improve my writing, but, more importantly, she allows me to see a world detached from my academic interests. My thanks as well to Ariel and Adrian, who reminded me to play.

Abbreviations

ANRW	*Aufstieg und Niedergang der Römischen Welt*
CAG	*Commentaria in Aristotelem Graeca*
CH	*Corpus Hermeticum*
CMAG	*Catalogue des Manuscrits Alchimiques Grecs*
CO	*Chaldean Oracles*
De Abst.	*De Abstinentia* (Porphyry)
DA	*In De Anima* (Simplicius [?])
DCMS	*De Communi Mathematica Scientia Liber* (Iamblichus)
DM	*De Mysteriis* (Iamblichus)
Dub. et Sol.	*Dubitationes et Solutiones de Primis Principiis in Platonis Parmenidem* (Damascius)
Enn.	*Enneads* (Plotinus)
Entretiens	*Entretiens sur l'Antiquité Classique*, vol. 21: *De Jamblique à Proclus*
ET	*Proclus: The Elements of Theology* (Dodds)
GA	*De Generatione Animalium*
In Nic.	*In Nicomachi Arithmetica Introductionem* (Iamblichus)
In Remp.	*In Platonis Rempublicam Commentaria* (Proclus)
In Tim.	*In Platonis Timaeum Commentari* (Proclus)
La Rev.	*La Révélation d'Hermès Trismégiste*, 4 vols. (A.-J. Festugière)
NHC	*Nag Hammadi Codices*
Stob.	*Stobaeus: Anthologium*, 4 vols. (ed. C. Wachsmuth and O. Hense)
TA	*Theologoumena Arithmeticae* (Iamblichus [?])
Th. Pl.	*Proclus: Theologie Platonicienne*, 5 vols. (ed. H. D. Saffrey and L. G. Westerink)
VP	*De Vita Pythagorica Liber* (Iamblichus)

Foreword

Neoplatonic Theurgy
and Christian Incarnation

European culture and the Christian religion from which it is inseparable are constituted in, and founded upon, a double inheritance: the Law of the Old Covenant and the wisdom of Greek thought. In modernity this double inheritance has tended to be tidily parsed, as if the former concerned the substance of cultic practice and salvation, concrete and "material," while the latter concerned the pure disembodied act of reason and of philosophical wisdom. And so the Hebrew basis of Christian culture and religion is thought of as meaty and incarnational, while the Hellenistic contribution is colored by a superficial (and false) sense that Hellenism, and especially Platonic thought, rests on an unequivocal body-soul, matter-spirit dualism.

This division is highly distortive. The sapiential literature of the Hebrew Bible itself proves that no such tidy division exists, since herein the Scriptures themselves already bears traces of the Hellenistic culture and thought that would later permeate Christianity. And if on the one hand we are seeing that Christianity inherited a certain "Hellenism" already within its Scriptures, on the other hand we are discovering more and more that, inasmuch as the philosophy of the Greeks was itself fully "religious"—concerned above all not with "philosophizing" in a modern sense, but rather with the cultivation of spiritual practices that would realize the communion of the soul with the gods through concrete practices—the liturgical practice of Christianity, too, inherits significantly from the cultic practices of Greek philosophy. In this regard the recovery of the thought and influence of the Syrian Neoplatonist Iamblichus (c. 245–c. 325) may prove, in time, to stand at the very heart of a new self-understanding of Western culture and religion—one less dominated by the old mischaracterization and now freshly aware of the integrity of the double inheritance; and in particular how Christian liturgy, the sacramental practice of the Church and the metaphysics of the Incarnation owe a perhaps significant debt to the pagan Platonic tradition. The seminal work of Gregory Shaw stands at the crossroads of this new realization.

Theurgy and the Soul is a profound introduction and account of Iamblichian theurgy, "a 'work of the gods' capable of transforming man to a divine status" (5). Theurgy, as Shaw shows us, originated with the second-century Platonists, who used the term to explain the divinizing power of the rites of the Chaldean Oracles, some of which were thought to have been transmitted by the soul of Plato himself. In the performance of these rites, Iamblichus understood the goal of philosophy to be accomplished, namely, union with the divine. And thus, as Shaw outlines, Iamblichus sets out the definitive Platonic apology and rationale for theurgy, which after him became integral to the Neoplatonic tradition from the pagan Proclus to the Christian Denys the pseudo-Areopagite. These theurgic rites, as far as we can tell, approximate something of the "sacramental," in that "matter" (*hyle*) is used within a cultic rite to effect divine union. As Iamblichus puts it in *De Mysteriis*, in a passage outlined by Shaw,

> Since it was necessary that earthly things not be deprived of participation in the divine, the earth received a certain divine portion capable of receiving the Gods. The theurgic art, therefore, recognizing this principle in general, and having discovered the proper receptacles, in particular, as being appropriate to each one of the Gods, often brings together stones, herbs, animals, aromatics, and other sacred, perfect, and deiform objects of a similar kind. Then, from all these it produces a perfect and pure receptacle. (*DM* 233, 7–16)

Through the exercise of the rite, *hyle*—the technical term for "matter" coined by Aristotle—is made a receptacle of divine energy. What may perhaps startle the modern reader is the fact that all of this was proposed and executed by Iamblichus as a retrieval of the cosmic vision of Plato's *Timaeus*, which Iamblichus understood as threatened by the dualistic and quasi-gnostic impulses of Plotinian Neoplatonism.

With acumen and mystical love of his theme, Shaw expounds the contours of the theurgic vision and how, through cultic rites, Iamblichian Neoplatonism realized that "the highest good was not realized by escaping from materiality but by embracing matter and multiplicity in a demiurgic way" (26). In this way, he illustrates how Iamblichus realized an integral relation between rituals of cultic worship and the intellectual discipline of philosophical *paideia*. Key in this regard is the function of Plato's doctrine of *anamnesis*, which here works a process of the soul's reawakening though contact with the sensible world, coupled with a ritualistic extension of the cosmology of the *Timaeus*. All of this, outlined in detail by Shaw, decisively shatters the old modern idea of "Platonic philosophy" as disembodied and merely mental, a contemplating soul essentially divestible from religious, spiritual, and cultic practices. For Iamblichus, as Shaw masterfully shows, philosophy finds its apex not in a disembodied "reason" but in a cultic participation in the divine works, known as theurgy. Indeed for Iamblichus, the power of theurgic rites, and not the philosophical theory, became the key to realize a philosophical vocation of union with the divine. In this regard, Iamblichus's non-dualistic sense of the interrelation of the material and the divine, along with his emphasis of rite and "liturgy," found a remarkable common cause with orthodox Christianity (as opposed to its Manichean and Gnostic variants).

As Shaw shows, for Iamblichus—in contradistinction to the dualistic and gnostic deprecation of matter which marred so much non-Christian thought of the era—incarnate being is precisely the vehicle of salvation through theurgy, rooted in a very careful and precise understanding of embodiment as depicted in the *Timaeus* of Plato, where the individual soul is called to imitate the activity of the Demiurge. This imitation lies at the heart of the rites of theurgy. All of this is based on Iamblichus's modification of Plotinus, for whom the individual soul is not fully descended and so in no need of divinizing ascent to the realm of the gods. For Iamblichus, on the contrary, the soul is fully descended, fully incarnate, and so has no unmediated access to the divine. There is no escape from mediation, from the "sacramental," and from images; indeed it is only *via* these material facts that the soul receives (as by a quasi-"Grace") the theurgy of the gods, the divine action that transforms the soul into godlikeness. All of this is remarkably akin to the sacramental and liturgical practice of Christianity, which finally understands the ascent of the human soul to God, not so much as a mere ascent of the soul, but rather as a paradoxical ascent of the soul rooted in the Incarnate descent of God from heaven relived and participated in Christian liturgy, which insofar as it is a "work-of-the-people" is finally and most truly a grace imbued by the power and action of the Holy Spirit.

The cultic presupposition of Iamblichian Neoplatonism is based on a radical and tensively paradoxical doctrine of participation. The doctrine was received by his chief intellectual heir, Proclus (412–485) who, in the form of the *Liber de Causis*, exercised an unparalleled influence on the metaphysical vision of the mediaeval schoolmen, and crucially on Thomas Aquinas. But undoubtedly the strongest current of Iamblichian Neoplatonism entered already through the mysterious sixth-century Syrian-Christian author of the *Corpus Dionysiacum*, who in order to express the Christian view of the cosmos—the *ratio* of the monastic life and the emoting of the Christian liturgy—drew profoundly on Proclus. All three presume and expound Platonic *methexis* as a radical "sharing out" of the divine life in which, paradoxically, divine simplicity and divine self-partition converge and invert, entailing a mysterious and ontological kenosis at the heart of being. Finally this paradox can only be understood through the logic of gift: that being is perfected in giving, such that to give oneself away is to receive oneself most perfectly.

This suggests that there is an aspect of inversion and of super-transcendence in excess of every discrete hierarchy of being. And this forms, as it were, the basis of the logic of the theurgic re-conception of the One and, in a different way, in the Christian recapitulation of God realized in Incarnation and in the proclamation of the Crucified Lord. In the case of Iamblichus and Proclus it is clear that when they speak of the absolute One as "imparticipable," this means that the One cannot be parceled out—not only on account of its inaccessibility but also on account of its unequalizably intimate

relation to everything that proceeds from it.[1] The point is that the "participated" for these thinkers refers to elements within a hierarchy that have something that is already always specific to share, and that they can only impart in diminishing degrees. But at the very summit of the hierarchy stands something that does so by virtue of the fact that it *exceeds* all hierarchy. What is absolute and first is really only so in terms of "aristocratic height" because it is greatest in terms of "democratic scope," as the very first proposition of Proclus's *Elements of Theology* makes clear.[2] The One is supremely intimate with everything because nothing exists except by virtue of some sort of unity. Indeed, after the energy of emanation has run out, at the bottom of the material scale the power of unity still remains, which is why for Proclus matter retains in the very pit of being a certain simplicity characteristic of its trans-existential summit.[3] All of this is brought into clearest relief in terms of intellect.

For from a strictly hierarchical point of view, intellect is more than life, which is in turn more than being—but the greater reach of being and then life in terms of scope is taken by Proclus to reverse the normal hierarchical succession. In this way the "non-participability" of the One is in fact something like a *hyberbolic* degree of self-sharing, such that unity gives everything into being, yet without dividing itself. Somehow it gives itself absolutely and without stint, yet because it really does give, it is not identical with its diversity of gifts, which can only be gifts because they remain other than the giver. Hence each reality is only real because it has fully received unity, yet its unity is after all but particular and incomplete: as a particular limited mode of coherence it only "shares" in the One. It must be for this reason that Proclus with seeming inconsistency does after all speak of "participation in the One," even though he often deems the One to be imparticipable.[4]

The same paradox is revealed in both Iamblichus and Proclus at every level of the scale of being before that of matter—unity, intel-

---

1. Proclus, *Elements of Theology*, 53, 57.
2. Ibid., 1, and cf. 21.
3. Ibid., 59.
4. Ibid., 3, 5, 21.

lectuality, psychic existence—which always consists within itself in a triad of remaining, outgoing, and reversion. This triad can also be constituted as imparticipable, participated, and participating. However, it is clear that the "imparticipable" element at the top of the triad itself shares in the next level above it and transmits this upper level economically within its own level via the outgoing to the lower elements within its own triadic series, which "rebound" upwards. More evidently than Plotinus, the theurgic Neoplatonists assume that such procession involves also participation, and therefore one must conclude that by "imparticipable" they mean that which cannot be communicated within the very act of communication as the very condition for the possibility of communication.[5] Moreover, the fact that "imparticipability" recurs at every lower level of the ontological series (or hierarchy) shows that this paradox can be inverted: what is communicated down the series is supremely that which cannot be communicated, since the "imparticipable" element always takes the lead at each stage. It is perhaps for this reason that Proclus says that the descending scale of internally triadic levels can also be considered (beginning at any point upon this scale) as *two different series* of "complete" imparticipables and "dependent" participations.[6] In strict parallel, what descends is the complete and so *indeclinable*, as it were, *alongside* the declinable.

This paradoxical model of *methexis*, characteristic of theurgic Neoplatonism, can be described as "participation all the way up"— or "radical participation," since it does not allow that there is any literal "reserve" in excess of communication, precisely because it is this very reserve that is "impossibly" communicated. This model of participation, of metaphysical vision, was adopted and Christianized because, finally, it expressed metaphysically the most basic truth of Christianity: "Whoever finds his life will lose it, and whoever loses

5. On the divergent inheritances of Proclus and Plotinus in Christian theology, cf. John Milbank, *Beyond Secular Order* (Oxford: Wiley-Blackwell, 2014), 208–11. A double genealogy is here intimate: first lineage deriving from Plotinus through Avicenna, then to Scotus, Descartes and finally Kant; while another derives from Proclus to Thomas Aquinas, a minority theurgic tradition, which is taken up by Nicholas Cusa and later Vico.

6. Proclus, *Elements of Theology*, 64.

his life for my sake will find it" (Matt. 10:38); "unless a grain of wheat falls into the earth and dies, it remains alone; but if it dies, it bears much fruit" (John 12:24); "This is my body, which is given for you" (Luke 22:19). The law of existence, from a Christian point of view, is based in the dynamic of radical love, of gift of being that is the only perfection of being. Or as the Second Vatican Council put it, "man ... cannot fully find himself except through a sincere gift of himself."[7]

The basic convertibility of Christianity and the Iamblichian paradox of participation is twofold. First, Christianity as a monotheism insisted on the absolute simplicity of God: a simplicity incompatible with different "aspects" or "ontological regions" within the Godhead. Secondly, in terms of the doctrine that "God is Love," especially as spelled out in Trinitarian terms, Christianity saw "sharing" not only as an attribute of God's very essence (even if it also held for monotheistic reasons that this essence is radically incommunicable) but that this is the condition of the possibility of both *creatio ex nihilo* and of Incarnation. Such an affirmation was a crucial aspect of the Christian view that God was eminently "personal" in nature. Christianity was therefore committed to both gift and paradox as fundamental dimensions of its theology. To *paradoxa*—an incomprehensibly original excess of glory, which is to say also, an incomprehensibly original excess of gift.[8]

If the current of Iamblichian participation flows into Christianity through the *Liber de Causis* and the *Corpus Dionysiacum*, the extremity of paradox the Iamblichian doctrine represents finds already equivalences prior to composition of the *Corpus* and thus long before the mediaeval reception of the *Liber*. In Augustine already, in whom we find a firm opposition to what he saw as the magical, demon-invoking character of pagan theurgics, there is nevertheless a certain equivalent of the theurgic moment in the

---

7. *Gaudium et spes*, 24.
8. This is true conceptually and probably also etymologically. Whatever may be claimed by some, nothing really forbids us from supposing that all Indo-European "do" and "da" roots are originally concerned at once with gift and outgoing manifestation or intentional action—as in "I do."

Confessiones.[9] It is the singing of a psalm that "shows" (in a Wittgensteinian sense) the answer to the conundrum of time. For Augustine quite clearly, the liturgical action is only possible because God himself has descended into time at the Incarnation in order to counteract its fallen tendency to "dispersal"; and this stipulation later becomes *the* key difference between the Iamblichian and Dionysian "theurgies."[10] Nevertheless the resonance here is remarkable. Finally, the entire book concludes with a joining of the self with the cosmos to sing a cosmic hymn of praise.

It has often been argued that Augustine's later critique of both empire and pagan magic in the *City of God* implies a complete rejection of this earlier Pythagorean approach to the political,[11] and moreover that this underpins a *tout court* rejection of every quasi "theurgic" integration of *theoria* and politics that would regard political life on earth as training for the divine life, or any earthly city as a reflection of an archetypal heavenly one. The truth is more complex. And it is a fact, moreover, that Augustine, drawing out Biblical themes, makes participation in "Jerusalem, our mother who is above" an important theme of his oeuvre up until the end. The "City of God," for Augustine, is an eternal and eschatological as well as temporary reality. In the latter respect it is *not* the mere aggregate of the truly saved, but a literal earthly polity that combines elevated theory and popular practice as crucially conjoined elements for the way of ascent.[12]

Most importantly of all, one can construe Augustine's reworked account of deification in terms of a greater stress upon free divine

9. It is not impossible that Augustine knew something of Iamblichus's works: see Dominic J. O'Meara, *Platonopolis: Platonic Political Philosophy in Late Antiquity* (Oxford: OUP, 2003), 151. And see also Jason Parnell's important *The Theurgic Turn in Christian Thought: Iamblichus, Origen, Augustine and the Eucharist* (Ann Arbor MI: ProQuest, 2010), which shows that besides Augustine, Origen too evidences equivalents to theurgy.

10. Cf. Andrew Louth, "Pagan Theurgy and Christian Sacramentalism," *Journal of Theological Studies* 37 (1986), 432–38.

11. Augustine, *De Ordine* II, xiv.39-xvi.44; noted by O'Meara in *Platonopolis*, 152–53.

12. See John Milbank, *Theology and Social Theory: Beyond Secular Reason* (Oxford: Blackwell, 2006), 382–442.

descending grace as parallel to the greater emphasis upon divine descent within later Neoplatonism. This parallel seems counter-intuitive only in the light of a narrow understanding of divine pre-destination in Augustine's final anti-Pelagian writings—an excess that the Western Church mostly retreated from. But so long as divine grace remains linked to synergy of divine and human will and to sacramental mediation (as it is in the bulk of Augustine's writings), one can see how the critique of "Pelagian ascent" in the case of inner-Christian debates is truly comparable to the critique of "Plotinian ascent" in the case of Neoplatonic discussions. This is perhaps most clearly stated by Augustine in the *Psalmos vox totius Christi* theme; here Christ with us, as the incarnate body of God, alone performs the true and atoning liturgy in such a way that this action is wholly complete in him alone and yet even so completed by us.[13]

The basic metaphysical convertibility between Christianity and theurgic Neoplatonism lies in the way the paradox of participation entails for both a non-contrastive and non-dualist construal of the relation of divinity and even *hyle*, the lowest form of creation: matter and images can therefore truly communicate the transcendent, the world is therefore truly "sacramental." For Christianity, of course, the basis of this is the Incarnation through which "matter ... becomes by its participation in Christ's mystery the medium through which salvation is accomplished."[14]

In the eighth century, facing contrastive and dualist iconoclasm of both the growing fact of Islam and iconoclast Christians within the Church, John of Damascus was moved to defend the Christian veneration of the "icon" (which included cloth, metal, ivory, wood, manuscript illustrations, frescoes, mosaics and statues) in terms highly reminiscent of Iamblichus:

> I do not venerate matter (*hyle*), I venerate the fashioner of matter, who became matter for my sake and accepted to dwell in matter and through matter worked my salvation, and I will not cease

13. See Augustine, *Enarr in Psalmos*, 60: 1–3, 61:4, 85: 4–5.
14. Christoph Schönborn OP, *God's Human Face: The Christ-Icon*, trans. Lothar Krauth (San Francisco: Ignatius Press, 1994), 196.

from reverencing matter, through which my salvation was worked.... [For] if the body of God has become God unchangeably through the hypostatic union, what gives anointing remains, and what was by nature flesh animated with a rational and intellectual soul is formed, it is not uncreated. Therefore I reverence the rest of matter and hold in respect that through which my salvation came, because it is filled with divine energy and grace.[15]

For John matter has been transformed by the Incarnation, the descent of the divine into the lowest order of creation, in order to draw the soul of the lost human being back to God. A concrete trace of Iamblichus in Christian theology lies, perhaps, most strongly here, in this realization of John: matter is pregnant with power to communicate what is most radically beyond matter.

In this defense of the icon it is possible that John relied directly on Iamblichus, who had also defended the intrinsic worthiness of matter (*hyle*), which for him even in its cosmological "lowliness" is nevertheless a work and expression of the paternal source.[16] And this means that matter is capable, through images and image-making, of becoming a true icon of the divine.[17] In John as in Iamblichus, the conviction of matter's worthiness to image the divine origin means that matter itself is receptive of the divine,[18] and can therefore be a vehicle of communication of divine energy.[19] Through rites and prayers, the divine power of matter to be receptive to the divine

15. John of Damascus, *De imaginibus, Oratio* I.16 (PG 94.1245 A–B).

16. Cf. Iamblichus, *De Mysteriis*, VIII.3. That the Damascene read Iamblichus seems likely. He was brought up outside the boundaries of the Byzantine Empire in Damascus, where his father held the high hereditary public office of chief financial officer for the caliph of Syria. The civil status of John's family and the command of Greek verse and prose he evidences in his own oeuvre leads Andrew Louth to conclude that John clearly "benefited from a classical education (the *enkyklios paideia*)" (Louth, *St. John of Damascene*, 6, cf. 19). The *Enkyklios Paideia* of the Middle Eastern seventh century context was one in which Hellenistic learning flourished. John is indeed well versed in Plato and Aristotle, and his writing evidences familiarity with Neoplatonic themes. All this seems to support the suggestion that he knew Iamblichus; that he deliberately and echoed Iamblichus would, however, require more scholarly substantiation than we are providing.

17. Cf. Iamblichus, *De Mysteriis*, III.28.

18. Ibid., V.23.

19. Ibid., V.12.

energy is unlocked, making it thereby a vehicle of the soul's receptivity to the divine energy.[20] In this way the logic of Neoplatonic theurgy involves a kenosis of mind, a recollection that plunges downwards into matter, into the simplicity and non-reflexivity of material being. In a sense, then, better than abstract thought, material images reflect the divine simplicity and non-reflexivity of the original One at a highest pitch. In any event, for John the most profound theurgical *anamnesis* involves recapturing what Iamblichus calls the "pure and divine form of matter,"[21] what Denys calls, "Using matter, one may be lifted up to the immaterial archetypes."[22] But whereas for Iamblichus the pure divine form is beyond form and matter, for the Damascene and the Areopagite the pure divine form is Jesus Christ.[23]

If the structural parallels between Christianity and theurgic Neoplatonism extended beyond the bounds of the direct influence of the latter upon the former, this is because, at their heart, they discern the common paradox that is the heart of being, whom Christians profess in Jesus Christ, the Paradox Incarnate. All the specific impulses within Christianity supporting the double and co-belonging ideas of "descent all the way down" and "participation all the way up" are clearly Biblical, yet one should not atavistically seek to deny the extent to which pagan attention to its own oracles could lead it to go in a convergent direction. In the case of Iamblichus one sees above all the idea (highly consonant with Christianity) that

20. See Iamblichus, *De Mysteriis*, III.30 and V.15. And see John of Damascus, *De imaginibus, Oratio* I.36 (PG 94.1264A–D). Cf. Proclus, *The Elements of Theology*, 57.

21. Iamblichus, *De Mysteriis*, V.23.

22. Denys the Areopagite, *Coelesti hierarchia*, 2 (PG 3.144C). Cf. Andrew Louth, "St Denys the Areopagite and the Iconoclast Controversy" in Ysabel de Andia (ed.), *Denys l'aréopagite et sa postérité en orient et en occident: Actes de colloque international, Paris, 21–24 septembre 1994* (Paris: Institut d'Études Augustiniennes, 1997), 329–40.

23. Andrew Louth has shown that Denys's notion of theurgy is essentially a Christocentric theology of Incarnation, see Louth, "Pagan Theurgy and Christian Sacramentalism in Denys the Areopagite," *The Journal of Theological Studies* 37 (1986), 432–38. Further, on the importance of the Dionysian absorption of Neoplatonic theurgy, see Ysabel de Andia, *Henosis L'Union à Dieu chez Denys l'Aréopagite* (Leiden: Brill, 1996).

while prayer is not about changing the minds of the gods, neither is it mere self-therapy. Instead it is the theoretical and practical endeavor to arrive at a kind of "attunement" with the divine that will truly allow the divine influence to flow into reality. No doubt our "attuning" is also ultimately the work of the gods, but that issue of causality lies at another ontological level. On the finite level there is a genuine synergy. When it comes to the issue of how far the divine side of causal influence belongs to the divine essence itself, it is clear that increasingly Iamblichus ascribes to the notion of a single "divine world" comprised of the One, the Good, gods, daemons and heroes, over against the non-divine world.[24]

The drive towards "monotheism" in Iamblichus's writings lies here and *not* in a tendency to posit a "one beyond the one" as a counter-movement to the general efflorescence of divine beings that was part of his deliberate defense of pagan polytheism. Indeed, as with Iamblichus's later successor Damascius of Athens, the positing of ever-yet greater absolutes was not an attempt to define an area absolutely reserved from all communication, but rather an attempt to indicate an "Ineffable" that could comprise both the one and the many, both absolute reserve and generous outflowing.[25] Certainly in one respect this all-encompassing "One" is thereby all the more replete and withheld, yet only to the degree that no act of self-donation lies outside its sway. No doubt the arising *aporiae* here (how to avoid both pantheism and acosmism) anticipates, on one level, the Trinitarian elaboration of classical Christian orthodoxy, which is a resolution through a heightened intensity of paradox, fully articulating the idea that God is in himself an ecstasy beyond himself, which includes an ecstatic reach towards the "external" beyond of Creation. All the same, pagan theurgic philosophy increasingly approached the question of participation in terms of paradox and mediation, which accomplished a remarkable synthesis of common religious piety open to all, and not merely the philosophically ini-

24. See Iamblichus, *On the Mysteries*, I. 9–15.
25. See Damascius, *De Principiis*, R. 76–77, 83; John Milbank, "The Mystery of Reason," 68–117, esp. for Damascius see 85–91. It is relevant to the argument of this essay that Damascius sees "participation" as more ineffable than "procession."

tiate. Achieving this synthesis, as Shaw shows to brilliant effect in *Theurgy and the Soul,* was the prestige of Iamblichus. That theurgic Neoplatonism aimed to do nothing other than return to the non-dualist essence of authentic Platonism through cultic ritual suggests that one current of Platonic thought was always running rather near to the ritual *anamnesis* at the heart the Christian Mass. And herein may lie the most lasting contribution of the Iamblichian theurgical vision: "the Church, with its ecclesiastical embodiment of the divine hierarchy, its initiations, and its belief in salvation through sacramental acts, may have fulfilled the theurgical program of Iamblichus in a manner that was never concretely realized by Platonists" (271).

JOHN MILBANK and AARON RICHES

Preface

To the Second Edition[*]

I wish to thank John Riess of Angelico Press for making possible the republication of *Theurgy and the Soul*. John initially suggested that I consider republishing my book two years ago, and after patiently sticking with the project, and with me, he has seen the process through. The present volume is an exact facsimile of the 1995 edition with the exception of a few typographical errors corrected from the original. Nothing else has been changed, which means that the scholarship on Iamblichus since 1995 has not been integrated into this republished text. Most significantly, my references to Iamblichus's work on theurgy use Édouard des Places' *Jamblique: Les mystères d'Égypte* (1966)—the standard academic text in 1995—rather than the fine English translation and text, *Iamblichus: On the Mysteries* by Emma C. Clarke, John M. Dillon, and Jackson P. Hershbell (2003) or the impressive text, translation, and annotation by Henri Dominique Saffrey and Alain-Philippe Segonds, *Jamblique: Réponse à Porphyre (De Mysteriis)* (2013). I also want to thank John Milbank and Aaron Riches who, when they learned of Angelico's plan to republish my book, generously offered to write a Foreword in which they draw connections between Iamblichus's theurgy and the theology of the Incarnation. Of their stimulating Foreword and the connections they make between the Christian sacramental vision and Iamblichean theurgy I have more to say. Firstly, however, I want to reflect briefly on this book after living with it for nearly twenty years.

In his profoundly Neoplatonic essay, "The Poet," Ralph Waldo

---

[*] I thank Peter Durigon for his fiery insight that helped me think through questions in the writing of this preface; I also thank Joel Feldmann for showing me how to let the questions go.

Emerson says the poet "speaks adequately . . . only when he speaks somewhat wildly."[1] The author of a poem touched by this wildness knows that what he speaks is past his understanding, and so too what he writes. When I initially completed *Theurgy and the Soul* I scarcely understood what I had written.[2] My engagement with Neoplatonic thinkers was like someone who has stumbled into a cave of gems. I found myself captivated by the depth and beauty of their ideas and then was even more fortunate to have been initiated into the intellectual subtlety of their vision by the late Neoplatonic scholar, Jean Trouillard. Through his writing, generosity, and hospitality, Trouillard revealed to me the living architecture of the world imagined by the Neoplatonists, and again, thanks to Trouillard, I was able to find my place in their world. *Theurgy and the Soul* is a work of imagination inspired by his lucidity and warmth. It has passed successfully for twenty years as an academic study of the theurgic phase of Neoplatonism, but it is more the product of my exploration of the beauty I stumbled upon in that cave of gems—the imagined world of the Neoplatonists.

As conceived by its principal architect, Iamblichus, theurgy may be defined as *divine activity communally shared*. It is not transcendent knowledge, something that might be grasped or experienced by an individual for, as Iamblichus put it, "it is impossible to participate individually in the universal orders, but only in communion with the divine choir of those lifted up together, united in mind."[3] As distinct from what often passes for Neoplatonism, even today, theurgic Neoplatonism did not culminate in an elevated state disengaged

1. Ralph Waldo Emerson, *Self-Reliance and Other Essays* (New York: Dover Publications, Inc., 1993), 75.

2. Fortunately, my dissertation director at UC Santa Barbara, Birger A. Pearson, understood very well what I had written. Without his guidance and support my thesis would not have been completed.

3. Quoted by Damascius in *Damascius Lectures on the Philebus*, tr. and text by L. G. Westerink, 3rd edition (Wiltshire: The Prometheus Trust, 2010), 106. Elsewhere Iamblichus says "the way of ascent to the One is not available to each thing by itself unless it first coordinates itself with the all, and so returns back to the common principle together *with all things*." See *Damascius' Problems and Solutions Concerning First Principles*, translated with introduction by Sara Ahbel-Rappe (Oxford: Oxford University Press, 2011), 154.

from the messiness of our day to day existence (the *escape* from mundane reality often associated with Plotinus). The inequalities and suffering of mortal life, all that we experience in our mundane lives, was *included* in the theurgic vision of Iamblichus. It is a radically non-dual vision that sees the physical world as radiantly transformed, not rejected or denied in favor of a "spiritual" reality. I was drawn to Iamblichus's vision and my feeling today about *Theurgy and the Soul* is largely unchanged. In the last twenty years, significant scholarship on theurgy has been published in the fields of Neoplatonism, Gnosticism, Magic, and Sacramental Theology. These studies have taken us much further into the subtleties of theurgic Neoplatonism and the cultural contexts in which it developed; I hope that my work on theurgy may have contributed to some of this impressive research.[4] Most notably the fine scholarship of Wayne Hankey has shown the crucial importance of Iamblichean theurgy in the history of Western philosophy and in the development of contemporary French Neoplatonists in particular. In the practical appropriation of theurgy I have been impressed by Sam Webster's measured integration of theurgic Neoplatonism with his Open Source community of the Golden Dawn, indicating an interface between what has long been an occult magical tradition and academic scholarship.[5] Perhaps most striking is the importance given to Iamblichean theurgy by John Milbank and other theologians of Radical Orthodoxy for whom the metaphysics and *praxis* of Iamblichus's sacramental vision play a critical role in transfiguring a world that has been drained of all depth, meaning, and divinity. The spiritual wasteland of our age, rightly lamented by Milbank, had been predicted by Iamblichus himself to Porphyry, the editor of Plotinus' *Enneads*. Iamblichus prophesied darkly that Porphyry's conviction

---

4. Scholars who have deepened my understanding of Neoplatonic theurgy since 1995 include Sara Rappe, Algis Uždavinys, Robbert Van Den Berg, John Dillon, John Finamore, Henri Saffrey, Sarah Johnston, Emma Clarke, Wayne Hankey, Edward Butler, Dominic O'Meara, Zeke Mazur, John Bussanich, Angela Voss, Radek Chlup, Tuomo Lankila, Ilinca Tanaseanu-Döbler, and Polymnia Athanassiadi. I am sure to have overlooked others since our discipline has grown tremendously.

5. http://osogd.org/.

that gods are too spiritual to be engaged in material rites is a belief that empties our world of divinity:

> This doctrine [Iamblichus says] spells the ruin of all holy ritual and theurgic communion between gods and men, since it places the presence of superior beings outside the earth. It amounts to saying that the divine is at a distance from the earth and cannot mingle with men, and that this lower region is a desert, without gods.[6]

In direct contrast to this bleak vision, Iamblichean theurgy aims to sustain the continuity of the gods with our physical world—this lower region—by recognizing their presence in material existence: in animals, plants, and even in stones, and further, that human beings have the capacity to engage this presence by ritually embodying the divine activity, the *theurgy*, through which it is revealed.

For a Platonist and Pythagorean the cosmos is theophany, and theurgy is the *praxis* through which human beings enter and embody the divine revelation that is the cosmos and natural world. Iamblichus thus avoided the temptation, so prevalent in his age, to escape from material reality and split the world in two. For Iamblichus *the highest is in the lowest*. The ineffable One beyond being is present in the densest material reality. The ineffable unities, the henadic gods, are not isolated in some exalted "place" but are revealed symbolically in *unifying activities* seen, felt, and encountered in our mundane world.[7] In Iamblichus's cosmology, the powers emanating from the One are received and orchestrated by a noetic activity personified by Plato as a Demiurge who weaves these divine powers into a living cosmos. Thus, the highest and most

6. *On the Mysteries*, 28.4–8, translated by Peter Brown, *The Making of Late Antiquity* (Cambridge: Harvard University Press, 1978), 101. I have modified his translation. The reference to *On the Mysteries* in the Preface is to *Iamblichus: On the Mysteries*, translated with introduction and notes by Emma C. Clarke, John M. Dillon, and Jackson P. Hershbell (Atlanta: Society of Biblical Literature, 2003); the numeration refers to the Parthey marginal numbers of Iamblichus's text.

7. Iamblichus says that daimons reveal the will of the gods "neither by disclosure nor by concealment," that is, not as one would reveal or conceal objective information. In Iamblichean theophany the divine *remains hidden in its disclosure*. Iamblichus believes this is the way of cosmogenesis and of the sacred traditions that embody it: an activity he describes as *symbolic* (*On the Mysteries*, 136.1–7).

hidden spiritual principles unfold and are revealed through our evanescent and material reality—including all the passions of the human condition—and theurgy is the art of learning how to receive this procession in a way that mimics—no, even more—that *incarnates* the demiurgy that continually creates and sustains our world. To ignore and disparage material reality would thus ignore its divinity and, inevitably, our own. It would make the world, as Iamblichus feared, "a desert, without gods." Yet we live in that desert and have lived in it for a very long time, so it is difficult for us to recover the non-dual vision of Iamblichean theurgy, difficult to rediscover life-giving water hidden in our desert.

It is here that I fully appreciate the work of John Milbank, Aaron Riches, and others in Radical Orthodoxy in their effort to recover the sacramental in human existence. With their vision of the Incarnation as center-piece to Christian theology, they seek to free us from the dark spell of a world ruled by a technologized rationality applied to merely material and physical existence. It is a kind of enchantment that one can only describe as grotesque and abysmal: the numbing weight of the world we live in. It is clear that we need a sophisticated response to this dark spell, and it will do us no good to embrace a pre-modern and idyllic vision. It requires integrating and redirecting the intellectual currents that have shaped our world. Most importantly, it requires that we recover a deep symbolic imagination that has the power to effect our transformation but—and this is critical—at the same time, re-coordinate our discursive powers in relation to this imagination. This is the monumental task that Milbank has heroically—*madly*—taken on his shoulders and I admire him for it.

The linchpin of Milbank's theology is the symbol, the living reality, of the Incarnation, for in the full descent of divinity into our world, the world becomes saturated with divine presence that allows it, henceforth, to be experienced as sacred. Much of the work of Radical Orthodoxy, it seems to me, is concerned, on the one hand, with examining the intellectual habits that prevent us from being able to experience this sacramental presence and, on the other, with attempting to redirect our thinking to the poetic sources that open us to the sacramental. In theurgic terms, they are performing an intellectual incantation to free us from our dark trance. In the imagination of Milbank and Riches, the Incarnation is far greater in scope than the singular event of the life of Jesus. Rather, the Incarnation initiates the valorization of all material reality as evident in their quotation of John of Damascus who, in light of the Incarnation, imagines that *all* matter has become "filled with divine energy and grace." It is here that Iamblichus's emphasis on the penetration of the One throughout all material existence,[8] provides precisely the metaphysical principle needed to support a more profound and expansive understanding of the Incarnation. Like the vision of Iamblichean theurgy—and the theology of John of Damascus—Milbank and Riches extend the boundaries of the Incarnation to include the entire material world. And in this sense they rightly see a "convergence" between Neoplatonic theurgy and Incarnational theology.

Yet, despite this convergence, Milbank and Riches also point to a difference, the *key* difference, between the theurgy of Iamblichus and Christian theurgy. It is this: in Neoplatonic theurgy the material cosmos is an *agalma*, a shrine of the Demiurge (*Timaeus* 37c); the cosmos itself reveals the presence of gods. That is, the natural world for Iamblichean Platonists is a theophany. Far from being "fallen," nature itself is the face and living symbol of the divine: nature is the *incarnation* of divine realities *ab ovo*. From this perspective, the Incarnational theology of the Church enters this theophanic current *downstream* and embraces theurgic realities that had already been spelled out by Platonists and in a manner significantly different from Christian theology. Jean Trouillard addressed these issues in a different context but one that is germane. He observed that "certain Christian authors speak of the presence of the divine in the same terms as the Neoplatonists," leading some to assert an "influence or spontaneous convergence" of thinking. Yet, he observes, identical language can "mask heterogeneous thoughts"

---

8. Iamblichus says that the influence of higher principles is *more piercing* (*driumterai*) than the influence of lower realities; Proclus characterizes this influence as being *more extensive*. This explains the ineffable presence of the One even in the densest levels of existence. See *Iamblichus Chalcidensis: In Platonis Dialogos Commentariorum Fragmenta*, translated and edited by John Dillon (Leiden: Brill, 1978), 236.

(*recouvrir pensées hétérogènes*).[9] I would like to explore these differences, not to rebut the insights of Milbank and Riches concerning
the Christian Incarnation and Neoplatonic theurgy, but to provide
a richer context for understanding both.

In Christian theology the cosmos is not the privileged revelation
of the divine, the shining *agalma* of the *Timaeus*. Here the Christian and Platonic myths diverge: the Platonic myth is cosmocentric,
the Christian anthropocentric. In the Christian myth nature
becomes "fallen" and needs redemption. The Incarnation of the
Divine Man in history is necessary to redeem nature and the material order; yet, after the event of the Incarnation, the material cosmos has the same function as the material cosmos of Iamblichus
with one significant difference: for Iamblichus the sacramental
power of matter does not require the Incarnation of Christ. The
material realm is, and has always been, inalterably and intrinsically
sacramental. For the Neoplatonist there is no need for a "new creation," no need to be redeemed *from* a fallen nature, for *nature itself
is the body of our salvation*. The ongoing and natural expression of
demiurgy reveals the choreography of an ancient and everlasting
theophany. This is why Iamblichus insists that all theurgy must be
in "*analogia* with creation." Theurgic activity was always—in *analogia*—cosmogonic activity, and this is what distinguishes it from
sorcery (*goeteia*).[10] Iamblichus thus honored the Egyptians as
sacred people precisely because their rituals mimetically reflect the
demiurgy of the gods. Theoretically, any culture could be theurgic
if its rites and prayers preserve the "eternal measures" of creation.[11]
The question is whether this difference between the Platonic and
Christian myths has significant consequences "downstream," i.e.,
after the Incarnation.

It may. For Iamblichus the theurgic rites of each sacred race

---

9. Jean Trouillard, *L'Un et l'âme selon Proclos* (Paris: Les Belles Lettres, 1972), 5.

10. *On the Mysteries*, 168.10–12. Elsewhere Iamblichus explains that those who
divert spiritual powers from their demiurgic purpose are sorcerers whose perversity
will ultimately destroy them (182.11–13). See also, G. Shaw, "Neoplatonic Theurgy
and Dionysius the Areopagite." *Journal of Early Christian Studies* 7:4 (December
1999), 595–98.

11. *On the Mysteries*, 65.4–11.

revealed the gods in modes appropriate to their respective cultures. Neoplatonic theurgy was imagined within a polytheistic and pluralistic cosmos: the varieties of culture and geography corresponding to the diversity of theurgic societies. This was also consistent with Iamblichus's metaphysics where the utterly ineffable One can only be "known" in the Many, the henophany of each culture both veiling and revealing its ineffable source. To privilege any one of these henophanies over the others, to proclaim that it alone is true, is an assertion that would have been treated with contempt by theurgic Neoplatonists.[12] For such a claim betrays the very principle of theurgy understood as cosmogonic activity rooted in an *ineffable* source, one that necessarily expresses itself in *multiple* forms of demiurgic generosity. Theurgists would find claims to an exclusive possession of truth equivalent to the deranged assertion that the sun shines only in my backyard! These are delicate matters, but it needs to be explored in what sense Christian theology remains divergent from Neoplatonic theurgy, and I believe we may find clues in that most theurgic and Neoplatonic of Christians, Dionysius the Areopagite.

It is now well-known that Dionysius appropriated theurgy to shape his understanding of the sacraments. Indeed, in the writings of the Areopagite we find some of the richest evidence for theurgic worship, and since Iamblichus gives few concrete examples one could find no more striking evidence of how theurgic rites were performed than in the liturgical writings of Dionysius. Yet there is an almost imperceptible shift in Dionysius away from the cosmocentric roots of Platonic myth. For example in *Divine Names* Dionysius uses the term *para phusin* (opposed to nature) synonymously with *huper phusin* (above/before nature) to describe the miracle of the Incarnation.[13] For Iamblichus, the term "supernatural" (*huper phuēs*)—

---

12. Thus, Julian's effort to re-Hellenize the Empire based on Iamblichean teachings was inevitably a distortion of Iamblichus's less hegemonic vision. Yet, it is one thing to serve as a sage, surrounded by one's students in Apamea, quite another to attempt to govern an Empire. The social context is inevitably important in shaping one's metaphysical system. Now see Radek Chlup's interesting comments on this issue among later Platonists in *Proclus: An Introduction* (Cambridge: Cambridge University Press, 2012), Chapter 9: "Worldview," 255–78.

13. Pseudo-Dionysius, *Divine Names*, 648A.

which he coined—could never be opposed to nature (*para ten phusin*). To be *para phusin* was to be opposed to *phusis*, to nature, and thus, to theophany.[14] *Huper phuēs* is not in any way opposed to nature nor did it refer to a separate "supernatural world" as it has come to be conceived; rather, it refers to divine powers that are continually revealed *through* nature. For Pythagoreans like Iamblichus, numbers, like gods, are also supernatural: they are anterior principles that unfold into the physical world. With Dionysius the sensitivity to *phusis* as theophany is diminished, if not lost, and we see a shift away from Platonic cosmocentricism. The *ecclesia* assumes the divine status that had previously been ascribed to the material cosmos in Neoplatonic theurgy. This shift was noted by A.H. Armstrong who said: "It is the ecclesiastical cosmos, not the natural cosmos, which appears to be of primary religious importance for the Christian. There is here a new and radical sort of religious anthropocentricism. . . ."[15] Despite the homologization of the Church to the world in the *Mystagogia* of Maximus the Confessor,[16] the shift from cosmocentric to anthropocentric had been established. One must ask, then, if Christian theurgy can still claim to be—in *analogia*—cosmogonic and, if not, whether it is theurgy at all. Such questions go beyond the bounds of this Preface, but it seems to me from the evidence of Milbank's and Riches' reading of their tradition that this divergence may not be altogether definitive. For example, their understanding of prayer as an "attunement" with the divine that allows its influence to "flow into reality" is entirely theurgic *and* Christian. The question, however, has to do with how that flow is imagined and here, again, we might discern an even more interesting convergence *and* divergence of the two traditions.

14. See Iamblichus's discussion of two kinds of ecstasy: the divine and the deranged. The former are *huper phuēs*, the latter *para phuēs* (*On the Mysteries*, 158.8–159.4).

15. A.H. Armstrong, "Man in the Cosmos: A Study of Some Differences Between Pagan Neoplatonism and Christianity," in *Romanitas et Christianitas*, ed. W. den Boer et al. (London: North-Holland, 1973), 11.

16. St. Maximus the Confessor, *The Church, the Liturgy and the Soul of Man: The Mystagogia of St. Maximus the Confessor*, tr. Dom Julian Stead (Still River, Massachusetts: St. Bede's Publications, 1982), 71.

Milbank and Riches invite us to consider a convergence in the "common paradox that is the heart of being" for both theurgic Neoplatonism and Christianity. Neoplatonic theurgy—they observe, alluding to a central Incarnational theme—requires a kind of "kenosis of mind . . . that plunges downward into matter, into the simplicity and non-reflexivity of material being" to give the soul a receptacle *undivided by thought* and thus capable of receiving the powers of the One. This paradox of going *below* form to receive what is *above* form is already evident in the *Timaeus* since the maternal principle of matter, the *chōra*, must be utterly formless to serve as receptacle and nurse through whom all Forms come to exist.[17] This paradox, at the core of demiurgy, is necessarily re-enacted in theurgic rites that employ what Iamblichus calls the "pure and divine form of matter."[18] The nature of this theurgic-demiurgic paradox has its correspondence, as one might expect, in the human soul. For Christians the paradox is represented through the image of Jesus Christ, the Paradox Incarnate, while for theurgical Neoplatonists paradox defines every human soul and reflects the paradox of the One itself.[19] Again, there is thematic convergence between Neoplatonic theurgy and Christianity: paradox as essential for continuity with the divine; and yet there is also divergence: this paradox is conceived in distinctly different ways. The paradox of the incarnate Christ is at the very core of Christian sacramental life, a

17. *Timaeus*, 50e.
18. See G. Shaw, "The *Chōra* of the *Timaeus* and Iamblichean Theurgy," *Horizons: Seoul Journal of Humanities*, Vol. 3, No. 2, 2012, 103–29.
19. The One of Plato's Parmenides, after all, is not "one," *cannot* be one (*Parmenides*, 141d–142), and is certainly not a Supreme One since it is not "one" at all. Iamblichus maintained that the power of the One pervades all things undividedly and thus establishes the *continuity* of all existence, yet since the One stops to define each existence as "one" it also establishes *discontinuity*. As Iamblichus puts it: "its power encompasses both halting and proceeding at the same time" (Simplicius, *In Categ.* 135.8ff). The theurgist would realize that the soul's contraction into an isolated and individual mortal life was as much an expression of the power of the One as was its reintegration into the continuity of the whole. To deny discontinuity in favor of continuity, the material in favor of the immaterial, mortal for immortal, would cut the soul out of the activity the One and its demiurgic expression. In sum, for human souls to become divine, they must remain mortal. Such reflections on the One are radically non-dual, and this is explored in remarkably clear terms by

mystery that has virtually been forgotten. In the formula of the Council of Chalcedon Jesus Christ is defined as "truly god and truly man ... consubstantial (*homoousios*) with the Father according to the Godhead and consubstantial (*homoousios*) with us according to his humanity." These two natures, divine and human, are present in one person, and through this utterly paradoxical image of the God who has become man, an immortal mortal, Christians find their continuity with the divine.

The divergence with Neoplatonic theurgy may appear significant here, but the formal heterogeneity masks an underlying similarity that can best be described as *incarnational.* One of the most significant contributions of Iamblichus to Neoplatonism is his insistence—against Plotinus and Porphyry—that the human soul descends fully into a body and is subject to all the consequences of mortal existence. According to Iamblichus the soul is defined as

> the mean between divisible and indivisible, corporeal and incorporeal beings; [it is] the totality of the universal ratios (*logoi*) which, after the Forms, serves the work of creation; [the soul is] that Life which, having proceeded from the Intellect, has life itself and is the procession of the classes of Real Being as a whole to an inferior status.[20]

The Iamblichean soul unfolds the *logoi* of the universe into manifest multiplicity. To "serve the work of creation" the soul must animate a mortal body, that is, to participate in demiurgy we must become

Damascius. He says, "the One is without differentiation, though not in the sense of being undifferentiated as opposed to differentiated, but it is entirely simple and is at the same time all things in an undifferentiated way. It is all things as the One; that is to say, the One is *all* things and not only One" (*Damascius' Problems and Solutions Concerning First Principles*, op. cit., Ahbel-Rappe, 154, modified). Again, the One of the Neoplatonists is no more present in unity than in diversity, in spirit than in matter, in the immortal than in the mortal.

20. Iamblichus, *De Anima*, preserved in Stobaeus, I.365, 25–366, 5; now see *Iamblichus, De Anima*, text, translation and commentary by John F. Finamore and John M. Dillon (Leiden: Brill, 2002). My translation of this passage is based on that of John Dillon, modified slightly, "Iamblichus of Chalcis," *Aufsteig und Niedergang der Römischen Welt*, Part II, 36.2 (New York: de Gruyter, 1987), 893. This definition of the soul, Iamblichus said, was shared by "Plato, Pythagoras, Aristotle, and all of the Ancients. . . ." (Stobaeus, I.366, 6–8).

mortal. This no longer allows the soul to return by introspection to an "unfallen" state, as Plotinus had taught. The soul is more deeply implicated in the material world, and yet, as a Platonist, Iamblichus believed the soul is also immortal, which leads him to some profoundly paradoxical conclusions. Iamblichus's definition of the human soul, of *every* human soul, includes paradoxes as dramatic as those invoked at Chalcedon. According to Iamblichus

> the soul is a mean (*mesē*), not only between the divided and the undivided, the remaining and the proceeding, the noetic and the irrational, but also between the ungenerated and the generated.... Thus, *that which is immortal in the soul is filled completely with mortality and no longer remains only immortal.*[21]

The kenosis of a Savior who empties himself of divinity to take on mortality, the paradoxical generosity of the God who becomes mortal man is, for Neoplatonic theurgy, the condition of *every* human soul. The convergence *and* divergence with Christianity are here. We ourselves are the Paradox Incarnate: immortal beings filled completely with mortality. This paradox of the soul is heightened by Iamblichus to such an acute degree that only Damascius in the 5th century was able to endure it. The Iamblichean soul is a *coincidentia oppositorum;* becoming incarnate changes not merely its activities but its very essence: our unity becomes divided, our immortality mortal, and our identity a form of self-alienation. As Iamblichus puts it, as embodied souls we are "made other" (*heteroiousthai*) to ourselves.[22] "Self-alienation" (*allotriōthen*) constitutes our existence.[23] Yet it is only through this experience of self-alienation that we are able to mediate the ongoing demiurgy of the cosmos. Herein lies the paradox for Neoplatonic theurgy. As the

21. Simplicius [Priscian], *In De Anima* 89.33–37; 90.21–23. Carlos Steel has argued persuasively that the author of the Simplicius commentary on Aristotle's *De Anima* was Priscian. See C. Steel, *The Changing Self*, tr. E. Haasl (Brussels: Paleis der Academien, 1978), 16–20. Steel's book continues to be the single most important source for understanding the consequences and paradoxes of Iamblichus's psychology.

22. For citations, see *Theurgy and the Soul*, 114.

23. Simplicius, *In Libros Aristotelis de Anima Commentaria*, edited by M. Hayduck *CAG*, vol. 11 (Berlin: G. Reimeri, 1882), 223.26.

mean of cosmogenesis, the human soul cooperates with the Demiurge by creatively weaving unity with multiplicity and allowing the Forms to become embodied. Milbank and Riches have this precisely correct: in theurgy the soul is called on to imitate and to cooperate with the activity of the Demiurge. Yet to perform this mediation the soul must necessarily embrace dividedness, weakness, and mortality. Ironically and paradoxically, the soul's identity with the Demiurge is realized only through self-alienation and division; only through our dividedness and contingency can we enter the unifying activity of the Demiurge. It is the unique character of the human soul that its immortality and universality are discovered and expressed in a particular and mortal form. To escape mortality, therefore, would forego our only path to immortality. Christianity expresses this paradox through the Incarnation that redeems the world and presents a paradoxical model of losing-finding/giving-receiving, that Christians emulate in order to participate in the mystery of the Incarnation. Neoplatonic theurgists recognize this paradox but, again, they see it as an expression of cosmogenesis and as rooted in the essential structure of *every* human soul.

For Iamblichus, the paradox at the heart of being is manifest to an acute degree in theurgic rites where the soul experiences its paradox fully. Iamblichus says:

> The whole of theurgy presents a double aspect. One is that it is conducted by men, which preserves our natural rank in the universe; the other is that, being empowered by divine symbols, it is raised up through them to be united with the gods and is led harmoniously into their order. This can rightly be called taking the shape of the gods.[24]

The theurgist takes the shape of a god while remaining human and preserving our mortal rank in the universe. Iamblichus was careful not to erase the distinction between humans and gods as he believed Plotinus had done.[25] In *On the Mysteries* he tells Porphyry

---

24. *On the Mysteries,* 184.1–8.
25. See his critique of Plotinus' and Porphyry's blurring of the distinctions among incorporeal beings in his *De Anima* commentary, preserved by Stobaeus, I.365.7–21; see Finamore and Dillon, op. cit.

that human beings are "weak and small, possessed by a congenital nothingness (*oudeneia*)."[26] He protects the experience of deification from our titanic intellectual appetite by maintaining a clear distinction between the divine and human. Yet, while he tells Porphyry plainly that "the divine has nothing in common with us,"[27] he also says theurgic prayer "increases our divine eros (*theion erōta*) and kindles the divine element of the soul (*to theion tēs psychēs*)."[28] The paradox of Iamblichean theurgy is that both statements are true; both reflect the itinerary of theurgic deification. The theurgist remains human yet takes the shape of the gods. The language of Chalcedon is remarkably similar. Christ is described as possessing two natures, divine and human, that remain unmixed despite their "union" in the person of Christ. The theurgist also possesses two natures, divine and human, that remain distinct while being embodied by the theurgist. The expression of paradox in theurgic ritual is the culmination of a mediating itinerary that begins when the immortal soul becomes mortal and ends when the embodied soul recovers its immortality and "takes the shape of the gods," yet it is a deification that occurs only by virtue of the theurgist *remaining* mortal.

The convergence Milbank and Riches see with Neoplatonic theurgy lies not merely in this incarnational paradox; there is, in the Neoplatonic vision an essential element that breathes through the entire cosmos and is felt most especially in theurgic activity: the generosity of the Demiurge (*Timaeus* 29e). For theurgists the world is the manifestation of this generosity, our descent into bodies is an expression of this generosity, and our deification in theurgic rites is effected, Iamblichus says, by this same generosity (*apthonōs*).[29] In Christian terms, as articulated by Milbank and Riches, this generosity is imag-

---

26. *On the Mysteries*, 144.10–11. In his *De Anima* commentary Iamblichus says that embodied souls are "confined in one single form and divided out among bodies" (Finamore and Dillon, op. cit., 373.26). Thus, as embodied, the human soul is identified with and limited by its physical body.

27. Ibid., 204.14.

28. Ibid., 239.6.

29. Ibid., 41.3–8. The generosity in the soul's descent is explored beautifully by Jean Trouillard, "Proclos et la joie de quitter le ciel," *Diotima* 11 (1983): 182–92.

ined in a different cosmological context but with a similar function. They describe it as God's love and—as in Neoplatonic theurgy—they see this expressed through the paradox and gift of the Incarnation: gift and paradox being the "fundamental dimensions" of Christian theology.

In *On the Mysteries*, Iamblichus's defense of worship seems to anticipate modern critics of religion and may also help to situate theurgy in today's Church. He says:

> If these forms of worship were only human customs and received their authority from our cultural habits, one might argue that the cults of the gods were inventions created by our thinking. But in fact the one invoked in sacrifices is a God, and he presides over these sacrifices,[30] and a great number of gods and angels surround him. And every race on earth is allotted a common guardian by this God, and every temple is also allotted a particular guardian.[31]

In a world replete with divine powers, the task of theurgists was to discover a way of honoring each divinity in a manner appropriate to its specific qualities and related to the place in which it was received. The geographic features of each place would reveal the appropriate mode of worship to a discerning eye. Yet our culture has long since moved out of this cosmocentric vision of the Neoplatonists. Nature is no longer an imaginal landscape of divinities. The world has been drained of its sanctity, and with it, so have we. Yet, in a way that would surely have surprised Iamblichus, who deigned not even to speak of Christians,[32] it is clear that elements of his theurgic vision have survived within the church and are now being applied creatively to a community and culture—Christian *and* post-Christian—that are in desperate need of revival. While the formal character of Milbank's and Riches' theology may be foreign to Iamblichus's Platonism, they share an underlying impulse that, to my mind, reflects Iamblichus's statement that to "*every race on earth is allotted a Common Guardian.*" These Christian thinkers, these

---

30. John Dillon suggests that this god is the Demiurgic Nous who presides over all other gods and divinities; see *On the Mysteries*, 273, footnote 350.

31. Ibid., 236.1–6.

32. Ibid., 179.10–180.3.

theurgists, are heroically addressing the aching need of their Christian and post-Christian community. In their service to this community they serve its Guardian and, with their Incarnational theology, they are breathing life back into a culture that desperately needs to become *incarnate*. I may be more securely held by the parameters of the Platonic myth than the Christian, but I have learned a great deal from Milbank and Riches about the theurgic function of the incarnate soul in Christianity *and* in Neoplatonism. For this, especially, I thank them.

Introduction

To Preserve the Cosmos

To no man is it permitted to change these prayers....

A t the end of the fourth century C.E. the decline of traditional pagan culture had come to focus on the temples of the gods, the last vestige of the *"old ways."* By 386 sacrifices to the gods had been outlawed and temples were being vandalized by Christian monks. To protect the pagan shrines the orator Libanius appealed to Emperor Theodosius, saying:

> They [the monks] are spreading out like torrents across the countryside; and in ruining the temples, they are also ruining the countryside itself at one and the same time. *For to snatch from a region the temple which protects it is like tearing out its eye, killing it, annihilating it.* The temples are the very life of the countryside; around them are built houses and villages, in their shadow a succession of generations have been born up until the present day. It is in those temples that farmers have placed their hopes for themselves and their wives and children, for their oxen and for the ground they have sown or planted. A country region whose temple has been destroyed in this manner is lost, because the despairing villagers no longer have the will to work. It would be pointless to exert themselves, they think, because they have been deprived of the gods who made their labors prosper.[1]

Despite Libanius's plea it was too late. The countryside had already been "blinded" and the gods were being driven from the land.[2] For

---

1. Libanius, *Pro templis* 30.8; quoted by H.D. Saffrey, "The Piety and Prayers of Ordinary Men and Women in Late Antiquity," in *Classical Mediterranean Spirituality*, ed. A.H. Armstrong (New York: Crossroad, 1986), 200.

2. See Pierre Chuvin, *A Chronicle of the Last Pagans*, trans. B.A. Archer (Cambridge: Harvard University Press, 1990) for a succinct description of the end of traditional pagan religions in the fourth and fifth centuries.

pagans, the loss of these shrines marked the end of a way of life: it severed their contact with the gods, threatened their society, and disturbed the order of nature.

The sentiments of Libanius reflect the despair of a culture that only two generations earlier had been far more hopeful. When the Roman imperial court first came under Christian influence during the reign of Constantine (312–336 C.E.), the leading thinkers of the pagan world turned to the Syrian Platonist, Iamblichus (c. 240–c. 325 C.E.), for spiritual and intellectual leadership.[3] An official of Emperor Licinius praised Iamblichus as "benefactor of the entire world," "universal blessing of the Hellenes," and "[the] one appointed by the gods to be the savior of the entire Hellenic world."[4]

Such praise was not mere hyperbole. Only one generation after Iamblichus's death, the emperor Julian employed the Platonic and theurgic doctrines of Iamblichus in an attempt to wrest control of the empire away from the "Galileans" and return it to the ancestral practices of the "Hellenes." In "the divine Iamblichus" Julian saw a philosopher equal to Plato, for Iamblichus's teachings had led Julian and other pagans to a deeper understanding of their traditional religious practices. Specifically, Iamblichus revealed the integral connection between the rituals of cultic worship and the intellectual disciplines of philosophic *paideia*. Such an integration had been the goal of Plato himself, and by the fourth century C.E. it was crucial for the survival of Hellenic (i.e., non-Christian) religions. Julian recognized this and intended to re-paganize the empire on Iamblichean lines.[5] In his short reign (361–363) he refurbished the temples, restored a state priesthood, and praised the gods in hymns following

3. For a biographical sketch of Iamblichus see John Dillon, "Iamblichus of Chalcis," *Aufstieg und Niedergang der Römischen Welt* (*ANRW*), vol. 2, 16.2 (New York: de Gruyter, 1987), 863–78.

4. Julian, *The Apocryphal Letters*, nos. 75 and 76; *The Works of the Emperor Julian*, trans. W.C. Wright (Cambridge: Harvard University Press, 1980), 3:243–45. For the identity of the author, thought to be a student of Iamblichus, see T.D. Barnes, "A Correspondent of Iamblichus," *Greek, Roman, and Byzantine Studies* 19 (1979): 99–106.

5. I have benefited from Jay Bregman's unpublished essay: "The Theurgic Bases of Late Pagan 'Theologico-Political' Theory."

Iamblichean doctrine. Yet Julian's enterprise ended abruptly with his death in 363 C.E. and by the end of the fourth century—apart from a small group of philosophical elite—the death of his world had all but transpired and the pagan gods had been exiled from the Christian empire.

Iamblichus lived at a critical juncture in the history of the late antique world. As foremost Platonist of his time and designated "savior" of Hellenic culture, one might expect the "god-inspired Syrian" to have been a leading figure in the pagan polemic against Christianity. After all, his teacher Porphyry had been one of Christianity's most formidable opponents. Yet there is no extant writing of Iamblichus in which he criticizes, or even mentions, Christianity. For Iamblichus, the central issue of his age was not the polemic between pagans and Christians but the far more serious conflict between "old ways" and "new ways," between the ancient traditions inspired by the gods and those recently invented by man.

Iamblichus was not a proponent of "Hellenic" culture in the manner of his enthusiastic student Julian. Indeed, writing in the persona of Abammon, an Egyptian priest, Iamblichus claimed in the *De Mysteriis*[6] that "Hellenes" had already abandoned their religious heritage, and he blamed them for the loss of sanctity in his age:

> At the present time I think this is the reason everything has fallen into a state of decay—both in our [sacred] words and prayers—it is because they are continually being changed by the endless innovations and lawlessness of the Hellenes. For the Hellenes are by nature followers of the latest trends and are eager to be carried off in any direction, possessing no stability in themselves. Whatever they may have received from other traditions they do not preserve, but even this they immediately reject and change everything through their unstable habit of seeking the latest terms. (*DM* 259, 5–14)

Iamblichus's tirade against the Greeks should not surprise us, for Plato himself censured the Greeks with almost identical charges,

---

6. The standard edition is *Jamblique: Les mystères d'Egypte*, trans. and ed. E. des Places (Paris: Les Belles Lettres, 1966). Also useful is Thomas Taylor's translation, *Iamblichus on the Mysteries of the Egyptians, Chaldeans, and Assyrians*, 2d ed. (London: Bertram Dobell, 1895). References to the *De Mysteriis* will be noted by *DM*.

and he blamed the cultural demise of his own era on the innovations of Hellenic thinkers (*Laws* 657a). Such anti-Hellenic criticism was, in fact, a topos in Plato's writings, as was his exaltation of barbarian races (especially Egyptian) in contrast to the unstable Greeks. Iamblichus similarly praised the Egyptians and explained the power of their hieratic rites:

> Understand that since the Egyptians were first to be allotted the participation in the Gods, the Gods are pleased when invoked according to the custom of the Egyptians [*DM* 258, 3–6].... The barbarians, since they are fixed in their manners, firmly continue to employ the same words. Thus they are beloved by the Gods and offer invocations pleasing to them. To no man is it permitted to change these prayers in any way. (*DM* 259, 14–19)

For Iamblichus, the crisis of the fourth century had little to do with Christianity. As a Platonist he felt responsible to preserve humanity's contact with the gods, so his concern was not with Christians or with any other group that promised to replace the "old" order with a "new" one. As Plato put it, such purveyors of "new styles" could never corrupt the "sacred" traditions rooted in the cosmic gods (*Laws* 657b). Yet Iamblichus was more than a Platonist, he was also one of the holy barbarians of whom he speaks. A Syrian by birth, Iamblichus chose not to hellenize his Semitic name, as was the fashion among educated and well-to-do families;[7] rather, like his own pious barbarians he remained loyal to a holy ancestry. Descended from the royal blood of the priest-kings of Emesa—several of whom bore his name[8]—Iamblichus possessed a unique perspective to reinterpret Plato's esteem for those races who maintained an unbroken contact with the gods. In Iamblichus's estimation the responsibility of Platonists to value and explore this contact had recently been ignored and Plato's cosmological principles overlooked due to an excessive rationalism in Platonic schools. This rationalism exalted the powers of the mind while diminishing the

7. His contemporary, Porphyry, by contrast, was born with the Phoenician name Malchos; John Dillon, "Iamblichus of Chalcis," 864.

8. The Syriac or Aramaic original is *ya-mliku*, which means "(El) is king" or "May he rule." Dillon, "Iamblichus of Chalcis," 863–65.

prestige of the traditional cults of the gods that, in Iamblichus's view, were the basis for all genuine culture and wisdom. It is ironic, but the exile of the Hellenic gods lamented by Libanius in the fourth century may well have been initiated by the antipathies of leading Hellenic thinkers toward the powers of the sensible cosmos and the cults that venerated them.[9]

To appreciate Iamblichus's contribution to the late antique world and to the Platonic tradition we must understand the crisis of the age as he did. Only then can we understand why Iamblichus placed *theourgia* (god-work) at the heart of Platonic disciplines, why he preferred it to *theologia* (god-talk), and why his soteriology was intimately tied to the invocation of the natural powers of the cosmos. Iamblichus believed that the world described by Plato in the *Timaeus* was being torn apart by a new kind of Platonism that denied the sanctity of the world and elevated the human mind beyond its natural limits. According to Iamblichus such rationalistic hubris threatened to separate man from the activity of the gods, and he presented theurgy as the antidote to restore contact with the divine order.

Iamblichus's distinction between theurgy and theology is crucial for understanding his Platonism.[10] For theology was merely *logos*, a "discourse about the gods," and however exalted, it remained a human activity, as did philosophy. Theurgy, on the other hand, was a *theion ergon*, a "work of the gods" capable of transforming man to a divine status. Although the term *theourgia*, originated with second-century Platonists to describe the deifying power of Chaldean rituals—some of which were believed to be transmitted by the soul of Plato himself[11]—it was Iamblichus who provided a philosophic rationale for the performance of these rites and ensured that theurgy

9. The pronounced rationality among philosophers of late antiquity, including their distaste for cultic activity, is described by Pierre Hadot, *Exercices spirituels et philosophie antique* (Paris: Etudes Augustiniennes, 1981), 237–38.

10. For the history of the term theourgia in later Platonism see Hans Lewy, *Chaldean Oracles and Theurgy*, ed. M. Tardieu (Paris: Etudes Augustiniennes, 1978), 461–66.

11. H.D. Saffrey, "Les Néoplatoniciens et les oracles, chaldaïques," *Revue des Etudes Augustiniennes* 27 (1981): 218–19.

would become an integral part of the Platonic vocabulary. In Platonic terms, theurgy fulfilled the goal of philosophy understood as a *homoiōsis theō*. The rituals themselves, Iamblichus explained, varied according to the capacities of its participants, and though he provided little information about particulars, it is clear that many "theurgic" rites were already well known to the Hellenic world. In the hands of Iamblichus, theurgy represented a revaluation of traditional cult practices. Iamblichus maintained that the divine principles invoked in these rites were exemplified abstractly and theoretically in the teachings of Pythagoras, Plato, and Aristotle, and that both cultic acts and philosophic *paideia* were rooted in one source: the ineffable power of the gods. In theurgy these divine principles were embodied and enacted, not merely contemplated, and in whatever context this occurred it was a "work of the gods," a *theourgia* in which the human soul participated both as recipient and beneficiary.

As a Platonist, Iamblichus defended the practice of theurgy according to the canons of the Platonic tradition. Therefore, any attempt to understand Iamblichean theurgy must follow the Platonic themes that Iamblichus himself was so careful to explain. Of central concern to Iamblichus was Plato's description of the cosmos and its role in the education and deification of the soul. As we shall see, it was the issue of the soul's place in the sensible cosmos that divided Iamblichus and all subsequent theurgical Platonists from the nontheurgical Platonism of Plotinus and Porphyry.

In the *De Mysteriis*, Iamblichus the philosopher argued that Plato's teachings were integrally related to the sacred traditions of the Egyptians, Chaldeans, and Assyrians; and as a theurgist, he explained and defended his tradition using Platonic categories. In so doing Iamblichus established a new synthesis of cult and philosophy, becoming the first leader of a Platonic school to function simultaneously as hierophant of a sacred cult.[12] The synthesis of

---

12. Not surprisingly, Iamblichus's Pythagoras was portrayed as the exemplary spiritual man, combining cultic worship and philosophy in his teachings. See *Iamblichus: On the Pythagorean Life*, para. 85, translation with notes and introduction by Gillian Clark (Liverpool: Liverpool University Press, 1989). See also *Iamblichus: On the Pythagorean Way of Life*, text, translation, and notes by John Dillon and Jackson Hershbell (Atlanta, Ga.: Scholars Press, 1991).

these diverse modes of thought in Iamblichus's school deeply influenced and, in some measure, defined the soteriological thinking of the later Platonists and other inheritors of Platonic thought.

The great influence Iamblichus exercised over subsequent Platonists was due, in large part, to the theoretical framework he outlined in the *De Mysteriis* for a wide variety of divinational rites practiced in the late antique world. On the one hand it was a great theoretical achievement to have demonstrated how the abstract tenets of the Platonists were exemplified concretely in time-honored divinational rites. Yet in practical terms, as the Church increasingly began to persecute pagans and outlaw their religious practices in the later fourth century, Iamblichus's apology for traditional pagan forms of worship and divination gained far more than theoretical significance. The *De Mysteriis* and Iamblichean theurgy became the foundation for the resurgence and continued life of Platonic communities until the closing of the Athenian Academy by Justinian in 529 C.E. and later—for Platonists in exile—in the frontier city of Harran where Iamblichean Platonism ultimately passed into Arab hands and thrived until the tenth century.[13]

It should be recognized that the author of the *De Mysteriis* eventually came to play a far different role from any that he might have imagined as a Platonic teacher living on one of his estates in the predominantly pagan Apamea of the late third and early fourth centuries. Even the title of his best-known work, the *De Mysteriis*, is not his own but that of the Renaissance "magus," Marsilio Ficino, who attempted to revive Iamblichean Platonism in fifteenth-century Florence.[14] The true title of the work, though less sensational, more accurately describes its contents: "The Reply of the Master Abammon to the 'Letter of Porphyry to Anebo,' and the solutions to the difficulties that it contains."[15] In effect, this treatise, which today has

---

13. For an excellent account of the influence of Iamblichus on the struggle of later Platonists against Christian persecution, see Polymnia Athanassiadi, "Persecution and Response in Late Paganism: The Evidence of Damascius," *Journal of Hellenic Studies* 113 (1993): 1–29. See also Michel Tardieu, "Sabiens Coraniques et 'Sabiens' de Harran," *Journal Asiatique* 274 (1986): 1–44.

14. Ficino's full title is *De Mysteriis Aegyptiorum, Chaldaeorum, Assyriorum.*

15. H.D. Saffrey, "Les livres IV à VII de *De Mysteriis* de Jamblique relus avec la

become notorious as an apology for the practice of magic and divination, formed part of the correspondence between two of the most learned Platonists of the later third century. Porphyry, who directed a Platonic school in Rome, posed the questions and was therefore responsible for the structure of the work. Yet it was Iamblichus's answers that changed the course of Platonism; in his lengthy replies to Porphyry's questions Iamblichus solved problems that had long vexed Platonists, and he provided a philosophically viable framework for a religious way of life that Porphyry himself had longed to create.

Yet why would Iamblichus adopt the pseudonym of an Egyptian priest in order to explain his Platonic mystagogy? According to the later Platonists the answer was clear.[16] Plato himself had acknowledged that his writings were merely a *propaideia* to deeper mysteries,[17] and in several dialogues he spoke of the influence of "Oriental," particularly "Egyptian," wisdom on his thought.[18] Although Plato probably never participated in Egyptian or Chaldean mysteries, he was believed to have done so by Platonists,[19] and therefore the Oriental element in Iamblichus's Platonism should not be seen as alien but as an attempt to reveal more completely the wellspring of

---

Lettre de Porphyre à Anébon," in *The Divine Iamblichus: Philosopher and Man of Gods*, ed. H.J. Blumenthal and E.G. Clark (Bristol: Bristol Classical Press, 1993), 144–45.

16. In his *Théologie platonicienne* (*Th.Pl.*), vol. 1 (Saffrey-Westerink, 1968), Proclus says that Plato received his philosophy from the gods (5, 1–6), and that in writing the dialogues he functioned as a mystagogue: "the primary leader and hierophant of those true mysteries into which souls separated from terrestrial places are initiated" (6, 2–7). It was a commonplace among Platonists that Plato received his mathematic and hieratic teachings from the Egyptians; see *Anonymous Prolegomena to Platonic Philosophy* (4, 8–10), trans. L.G. Westerink (Amsterdam: North-Holland, 1962), 8–9; cf. Aristotle, *Metaphysics* 981a, 21–26. For a discussion of the Oriental origin of Platonic philosophy see B.D. Larsen, *Jamblique de Chalcis: Exégète et philosophe* (Aarhus: Universitetsforlaget, 1972), 150–52; cf. J. Bidez, *Eos, ou Platon et l'orient* (Brussels: M. Hayez, 1945; reprint, New York: AMS Press, 1979), 21–23.

17. See esp. *The Seventh Letter* 341c–d.

18. *Statesman* 290c–e; *Timaeus* 21; *Phaedrus* 275b; *Laws* 819b; *Philebus* 18b; *Charmides* 156b–157c.

19. Larsen, *Jamblique de Chalcis*, 151–52.

Platonic wisdom.[20] Just as Plato turned to his Lady of Prophecy, Diotima Mantinikē,[21] to reveal erotic mysteries, so Iamblichus deferred to his persona, the Egyptian priest Abammon, to explain theurgic mysteries, the *hieratikē technē*. In the role of Egyptian mystagogue responding to the questions and criticisms of Porphyry the "philosopher," Iamblichus played "divine revealer" to the wayward Hellene, guiding Porphyry back to the primitive intuitions that Plato and Pythagoras received from the Egyptians.[22] Since Plato's dialogues had already become a kind of scripture for fourth-century Platonists,[23] the hieratic posture adopted by Iamblichus would not have seemed unorthodox.

To understand theurgical Platonism, however, one must first understand Iamblichus's cosmology and soteriology. He believed that it was necessary for the soul to inhabit its proper "place" in the cosmos, so we must try to picture the place of the soul according to the later Platonists. For Iamblichus, Plato's *Laws* provide the model of a community properly placed in the cosmos.

Plato says that in man's Golden Age humanity was ruled by a divine hierarchy that ensured the well-being of all. The god Kronos established religious and political law, and society was governed by daimons. Plato says:

> *Kronos* gave our communities as their kings and rulers, not men but *Daimones*, beings of diviner and superior kind just as we still do the same with our flocks of sheep and herds of other domesticated animals. We do not set oxen to manage oxen, or goats to manage goats; we, their betters in kind, act as masters ourselves. So, the god, in his kindness to man, did the same; he set over us the superior race of *Daimones*. (*Laws* 713cd; trans. A.E. Taylor)

---

20. Ibid., 155–57.
21. *Symposium* 201d, 2. For the connection between Mantinea and *mantis* see *Plato: Symposium*, ed. K.J. Dover (New York: Cambridge University Press, 1980), 136–38.
22. Larsen, *Jamblique de Chalcis*, 150–57.
23. H.D. Saffrey, "Quelques aspects de la spiritualité des philosophes néoplatoniciens," *Revue des Sciences Philosophiques et Théologiques* 68 (1984): 170–71. Cf. Philip Merlan, "Religion and Philosophy from Plato's *Phaedo* to the Chaldaean Oracles," *Journal of the History of Philosophy* 1 (1963): 163–76.

Guided by these daimons, man enjoyed peace, prosperity, and justice until he usurped their authority, began to rule himself, and ignored the hierarchical law that each species must obey its superior order (*Laws* 716ab). In accord with this principle, Plato believed that humanity should seek to re-establish the order and hierarchy of the Golden Age (*Republic* 500c).

This myth reveals Plato's model for cosmic and social order. It describes a taxonomy in which the gods stand as the principle and basis for human society.[24] Acting as intermediaries between the gods and man, daimons revealed the rhythms of the year through which human society contacted the gods in ritual and sacrifice and thus became properly "placed" within the unity of the cosmos. As Plato observes, for a city to be kept alive "its sacrifices and feasts must fit the true natural order" (*Laws* 809d), and this co-ordination of human acts to the cosmos "increases the intelligence of men" (*Laws* 809e). Thus, Plato's *homoiōsis theō*, recognized as the goal of *paideia*, was measured by the soul's *homoiōsis kosmō*; to be assimilated to the gods one had to enter into communion with the daimons who revealed them in the natural world.

Plato's taxonomy of the cosmos and society exemplifies what Jonathan Z. Smith has termed a "locative" view of existence.[25] Quoting Cornelius Loew's outline of this worldview Smith describes the locative orientation as centered in five basic propositions: "(1) there is a cosmic order that permeates every level of reality; (2) this cosmic order is the divine society of the gods; (3) the structure and dynamics of this society can be discerned in the movements and patterned juxtapositions of the heavenly bodies; (4) human society should be a microcosm of the divine society; and (5) the chief responsibility of priests and kings is to attune human order to the divine world."[26] In a locative orientation, evil and the

---

24. Cf. *Republic* 441c where Plato says that the elements of the city are equal in number to the elements of the soul and that these are displayed perfectly in the order of the heavens.

25. Jonathan Z. Smith, *Map Is Not Territory* (Leiden: E. J. Brill, 1978), 88–103.

26. Ibid., 160.

"demonic"[27] arise only when something is "out of place"; in Plato's taxonomy, the demonic was relegated to the province of the inverted soul,[28] turned "upside-down" (*anatropē*) and alienated from the Whole.

Platonic *paideia* was supposed to reorient the soul to the cosmic (locative) order and exorcise it of its self-assertion. The "demonic," in the Platonic view, was a symptom of the soul's confusion, the cosmic order gone haywire.[29] Since Platonic taxonomy was locative as well as monistic, the demonic element was only relatively evil, an unbalanced expression of divine elements. Therefore the power of evil was temporary and limited to the province of the upside-down soul.

The pervasive acosmic mood of late antiquity effected a change in this locative orientation, and its influence was felt even in Platonic circles where it reversed the traditional locative taxonomy. In the late imperial period, man's "cosmological conviction" was shattered.[30] The all-pervasive and beneficent order of a cosmos articulated in its most sophisticated form by Plato—and less subtly by others—was transformed into a maleficent system of repression and punishment meted out by cruel demons.[31] As Smith puts it:

27. The term "demonic," as employed here and by Smith in his taxonomy, represents chaos, disorder, and evil; in short, that which threatens the cosmos. It should not be confused with the daimons of traditional Platonism. The Platonic *daimōn* was a cosmogonic entity and certainly not evil, although the question surrounding its cosmogonic function did lead, eventually, to dualist interpretations that transformed the Platonic *daimōn* into a demon.

28. See Plato's description, *Tim.* 43b–e.

29. I have borrowed Jonathan Z. Smith's use of the term "demonic" as discussed in his article: "Towards Interpreting Demonic Powers in Hellenistic and Roman Antiquity," *ANRW* 2, 16.1, see esp. 429–30. While I find Smith's terminology and analysis useful, I disagree with his description of the theurgist's worldview as "utopian" (438). The "utopian" view described in his essay seems less a worldview than a view of the self and should not be equated with the utopian worldview as described in Smith's articles: "Birth Up Side Down or Right Side Up?" in *Map Is Not Territory*, or "The Temple and the Magician."

30. See E.R. Dodds, *Pagan and Christian in an Age of Anxiety* (New York: Norton, 1965).

31. Larsen, *Jamblique de Chalcis*, 150–57.

Hellenistic man suffers from what might be called cosmic paranoia. He experiences himself to be naked and helpless; he sees
danger and threat everywhere. Looking up at the heavens, at the
stars, and the motions of the heavenly bodies, he no longer sees
guarantors of order; the guardians of a good cosmic and human
destiny ... but rather a grim system of aggressors, an openly hos-
tile army which seeks to chain him. (*Map Is Not Territory*, 138)

In such a world, Smith says, man's salvation is no longer measured
by the degree of his assimilation to the patterns of the cosmos "but
rather by the degree to which he can escape the patterns" (139).
Smith aptly terms this inverted locative orientation "utopian,"
meaning that there is no place in the cosmos that is good.[32]

Iamblichus's position developed in the context of this cosmic
pessimism: he was the inheritor of a Plotinian Platonism where the
soul never descended into a body; it remained in the heavens, above
the flesh and the physical world. Plotinus's (c. 205–270 C.E.) view of
the soul, which may have been influenced by Gnostic dualists, was
unorthodox from a Platonic perspective. Plotinus admitted as
much (*Enn.* IV, 8, 8, 1–4), yet his psychology had a profound influence on the Platonism of his time.

With respect to Smith's locative and utopian categories, the
Gnostics and Plotinus were in the same camp and represent two
possibilities within the utopian orientation: the Gnostics, by identifying the cosmos as evil and the soul as a fallen spirit; and Plotinus,
by denying the soul's descent and identifying sensible matter as evil
and the cause of the soul's confusion. They seemed to concur that
traditional Platonic taxonomy was no longer valid, for both project
the demonic *outside* the soul. For Gnostics the soul was pure but
polluted by material demons; for Plotinus the soul never descends at
all. And with the effects of *anatropē* denied, or presumed to inhibit
only a nonessential aspect of the soul, Plotinus, as much as the
Gnostics, rejected the locative taxonomy of his inherited tradition.
By placing the demonic outside the soul, in the demon enchantress

---

32. Smith pursues this theme with examples drawn from Gnostic and gnosticizing literature that demonstrate a reversed evaluation of the structures of the cosmos. See also *Map Is Not Territory*, 172–89.

Nature (*Enn.* IV, 4, 43, 23–26) and by denying the soul's descent from the noetic realm, Plotinus reversed Platonic taxonomy. Whereas traditional Platonic *paideia* had traced an ascent to the gods through a deepening assimilation to cosmic orders, Plotinus's utopian orientation tended to devalue the cosmos as a divine revelation; this, in turn, denied the value of religious rituals tied to the rhythms of the sensible world.

A.C. Lloyd has argued that Iamblichus's metaphysics of the completely descended soul served to justify his practice of theurgic rituals, and conversely, that Plotinus's rejection of ritual practices and Porphyry's low evaluation of them reflected their view of the soul as undescended.[33] Important as this may be to distinguish the metaphysics of Plotinian and Iamblichean Platonism, it does not sufficiently account for the pronounced significance that Iamblichus gave to this issue. Iamblichus's doctrine of the completely descended soul may, in part, be explained as his intellectual justification for theurgy; but it was far more than that. Tied to this doctrine were issues central to the principles of the Platonic tradition. For Iamblichus, the doctrine of the undescended soul struck at the heart of Platonic *paideia* because it threatened to desacralize and demonize the cosmos. This consequence, clearly, was not foreseen by Plotinus, who would have opposed it. Indeed, Plotinus argued eloquently for the divinity of the cosmos against the Gnostics (*Enn.* II, 9), but for Iamblichus such arguments were futile without the corollary doctrine of the soul's descent. If, as Plotinus believed, the soul's confusion does not derive from the soul, if the soul does not undergo a complete change in embodiment, and if it does not, in fact, truly become embodied, then the manifestation of the divine as *kosmos* would have little or no role in the soul's *paideia*. In addition, with the demonic projected from the soul to the sensible cosmos, Plotinus gave to it a permanence it never held in traditional Platonism. In effect, the doctrine of the undescended soul split the cosmos into

33. See A.C. Lloyd, "The Later Neoplatonists," in *The Cambridge History of Later Greek and Early Medieval Philosophy*, ed. A.H. Armstrong (Cambridge: Cambridge University Press, 1967), 287–93; cf. R.T. Wallis, *Neoplatonism* (Duckworth: London, 1972), 118–20.

two opposed worlds, and if the physical world was upside-down (*anatropē*) and not the soul, then the performance of sacrifices and rituals to assimilate oneself to its orders would be worse than useless; they would be positively harmful.[34]

The doctrine of an undescended soul also had significant social consequences. If the traditional agricultural and civic religious festivals were tied to nature's powers, to take part in them would commit oneself to the demonic order. The philosopher of the Plotinian school, therefore, should refuse to acknowledge demonic gods or participate in civic religious rites and all corresponding social customs. To paraphrase the words of Plotinus, it is for the gods of the cosmos to come to the philosopher, not for him to go to them.[35]

While traditional Platonism had long recognized hierarchical distinctions in one's ascent to the gods, it never opposed one stage of *paideia* to the next in the manner described above. From the soul's prenatal "lessons" given through the mother's rhythmic chants and movements (*Laws* 790d), to the increase of intelligence from daily rituals (*Laws* 809d) and the rigorous program of training in gymnastics, music, mathematics and dialectic (*Republic* 535a–541b), *paideia* was conceived by Plato as a hierarchical unfolding of the powers of the soul through a corresponding enfolding of the soul into the harmonies and powers of the cosmos. Higher degrees of *paideia* included lower degrees, just as primary orders of the cosmos contained subordinate orders. With the desacralization of the cosmos, however, this paradigm was lost, and despite Plotinus's profound testament to the divinity of the world in *Against the Gnostics* (*Enn.* II, 9), his doctrine of the undescended soul, in principle, has already severed the body from its head. A complete separation was inevitable, ontologically separating the sensible cosmos from the noetic, and politically pitting the philosopher against the common man.

---

34. That this was not Plotinus's intention has been argued convincingly by A. H. Armstrong, "The Apprehension of Divinity in the Self and Cosmos in Plotinus," in *The Significance of Neoplatonism*, ed. R. B. Harris (Norfolk, Va.: International Society for Neoplatonic Studies, 1976), 187–97. Indeed, Armstrong suggests that Iamblichus's use of the term *huperphuēs* in the *De Mysteriis* led to a "two world" way of thinking. See "Iamblichus and Egypt," *Etudes Philosophiques* 2–3 (1987): 179–88.

35. Porphyry, *The Life of Plotinus*, 10.

Plotinus's position was reflected in the writings of his disciple, Porphyry, the historical and ideological mediator between Plotinus and Iamblichus.[36] In his treatise *On the Abstinence of Animal Food*,[37] Porphyry attacked the practice of animal sacrifice and said such rites did not pertain to gods but to evil daimons: "For he who is studious of piety knows very well that no animated being is to be sacrificed to the Gods; but a sacrifice of this kind pertains to *Daimones* and to other Powers" (*De Abst.* II, 36, 5). In an explanation that was sure to delight Christians, Porphyry attributed the origin of these rites to the devices of bloodthirsty daimons whose life depended on ingesting the vapors of blood sacrifice (II, 42, 1). He continued: "Falsehood is allied to these malevolent beings, for they want to be considered as Gods, and the power which presides over them is ambitious to appear as the greatest God. These are they who rejoice in libations and the savour of sacrifices" (II, 42, 2; trans. T. Taylor). The philosopher should stand aloof from this superstitious cult and become godlike by dissociating himself from daimons and their misguided worshipers (II, 43, 3–4). Employing the formula of his master Plotinus, Porphyry advised the philosopher to forgo all ritual activities in order to return "alone, through himself, to God alone" (II, 49, 1); while the philosopher should understand the enchantments of nature and the cults tied to its daimons, he should have nothing to do with them. "In every respect," Porphyry says, "*the philosopher is the savior of himself*" (II, 49, 2).

I would argue that Porphyry's repudiation of the value of cult sacrifice and his belief that man can save himself depend entirely on his accepting the doctrine of the undescended soul and its corollary that the human self is identical to the divine *Nous*. On this latter point Porphyry maintained flatly that "the true self is the *Nous*" (I,

36. See Garth Fowden's essay describing the "shift" in the Platonic tradition from the Plotinian/contemplative to the Iamblichean/theurgical mode, "Late Antique Paganism Reasoned and Revealed," *Journal of Roman Studies* 71 (1981): 178–82.

37. Porphyry, *Porphyre: De L'Abstinence* (*De Abst.*), 2. vols., translation and introduction by Jean Bouffartigue and Michel Patillon (Paris: Les Belles Lettres, 1977). See also the English translation by Thomas Taylor, *Porphyry On Abstinence From Animal Food* (1823), edited and introduced by E. Wynne-Tyson (New York: Barnes and Noble, 1965).

29, 4). This new metaphysics undercut the traditional basis of *pai-deia*, for it transformed the Platonic *homoiōsis theō*, measured by the soul's assimilation to the cosmic gods, into a *homoiōsis heautō* with the "self" understood as the divine *Nous!* The soul's identification with the cosmos, therefore, was no longer necessary or desirable, for the cosmos had been altogether short-circuited: it was something to escape from, not assimilate oneself to. Consequently, Porphyry conceived of salvation as the soul's permanent escape from the cosmos, "never again to find itself held and polluted by the contagion of the world."[38] In this, he abandoned the Platonic doctrine of rebirth,[39] yet his unorthodoxy with respect to traditional Platonism was consistent with its "gnosticized" form where the cosmos, and not the soul, carried the burden of the demonic. Porphyry maintained that permanent escape was possible only for the philosopher, not for the common man, and this again exemplifies the social as well as ontological oppositions tied to the doctrine of the undescended soul. Those incapable of the philosophic escape, says Porphyry, performed theurgic rites to purify their irrational elements, but such souls were never free.[40]

Iamblichus had been led to the higher reaches of Platonism by Porphyry, and although Porphyry also introduced Iamblichus to theurgy it was Iamblichus who discovered its deeper significance. For Porphyry, theurgy functioned as a mere *preparatio* for the philosophic life and was to be left on the periphery of its higher disciplines. Iamblichus, on the other hand, moved theurgy from periphery to center, not only in the life of the philosopher, but for anyone who worshiped the gods.

With theurgy Iamblichus hoped to recover Plato's positive orientation to the cosmos. At issue was the divinity of the world, and for Iamblichus the most effective means to acknowledge this was through the performance of rites that conformed the soul to its

---

38. *De regressu animae* 40*, 15–16, in J. Bidez, *Vie de Porphyre* (Hildesheim: Georg Olms, 1964). See the discussion of Andrew Smith, *Porphyry's Place in the Neoplatonic Tradition: A Study in Post-Plotinian Neoplatonism* (The Hague: Martinus Nijhoff, 1974), 59.

39. Augustine, *City of God*, book 10, chap. 30.

40. Porphyry, *De regressu animae* 32*, 5–25.

orders. At issue as well was the future of the Platonic philosopher in society. Porphyry's metaphysics of an undescended soul and "demonized" cosmos opposed the philosopher to the sensible world and the social order. For Porphyry, Platonism was limited to an intellectual elite. The theurgical Platonism of Iamblichus, by contrast, allowed for gradations of religious experience that corresponded to the different levels of the cosmos and society. In theurgy, Iamblichus provided a soteriology that theoretically could touch any soul, from the most material to the most spiritual, while preserving their communal affiliations. With a more consistent metaphysics[41] Iamblichus succeeded in restructuring Plato's teachings in a way that preserved the mystical elements of Plotinus's soteriology without losing contact with the physical cosmos or society.

To return to Smith's categories, Iamblichus's theurgical Platonism was "locative" in a highly sophisticated way. In both traditional and theurgical Platonism the demonic was not an external evil on the fringe of the cosmos,[42] for the cosmos was all-embracing and entirely good.[43] Iamblichus, like Plato, placed the demonic within the embodied soul, the only chaos untamed by the Demiurge. Yet, in Iamblichus's Platonism the purpose of this alienation was made clearer: while Plato's Demiurge gave to each soul a spark of himself (*Tim.* 41c), Iamblichus understood this to mean that each soul had the responsibility to perform its own demiurgy, that is to say, its own *theurgy*. The task for every soul was to partake in divine mimesis by creating a cosmos out of the initial chaos of its embodiment. Therefore, the "demonic" condition of the embodied soul was a *felix culpa* without which the soul could not participate in cosmogenesis, including its own creation and salvation.

Platonists of the second and third centuries C.E. had disowned this confusion of the soul. In direct contrast to the traditional taxonomy, Numenius had shifted the demonic from the soul to the

---

41. For a discussion of the greater consistency in Iamblichus's metaphysics than in Plotinus's, see J.M.P. Lowry, *The Logical Principles of Proclus' STOICHEIŌSIS THEOLOGIKĒ* (Amsterdam: Rodopi, 1980), 18–25.

42. See J.Z. Smith, "Towards Interpreting Demonic Powers," 429–30.

43. As attested to in *Tim.* 36b.

sensible world and both Plotinus and Porphyry followed him. These twin doctrines of an upside-down world and an undescended soul were rejected by Iamblichus, who warned Porphyry that such teachings would destroy their entire way of life, saying: "This doctrine spells the ruin of all holy ritual and theurgic communion between gods and men since it places the presence of superior beings outside this earth. For it amounts to saying that the divine is at a distance from the earth and cannot mingle with men and that this lower region is a desert, without gods."[44]

Like Plato, Iamblichus believed his age was threatened by the loss of the gods, and he yearned for the time when gods and men were joined concretely through ritual. With theurgical Platonism, Iamblichus tried to recapture this Golden Age, and although he succeeded only within Platonic circles, his Syrian school presents probably the best synthesis of philosophy and ritual in the late antique world. In the *De Mysteriis* Iamblichus explained in a coherent and systematic way the raison d'être of the rituals he performed and prescribed for others, and he attempted to prove the necessity for these rites through a careful reflection on the intellectual canons of his time: the corpus of Platonic, Aristotelian, and Pythagorean writings.

Since much of Iamblichus's writing is fragmentary, I have had to make speculative interpretations concerning some aspects of theurgy. However, these have been made in accord with the extant literature, and if apparently contradictory or unintelligible material begins to "make sense" without doing violence to the extant literature then I believe the interpretive framework has been justified and may at least be considered a viable hypothesis for understanding Iamblichean theurgy. The ineffability of the "divine acts" means that although theurgy was the centerpiece of Iamblichus's Neoplatonism, it remained undefined. I shall, however, reveal its significance through an examination of the issues that were directly relevant to theurgy and of crucial importance to Iamblichus and other fourth-century Platonists: the status of matter and the material world, the nature of the embodied soul, and the way to achieve

---

44. *DM* 28, 6–11. Translation by Peter Brown; see *The Making of Late Antiquity* (Cambridge: Harvard University Press, 1978), 101.

salvation. By examining theurgy in each of these contexts successively, I believe we may begin to understand its function and meaning without violating its essentially indefinable character.

Without the goodness of a material world connected to the gods, Iamblichus, as a Platonist, could not have encouraged rituals that invoke the powers of the physical cosmos. If matter was the cause of evil and human suffering—as many argued—a Platonic theurgy would have been inconceivable. Therefore, in Part I, I examine Iamblichus's arguments against Platonic dualists who had demonized the material world. Using Neopythagorean theories, which he presented as the "old ways" of the Egyptians, Iamblichus argued that matter derived from a divine principle and that the physical cosmos was directly generated by the gods.

Once the material world has been exorcised of evil and is seen to be an expression of divine activity, we turn to the confusion of the human soul, perhaps the most vexing problem for Platonists. In Part II, I examine Iamblichus's understanding of the soul and his rationale for the performance of theurgic rites. The defining issue for Iamblichus and other Platonists was whether or not a divine soul descended completely into a mortal body, and profoundly different soteriologies developed depending on one's answer. Since Iamblichus believed the soul fully descended and was, paradoxically, both mortal and immortal, he had to create a soteriological practice that incorporated the soul's physical actions into a divine pattern—the specific function of theurgic rites. Theurgy allowed the embodied soul to tap the divine power hidden in its mortality and to realize that its paradoxical nature, being both mortal and immortal, allowed it to participate directly in the creation and salvation of the cosmos.

After a careful study of Iamblichus's psychology and theurgy's role in the cure of souls, I turn to the actual performance of theurgic rites and the guidelines suggested by Iamblichus. In Part III, I examine the tripartite schema Iamblichus employed to co-ordinate the mortal activities of souls with their immortal archetypes. For Iamblichus, the cosmos itself was the paradigmatic theurgy: the act of the gods continually extending themselves into mortal expression. Without first appreciating Iamblichus's conception of the divinity of the material world as well as his views on the paradox of the embodied soul, the full significance of theurgy and the guidelines for its practice could not be properly understood. In short, theurgy was Iamblichus's attempt to ensure the deification of souls through their assimilation to the orders of the cosmos—a traditional Platonic teaching.

It is with Iamblichean Platonism that my study of theurgy concludes. In Part IV, I argue that theurgy represented Iamblichus's attempt to bring traditional pagan divinational practices in line with Platonic and Pythagorean teachings. Through discovering metaphysical principles in time-honored sacrifices and divinational rites, Iamblichus believed he was following the example of both Plato and Pythagoras. As the scion of Syrian priest-kings who were, themselves, oracular figures, Iamblichus was ideally suited to refashion the Platonic tradition to meet the cultural and intellectual needs of fourth-century pagans. Iamblichean Platonism, with its emphasis on theurgy, succeeded in incorporating pagan religious rites into the intellectual edifice of Platonism while, at the same time, infusing the Platonic school with the vitality of popular cultic practices. It was a synthesis that other Platonists—for a variety of reasons—had not accomplished, and I hope this study will shed light on the significance of Iamblichus's achievement.

I

Matter and Embodiment

1

Embodiment
in the Platonic
Tradition

[Plato] ... does not always speak consistently.

I n his introduction to Egyptian theology in the *De Mysteriis*, Iamblichus says: "The Egyptians, imitating the nature of the universe and the creative energy of the Gods, themselves produce images of mystical insights—hidden and invisible—by means of symbols, just as nature symbolically reveals invisible measures through visible shapes and the creative energy of the Gods outlines the truth of the Forms through visible images" (*DM* 249, 14–250, 7). Writing under the pseudonym of "Abammon," an Egyptian priest, Iamblichus dedicated book VII of the *De Mysteriis* to the exegesis of the symbols and theology of Egyptian religion.[1] In this passage Iambli-

1. H.D. Saffrey says that Abammon was a theophoric name combining the Syriac word for father "ab(ba)" with the Egyptian god Amon who had been assimilated by the Greeks to Zeus; see his "Abamon, pseudonyme de Jamblique," *Philomathes— Studies and Essays in the Humanities in Memory of Philip Merlan* (The Hague: Martinus Nijhoff, 1971), 227–39. Thus, "Abammon" was a popularized transcription of the Greek *pater theou or theopatōr*, which Saffrey says was descriptive of the theurgist in the Iamblichean scheme of virtues. Iamblichus's list differs from Porphyry's in that his highest virtue was called "hieratic" or "theurgic" rather than "paradigmatic" as in Porphyry's scheme. Porphyry's list of the virtues is as follows:

virtue	activity	agent
political	curbing of passions	virtuous man
cathartic	cleansing of passions	daimonic man/ good daimon
theoretic	intellectual activity free from passions	god
paradigmatic	conjunction with the intellect	father of gods

(*Sent.* 32; 30, 6–31, 8; ed. E. Lamberz [Leipzig: Teubner, 1975])

23

chus referred to the theme of divine mimesis, which is of central importance in his apology for theurgy.

Reverence for Egyptian wisdom was already well established in the Platonic tradition in the fourth century c.e., but Iamblichus's[2] Syrian school exhibited an unmatched admiration for their rites and theology. Iamblichus explained that he revered Egyptian theology because it possessed real power, "imitating the nature of the universe and the creative energy of the Gods." In Platonic terms this meant taking an active part in the demiurgy of the cosmos and becoming a co-creator with the god of creation. The power and authority of Egyptian rites derived from this co-operative mimesis: according to Iamblichus, they embodied the eternal ratios (*metra aidia*; *DM* 65, 6) which were the guiding powers of the cosmos. The Egyptians praised by Iamblichus worshiped the true gods of Platonism: the unchanging patterns of nature; they were a community perfectly integrated with the natural world, reproducing in cult and ritual the activity of the Demiurge in the cosmos.[3] For Iamblichus, Egyptian

---

Iamblichus interpreted Porphyry's theoretic and paradigmatic virtues as degrees of "human" intelligence and distinguished them from the *hieratikai* (or *theourgikai*) *aretai* (cf. Damascius, *In Phaed.* paras. 138–44, in L.G. Westerink, ed. and trans., *The Greek Commentaries on Plato's Phaedo*, 84–87; (New York: North-Holland, 1977). For Iamblichus, the theurgic virtues were "father, in the soul, of all in it which exists from god" (Saffrey, "Abamon," 238), not intellectual virtues as listed by Porphyry. Thus, the term *theopator*, which Porphyry gave to the one who practiced "paradigmatic" virtues, was transferred by Iamblichus to the theurgist.

By using the pseudonym Abammon (father of gods) Iamblichus avoids the indiscretion of refuting his teacher directly; at the same time, he plays on Porphyry's scheme of the virtues, adopting a name as an apologist for theurgy, which describes the highest degree of virtue in Porphyry's own system.

2. For a discussion of the influence of Egypt and the Orient on Plato, see J. Bidez, *Éos, ou Platon et l'orient* (Brussels: M. Hayez, 1945; reprint, New York: AMS Press, 1979). Cf. H. Joly, "Platon égyptologue," *Revue Philosophique de la France et de L'Étranger*, no. 2 (1982): 255–66. For studies of the "sacerdotal" mode of philosophizing in late antiquity, see A.-J. Festugière, *La Révélation d'Hermès Trismégiste* (Paris: Gabalda, 1950), 1:10–44. See also Philip Merlan, "Religion and Philosophy from Plato's *Phaedo* to the Chaldaean Oracles," *Journal of the History of Philosophy* 1 (1963): 163–76.

3. A.H. Armstrong contrasts the community of Christians, for whom divine revelation was reserved to a particular social group with the traditional Hellenes for

mysteries represented the highest possible appropriation of the divine in mortal life, and he looked to their rites as a model for the religious rituals he introduced to the Platonic tradition under the name of *theourgia*, a term borrowed from second-century Chaldean Platonists.[4]

Theurgical Platonism represents Iamblichus's attempt to introduce the divine mimesis of Egyptian cult to the Platonic community and the Hellenic world. It was a contribution that Iamblichus believed was sorely needed by Hellenes because of their obsession with discursive novelties that lacked power and a vital connection to the cosmos (*DM* 259, 9–14). Like the Egyptian cult, theurgy imitated the gods, and Iamblichus said that every theurgic observance was a ritualized cosmogony (*DM* 65, 4) that endowed embodied souls—regardless of their station in life—with the divine responsibility of creating and preserving the cosmos. From a theurgic perspective, embodiment itself became a divine service, a way of manifesting the will and beauty of the gods.[5]

Iamblichus's position irrevocably changed the attitude of Platonists toward embodiment and the physical world, yet the basis for this change and the central role of theurgy in later Neoplatonism have largely been ignored. If theurgy is understood as co-operative demiurgy, then the attitude of a theurgist toward the physical world would be of decided importance. By sharing in the activity of creation the theurgist would participate in the ordering of matter, which was the specific function of the Demiurge as described in Plato's *Timaeus*. One's attitude to the body and matter, then, would

---

whom divine wisdom was universal; see his "Christianity in Relation to Later Platonism," *Jewish and Christian Self-Definition*, ed. E. P. Sanders, 1:87 (London: SCM Press, 1980). Cf. Armstrong, "Man in the Cosmos: A Study of Some Differences between Pagan Neoplatonism and Christianity," in *Romanitas et Christianitas*, ed. W. den Boer et al. (London: North-Holland, 1973), 5–14. Cf. Peter Brown, *The World of Late Antiquity* (New York: Harcourt Brace Jovanovich, 1971), 73–74.

4. Though Porphyry was the first Platonist to adopt theurgical practices, it was Iamblichus who elevated its importance. For a discussion of the origin of the term, see Hans Lewy, *Chaldean Oracles and Theurgy*, ed. M. Tardieu (Paris: Etudes Augustiniennes, 1978), 461–66.

5. *DM* 272, 10–12. Cf. Iamblichus's discussion of the school of Calvenus Taurus in the *De Anima* (*Stob.* I, 378, 25–379, 6).

be an index of the degree and manner of one's participation in the Demiurge; more specifically, Iamblichus held that the worship of embodied souls was determined precisely by their degree of material involvement (*DM* 219–228, 13).

The theurgist's highest good was not realized by escaping from materiality but by embracing matter and multiplicity in a demiurgic way. In this, Iamblichus virtually reversed the symbolic language of his age: apotheosis in theurgy could no longer be imagined as the ascent of the soul (the well-known Plotinian metaphor), without a corresponding descent and demiurgy. The pivot on which the metaphor turned was Iamblichus's understanding of the soul's relation to matter, and his solution to this question is critical for understanding the central role he gives to theurgy. Indeed, in the view of Iamblichus and other hieratic Neoplatonists, embodied souls were able to attain salvation *only* through the theurgic use of matter.

That the soul's ritual use of matter could itself bring about the salvation of the soul was certainly a new development in the Platonic tradition, yet despite its apparent unorthodoxy, there are elements in the dialogues that lend it support—most obviously the doctrine of *anamnēsis*, the core of Plato's epistemology (*Phaedo* 75e; *Meno* 81cd). In the doctrine of recollection, the soul's education is described as a process of reawakening by means of contacts with the sensible world that functioned as mnemonic prods, reminding the soul of the Platonic Forms. Theurgy should be seen as the development and translation of this epistemological theory into a ritual praxis where the prods of sensate experience were carefully controlled in rites designed to awaken the soul to the Forms.[6] While the doctrine of recollection lent itself specifically to a theurgic development, the cosmology of the *Timaeus* provided the necessary framework: without the descent of souls into mortal bodies and the physical appearance of Forms, Plato says the work of the

---

6. For an illuminating discussion of ritualized recollection among neoplatonizing Muslims, see Henry Corbin, *Avicenna and the Visionary Recital*, tr. W. Trask (Dallas: Spring Publications, 1980), 115–16. Pierre Hadot says that the notion of innate or pre-intellectual knowledge of the Forms had assumed a "mystical value" for Iamblichus since, for him, each soul has "innate knowledge of the gods" (*DM* 7, 14); *Porphyre et Victorinus* (Paris: Etudes Augustiniennes, 1968), 1:117 n. 6.

Demiurge would remain incomplete. The embodiment of the soul and its perfection in theurgy was seen by Iamblichus as essential to cosmogenesis.

Although there is evidence in Plato's dialogues that seems to contradict Iamblichus's positive view of matter and embodiment, this conflict is in the dialogues themselves and was the inheritance of any Platonist who attempted to resolve the problem of embodiment. Plotinus, for example, in his discussion of embodiment, said that the *Timaeus* supported an optimistic view of the soul's descent, while the *Phaedo* and *Phaedrus* presented the soul's descent in a far more negative light, one that Plotinus himself emphasized. As Plotinus put it: "[Plato] ... does not always speak consistently, so that his meaning might be grasped easily" (*Enn.* IV, 8, 2, 27–28), and Platonists quoted the dialogues to support positive and negative views of matter and embodiment. However, due to the canonical authority of the dialogues in late antiquity and the demand by Platonists for consistency in the writings of their master, the ambiguities on this issue needed to be brought into accord.[7] E.R. Dodds explained that the task specifically was to reconcile the cosmology of the *Timaeus* with the psychology of the *Phaedo* and *Phaedrus*, and he noted that Plotinus had not been altogether successful in this as he leaned too much toward the psychological perspective, which presented matter negatively.[8]

A.-J. Festugière catalogued the optimistic and pessimistic views of embodiment outlined in Iamblichus's treatise *De Anima*, which shows the Syrian's thorough familiarity with this issue.[9] In the

---

7. For a discussion of the "canonization" of Plato's dialogues, see Michael Dunn, "Iamblichus, Thrasyllus, and the Reading Order of the Platonic Dialogues," in *The Significance of Neoplatonism* (Norfolk, Va.: International Society for Neoplatonic Studies, 1976), 59–80. See also *Anonymous Prolegomena to Platonic Philosophy*, ed. L.G. Westerink (Amsterdam: North-Holland, 1962), xxxvi–xl; H.D. Saffrey, "Quelques Aspects de la spiritualité des philosophes néoplatoniciens: De Jamblique à Proclus et Damascius," *Revue des Sciences Philosophiques et Théologiques* 68 (1984): 169–82.

8. E.R. Dodds, *Pagan and Christian in an Age of Anxiety* (New York: Norton, 1965), 25.

9. *La Rev.* 3:69–82.

context of this problem, theurgy may be seen to bridge the gap between the psychological matter of the *Phaedo* and *Phaedrus*, with their pessimistic view of embodiment, and the cosmological matter of the *Timaeus*, which presents embodiment optimistically. The theoretic structure of this bridge was outlined in Iamblichus's metaphysical solution to the problem of how the One becomes Many. By postulating a middle term, or, as it turns out, middle *terms*, Iamblichus allowed for continuity between irreconcilable extremes, a principle of mediation that became an integral part of post-Iamblichean Platonism.[10]

In the existential situation of embodied souls, Iamblichus's introduction of theurgic rituals provided a mediation between man's experience of matter as an oppressive weight, separating him from the divine, and his innate awareness of matter as the vehicle that joined him with the gods (*DM* 7, 13–8, 2). Theurgy was the dynamic expression of the mathematical mean, establishing a continuity between mortal and immortal realms by allowing embodied souls to enter divine energies through the performance of ritual.

Iamblichus solved the Platonic problem of matter and embodiment as a "Pythagorean," for he viewed all aspects of creation, however dense, as expressions of the primary and divine principles: *peras-apeiron*. Theurgic rites allowed the soul to enter these measures directly, ritually enacting divine principles whose power was shared by those who embodied them.

Iamblichus's solution must also be seen in the context of the late third and fourth centuries and the increasing popularity of religions of radical dualism exemplified in Gnosticism, Manichaeanism, and, to some degree, Christianity.[11] The question of the value of life in a body and the status of the physical world had become highly charged issues on which often depended the salvation or damnation of one's

---

10. *Proclus: The Elements of Theology*, 2d ed., revised text, translation, introduction, and commentary by E. R. Dodds (Oxford: Clarendon Press, 1963), xxi–xxii.

11. For a brief description of dualist vs. monist systems in late antiquity, see Peter Brown, *World of Late Antiquity*, 73–74. Cf. A. H. Armstrong, "Man in the Cosmos," 5–14.

soul.[12] In this light, it was not Iamblichus as Platonic scholar and mathematician that attracted the adulation of his successors. It was Iamblichus as savior, *theios Iamblichos*, who revealed mysteries that transformed the suffering and weight of material experience into a foundation for communion with the gods.[13] The body-as-tomb (*sōma = sēma*), "riveted to the soul by sense experience" (*Phaed.* 83d), became the vehicle through which the soul found its proper limits,[14] thereby "saving itself" and "becoming liberated while still in a body" (*DM* 41, 10). Thus, matter and the soul's use of matter played an indispensable role in theurgy as it did in cosmogony. The soul could no more realize its salvation without embracing matter than the Demiurge could create the cosmos without the formless receptacle that gave expression to the Forms (*Tim.* 48e–49a). The difference, however, is that while the soul's embrace of matter was piecemeal, following the cycles of time, the act of the Demiurge on matter was simultaneous and complete, and it is precisely in this "difference" that Iamblichean theurgy must be understood.

At this point we should bear in mind that Iamblichus's term for "matter" was coined by Aristotle who said that Plato's material principle, which was called "space" (*chōra*) (Tim. 52b), "receptacle" (*hupodochē*), "mother" (*mētēr*), and "nurse" (*tithēnē*) (*Tim.* 49b), was equivalent to the term *hulē*: "the receptive space (*chōra*) of Plato's *Timaeus* is the same as matter (*hulē*)" (*Physics* 209b, 11–13). *Hulē*, originally meaning "wood" or "timber," henceforth became the technical philosophical term used by Platonists to refer to

---

12. This theme is examined in the social and institutional life of late antiquity by Jonathan Z. Smith in three essays: "The Influence of Symbols on Social Change: A Place on Which to Stand," "Birth Upside Down or Right Side Up?" and "The Temple and the Magician," in *Map is Not Territory* (Leiden: E. J. Brill, 1978), 129–89.

13. The attestations for Iamblichus as *theios* are numerous. See Eduard Zeller, *Die Philosophie der Griechen* (Hildesheim: Georg Olms, 1963), 3: part 2, 378–79 n. 2.

14. *Cratylus* 400c. C. J. de Vogel has corrected misconceptions in our understanding of Plato's view of the body as a tomb. She argues that, for Plato, the body was not simply the soul's prison but provided the soul its limits, its enclosure (*peribolos*), "in order that it might be saved" (*Crat.* 400c); see de Vogel, "The SŌMA–SĒMA Formula: Its Function in Plato and Plotinus Compared to Christian Writers," in *Neoplatonism and Early Christian Thought*, 79–99 (London: Variorum, 1981).

"matter." Like most Neoplatonists, Iamblichus believed Aristotle and Plato were essentially in agreement, and he translated many of Aristotle's theories about the physical world to the intelligible.[15] Aristotle's influence on Iamblichus, however, remained terminological and to some degree structural, for his meanings were transformed entirely in Iamblichus's theurgical Platonism.

15. See Stephen Gersh, *From Iamblichus to Eriugena: An Investigation of the Prehistory and Evolution of the Pseudo-Dionysian Tradition* (Leiden: E.J. Brill, 1978), 33–45. Cf. B.D. Larsen, "La Place de Jamblique dans la philosophie antique tardive," in *Entretiens sur l'antiquité classique*, vol. 21: *De Jamblique à Proclus* (hereafter *Entretiens*), 10–14 (Geneva: Fondation Hardt, 1975).

2

Matter as Cosmic Instrument

It would be far from true to suggest that the material principle is evil.

I amblichus's description of the origin of matter in the *De Mysteriis* concludes his explanation of Egyptian and Hermetic theology. After asserting a primordial and ineffable god, Iamblichus describes the "first God and king" (*DM* 261, 10), "God and principle of God" (*DM* 262, 4), who derived self-begotten as a "monad from the one" (*DM* 262, 4–5); and it is from this god, the "father of essence" (*DM* 262, 6), and "principle of intelligibles" (*DM* 262, 7–8), that matter is created. He says: "God produced matter out of the scission of materiality from substantiality, which the Demiurge, receiving as a living substance, fashioned into simple and impassible spheres and organized the last of this into generated and mortal bodies" (*DM* 265, 6–10). This is repeated almost verbatim in Iamblichus's commentary on the *Timaeus* quoted by Proclus: "The divine Iamblichus relates that Hermes wishes materiality to be created out of substantiality; and it is likely that it is from this source that Plato derived such a doctrine of matter."[1]

Iamblichus's portrayal of matter here is clearly positive, and the reference to Hermes was meant to lend authority to his view. Iamblichus's metaphysical position was monistic, as can be seen in his

---

1. See John Dillon, trans. and ed. *Iamblichi Chalcidensis* (Leiden: E.J. Brill, 1973), 141.

summary of the Egyptian hierarchy: "And thus, from on high to the lowest things, the Egyptian doctrine concerning principles (*archai*) begins from the One and proceeds into multiplicity, and the multitude in turn is governed by the One; and everywhere the indefinite nature is ruled by a certain defined measure and by the highest uniform cause of all things" (*DM* 264, 14–265, 6). Not only was matter divinely created; even its furthest sensible expression was dominated by the supreme principle.[2]

Iamblichus's Hermetic position opposed Platonic dualists such as Numenius, who viewed matter as autonomous and evil, and Plutarch, who postulated an evil soul that preceded the World Soul.[3] Iamblichus also disagreed with Plotinus's portrayal of matter; although Plotinus said that intelligible matter was divine and essentially good (*Enn.* II, 4, 5, 12–22), he condemned sensible matter as the "cause of all evils" and "evil in itself" (*Enn.* I, 8, 3, 38–40). Plotinus left a breach between intelligible and sensible matter, with the latter carrying the pejorative imagery of his dualist predecessors.[4] Iamblichus, on the other hand, asserted an unbroken continuity between divine and sensible matter. The implications of this argument will be treated later, but in sum, Clemens Bäumker has characterized the difference by pointing out that while the Plotinian cosmos was diminished in value in proportion to its degree of sensible expression, in the Iamblichean world sensible matter represented no subtraction of intelligible power because it was derived directly from the

2. For a description of the continuity of Iamblichus's Hermetic cosmos see Garth Fowden's summary of cosmic sympathy in the Hermetica; Garth Fowden, *The Egyptian Hermes: A Historical Approach to the Late Pagan Mind* (New York: Cambridge University Press, 1986), 77–78.

3. Numenius, ed. E. des Places (Paris: Les Belles Lettres, 1973), frag. 52; 97, 76–91. Plutarch, *On the Generation of the Soul* 1014bc, in *Plutarch's Moralia*, vol. 13, ed. Harold Cherniss (Cambridge: Harvard University Press, 1976).

4. For a discussion of Plotinus's attempt to integrate Persian dualism see J. Trouillard, "La médiation du verbe selon Plotin," *Revue Philosophique de la France et de L'Etranger* 146 (1956): 66–69. For the problem of evil in Plotinus with a catalogue of current interpretations see D. O'Brien, "Plotinus on Evil: A Study of Matter and the Soul in Plotinus' Conception of Human Evil," *Downside Review* 87, no. 286 (1968): 68–110.

highest intelligible being, the *aoristas duas*.[5] Iamblichus, under the influence of Pythagorean arithmology, viewed all manifestation, sensible or intelligible, as reducible to numerical principles, and it is possible that many important differences between pre- and post-Iamblicheans were due more to the influence on Iamblichus of an "immanentist" Pythagorean metaphysics than to his reputed "Oriental" predisposition to "alien ideas."[6]

Festugière demonstrated that Iamblichus's description of the origin of matter was a well-known Pythagorean teaching, as evidenced in the writings of the Neopythagorean Moderatus of Gades (first century C.E.). In Moderatus's description of first principles, "quantity" (*posotēs*) is derived from Unifying Reason (*heniaios logos*), after it has been separated from it and deprived of all "formal qualities," and in Iamblichus's system materiality is derived from the Paternal Monad when it is separated from substantiality (i.e., all formal qualities).[7] The *posotēs* of Moderatus and the *hulē/hulotēs* of Iamblichus were functionally the equivalents of the material principle in the *Timaeus*, which was able to receive the Forms without distortion because it lacked all "formal" qualities (*Tim.* 49b).

In his *Introduction to the Arithmetic of Nicomachus*, Iamblichus

---

5. Clemens Bäumker, *Das Problem der Materie in der Griechischen Philosophie* (Frankfurt am Main: Minerva, 1963; reprint of 1890 ed.), 419.

6. C.J. Vogel has discussed the difference between Plato's "metaphysic of the transcendent" and the Pythagorean "metaphysic of immanent order"; see de Vogel, *Pythagoras and Early Pythagoreanism* (Assen: Van Gorcum, 1966), 197–200. In the hands of Pythagoreans such as Iamblichus the transcendence/immanence distinction of Plato and Pythagoras was fused into an ineffable principle at once transcendent and immanent. As regards Iamblichus's supposed infection by alien (Oriental) ideas, see E.R. Dodds, "Iamblichus," *Oxford Classical Dictionary*, 2d ed. (Oxford: Oxford University Press, 1970), 538. Festugière, however, argues that Neopythagorean notions of a transcendent god and material dyad need not derive from Oriental sources: "On le voit donc, quelque route qu'on suivît, qu'on distinguat Monade et Dyade *aoristos* comme un couple antithétique, on qu'on les réunait en une même Monade *arsenothelus*, on révenait à la notion de l'*hen* absolutement transcendant. Ces speculations, purement grecques, sont anterieures à Eudore. Et il n'est donc nul besoin de recourir à l'Orient pour éxpliquer la transcendance de Dieu." *La. Rev.* 4:53.

7. *La. Rev.* 4:38–40.

again discussed the origin of the matter that was shaped by the Platonic Demiurge: "The God, *Demiurgos*, is not the creator of matter, but when he receives it, as eternal, he molds it into forms and organizes it according to numerical ratios."[8] Having already explained that form and matter in the cosmos are analogous to the monad and dyad in number (*In Nic.* 78, 11–14), Iamblichus maintained that just as numbers are derived from combinations of the monad and dyad, the manifest world is derived from a demiurgic activity that he called the "rhythmic weaving" of monadic and dyadic *archai*.[9] Arithmogony, for Iamblichus, was the analogue of cosmogony, and both expressed the harmony of opposed principles.[10] Thus Iamblichus: "If, as the Pythagoreans say, 'there is a combination and unification of disagreeing parts and a harmony of things naturally at war,' the essence of harmony necessarily holds rule."[11] Quoting another Pythagorean dictum, Iamblichus says: "There is nothing in existence in which opposition is not present."[12] These oppositions, held in measured grades of tension and proportion, made up the framework for physical manifestation.

Iamblichus maintained that the "wisest men" (the Pythagoreans) grasp all things according to number (*In Nic.* 72, 6–9), and following their example, he believed that all matter—from its intelligible

8. *In Nic.* 79, 5–8. Text: ὁ δημιουργὸς θεὸς μὴ ὢν τῆς ὕλης γεννητικός, ἀλλὰ καὶ αὐτὴν ἀίδιον παραλαβών, εἴδεσι καὶ λόγοις τοῖς κατ᾽ ἀριθμὸν διαπλάττων καὶ κοσμοποιῶν.

9. *In. Nic.* 78, 22–24. Text: οὕτως καὶ αἱ τῶν ὄντων ἀρχαὶ ἄμικτοι τῶν ἄλλων δυνάμεων οὖσαι πάντα τὰ μεταλαμβάνοντα αὐτῶν κατὰ τὰς οἰκείας δυνάμεις ῥυθμίζουσι.

10. Iamblichus said that according to the Pythagoreans there were "ten" such kinds of relations (*scheseis*) being explained arithmetically as the ten proportions or "means" that developed out of the initial opposition of the "odd" and "even" (*In. Nic.* 72, 9–13). "Ten," for the Pythagoreans, was the glyph for the perfectly manifested cosmos; it culminated the arithmogonic progression symbolized in the tetractys. All manifest possibilities were contained in the decad-tetractys.

11. *In. Nic.* 72, 26–73, 3. Text: ἡ τῆς ἁρμονίας οὐσία χώραν ἀναγκαίως ἔχει, εἴ γε ῾συναρμογά τίς ἐστι καὶ ἕνωσις τῶν διχοφωεόντων καὶ τᾷ φύσει πολεμίων ἁρμονία᾽ κατὰ τοὺς Πυθαγορείους.

12. *In. Nic.* 73, 4–5. Text: ῾μηδὲν εἶναι ἐν τοῖς οὖσιν οὗ τὸ ἐναντίον οὐκ ἔστιν᾽.

to sensible expression—simply manifested the dyadic principle.[13] In his treatise *On General Mathematical Science*, Iamblichus gives an account of this principle and describes the place of evil in the cosmos:[14]

> Now, of the mathematical numbers let the two first and highest principles be set forth: the One (which one must not yet call "being" on account of its being simple, the principle of beings and not yet that sort of being of which it is principle), and the other is the principle of the Many which—of itself—is able to provide division. Because of this, as much as it is in our power to say, we compare it to a completely fluid and pliant matter.[15]

The *archai*, One and Many, were nonexistent in themselves, but in combination they gave rise to intelligible differentiation and being. Evil arose as a subsidiary and was not identified with matter. Thus Iamblichus:

> Let it be thus for us. In the elements from which numbers arise neither beauty nor the good yet exist, but out of the combination of the One and the causal matter of the Many, number subsists. In these first existences [numbers], being and beauty appear, and, in turn, from the elements of lines, geometrical existence appears in which being and beauty are similarly found and in which there is nothing ugly or evil. But, in the last of things, in the fourth and

---

13. For the dyad as source of matter in Neopythagorean thinking see Dominic J. O'Meara, *Pythagoras Revived: Mathematics and Philosophy in Late Antiquity* (Oxford: Clarendon Press, 1989), 60–64.

14. Philip Merlan was the first to argue that chapter IV of *De Communi Mathematica Scientia Liber* (*DCMS*) was taken directly from Speusippus. John Dillon has recently supported Merlan's thesis against Tarán's criticism. See J. Dillon, "Speusippus in Iamblichus," *Phronesis* 29, no. 3, (1984): 325–32. Whether chapter 4 of *DCMS* draws directly or indirectly from Speusippus, Iamblichus certainly stands behind it.

15. *De Communi Mathematica Scientia Liber* (*DCMS*), ed. N. Festa (1891; Stuttgart: Teubner, 1975), 15, 6–14. Text: Τῶν δὴ ἀπιθμῶν τῶν μαθηματικῶν δύο τὰς πρωτίστας καὶ ἀνωτάτω ὑποθετέον ἀρχάς, τὸ ἕν (ὅπερ δὴ οὐδὲ ὄν πω δεῖ καλεῖν, διὰ τὸ ἁπλοῦν εἶναι καὶ διὰ τὸ ἀρχὴν μὲν ὑπάρχειν τῶν ὄντων, τὴν δὲ ἀρχὴν μηδέπω εἶναι τοιαύτην οἷα ἐκεῖνα ὧν ἐστιν ἀρχή), καὶ ἄλλην πάλιν ἀρχὴν τὴν τοῦ πλήθους, ἣν καὶ διαίρεσιν οἷόν τ᾽ εἶναι καθ᾽ αὑτὸ παρέχεσθαι, καὶ διὰ τοῦτο ὑγρᾷ τινι παντάπασι καὶ εὐπλαδεῖ ὕλῃ, προσηκόντως εἰς δύναμιν παραδεικνύντες, ἀποφαίνοιμεν ἂν ὁμοίαν εἶναι·

fifth levels, which are composed from the last elements, evil appears, not as a guiding principle, but from something falling out and not maintaining the natural order.[16]

Evil came to exist only accidentally, from a falling out and lack of control in the fourth and fifth grades of existence, not, as Tarrant translates: "from . . . failing to control nature's ways,"[17] as if nature were evil, for in the *Theology of Numbers*, attributed to Iamblichus,[18] he says that *phusis* is good and the same as *pronoia*, that is, nature *is* providence and manifests the order of the gods.[19] Although Iamblichus gives no explanation for the fourth and fifth levels, Merlan, Kramer, and Tarrant suggest that he was following a Speusippan design but they disagree on its ontological order.[20] John Dillon argues that Iamblichus is either quoting Speusippus directly or paraphrasing him.[21]

Iamblichus flatly denied that the material principle of number was evil. In *On General Mathematical Science* he says: "It is not

16. *DCMS* 18, 1–13. Text: Καὶ τοῦτο μὲν οὖν οὕτως ἡμῖν ἐχέτω. τὰ δὲ στοιχεῖα, ἐξ ὧν οἱ ἀριθμοί, οὐδέπω ὑπάρχει οὔτε καλὰ οὔτε ἀγαθά· ἐκ δὲ τῆς συνθέσεως τοῦ ἑνὸς καὶ τῆς τοῦ πλήθους αἰτίας ὕλης ὑφίσταται μὲν ὁ ἀριθμός, πρώτοις δὲ ἐν τούτοις τὸ ὂν φαίνεται καὶ κάλλος, ἐφεξῆς ἐκ τῶν στοιχείων τῶν γραμμῶν τῆς γεωμετρικῆς οὐσίας φανείσης, ἐν ᾗ ὡσαύτως τὸ ὂν καὶ τὸ καλόν, ἐν οἷς [οὔτε] οὐδὲν οὔτε αἰσχρόν ἐστιν οὔτε κακόν· ἐπ᾽ἐσχάτῳ δὲ ἐν τοῖς τετάρτοις καὶ πέμπτοις τοῖς συντιθεμένοις ἀπὸ τῶν στοιχείων τῶν τελευταίων κακίαν γενέσθαι οὐ προηγουμένως, ἐκ δὲ τοῦ ἐκπίπτειν καὶ μὴ κατακρατεῖν τινα τοῦ κατὰ φύσιν.

17. H. Tarrant, "Speusippus' Ontological Classification," *Phronesis* 19 (1974): 130–45.

18. Although Iamblichus is not believed to have written this treatise, it is Iamblichean in character and surely represents his thinking, often repeating passages found in the fragments of Iamblichus's Pythagorean writing translated by D.J. O'Meara, *Pythagoras Revived*. See also *The Theology of Arithmetic*, trans. Robin Waterfield (Grand Rapids, Mich.: Phanes, 1988). Waterfield suggests that the present treatise may have been a compilation of notes taken from Iamblichus's lectures. As a matter of convenience I shall refer to the author as Iamblichus.

19. *Theologoumena Arithmeticae* (*TA*) 42, 9. Text: φύσις δὲ ἀγαθή, ταὐτὸν καὶ πρόνοια.

20. Philip Merlan, *From Platonism to Neoplatonism*, 2d ed. (The Hague: Martinus Nijhoff, 1960), 110–24; H.J. Kramer, *Der Ursprung der Geistmetaphysik* (Amsterdam: P. Schippers, 1964), 212–14; See Tarrant's diagram of their respective interpretations of this passage, "Speusippus' Ontological Classification," 144.

21. See Dillon, "Speusippus in Iamblichus," 325–32.

appropriate to contend that this [material principle] is evil or ugly.[22] ... It would be far from true to suggest that the material principle is evil."[23] Iamblichus argues that if the One is praised on account of its independence (*autarcheia*) and being the cause of beauty in numbers, "would it not be senseless to say that the natural receptacle of such a thing is evil or ugly?"[24] Just as the principles of the "same" and "different" were mixed together by "persuasive necessity" in the *Timaeus* (35a), so, Iamblichus said, the principles of unity and multiplicity were combined by "a persuasive necessity" (*tinos pithanēs anagkēs*; *DCMS* 15, 17) and in both cases the resulting *harmonia* served as the framework for the manifest world.

The dualism that Iamblichus described in *On General Mathematical Science* held only at the level of mathematical numbers; the *Theology of Numbers* said that the dyad itself, the principle of multiplicity and matter, not only is derived from the One, but, in a certain sense, *is* the One: "According to one designation they [the Pythagoreans] call the monad 'matter' and 'receptacle of all' since it is the cause of the dyad and of all receiving ratios."[25] In short, prior to the two primary principles of the One and the Many (*DCMS* 15, 6–14) Iamblichus asserts a monad from which these principles derive and in which they remain essentially contained. This was consistent with what we know of Iamblichus's metaphysics in the *De Mysteriis* where he described a paternal monad (itself derived from a higher unity) that gave rise to the division of materiality and substantiality (*DM* 265, 6–10). The consistency of Iamblichus's metaphysics is borne out by Damascius, who said that Iamblichus asserted an "entirely ineffable" One (*pantelōs arrheton*) prior to the simple unity (*ho haplōs hen*) that preceded the limit (*peras*) and

---

22. *DCMS* 15, 23–24. Text: κακὸν δὲ ἢ αἰσχρὸν τὸ τοιοῦτον οὐ προσῆκον ἴσως ἐστὶ τιθέναι.

23. *DCMS* 16, 1–2. Text: ὥστε πολλοῦ δέον ἂν εἴη κακὸν προσαγορεύεσθαι αὐτό.

24. *DCMS* 16, 4–6. Text: πῶς οὐκ ἄλογον ἂν εἴη λέγειν τὸ κακὸν ἢ τὸ αἰσχρὸν δεκτικὸν κατὰ φύσιν τοῦ τοιούτου πράγματος εἶναι.

25. *TA* 5, 12–15. Text: κατὰ δέ τι σημαινόμενον καὶ ὕλην αὐτὴν καλοῦσι καὶ πανδοχέα γε, ὡς παρεκτικὴν οὖσαν καὶ δυάδος τῆς κυρίως ὕλης καὶ πάντων χωρητικὴν λόγων.

unlimited (*apeiron*) and whose mixing gave rise to the One-Being (*to hen on*).[26]

The dyad, Iamblichus said more specifically, served as a border-land (*metaichmion*) between the multiple *arithmoi*, represented by the triad, and the monad.[27] This he demonstrated by the fact that while the monad is made greater by addition than by multiplication ($1 + 1 > 1 \times 1$), and all other numbers become greater by multiplication than by addition ($3 \times 3 > 3 + 3$; $4 \times 4 > 4 + 4$, etc.), the dyad alone remains equal by addition or multiplication ($2 + 2 = 2 \times 2$) (*TA* 10, 10–11, 1). It was the "mother of numbers" and served as the matrix that transformed the monad into *arithmoi*.[28]

Though Iamblichus held a positive view of matter, as a Platonist, he needed to account for Plato's description of matter as the discordant and chaotic mass ordered by the Demiurge.[29] In his commentary on the *Timaeus* (30a), Iamblichus argued that this passage should not be taken literally so that chaos is understood to exist prior to an ordered cosmos. This, Iamblichus says, would be "impious, not only about the cosmos, but about the Demiurge himself, utterly abolishing either his supremely good will or else his creative power."[30] Rather, Iamblichus said that Plato described a cosmos

26. *Damascius: Dubitationes et Solutiones de Primis Principiis in Platonis Parmenidem* (*Dub. et Sol.*), 2 vols., ed. C. A. Ruelle (1889; Brussels: Culture et Civilisation, 1964), 103, 6–10. While my references to Damascius are taken from Ruelle's edition, I have checked my citations with the improved text and translation of Damascius, *Traité des premiers principes*, 3 vols., text established by L. G. Westerink and translation by J. Combes (Paris: Les Belles Lettres, 1986–91). See also the diagram of Iamblichus's metaphysical hierarchy based on this passage; J. Dillon, *Iamblichi Chalcidensis*, 32.

27. *TA* 10, 9–10. Text: ὅτι νοουμένου πλήθους κατὰ τριάδα τοῦ δ᾽ ἀντιθεμένου τῷ πλήθει κατὰ τὴν μονάδα μεταίχμιον ἡ δυὰς ἂν εἴη.

28. Iamblichus gave the dyad the epithets "Isis" based on the false etymology with *isos* "equal" (*TA* 13, 12) and "Rhea" because of the "flowing" (*rhusis*) of the material principle (14, 7). Though the dyad was needed to mediate the appearance of the intelligible *arithmoi*, in itself it was without "form" either *en dunamei*, as the monad (*TA* 1, 9), or *en energeia*, as all other numbers (1, 10).

29. *Tim.* 30a. It was from this passage that Plutarch developed his theory of a discordant World Soul that was brought to order by the Demiurge. See *On the Generation of the Soul* 1014bc, ed. Cherniss.

30. J. Dillon, *Iamblichi Chalcidensis*, 141.

after chaos in order to emphasize the dependence of the sensible world on: (1) the providence of the Demiurge, (2) the choreography of the *Nous*, and (3) the presence of the soul, without which the cosmos would fall into disarray.[31] The separation of corporeality from its form-giving qualities was merely a necessity of discourse. Iamblichus explains: "although the cosmos is eternally in being the exigencies of discourse separate the creation from the creator and bring into existence in a time sequence things which are established simultaneously."[32]

Thus, although in the *Timaeus* Plato describes creation as a sequence of events, the work of the Demiurge was simultaneous. For Iamblichus this meant that the cosmogony did not take place in a chronological past but was always present *in illo tempore*, and was therefore always accessible by means of theurgic ritual. The chronology of the *Timaeus* simply portrayed ontological grades of being simultaneously present in the corporeal world. The separation of corporeality from its principles was an impossibility that could occur only in abstraction, not in actuality. In other words, at the "moment" the Demiurge exists the entire corporeal world exists, and in every sense. There was no spatial or temporal separation between the Forms and their sensible expression.

Post-Iamblicheans no longer impugned matter as the cause of evil, and their solution to the problem was summed up by Jean Trouillard who said: "On exorcise la nuit en l'introduisant parmi les valeurs divines."[33] This followed Pythagorean thinking where the dyad became the mother of divine numbers. In any case, Iamblichus's strong monism made no allowance for a principle of evil; it was merely an accident within the flux of nature.[34] Yet, as Iamblichus noted, evil does appear in the composite lives of the last elements, in the fourth and fifth levels of existence, when something

---

31. Ibid., 140.
32. Ibid.
33. J. Trouillard, *L'un et l'âme selon Proclos* (Paris: Les Belles Lettres, 1972), 19.
34. Proclus coined the term *parhupostasis* to describe the quasi-existence of evil. It was entirely parasitic on the Good. See *Proclus: Trois études sur la providence*, vol. 3, *De l'éxistence du mal*, ed. D. Isaac (Paris: Les Belles Lettres, 1982), 13–17.

"falls out of the order of nature" (*tina ekpiptein . . . tou kata phusin;* *DCMS* 18, 13).

I follow Merlan and Tarrant in assigning the fourth and fifth levels to "bodies" and "unordered masses" respectively, for Iamblichus emphasized that the soul was not a composite.[35] In the *De Mysteriis* he says: "Whenever the soul comes into the body it does not suffer nor do the *logoi* which it gives to bodies, for the *logoi* are forms (*eidē*), simple and uniform, allowing no disturbance to come in or out of themselves. The soul, moreover, is *the cause of the suffering* for the composite, and the cause is surely not identical with its effect" (*DM* 35, 8–14). This would seem to refute Kramer's assigning souls and bodies to the fourth and fifth levels respectively, yet, according to Iamblichus, the soul maintains an intimate connection with the composite lives that it sustains. Despite the fact that the soul, *kath' heautēn,* is ungenerated and free of suffering, it nevertheless "inclines and is turned to the generated composites over which it has jurisdiction" (*DM* 21, 6–7), and to the degree that the soul's attention falls into these lives it is subject to the suffering and evils that are their lot.[36]

---

35. *Suntithēmi* is the key term in both the *DM* and *DCMS* to designate lives in the "last orders" in generated and composite existences. In the *DCMS* Iamblichus says evil appears *en tois tetartois kai pemptois tois suntithemenois* (18, 10), and in the *DM* Iamblichus says the soul is the generative cause of *gignomenon te kai phtheiromenon tōn sunthetōn* (35, 14–16).

36. Cf. Iamblichus's *Letter to Macedonius on Fate,* Stob. II, 173, 5–174, 27, Stobaeus: *Anthologium,* 4 vols., ed. C. Wachsmuth and O. Hense (Berlin: Weidmanns, 1958).

3

Matter as Obstacle to the Embodied Soul

What good ... can be generated from matter?

I t is precisely in the turn to composite lives that the perspective on matter changes from that of the World Soul to that of particular embodied souls; in turn, the portrayal of matter becomes pessimistic. Even the "optimistic" *Timaeus* touched briefly on the cause for this pessimism in its description of the confusion that attends the embodiment of the soul (*Tim.* 44). In this regard, the pessimistic language of the *Phaedo* should be understood within the context of the soul's entire incarnational itinerary. The perception of the body as a "prison" would be an important and necessary step in the soul's progress toward a complete incarnation. The negative imagery functioned as a catalyst to purge the soul of an identity anchored in the sensible world; in light of Iamblichus's itinerary for the study of the Platonic dialogues, where the *Phaedo* is read early on,[1] its negative view of embodiment should be seen as a medicinal shock, intended to disturb the soul's complacency and later to be ameliorated with a more complete understanding.[2]

1. Iamblichus's itinerary for the reading of the Platonic dialogues and their relation to the development of the virtues is explained in *Anonymous Prolegomena to Platonic Philosophy*, intro., text, and trans. L.G. Westerink (Amsterdam: North-Holland, 1962), xxxvii–xl.

2. In support of this interpretation I refer the reader to Iamblichus's definition of *katharsis* in *De Anima* where he contrasts the "lesser" perfections of catharsis, which are simply purgative and remove the soul from somatic attachments, with the complete catharsis that follows purgation and withdrawal with a reinvestment into particulars in a divine manner (*Stob.* I, 455, 25–456, 8).

41

That matter and embodiment were described both negatively and positively by Plato suggests that his writings were not to be taken as univocal truths but—as Iamblichus believed—spiritual exercises employed by students at different stages of development and under the careful guidance of teachers.[3] While one student would be encouraged to dwell on the ascetic themes of the *Phaedo*, another would be directed to the *Symposium* to contemplate erotic connections that would be impossible unless the soul had already practiced the asceticism and withdrawal encouraged by the *Phaedo*. The Platonic worldview was hierarchical, and in Iamblichus's Syrian school each dialogue had a specific purpose (*skopos*), the realization of which was dependent upon the student fulfilling its precedents.[4] They were not simply intellectual exercises but demanded profound transformations in the students who practiced them as part of their spiritual discipline.

Without taking into consideration Iamblichus's hierarchical understanding of Platonic education and its relation to the cosmos, his negative descriptions of matter in the *De Mysteriis* would appear inconsistent with his position on matter outlined above. For example, in book III, chapter 28, Iamblichus condemned the makers of magical talismans and idols on the grounds that their work was artificial (*technikōs*) and not theurgic (*theourgikōs*) (*DM*, 170, 9–10). Iamblichus dissociated theurgy from such artifice with a twofold critique, expressing concern for (a) the character of the idol maker, and (b) the material of his work. Iamblichus argued that while theurgy revealed the creative powers of the Demiurge and was

---

3. Pierre Hadot recaptures this important, yet often unnoticed, aspect of philosophy in antiquity, "Exercices spirituels," in *Annuaire: Ecole Pratique des Hautes Etudes* (Paris: 1976–77), 63–70; republished in Hadot, *Exercices Spirituels et Philosophie Antique* (Paris: Etudes Augustiniennes, 1981), 13–58.

4. For a discussion of Iamblichus's organization of Platonic dialogues according to the "central theme" or *skopos* of each, and the influence of this method on this history of literary criticism, see James Coulter, *The Literary Microcosm: Theories of Interpretation of the Later Neoplatonists* (Leiden: E.J. Brill, 1976), 73–94. For an explanation of the *skopos* as a central hermeneutic tool in Iamblichus's exegeses of the Platonic dialogues see B. D. Larsen, *Jamblique de Chalcis: Exégète et philosophe* (Aarhus: Universitetsforlaget, 1972), 429–46. Iamblichus's notion of the *skopos* as a hermeneutic tool became the central principle for all Neoplatonic exegesis.

rooted in uniform essences, the art of the idol maker concerned merely the last efflux of nature and attempted to manipulate the material world with sympathetic attractions. The creator of the stars and planets, true images of the gods, was *theos*, but of artificial idols Iamblichus says: "God is not their maker, but man. Nor are they produced out of uniform and intelligible essences, but from matter which has been acquired. What good, therefore, can be generated from matter and from the corporeal powers around matter and in bodies?" (*DM* 168, 3–8). Iamblichus no doubt meant to refute Porphyry's depiction of theurgy as a *material* manipulation of the gods, and therefore emphasized the indigence of material things as compared to divine beings; nevertheless he does ask: "What good can be generated from matter?" (*DM* 168, 6), which seems to contradict his remarks in the *Theology of Numbers* and *On General Mathematical Science*. It is clear that the context of Iamblichus's discourse has changed significantly; here his description of matter was unquestionably negative.

Throughout his exposition of theurgic sacrifice in book V, Iamblichus referred to matter as a pollution from which souls must be cleansed. For example, he says: "the contamination from material things falls upon those who are held in a material body; and as many souls as are subject to defilement by matter should necessarily be purified" (*DM* 204, 4–7). Matter was the obstacle that kept souls from communion with the gods. Since the gods were free from the pollution of matter, to reach them souls had to break free from material bonds. Iamblichus says:

> Just as the Gods split matter with lightning and separate from it from things which are essentially immaterial but have been dominated and bound by matter, and from being passive render them impassive, so also our [sacrificial] fire, imitating the activity of the divine fire, destroys everything material in the sacrifices, purifies the offerings by fire, and *frees them from the bonds of matter*. It makes them suitable for communion with the Gods through the purity of nature and in the same manner it frees us from the bonds of generation, assimilates us to the Gods, makes us fit for their friendship (*philia*), and leads our material nature up to the immaterial. (*DM* 215, 15–216, 8)

In these passages matter is opposed to the gods and the body is seen as the prison from which souls are freed. Yet Iamblichus also said that matter was an impediment only for individual souls, not for the World Soul or celestial souls (stars). For these, embodiment produced no "injury" nor "obstacle" (*DM* 200, 7–8), but "to a particular soul the communion with the body is demeaning in both these respects" (*DM* 200, 8–10). What determined whether or not matter impeded souls was the kind of body they inhabited and the perspective this allowed them. While human souls were particular and had a partial perspective, the World Soul and celestial souls were "wholes," complete worlds with a global perspective—a critical difference to which we will return.

The "bonds of generation" from which souls had to be cleansed were personified by Iamblichus as *daimones*, mediating entities that tied souls to their bodies.[5] In the *De Mysteriis* Iamblichus says: "One must assign to daimones the jurisdiction over generative powers, as well as the responsibility over nature and of binding souls to bodies" (*DM* 67, 15–68, 1). To free the soul from the bonds of generation theurgic sacrifice had to overcome the daimonic powers of nature. For, Iamblichus says, "*Daimones* lead souls down into nature" (*DM* 79, 9–10), not up to the gods. Yet, these same daimons followed divine will. "[They] bring into manifest activity the invisible good of the Gods . . . reveal what is ineffable in the Gods, shape what is formless into forms, and render what is beyond all measure into visible ratios" (*DM* 16, 16–17, 4). In the *De Mysteriis* daimons were portrayed both as agents of the Demiurge and as powers that defiled the soul by tying it to matter. This ambivalence was due to their centrifugal activity: in being agents of the Demiurge in the "procession" of the gods, it was their task to exteriorize specific aspects of the divine, and in disseminating the divine presence into matter daimons also led the attention of particular souls into a centrifugal

5. The locus classicus of the doctrine of daimons for Neoplatonists was Plato's *Symposium* 202e–203a. For a development of the doctrine after Plato among the Stoics see A. D. Nock, "Posidonius," *Journal of Roman Studies* 49 (1959): 1–15. For a comparison between the daimons of Iamblichus and their portrayal in the Chaldean Oracles, see Friedrich W. Cremer, *Die Chaldaïschen Orakel und Jamblich de Mysteriis* (Meisenheim am Glan: Anton Hain, 1969), 68–86.

and extroverted attitude. This was what bound them to their bodies and caused them to suffer.

In his opening remarks to Porphyry in the *De Mysteriis* Iamblichus said that he would reply to his questions theologically, philosophically, or theurgically (*DM* 7, 2–6). Iamblichus's description of daimons surely was drawn from his theurgic vocabulary: daimons were the personified powers of matter, entities whose centrifugal influence on souls was encountered and turned around in theurgic rituals. Iamblichus, therefore, allowed for a functional dualism within his monism. In the imagery of theurgic rites he pitted spiritual gods against material daimons, but as the soul was gradually freed from the bonds of generation it began to participate in the fundamental unity of the cosmos. By fulfilling the commands of a theurgic rite, the soul began to share in the continuity that extended from the gods to matter and in which the materializing daimons played an important and beneficial role.[6]

The dualistic language of the *De Mysteriis* was even more evident in the Chaldean Oracles. Based on the extant fragments, the Oracles seem to have been more "hieratic" than the *De Mysteriis* and less "philosophical"; they pertain strictly to ritual phenomena and are in no way an apology for ritual practices as was the *De Mysteriis*. Hans Lewy and Frederick Cremer have proven that these oracles, "recorded" by second-century Platonists, had a significant influence on Iamblichean theurgy.[7] Their negative portrayal of the material world is evident in the following *logia*:

> Fragment 88: [Nature] persuades us to believe that *daimones* are pure, and that the offspring of evil matter are good and useful.[8]

6. "Continuity" was the sine qua non for all theurgy. See *DM* 31, 18–32, 7. For the role of daimons in this continuity see *DM* 16, 6–20, 19.

7. Hans Lewy, *Chaldean Oracles and Theurgy* (Paris: Etudes Augustiniennes, 1978), and F. Cremer, *Die Chaldäischen Orakel*. For text, translation, and commentary see E. des Places, *Oracles chaldaïques* (Paris: Les Belles Lettres, 1971); see also the excellent English translation, *The Chaldean Oracles*, text, translation, and commentary by Ruth D. Majercik (Leiden: E. J. Brill, 1989).

8. Majercik, *Chaldean Oracles*, 82.

Fragment 90: from the hollows of the earth leap chthonian dogs (i.e., daimons), who never show a true sign to a mortal.[9]

Fragment 135: they [*daimones*] enchant souls, forever turning them away from the [holy] rites.[10]

Yet, as in the *De Mysteriis*, the Oracles also said that matter was derived from the highest divinity, the "source of sources" (*pēgē pēgōn*).[11] Faced with this ambiguity, Cremer asks: "Wenn die Materie von Gott kommt, wodurch ist sie ein *kakon*?"[12] and answered that Iamblichus attempted to resolve this problem by recourse to the notion of "unsympathetic sympathy,"[13] of a "matter alien to the gods" (*hē hulē allotria tōn theōn*; *DM* 233, 17). Lewy said that the development of an "evil matter" represented the attempt by late antique thinkers, under Gnostic influence, to correct the portrayal of matter in Plato's *Timaeus*. This resulted in a conflation of monist and dualist themes whose precise origin, he says, "can no longer be known."[14] Nevertheless, in his study of the Chaldean goddess Hecate, Lewy provides the key for understanding the role of matter in the *De Mysteriis* as well as in the Oracles.[15]

According to the Oracles, Hecate was queen of the daimons, and as such she personified all the powers of nature and matter. Lewy explains: "The Chaldean Hecate encountered the human souls in forms *always adequate to their internal condition*: for those sunk in the body she was necessity; for the erring, demonic temptation; for the renegade, a curse; for those who recalled their divine nature, a guide; and for those who returned home, grace."[16] Hecate was a mirror of the embodied soul, reflecting the soul's experience of

---

9. Ibid., 85.
10. Ibid., 101.
11. des Places, *Oracles chaldaïques*, frag. 30, p. 73.
12. Cremer, *Die Chaldäischen Orakel*, 30 n. 73.
13. Ibid., 28 n. 73.
14. Lewy, *Chaldean Oracles and Theurgy*, 382.
15. The term *hulē* was used by Iamblichus interchangeably with *phusis*, *sōma*, *genesis* and, in the Oracles, one may add the deities "Hades" and "Hecate" to the list. On Hecate as salvific goddess see Sarah Johnson, *Hekate Soteira* (Atlanta, Ga.: Scholars Press, 1989).
16. Lewy, *Chaldean Oracles and Theurgy*, 365.

matter and its own internal condition. In this sense, matter (Hecate) functioned as an index of the soul's spiritual condition and was evil only in proportion to the soul's attachment to its material existence. From a theurgic perspective, therefore, matter could not be considered apart from the soul's existential situation.

In the *De Mysteriis* Iamblichus used the terms *hulē, phusis, sōma,* and *genesis* nearly synonymously to define the "place" of the soul's extension.[17] They made up the field in which the soul's faculties were developed and tested, and its use of power in a corporeal existence determined its evaluation of matter. Embodied life could be experienced as a bondage to fate or as an opportunity to live under divine providence, depending on how the soul used its powers. For Iamblichus, providence (*pronoia*) and fate (*heimarmenē*) were functional terms describing the soul's experience of one divine law: salvific for those who obeyed and embodied it, oppressive to those who resisted it.[18]

In a letter to his student Macedonius, Iamblichus explained the nature of the soul and its relation to fate and providence. He says:

> The essence of the soul, in itself, is immaterial and incorporeal, entirely ungenerated and indestructible, possessing in itself Being and Life; it is completely self-moved and yet is the principle of nature and of all movements [Cf. *DM* 35, 9–11]. The soul, therefore, to the degree that it is itself, contains in itself self-authority, freedom, and life. But, to the degree that it gives itself to generated things, it is put under the sway of the cosmos, and to that degree it is led by fate and serves the necessities of nature. (*Stob.* II, 173, 5–13)

Fate ruled only those whose attention had been given over to generated things, not those who participated in their guiding principle. Iamblichus continued:

---

17. See Cremer's remarks, *Die Chaldaïschen Orakel*, 91.

18. The term *pronoia* is inadequately translated by "providence." For Neoplatonists it suggested the unknowable/(pre)knowable presence of the divine in the world. See J. Trouillard, "Note sur *PROOUSIOS* et *PRONOIA* chez Proclos," *Revue des Etudes Grecques* 72 (1960): 80–87.

To be brief, the movements of fate around the world may be likened to immaterial and noetic activities and revolutions, and the order of fate resembles this intelligible and pristine order. Secondary powers [encosmic gods] are joined with primary causes [hypercosmic gods] and the multitude in generation, and thus all things under fate are joined with undivided essence and with providence as a guiding principle. In accord with this same essence, then, fate is interwoven with providence and, in reality, *fate is providence*, is established from it and around it.

This being the case, the principle of human actions moves in concert with both these principles of the cosmos [fate and providence]. But there is also a principle of action liberated from nature and free from the movement of the cosmos. On account of this it is not contained in the motion of the world. Thus, it is not introduced from nature nor from any motion but is pre-established as more ancient, not having been derived from anything.[19]

Wherefore, since the soul is allotted certain parts from all the parts and elements of the cosmos and uses these, it is contained in the order of fate, takes its place in this order, fulfills its conditions, and makes proper use of it. And to the degree that the soul combines in itself pure reason, self-substantiated and self-moved, acting from itself and perfect, it is liberated from all external things. But to the degree that the soul extends into different modes of life, falls into generation, and identifies with the body, it is sewn into the order of the world. (*Stob.* II, 173, 26–174, 27)

The "parts" given to each soul from the totality of the cosmos made up its astrological portrait, and it was this confluence of elements at a particular juncture in time and space that made up the

19. Iamblichus referred to this "more ancient" and "pre-existent" principle to distinguish theurgical divination from human divination (*DM* 165, 14–166, 1). In the *De Mysteriis* Iamblichus often referred to astrology, one of the important forms of divination in late antiquity, and this passage on "fate" should be understood in an astrological context. One's fate was commonly believed to be determined by one's astral nativity—a point Iamblichus denies (*DM* 270, 9–11). Note also in this passage that Iamblichus mentions repeatedly that the soul is free from astral determinism; the soul is *apolutos* (*Stob.* 174, 12), *aphetos* (173, 14), and *authairetos* (173, 15). Iamblichus's argument draws, in large part, from the Stoics' accommodation of "fate" and "providence." Cf. Auguste Bouché-Leclercq, *Astrologie grecque* (Brussels: Culture et Civilisation, 1963), 31–32.

soul's localized self, the somatic testing ground that measured the soul's ability to integrate corporeal existence into a divine pattern. Failure to fulfill the conditions of the body resulted in fixations, unfulfilled conditions, and the subsequent suffering of "fate." The proper care of the body and somatic life, however, freed the soul from these bonds and allowed it, as Iamblichus says, to see "the turnings of fate to be like the perfect revolutions of the stars" (*Stob.* II, 173, 26–28).

4

Theurgy as
Demiurgy   *... taking the shape of the Gods.*

I n the *De Mysteriis* Iamblichus described the human soul as the
eschatos kosmos, the last world and reality: "Recognize, if you will,
the lowest of divine beings: the soul purified from the body"
(*DM* 34, 8). Because the human soul was the lowest divinity it suffered with the mortal lives that it sustained. Identified with only
"certain parts" of the cosmos, the soul lost its perspective of the
"whole" and become absorbed into the flux of mortal life.

Since matter cannot be discussed, from an existential perspective,
apart from the soul's experience of it, one may assume that Iamblichus's negative remarks about matter in the *De Mysteriis* describe, in
fact, the soul's experience of matter. Though Iamblichus used the
same term, *hulē* (or its functional equivalents: *sōma, phusis, genesis*),
it was not the *hulē* of the *Theology of Numbers* or the *hulē* produced
from the paternal monad in the *De Mysteriis*. It is one thing to speak
about matter philosophically or theologically—in an abstract or theoretical way—quite another to experience matter and to outline a
practical discipline to free souls from its constraints. However, apart
from telling Porphyry that he will answer questions philosophically,
theologically, or theurgically as he deemed appropriate, Iamblichus
did not explicitly signal the shifts in his discourse (*DM* 7, 2–6). What
was undoubtedly clear to himself and his readers is not always clear
to us. Being accustomed to a more univocal use of terms, the modern
reader of the *De Mysteriis* will likely miss these contextual shifts and
find Iamblichus's use of terms inconsistent and confusing.[1]

---

1. Hadot describes this problem in "Exercices spirituels," in *Annuaire: Ecole Pratique des Hautes Etudes* (Paris, 1976–77), 63–70.

Therefore, in spite of Iamblichus's pejorative descriptions of matter in the *De Mysteriis*, it was not viewed negatively, nor was embodiment per se. For later Neoplatonists, the body was understood as an integral part of a larger process. As Trouillard put it: "The body that the soul animates and through which it is placed in the cosmos is not an extrinsic addition but *the circuit that it travels in order to be united with itself.*"[2] The body was connatural (*sumphuēs*) with the soul, the soul with the intellect, and the intellect with god. The physical body was simply the "point of condensation" in a long process/*prohodos* that followed the material function of creative dispersion.[3] Nevertheless, Iamblichus was aware of the problems of embodiment and believed that theurgy was able to cure souls of somatic identification by guiding them into divinely sanctioned postures. He believed that the soul's "fall" into a body followed a divine impulse, a cosmogonic law, and that this same impulse, leading souls into bodies through daimonic urges, could be rerouted and transformed by theurgic rites. Theurgy limited and redirected the soul's daimonic attractions, transforming these intermediary beings into the soul's receptacle of salvation.

In an excellent analysis of the role of matter in the Chaldean Oracles, Stanislas Breton says that the negativity of matter was compensated by the Chaldean view of an unbroken continuity that extended from the gods to matter. He says:

> Matter and the body, consequently, are subject to a two-fold interpretation according to whether one descends or ascends the degrees of an ontological and divine hierarchy.... [The negative gravitation of the daimons] is equilibrated and compensated by an inverse pressure which makes of matter, in its "very fury," a homeopathic remedy for the degradation that it provokes. This is the profound meaning of theurgy which, relying on the continuity

2. J. Trouillard, *La Mystagogie de Proclos* (Paris: Les Belles Lettres, 1982), 251.

3. This image is taken from Stanislas Breton, "Téléologie et ontogonie: Variations sur les 'Oracles Chaldaïques,'" *Recherches de Science Religieuse* 66, no. 1, (1978): 8. For the ways in which Iamblichus discussed the continuity of lower entities with higher, see E. des Places, *Syngeneia: La Parenté de l'homme avec dieu d'Homère à la patristique* (Paris: Librairie C. Klincksieck, 1964), 171–76.

51

and connaturality of which we have spoken, discovers and exploits the quasi-sacramental virtues of little things as useless as stones.[4]

Even the densest aspects of matter, therefore, were potential medicines for a soul diseased by its body, and the cure for a somatic fixation in this theurgic homeopathy was the tail of the (daimonic) dog which bound it.

According to the *Timaeus* (41d), each soul was constituted by the same ratios as the World Soul and so necessarily participated, to some degree, in the entire world.[5] Consequently, there was nothing essentially perverse about material things or embodied experience. Yet, as Iamblichus explained in his letter on fate, if the soul directed excessive attention to the body it became subject to the rules governing corporeal action. In theurgic terms this demanded that the soul be reconciled with the daimon who ruled the realm of nature governing this activity. Being tied to generated life, the soul was bound to laws administered by daimonic intermediaries, and until the soul achieved a proper relation with them it remained subject to the punishments of their administration.

How these theurgic rapprochements were conducted, remains unknown since there are no extant records of theurgic ceremonies.[6] Nevertheless, Iamblichus did refer to material objects used in theurgic rites and accounted for the hidden power in such things as stones, plants, and animals. He says:

---

4. Breton, "L'homme et l'âme humaine dans les *Oracles chaldaïques*," *Diotima* 8 (1980): 22.

5. Iamblichus referred to this point in his explanation of divine justice (*DM* 188, 7–10).

6. Philippe Derchain has suggested that one ritual described in the *De Mysteriis* was taken directly from the ceremony of the sun's renewal in the house of life at Abydos. If Derchain is correct it may be that Iamblichus's (Abammon's) dependence on Egyptian cult was far greater than has been supposed. In late antiquity it was customary for Platonists to defer to the greater wisdom of the Egyptians, and one might assume that Iamblichus, following the style of Hermetic authors, claimed an Egyptian origin for theurgy to lend it an aura of ancient authority. If Iamblichus incorporated Egyptian hieratic practices in concrete detail it may provide an important key for understanding the liturgical order of theurgic rites. See Philippe Derchain, "Pseudo-Jamblique ou Abammōn," *Chronique d'Égypt* 38 (1963): 220–26.

Since it was necessary that earthly things not be deprived of participation in the divine, the earth received a certain divine portion capable of receiving the Gods. The theurgic art, therefore, recognizing this principle in general, and having discovered the proper receptacles, in particular, as being appropriate to each one of the Gods, often brings together stones, herbs, animals, aromatics, and other sacred, perfect, and deiform objects of a similar kind. Then, from all these it produces a perfect and pure receptacle. (*DM* 233, 7–16; cf. *DM* 235, 6–12)

Such objects served as receptacles of the gods because they preserved an intimate relation with them and bore their "signatures" (*sunthēmata*) in the manifest world. As such they were pure specimens of divine presence in matter, and for souls suffering a specific imbalance within the administration of a divine being, the objects that bore its symbol/*sunthēma* became homeopathic antidotes if handled in a ritually appropriate manner. Iamblichus explains: "Therefore, whether (it is) certain animals or plants or any of the other things on earth governed by Superior Beings, they simultaneously share in their inspective care and procure for us an indivisible communion with the Gods" (*DM* 235, 5–9). Through the appropriate use of the gods' *sunthēmata* in nature the soul could awaken in itself the power of their corresponding symbols (*DM* 136, 6–10). This realigned the soul with the manifesting energies of a deity and freed it from servitude to the daimons who watched over its physical expression (*DM* 174, 9–10).

Iamblichus's extant writings do not describe these theurgical practices in detail, but it is unlikely that they could have been explained discursively, for Iamblichus said that theurgic knowledge was gained only through "practical experience" (*DM* 229, 17–230, 1). Nevertheless, Iamblichus's theoretical justification for the use of material objects in theurgy may be summarized under three principles:

1. The gods illuminate matter and are present immaterially in material things. (*DM* 232, 14–16)

2. There exists a filial and beneficent bond between the gods who preside over life and the lives which they produce. (*DM* 235, 3–5)

3. The sacrificial order in theurgy was connected to the order of
   the gods. (*DM* 217, 3–4)

Proclus includes more specific information in his treatise *On the
Hieratic Art*, an introduction to theurgic taxonomy that identified
sunthēmata in nature with their ruling gods.[7] Proclus's best-known
example of a *sunthēma* is the "heliotrope" that bears the signature
of the sun god Helios. As Proclus puts it:

> each thing prays according to the rank it occupies in nature, and
> sings the praise of the leader of the divine series to which it
> belongs . . . for the heliotrope moves to the extent that it is free to
> move, and in its rotation, if we could hear the sound of the air buf-
> feted by its movement, we should be aware that it is a hymn to its
> king, such as it is within the power of a plant to sing.[8]

Like the heliotrope, other things in nature bore the imprint of the
sun god: cock (*CMAG* IV, 150, 4), lotus (*CMAG* IV, 149, 12), lion
(*CMAG* IV, 150, 3), and bel stone (*CMAG* IV, 149, 22), each revealing
different characteristics of the god hidden in its premanifest unity.
For example, while the bel stone demonstrated a solar affinity by its
mimesis of the sun's rays, the lotus and heliotrope imitated its diur-
nal revolution (*CMAG* IV, 150, 26–30).

Iamblichus explained that the power of the gods who "illuminated matter" was undiminished by their manifestations (*DM* 140,
19–141, 4). The use of "base" objects in theurgical rites in no way
degraded the god who was present in them. In fact, the use of inanimate objects in divination was all the more proof and guarantee
that a god was responsible for the prognosis since the objects themselves could not have provided it. Iamblichus says:

> If the power of the Gods extends in revealing itself as far as to
> inanimate things like pebbles, rods, pieces of wood, stones, corn
> or wheat, this very fact is the most striking aspect of the divine

---

7. Proclus, *On the Hieratic Art of the Greeks*, in *CMAG* VI, ed. J. Bidez (Brussels:
Maurice Lamertin, 1928), 139–51.

8. Proclus, *On the Hieratic Art*, in *CMAG* VI:148, 14–18. See the translation and
discussion of this passage in Henry Corbin, *Creative Imagination in the Sufism of
Ibn Arabi*, trans. Ralph Manheim (Princeton: Princeton University Press, 1969),
106.

prognostic in divination, for it gives soul to soulless things and motion to things without the power of movement. It makes all things clear and known, participate in reason, and be defined by the measures of *noēsis* although they possess no reason in themselves. (*DM* 141, 14–142, 3)

That things without intelligence should be vehicles of divine wisdom followed a principal tenet of theurgy that communion with the gods did not take place through man's mental efforts or power (*DM* 97, 1–9). Iamblichus continues: "Just as God sometimes makes an innocent fool speak words of wisdom—by which it is clear to all that the speech is not human but divine—in this same way God reveals ideas (*noēmata*) that transcend all [human] knowledge through things deprived of knowledge" (*DM* 142, 5–10).

Iamblichus's use of material objects in theurgy and his praise of their divine power was a correlate to his critique of human intellectual power. Man's incapacity to achieve union with the gods was made particularly evident in rites that employed insentient objects to achieve an experience that surpassed reason. The point, in short, was that theurgy is "divine action, not human" (*DM* 142, 7), and the use of inanimate objects in theurgic divination clearly demonstrates this point.

The *sunthēmata* embedded in nature were not limited to dense matter but were also present in certain incantations (*DM* 133, 18), concoctions (*DM* 133, 18), characters traced [on the earth] (*DM* 129, 15–17), and in the ineffable names that were able to draw souls into the presence of the gods (*DM* 157, 13–16). Iamblichus also mentions certain melodies and rhythms that gave the soul direct (*euthus*; *DM* 119, 6) participation in the gods.[9] The *sunthēmata*, in whatever expression, were divinizing, and for the same reason: they bore the impress of the god and were able to awaken souls to the divinity they symbolized.

---

9. Cf. *DM* 118, 17–119, 5. Iamblichus's theurgic interpretation of the possession through music or rhythmic speech (cf. Plato's *Ion* 536c; *Symp.* 215e) might be considered by historians of religions as a viable alternative to the theory that such occurrences are the effect of "anxiety states." See, for example, E. R. Dodds, *The Greeks and the Irrational* (Berkeley and Los Angeles: University of California Press, 1951), 79 n.108.

In theurgy, anything that received the god and mediated its presence functioned as a sacred receptacle whether it was a stone, a plant, a smell, or a song. All functioned as *hulē* with respect to the divine agent which they received and revealed.[10] Thus, even a "vision" that mediated the presence of a god was a kind of *hulē*. Iamblichus explains:

> One must be convinced by secret teachings that a certain matter is given by the Gods by means of blessed visions. This matter is somehow connatural (*sumphuēs*) with those who give it. The sacrifice with this sort of matter stirs the Gods up into manifestation and immediately invokes their appearance, receives them when they come forth, and reveals them perfectly. (*DM* 234, 7–14)

Iamblichus compares this visionary matter to the "pure and divine matter" (*hulēn tina katharan kai theian*) that receives and reveals the gods in cosmogony (*DM* 232, 17). As the soul became increasingly purified by theurgy so that it received such visions, its experience of matter became less like that of the *Phaedo* and more like the cosmological matter of the *Timaeus*, transforming the entire world into an immense receptacle, a *sunthēma* revealing the "will of the gods."[11] From a theurgic perspective, the cosmos was a temple whose sacrificial orders were designed by the Demiurge (*DM* 65, 6–8).

To be in a body, for a theurgist, was to have a place in this *temenos*, and even union with the gods was not impossible for those whose embodiment was properly consecrated. Iamblichus says: "By means of this [divine] will, the Gods, being benevolent and gra-

---

10. Each level on the chain of continuity became the "receptacle" of its superior. Thus, the role of any level would be alternately "formal" or "material," depending on whether the movement was up or down the chain. This "functional" view of matter had been outlined by Aristotle in the *De Anima* (430a, 10–13), where he says that the soul's cognitive powers are "matter" for the forms which they receive, i.e., insofar as anything is receptive to an informing principle, it is matter/*hulē* with respect to that principle.

11. Cf. *DM* 44, 11–45, 1 where the "necessity" of the gods is mingled with their beneficent will; cf. 141, 6–13 where god is said to create all forms of divination with one beneficent will, and 209, 14–17 where natural life forms are said to preserve the will of their maker.

cious, shine their light generously on theurgists, calling their souls up to themselves and giving them unification (*henōsis*), accustoming them—while they are yet in bodies—to be detached from their bodies and turned to their eternal and noetic principle" (*DM* 41, 4–11). To be *in* the body in a divine manner was to be *out of the body* (i.e., free of its material constraints), and Iamblichus maintained that this paradox was integral to every theurgic experience. He says:

> All of theurgy has a two-fold character. One is that it is a rite conducted by men which preserves our natural order in the universe; the other is that it is empowered by divine symbols (*sunthēmata*), is raised up through them to be joined on high with the Gods, and is led harmoniously round to their order. This latter aspect can rightly be called "taking the shape of the Gods." (*DM* 184, 1–8)

The theurgist was simultaneously man and god; he became an icon and *sunthēma* in precisely the same way as the other pure receptacles described by Iamblichus.

By means of appropriate rites the theurgist directed the powers of his particular soul (*mikros kosmos*) into alignment with the powers of the World Soul (cf. *DM* 292, 5–9), which gave him direct participation in the "whole." He became a *theios anēr*, universal and divine yet particular and mortal (*DM* 235, 13–14); in somatic terms this was the result of having filled the measures of his immortal *augoeides sōma*, the soul's "star body," which was visualized as a sphere.

The doctrine of the "soul vehicle" (*ochēma*) in the Platonic tradition is essential for understanding the manner in which the later Platonists visualized immortality.[12] Referred to by Iamblichus as a

---

12. See Robert Kissling, "The *OCHĒMA-PNEUMA* of the Neoplatonists and the *de Insomniis* of Synesius of Cyrene," *American Journal of Philology* 43 (1922): 318–30; E.R. Dodds, trans. and intro., *Proclus: The Elements of Theology*, 2d ed. (Oxford: Clarendon Press, 1963), esp. appendix II, "The Astral Body in Neoplatonism," 313–21; J. Trouillard, "Réflexions sur l'*OCHĒMA* dans les Eléments de Théologie de Proclos," *Revue des Etudes Grecques* 70 (1957): 102–7. More recent studies include: Andrew Smith, *Porphyry's Place in the Neoplatonic Tradition: A Study in Post-Plotinian Neoplatonism* (The Hague: Martinus Nijhoff, 1974), appendix 2, "The *pneumo/ochēma*," 152–58; H.J. Blumenthal, "Some Problems About the Body and Soul in Later Neoplatonism: Do They Follow a Pattern?" *Platonismus und*

vehicle (*ochēma*) (*DM* 132, 12), or breath (*pneuma*) (*DM* 125, 6), the perfection of this aetheric and luminous body effected the soul's immortalization. Through the purifying light given by the gods in theurgy the embodied soul was freed of its particularity and established in its starry vehicle, the *augoeides ochēma* (*DM* 312, 9–18). Like the spherical bodies of the universe and stars, for whom embodiment was simply adornment and revelation,[13] the spherical body gained in theurgic rituals established the soul as immortal yet still allowed for the multitude of activities engaged in by a mortal and embodied soul.

Iamblichus often repeats the Neoplatonic principle that "like approaches like,"[14] and in the case of a particular embodied soul the only way to reach the universality of the World and celestial souls was to become like them, that is, spherical. Thus, Iamblichus says: "Wherefore, also our vehicle (*ochēma*) is made spherical and is moved circularly whenever the soul is especially assimilated to *Nous*."[15] It was within his luminous and spherical vehicle that the

---

Christentum: Festschrift für Heinrich Dörrie, eds. H.-D. Blume and F. Mann, *Jahrbuch für Antike und Christentum*, Ergänzungsband 10 (Münster: Aschendorff, 1983), 75–85. The most detailed description of the purification of the soul-vehicle in late antiquity is Hierocles, *Hierocles in Aureum Pythagoreorum Carmen Commentarius*, ed. F.G. Koehler (Stuttgart: Teubner, 1974), chap. 26, 46–49. For Hierocles' view see Ilsetraut Hadot, *Le Problème du néoplatonisme alexandrin, Hiéroclès et Simplicius* (Paris: Etudes Augustiniennes, 1978), 98–106.

Apart from the historical sources for this teaching, discussed in large part by Kissling, the question remains of how to understand it. Blumenthal suggests that the psychic vehicle/faculty (i.e., imagination) was used by Plotinus "to protect the higher soul from influence from below" ("Some Problems," 83), to keep the higher principles from being stained by the lower. While this may be the case for Plotinus, it was not so for the later Neoplatonists. In "Réflexions sur *l'OCHĒMA*," Trouillard argues that for Proclus the *ochēma*, while separating distinct levels of the soul in the cosmos, at the same time joins them, preserving a continuity through all levels. In terms of salvation, the vehicle of the soul and its "imaginal body" became the "place" where the soul forgot or remembered its immortality.

13. *DM* 200, 7–8; cf. 202, 13–203, 9 for the ungenerated and impassive "aetherial body" of the heavens, and 212, 5 for the "impassive light-vehicle" of daimons.

14. References to the notion of *similis similibus* are seen in the *DM* 16, 11–13; 20, 4–8; 46, 13–16; 49, 1–3; 211, 15–18.

15. J. Dillon, ed., *Iamblichi Chalcidensis, In Tim.* frag. 49, lines 13–15.

theurgist received visions and was unified with the gods, yet this unification did not deny the multiplicity of his mortal life, for the sphere, Iamblichus says, "is capable of containing multiplicity (*to plēthos*), which indeed makes it truly divine, that not departing from its oneness it governs all the multitude."[16] The theurgist became spherical. He "took on a divine appearance" (*DM* 184, 8) but remained a man. His apotheosis demanded not only that he activate his aetheric and immortal body but also that he remain bound to his mortal life.

To the degree that a theurgist was divinized and assimilated to the Demiurge (*DM* 292, 14–17) he necessarily shared the benign interest of the Demiurge in generated life, including his own. Any aversion he may have felt toward his mortal existence was therefore overcome by his experience of the "whole," and his physical body became the nexus through which he expressed this divine benevolence. In his person, he preserved a continuity between the "whole" and its "parts," between the gods and man. Iamblichus outlines this process in his description of catharsis in the *De Anima*. The cleansing of the soul's particular fixations by purgation and withdrawal from the body was merely a preliminary stage, to be followed by a positive reinvestment in particulars. Iamblichus says:

> Indeed, of catharsis, one must conceive its most useful aspects to be: [1] withdrawal from alien things; [2] restoration of one's own essence; [3] perfection; [4] fulness; [5] independence; [6] ascent to the creative cause; [7] conjunction of parts with wholes; and [8] contribution from the wholes to the parts of power, life, activity, and similar things. (*Stob.* I, 455, 25–456, 4)

---

16. Ibid., frag. 49, lines 27–29. Iamblichus refers to this same principle: the unity that contains multiplicity at *DM* 59, 9–15. Fragment 49 of Iamblichus's commentary on the *Timaeus* (33b) is called by Dillon, "an elaborate encomium of sphericity" (ibid., 326). The sphere, revered by Platonists and Pythagoreans as the most simple and inclusive of all forms, deserves a more detailed study. Note also Iamblichus's description of the priestess of Delphi being divinely possessed by a rotating fire (*DM* 126, 13). For an interesting study of the "sphere" and circularity in the Platonic tradition, see Lynne Ballew, *Straight and Circular: A Study of Imagery in Greek Philosophy* (Assen, The Netherlands: Van Gorcum, 1979), 79–128; 131–33.

Of the eight attributes, only the first is negative, and Iamblichus specifically faults the view of those who defined catharsis as a withdrawal from matter. He says: "Some give greater value to separation from the body, freedom from [material] bonds, liberation from mortality, release from generation and similar *lesser goals* of catharsis" (*Stob.* I, 456, 6–8). The greater goals that followed were theurgic: the unification with the creative cause, the demiurgic activity of joining parts of wholes, and the subsequent reinvestment of parts with the vitality of their universal sources.

The mistake of an embodied soul was not in having a body, nor in being fully aware of physical existence. The error lay in the weighing of the soul's attention. Its consciousness was to be anchored in the whole, the harmonic unity of the Demiurge, with only minimal attention given to one's localized self. The experience of the theurgist would still include suffering and evils, but these would be incorporated into the whole. Iamblichus says: "Therefore, due to corporeal necessities, certain evils and corruptions occur to parts, but they are salvific and good with respect to wholes and the harmony of the universe" (*DM* 192, 3–6). Even the imposition of one "part" on another, while apparently distressful to that part, was necessary and beneficial to the harmony of the "whole," a principle which, Iamblichus says, "we see exemplified clearly in a dance" (*DM* 56, 14–15).

Evils rooted in corporeal necessities were inevitable and unavoidable, but moral evils and perverse acts derived from man's poorly receiving the emanations of the celestial gods, manipulating them for selfish ends, or suffering them in an unbalanced way (*DM* 194, 4–6; 13–15). These evils, however, did not come from the gods themselves. Iamblichus explains: "That which is given in one manner [from above], is received in another by the things here below. For example, the emanation of *Kronos* tends to stabilize and that of *Ares* is kinetic, but the passive and generative receptacle in material things receives the former as rigidity and coldness and the latter as exaggerated inflammation" (*DM* 55, 4–11; cf. *DM* 192, 18–193, 2). Though the gods descended with unified sameness to preserve the cosmos (*DM* 55, 17–18; 194, 8–12) their powers were received by mortals in a partial and passionate manner; as Iamblichus says, "parts are incapable of receiving the energies of the whole" (*DM* 192, 7–8). Through his participation in the whole the theurgist became immortal and universal, but as a part he lived and died. He ritually encircled his mortal life with the providential care of a creator.

The whole/part dichotomy was of central importance to Iamblichus,[17] allowing him to reconcile experiences of evil and corruption within a good cosmos. Cosmologies that opposed spirit to matter or assigned to matter a positive evil force erred, in the view of Iamblichus, by assuming that the cosmos could be adequately measured by the dialectical oppositions of the discursive mind (*DM* 10, 1–7). A cosmology with matter evilly opposed to spirit indicated that one's vision was still partial and fixed in unresolved oppositions.

Iamblichus's whole/part theodicy held that the experience of evil was rooted in an incomplete perception, in a partial identity not yet sacrificed for the good of the whole (*DM* 186, 11–187, 3; cf. book IV, chap. 5). In this, Iamblichus was simply following Plato, who, in the *Laws*, discussed the whole/part dichotomy in a similar way. Having outlined the order of the world, the Athenian stranger says that individual souls must also make their contribution. They exist, he tells his listener, "in order that blissful existence be secured for the life of the whole; not for your sake was the world generated—but you were born for its sake" (*Laws* 903c).

The partial or whole experience of matter and embodiment correspond directly to the Platonic description of embodiment in the *Phaedo* and the *Timaeus*: the former being the perspective of a particular soul in a mortal body, and the latter a view of matter from the perspective of the whole, perpetual and perfect. For a Platonist, the *Timaeus* and the *Phaedo* defined the parameters in which the problem of embodiment was discussed, and Iamblichus's solution was that the blessedness of embodiment as portrayed in the *Timaeus* was available to the particular soul only by imitating the activity of the Demiurge, and this was possible only through theurgic rites.

---

17. Iamblichus refers to this theme throughout the *De Mysteriis*; see, for example, book IV, chap. 9.

The meaning of theurgy in the history of Platonism becomes clear if it is seen as the praxis that allowed souls to move from the experience of embodiment as an isolated prison to a participation in the World Soul, where its particularity was re-established in the unity of the whole.

By entering into the community of the gods as one of its bodies of light, the embodied soul was no longer alienated by matter nor passionately drawn to it. Embodiment was transformed from the psychic chaos of suffering into a cosmos, an adornment of the divine. The "lapse of time" in the *Timaeus* (30a) between material chaos and cosmos—though only a necessity of discourse when speaking of the World Soul—was an accurate description of the experience of the embodied soul on its path to demiurgy. In theurgy the soul gradually transformed the chaos of its embodied experience into the perfect measures of the cosmos.[18] In his mortal aspect the theurgist became the recipient of this beauty, while in his mediation of the gods, he became his own demiurge.

Throughout the theurgist's lifelong labor (see *DM* 92, 8–10; 131, 9–10) of building a divine body, matter was the mirror that reflected the condition of his soul. It was, as Iamblichus says, the "index" (*deigma*; *DM* 80, 15) of divine presence, and the intensity of the soul's contact with the gods was in direct proportion to its receptive capacity.[19] In his explanation of appearances (*phasmata*) in divination Iamblichus explains that the higher the divinity, the more completely it consumes matter: "Take the immediate consumption of matter by the Gods as no small indication for you; with Archangels

18. Interesting parallels exist between the praxis of later Platonists and the methods of yoga. Compare the theurgists' goal of identifying with the order of the cosmos with Eliade's description of the goal of the yogi: "all these [yogic] exercises pursue the same goal, which is to abolish multiplicity and fragmentation, to reintegrate, to unify, to make whole. . . . Indeed one can speak of the first yogic stages as an effort toward the 'cosmicization' of man. *To transform the chaos of biomental life into a cosmos . . . .*" (my emphasis). Mircea Eliade, *Yoga: Immortality and Freedom*, trans. Willard Trask (Princeton: Princeton University Press, 1973), 97.

19. Iamblichus refers to the ability of souls to intensify this presence when he says that continual prayer "renders the receptacle(s) of the soul far greater [for the communion] of the Gods" (*DM* 238, 15–239, 1).

it is consumed in a short time; with Angels there is a dissolution and elevation from matter; by *Daimones* matter is beautifully organized; Heroes bear a proportionate adaptation to matter in fitting measures and give a skillful attention to it" (*DM* 80, 15–81, 4). The rank of a divinity was indicated by its relation to, and command over, matter. Matter was the index that measured the degrees of divinity, and for particular souls their relation to matter also determined the kind of theurgy they were to practice. The *materia* of the rites varied from stones and plants to the visionary matter given directly by the gods, but in all stages matter was not something reluctantly accepted in the rites, it was the necessary vehicle through which souls were divinized.

In the *De Mysteriis* Iamblichus portrays the soul's experience of matter through the Egyptian hieroglyph of a young god seated on a lotus. The material principle, represented by "mud" (*ilus*) under the lotus, serves as the "foundation" (*puthmen*) to nourish the lotus until it develops a circular throne for the god.[20] Just so, each embodied soul, rooted in the "mud" of embodiment and the waters of psychic change, is nourished by this very condition until it is capable of receiving the god.

The matter of the *Phaedo* with all its negative effects was revealed progressively to the theurgist as the matter of the *Timaeus*, but only by virtue of the theurgist himself becoming demiurgic and ritually enacting the "eternal measures" (*metra aidia*; *DM* 65, 4) established in creation. His perfection, as soul, was realized only by first assimilating himself to the world,[21] co-ordinating his "particular" attractions, somatic or intellectual, with their causal principles. As the "lowest" divinity, the human soul achieved its highest condition only when it was conscious of being lowest, for only then did it realize its place in the divine hierarchy. When the soul's "receptacles" were cleansed of the accretions added in embodiment it could become a proper receptacle of the gods and, like the pure matter of the *Timaeus*, transfer this order to the phenomenal world. The per-

20. For "mud" see *DM* 250, 17–251, 5; for "lotus" see 251, 17–252, 12.
21. I have been influenced on this point by S. Breton, "L'homme et l'âme humaine," 23.

fect theurgist became an embodied Demiurge[22] whose presence was enough to create harmony out of discord and drive away evil. Iamblichus says:

> [E]very vice and every passion is entirely removed by theurgists, for a pure participation of the good is present with the pure, and they are filled from on high with the fire of truth. For theurgists there is no impediment from evil spirits, nor are there hindrances to the goodness of the soul. Nor does any affectation, or flattery, or the enjoyment of vapors or violent force annoy them. But, all these, as if struck by lightning, yield and recede without touching the theurgists, nor can they even approach them. (*DM* 178, 8–16)

Having situated his particularity into the circle of the whole, the theurgist was immune from particular threats in precisely the same way as the gods (cf. *DM* 201, 16–202, 2). In imitation of divine beings, the body of the theurgist became a vehicle through which the gods appeared to the physical world and through which he received their communion.

---

22. Though this point shall be pursued later in arithmogonic terms, a suggestive ritual parallel existed in the example of the pharaoh (and his priest functionaries) in ancient Egyptian cult. He was, as Serge Sauneron says, "the guarantor of the universal balance"; see Sauneron, *The Priests of Ancient Egypt*, trans. Ann Morrissett (New York: Grove, 1960), 31.

II

The Nature of the Embodied Soul

5

The Descent of the Soul

One must take into account the differences between the universal soul and our own...

Iamblichus's teachings on the soul were an essential correlate to his theurgical system, yet to be understood properly they must be seen in the context of alternative developments in Platonic schools from the second to the fourth century c.e. Iamblichus's emphasis on the descent of the soul was a response to what he perceived as unorthodox and dualistic forms of Platonism. The most significant in Iamblichus's era was the Gnostics' reversal of the Platonic creation myth and their reinterpretation of the Demiurge and World Soul. Though Gnostics drew their dramatis personae from Jewish myths, their cosmological framework was taken from Plato's *Timaeus*, and to some degree from the *Phaedo* and *Phaedrus*. For the Gnostics, creation was no longer the beneficent expression of the Demiurge but the result of primal sin and error. The sensible world was a maleficent prison, and the orders of the heavens, which for Plato served as media for a return to the divine, were transformed into spiritual oppressors who held souls captive in matter.[1]

---

1. Recent scholarship has shown that this anticosmic characterization of Gnosticism, while generally accurate, is not universally applicable. The tractate *Marsanes* (*Nag Hammadi* Codices [NHC] 10, 1), for example, presents a monistic view of the cosmos fully in line with Plato's *Timaeus* (see esp. *Marsanes* 5, 17–26). For a discussion of *Marsanes* and its relation to Platonism, see Birger Pearson, "Gnosticism as Platonism: With Special Reference to Marsanes (NHC 10, 1)," *Harvard Theological Review* 77, no. 1 (1984): 55–72. Pearson shows in this article that certain Gnostic ideas influenced and informed later Platonic thought (17). Cf. Pearson, "The Tractate Marsanes (NHC X) and the Platonic Tradition," in *Gnosis: Festschrift für Hans Jonas*, ed. Barbara Aland (Göttingen: Vandenhoech and Ruprecht, 1978), 373–84.

This inverted mythology may have been rooted in Jewish apocalyp-
ticism, but it came to influence Platonists of the third century.
There were several gnosticizing Platonists in attendance at Plotinus's lectures, and the second-century Platonist, Numenius, had
already explained the myth of the *Timaeus* in a manner similar to
the Gnostics by asserting a secondary Demiurge who *falls* into
Nature and whose longing for release is reflected in the drama of
human suffering. The Hermetic *Poimandres* is another example of a
gnosticizing Platonism where creation is portrayed as the result of
an error or fall.

Hans Lewy contends that these remythologizings of the *Timaeus*
were attempts to improve on a myth that failed to provide satisfactory answers to the problem of evil and human suffering.[2] The
obvious appeal of Gnostic dualism was its dramatic clarity and the
solution it offered through gnosis. Gnostics promised salvation to
those who felt dominated by foreign and insensitive rulers, social as
well as cosmic. Although Iamblichus never explicitly argues against
the Gnostics,[3] his description of the soul, as well as his theurgical
system, were surely influenced by the Platonic-Gnostic debate, particularly as it was taken up by Iamblichus's predecessor Plotinus.
Plotinus's arguments against the Gnostics, and the solutions he suggests for the problems of the embodied soul provide the appropriate
context to evaluate Iamblichus's position.

In his *Treatise Against the Gnostics*[4] Plotinus charged that the
Gnostics failed to differentiate between the ontological levels of the
World Soul, which is a whole, and individual souls, which are parts.

Nevertheless, the Gnostics with whom Plotinus and Iamblichus were familiar were
almost certainly dualists, possibly Sethian or Archontic Gnostics; see *Plotinus*, vol.
2, trans. by A. H. Armstrong (Cambridge: Harvard University Press), 264–65.

2. Lewy, *Chaldean Oracles and Theurgy*, ed. M. Tardieu (Paris: Etudes Augustiniennes, 1978), 382; cf. Plotinus, *Enn.* II, 9, 6, 25–28.

3. The only extant evidence of Iamblichus's familiarity with the Gnostics is in
his doxography of the descent of the soul in the *De Anima*. "According to the Gnostics," Iamblichus says, "the soul descends because of derangement (*paranoia*) or
deviation (*parekbasis*)"; *Stob.* I, 375, 9.

4. *Enn.* II, 9 is listed as thirty-third in the chronology of Plotinus's writings.

Contrasting the respected teachings of the Ancients (*palaioi*)[5] and Plato with those of the Gnostics, Plotinus says:

> They [the Gnostics] blame the soul for its association with the body and censure the director of this universe and identify its maker with the soul, and attribute to this universal soul the same affections as those which the souls in parts of the universe have [*Enn*. II, 9, 6, 59–63; trans. Armstrong].... But to apply conclusions drawn from our soul to the Soul of the All is as if somebody were to take the tribe of potters or smiths in a well-ordered city and make them a reason for blaming the whole. But one must take into account the differences between the universal soul and ours, in its management of the body; it does not direct it in the same way, and is not bound to it. (*Enn*. II, 9, 7, 5–9)

According to Plotinus, the Gnostics projected their psychological condition on the cosmos and shifted the burden for their suffering to the Demiurge and his astral regents. In other words, they mistakenly took the "part," the particular soul, for the "whole," the World Soul. The cause for this, Plotinus argued, was the Gnostics' attempt to go beyond their capacities as individual souls and "set themselves up next to god" (*Enn*. II, 9, 9, 48). This was nothing more than wishful thinking (*hōsper oneirasi petesthai*; *Enn*. II, 9, 9, 49), Plotinus said, and it diverted their souls from making the only possible ascent to the gods, realized not by rejecting the stars and World Soul but by imitating them as much as possible (*Enn*. II, 9, 18, 31–35). The cause for evil and the suffering of the soul did not come from the World Soul or its regents but from the inability of the individual soul to harmonize itself with the ordered movements of the whole. Plotinus says: "If any of the parts of the universe is moved according to its nature, the parts with whose nature the movement is not in accord suffer, but those which are moved go on well, as parts of the

5. It is interesting that Plotinus refers to the authority of the "Ancients" (*palaioi*) (*Enn*. II, 9, 6) over against the new opinions of the Gnostics, for Iamblichus refers to the "Ancients" in the *De Anima* in contrast to the views of Numenius (and possibly Plotinus) (*Stob*. I, 458).

whole; but the others are destroyed because they are not able to endure the order of the whole."[6]

Iamblichus would have agreed with Plotinus's distinction between universal and individual souls. It was a position argued by Iamblichus himself—probably with some degree of irony—in his defense of theurgy against Plotinus's pupil, Porphyry. Yet the basis for Porphyry's reversal of this teaching probably lay in the thinking of Plotinus himself who, apart from his distaste for Gnostic views, had never found a satisfactory answer for the cause of human suffering and evil.[7]

In his treatise on the descent of souls into bodies (*Enn.* IV, 8) Plotinus followed Platonic tradition by contrasting the somatic experience of partial souls (*para meros*) (*Enn.* IV, 8, 7, 24), who move gradually from embodied confusion to tranquility, with the Soul of the All (*tou pantos*; *Enn.* IV, 8, 7, 27), which is never distressed and remains in the divine world. Plotinus then admittedly diverged from Platonic doctrine: "And if one may be so bold as to express more clearly *one's own conviction against the common opinion of others*, even our soul has not sunk entirely, but there is always something of it in the Intelligible World."[8] In his later *Enneads*[9] Plotinus continued to maintain this opinion and denied that the soul completely descends into a body. Describing "descent" as an "illumination" he says:

> If the inclination (*neusis*) is an illumination (*ellampsis*) to what is below it is not a sin; what is illuminated is responsible, for if it did not exist the soul would have nowhere to illuminate. The soul is said to go down (*katabainein*) or decline (*neuein*) in the sense that

6. *Enn.* II, 9, 9, 33–36. This is essentially the same argument that Iamblichus employs. Like Plotinus (II, 9, 9, 37–40), Iamblichus uses the analogy of a "dance" to account for evil, though in a slightly different manner (*DM* 56, 7–15).

7. See E. R. Dodds, *Pagan and Christian in an Age of Anxiety* (New York: Norton, 1965), 24–26; R. T. Wallis, *Neoplatonism* (London: Duckworth, 1972), 76–79.

8. *Enn.* IV, 8, 8, 1–4; cf. *Enn.* IV, 3, 12, 1–5 where Plotinus says that although the soul descends, its "head" remains above in heaven; cf. *Enn.* I, 1 where Plotinus portrays the higher soul as undescended.

9. Following the accepted chronology, the treatise on the descent of souls is early in the Plotinus corpus, no. 6 of 54; *Enn.* IV, 3, 12 is no. 27, and *Enn.* I, 1 is no. 53, next to the last in the corpus.

the thing which receives the light from it lives with it. (*Enn.* I, 1, 12, 25–29; trans. Armstrong)

Plotinus's position betrays the influence of the Gnostic myth of Sophia's fall, which he had condemned in his *Treatise Against the Gnostics*. There he says: "It [Sophia] did not come down itself, did not decline (*mē katelthein*) but only *illuminated* the darkness (*ellampsai monon tō skotō*) and so an image from it came into existence in matter" (*Enn.* II, 9, 10, 25–27; trans. Armstrong [modified]). The undescended soul of Plotinus exhibits the same traits and is described with the same metaphors as the Gnostics' Sophia. These similarities cannot prove that Plotinus's doctrine of the undescended soul was influenced by Gnostics, but Plotinus himself admitted that his view was unorthodox and it was condemned by nearly all post-Iamblichean Platonists.

The problem Plotinus was attempting to solve with his doctrine of the undescended soul was how to account for the soul's suffering and experience of evil. His solution, that the soul never really descends into a body, proved unsatisfactory to anyone faced with the reality of suffering. According to Iamblichus, the answer could be reached only by first understanding the nature of the soul as embodied. After one gained a proper grasp of the soul's condition, its activities could be redirected into theurgic rites that transformed the passions of the soul into divine actions. For Iamblichus the pain of embodiment was not dismissed but ritually transformed into an act of cosmogenesis.

In strictly Platonic terms the *novum* for Plotinus was his view of the soul as undescended, which may have been influenced by his encounter with Gnostics; for Iamblichus it was ritual theurgy. Why Iamblichus felt that theurgy was more consonant with Platonic teachings may be made clearer against the following outline of Plotinus's debate with the Gnostics. The three positions on the suffering of the embodied soul represent the views of (1) the Gnostics, (2) Plotinus's counter position, and (3) Plotinus's later views on the soul:

1. Gnostics (as described in *Ennead* II, 9)
   (a) The suffering of individual souls is due to the fall of the World Soul.
   (b) Individual souls (collectively) = the World Soul.

2. Plotinus (A) (against the Gnostics)
   (a) The suffering of individual souls is *not* due to the fall of the World Soul because the World Soul cannot fall [*Enn.* II, 9, 7, 9–19]. The relation of individual souls to their bodies includes a temporary period of suffering and confusion [*Enn.* II, 9, 7ff.], which can be overcome by education and an increasing mimesis of the gods [*Enn.* II, 9, 18, 32–35].
   (b) The World Soul *is not equal to* the sum of individual souls [*Enn.* II, 9, 8, 36–39].

3. Plotinus (B)
   (a) The World Soul does not fall and neither do individual souls. The suffering of individual souls, therefore, is merely the suffering of their "images"; in truth, individual souls remain above, at the level of the World Soul.
   (b) The World Soul = unfallen individual souls.

Iamblichus believed that the Gnostics and Plotinus (B) erred by confusing ontological levels. To account for the experience of suffering, the Gnostics confused the part with the whole and interpreted the condition of the World Soul as if it were an individual soul. Plotinus (B) erred no less, but in the opposite way: he raised the part (the individual soul) to the level of the whole (the World Soul), perpetually unfallen. In contrast, theurgy may be seen to be in agreement with the principles of Plotinus (A). For Iamblichus, the problem of human suffering had to be solved without changing the ontological status of the soul.

Iamblichus's view of the embodied soul was influenced by the Pythagorean principle of the "mean." Explaining this principle in mathematic terms Iamblichus says: "If the Many is conceived as a triad and that opposed to the Many is conceived as a monad, the dyad would be a borderland between them. Therefore, *the dyad possesses the characteristics of both.*"[10] Iamblichus held that every realm of being followed this law and Proclus applied Iamblichus's principle of the "mean" to the *nous* and soul in *Timaeus* 37e, saying "he (Iamblichus) takes issue with those who connect the soul directly with the Absolute Intelligence (for the transition from the transcendent to the participating should not be immediate, but there should be as media those essences which are combined with things that participate)."[11] Following the law of the mean, every hypostasis had three expressions: (1) unparticipated (*to amethek-ton*); (2) participated (*to metechomenon*); and (3) participating (*to metechōn*), at every level of the cosmos.[12] In the *De Mysteriis* Iamblichus used a threefold distinction of souls according to wholes and parts:

> The conflict of views in the issue at hand may easily be solved by demonstrating the transcendence of wholes with respect to parts and by recalling the exempt transcendence of the Gods with respect to men. For example, I mean that the entire corporeal world is ruled by [a] *the World Soul*, and that the celestial body is presided over by [b] *the Celestial Gods*, nor is there injury in their reception nor impediment to their intellection; on the other hand, both these ills exist for [c] *the individual soul* in communion with a body. (*DM* 200, 1–10)

10. *Theologoumena Arithmeticae* 10, 9–11. Text: ὅτι νοουμένου πλήθους κατὰ τριάδα τοῦ δ᾽ ἀντιθεμένου τῷ πλήθει κατὰ τὴν μονάδα μεταίκμιον ἡ δυὰς ἂν εἴη· διὰ τοῦτο καὶ τὰ ἀμφοτέρων ἰδιώματα ἅμα ἔχει.

11. Proclus, *In Platonis Timaem Commentari* (*In. Tim.*) III, frag. 60, 4–7, Dillon, trans., *Iamblichi Chalcidensis* 170–71; cf. frag. 54, 6–8, 162–63.

12. Cf. *In. Tim.* III, frag. 54, 6–7, Dillon, trans. *Iamblichi Chalcidensis*, 33, 162–63, 335–36; Iamblichus also employs the principle of mediation to explain the Aristotelian categories *poien/paschein*. In opposition to Plotinus, who attributes to agent and patient "the same substance" (*tēn autēn ousian*) but viewed "agentially" or "patiently," Iamblichus says: "the motion of the agent and the patient is distinguished as something intermediate between the two and which proceeds from the agent and produces an effect in the patient." See Simplicius, *In Aristotelis Categorias Commentarium*, in *Commentaria in Aristotolem Graeca* (AG), ed. C. Kalbfleisch, 8:303, 27–9 (Berlin: G. Reimeri, 1907). Cf. Stephen Gersh, *From Iamblichus to Eruigena: An Investigation of the Prehistory and Evolution of the Pseudo-Dionysian Tradition* (Leiden: E.J. Brill, 1978), 43–44, 90–91.

Iamblichus's celestial gods (souls) mediate between the World Soul and individual souls. Like the dyad in the mathematical example, celestial gods are the "borderland" (*metaichmion*) between the exempt wholeness and unity of the World Soul and the multiplicity and division of individual souls. Celestial souls possess the characteristics of their extremes: like the World Soul they exist in noetic perfection, never departing from their pure condition, but like individual souls, they each possess a single and moving body.

Iamblichus believed that the perfection of an individual soul occurred only through its return to the celestial orders, and through them, to the Demiurge (Cf. *DM* 292, 5–18). This was an elaboration of the Platonic teaching that the ratios of the embodied soul, twisted at birth, were identical to the ratios revealed in the heavens (*Tim.* 90cd). Indeed, what distinguished the theurgical Platonism of Iamblichus from the "exalted soul" Platonism of Plotinus was its interpretation of how the soul attained its celestial identity. Unlike Plotinus, Iamblichus maintained a need for mediation and a triadic distinction of souls, as seen in his description of their appearances in rites of divination:

> [I]f the soul is universal and does not belong to any particular species, it appears as a formless fire revealing—through the whole world—the total, one, indivisible, and formless Soul of the World. But a purified soul [i.e., like the stars] exhibits a fiery form and a pure unmingled fire, its inner light and form appear to be pure and stable, and it follows in the company of its anagogic Leader, rejoicing in his good will while revealing its own rank through its activities. But the soul which verges downward drags with it the signs of bonds and punishments, is weighed down with the conflicts of material spirits, is possessed by irregular troubles of matter, and appears to have placed before itself the authority of generative *Daimones* (*DM* 84, 6–20).

The mediating entities in this schema are described as purified souls instead of celestial. Since theurgists were able to attain the spherical purity of the celestial gods while still living a mortal life (Cf. *DM* 41, 4–11), their souls, *qua* theurgic, were equal to these divinities. According to Iamblichus they were "seated in the order of the angels,"[13] and their appearance provided corporeal souls with "sacred hope" (*DM* 83, 4–5) to attain salvation. The angelic soul of the theurgist was the functional equivalent of Plotinus's undescended soul, yet the realization of this divine status was explained by the two Platonists in strongly contrasting terms. For Iamblichus, the theurgist attained this rank through ritual practices and a demiurgic assimilation of all the powers that he encountered in embodiment. For Plotinus, it was less an assimilation of cosmic powers than a realization that the soul, as undescended, somehow never really encountered them.

This admittedly portrays a distorted picture of Plotinus's view of the soul and its relation with the *Nous*. We should remember that Iamblichus's portrayal of Plotinus's views was polemical. While it is true that Plotinus does speak of the soul as undescended and as possessing a continued contact with the *Nous*, he also says that *Nous* transcends the soul's discursive awareness (*Enn*. V, 3, 3, 22–28). "The *Nous*," he says, "is ours *and* not ours" (*Enn*. V, 3, 3, 27–28), so there is a tension in Plotinus's position that Iamblichus does not sufficiently take into account.

For both Plotinus and Iamblichus, the background to their views on the soul's apotheosis was the *Phaedrus* (246–48) where Plato describes the celestial circuit of the gods and the vain effort of human souls to imitate them. Due to the unruly character of one of his steeds the charioteer of the soul cannot follow the gods and falls into a body. Since Plotinus denied that this fall was complete, he had to explain why the soul identifies with the body if—as he also maintained—evil only occurs to the soul through its association with the body (*Enn*. I, 8, 15, 12–21). Iamblichus criticized Plotinus's position and the contradiction it posed with regard to the soul's experience of suffering. Proclus reports:

> The divine Iamblichus is quite correct, therefore, in attacking those who hold this opinion [that there is something of the soul which does not fall], for what element in us is it that sins when the unreasoning principle in us is stirred, and we chase after a lawless

13. *DM* 83, 3; cf. *DM* 69, 9–12; Proclus, *In Platonis Rempublicam Commentaria* (*In Remp.*) 2 vols., ed. G. Kroll (Leipzig, 1903–6), 2: 154. 17–19.

notion? Is it not our free will (*prohairesis*)? And how would it not be this? For it is by reason of this that we differ from those beings that follow impressions without reflection. If the free will sins, then how would the soul remain sinless? ... And what is the Charioteer of the soul? Is it not the noblest, and, one might say, consummate part of us? And how can we avoid this conclusion, if indeed this is what directs our whole being and with its own head views the supracelestial sphere and is assimilated to the "great leader" of the gods, who "drives a winged chariot" and "journeys through the heaven as a first" charioteer? And if the charioteer is the highest element in us, and he, as is said in the *Phaedrus*, sometimes is carried up aloft and raises "his head into the region outside," while at other times he descends and (fills his pair) with lameness and moulting, *it plainly follows that the highest element in us experiences different states at different times.*[14]

The agent of the soul's descent was *prohairesis*, its "free will," "choice," or "disposition."[15] In his letter on fate Iamblichus again used this term to account for different conditions in human life: "Why, you ask, are goods undeservedly distributed? Rather, to begin with, is it not impious even to ask this? For the goods of life do not depend on anything else but on man himself and on man's choice (*hairesis*), and the most important goods are determined by free-will (*prohairesis*) alone."[16] For Iamblichus *prohairesis* was neutral. It verged to what was better or worse and its choices were a reflection of the character of the soul. In some sense the soul was its *prohairesis*, at least with respect to its spiritual condition,[17] and if its *prohairesis* determined the quality of its life, then for the soul to change—for better or worse—it had to change its *prohairesis*. This is why Iamblichus says that theurgy did not act through the intellect but through one's entire character to allow the soul to exchange one life for another, to sacrifice its mortal life for the life

14. *In Tim.* IV, frag. 87, Dillon, trans., *Iamblichi Chalcidensis*, 198–201.
15. For the uses of this term by Neoplatonists, see John M. Rist, "Prohairesis: Proclus, Plotinus et alii," in *Entretiens sur l'antiquité classique*, vol. 21: *De Jambliqueà Proclus* (hereafter *Entretiens*), 103–22 (Geneva: Fondation Hardt, 1975).
16. *Stob.* II, 175, 17–21. Iamblichus's position simply follows standard Platonic doctrine; cf. *Rep.* 617e.
17. Cf. Rist, "Prohairesis," 104.

of a god.[18] Theurgy transformed the soul's *prohairesis* by conform-ing it to the divine *actions* communicated in theurgic symbols: the sacred stones, plants, animals, prayers (*DM* 48, 5–6), and names (*DM* 255, 4–15; 157, 13–16) that "preserve the *will* of the gods" (cf. *DM* 209, 14–17).

18. See *DM* 270, 17–19. Plotinus also speaks of the exchange of one life for another, though for Plotinus it is the exchange of the fallen for the unfallen soul. Plotinus calls the former the *inferior companion* of the higher soul. See *Enn.* I, 2, 6.

6

Soul as
Mediator

*The existence of souls is lowest,
deficient, and imperfect…*

In the *De Anima*[1] Iamblichus outlined his differences with Plotinus on the doctrine of the soul and developed his own position in more detail. Although the treatise is valuable as a doxography of the philosophical schools of antiquity, Iamblichus's own position is evident, and the rationale for his psychology lends support to his adoption of theurgy as the praxis necessary for the embodied soul.

The first part of the treatise discusses the essence (*ousia*) of the soul and the philosophers who define it as incorporeal, including those who equate the soul with all other incorporeals. Iamblichus says:

> There are some who maintain that all parts of this incorporeal substance are alike and one and the same, so that the whole exists in any part of it. They even place in the individual soul the Intelligible World, the Gods, the *Daimones*, the Good, and all races superior to the soul; and in each soul they contend that all these exist in the same way, though for each in a manner appropriate to its essence. Holding this opinion without question is Numenius, and Plotinus agrees with it, though not entirely, Amelius vacillates towards it, and Porphyry is in doubt about it, sometimes

1. See A.-J. Festugière's translation and commentary, "Traité de l'âme," *La Rév.* 3:177–264. Compare B. D. Larsen's discussion of this treatise, B. D. Larsen, *Jamblique de Chalcis: Exégète et philosophe* (Aarhus: Universitetsforlaget, 1972), 197–213. Larsen argues that Iamblichus makes use of Aristotelian methods to pursue Platonic themes. By drawing parallels with Iamblichus's other writings Larsen demonstrates how Iamblichus's philosophic positions support theurgy.

he earnestly rejects it and sometimes he follows it completely as having been handed down from on high. According to this view, the soul, considering its entire essence, is in no way different from the *Nous*, the Gods, or the Superior Races. (*Stob.* I, 365, 7–21)

According to Iamblichus this view failed to make distinctions within the incorporeal realm itself, so that from the human soul to the Good all incorporeals were considered as more or less equivalent. In contrast Iamblichus drew clear distinctions between ontological levels of the incorporeal realm.[2] He says:

The doctrine opposed to this, however, makes the soul a separate entity, inasmuch as it is generated second after the *Nous* as a different hypostasis, and that part of it which is noetic is explained as being dependent on the *Nous* along with the power of subsisting independently on its own, and it separates the soul also from all the classes of being superior to itself and assigns to it, as the particular definition of its essence, either [1] the mean between the divisible and indivisible, the corporeal and the incorporeal beings, or [2] the totality of the universal *logoi*, or [3] that which, after the Forms, is at the service of the work of creation, or [4] that Life which has Life of itself, which proceeds from the *Nous*, or [5] again the procession of the classes of Real Being as a whole to an inferior status. Indeed, Plato himself, Pythagoras, Aristotle, and all of the Ancients whose great names are praised for wisdom, were absolutely convinced of these doctrines (as anyone would discover if he were to study their teachings with care). And truthfully, we will attempt to construct our entire treatise around these teachings.[3]

Iamblichus defined the essence of the human soul with characteristics that describe its function as mediator between irreconcilable extremes (*Tim.* 34c–36e). In the *Timaeus* it is through the mathematical mediation of soul that the indivisible appears as ordered divisions of the cosmos. The human soul's essence, therefore, lay precisely in its mediating role, and Iamblichus's strict

2. Cf. *DM* 50, 6 where Iamblichus says that it would be out of place to put such things as "time," a "line," and "god" in the same genus simply because they are "incorporeal."

3. *Stob.* I 365, 22–366, 11, in *Iamblichi Chalcidensis*, trans. Dillon (modified slightly), 42.

adherence to this teaching led him into paradoxes that were resolved only in theurgic ritual. If mediation defines the essence of the soul as Iamblichus believed, it is clear why he did not identify soul with *Nous* as Plotinus did, for *Nous* is entirely free of the "lower" end of the oppositions mediated by the soul. Consequently, for Iamblichus, the deification of the soul could not be effected by introspection because the embodied soul had no immediate access to the divine. In light of this, Iamblichus developed a soteriological practice that by its very name, *theourgia*, defines not what the soul does, but what gods do through the soul.

Iamblichus's *De Anima* was clearly influenced by the language and the method of Aristotle; its significance, however, remained Platonic. Like most Neoplatonists, with the exception of Plotinus, Iamblichus believed that Aristotle's teachings were entirely harmonious (*sumphōnos*) with Plato's.[4] Iamblichus even integrated Aristotle's seemingly unplatonic view of the soul as *entelecheia* of the body into his theurgical Platonism. In his commentary on the *Alcibiades* Iamblichus employed the Aristotelian distinction of *ousia, dunamis,* and *energeia* but transformed it into an emanative triad typical of later Neoplatonism.[5] Having explained that the essences (*huparxeis*) of daimons and the superior races were extremely difficult to grasp Iamblichus says:

> [E]ven the essence (*ousia*) of the [human] soul is not easily perceptible to everyone. (Only) the *Timaeus* at any rate has given a full revelation of its essence . . . but to make clear the powers (*dunameis*) of Daimons is easy enough. We attain to a perception of them through their activities (*energeiai*) of which the powers are the immediate mothers; for a power is a median between an

---

4. See H. J. Blumenthal, "Neoplatonic Elements in the De Anima Commentaries" *Phronesis* 21, no. 1 (1976): 64–87.

5. The Aristotelian dictum that essences are known by their activities (*De Anima* 146, 21) had precedents in the Platonic dialogues (*Rep.* 477c; *Soph.* 247e), a point that was certainly not overlooked by the later Neoplatonists. See P. Shorey, "Simplicius *de Anima* 146, 21," *Classical Philology* 17 (1922): 143–44; cf. Stephen Gersh, *From Iamblichus to Eriugena: An Investigation of the Prehistory and Evolution of the Pseudo-Dionysian Tradition* (Leiden: E. J. Brill, 1978), 32–45.

essence and an activity, put forth from the essence on the one hand, and itself generating the activity on the other.[6]

Using this method to differentiate species of "soul" by reference to their activities, Iamblichus placed human souls near the bottom of the psychic hierarchy and maintained that their actions revealed their ontological rank. This was in opposition, he says, to the opinion of the Stoics, Plotinus, and Amelius who did not distinguish between the acts of particular souls and the acts of the World Soul (*Stob.* I, 372, 7–14). Thus Iamblichus says:

> There may be another opinion which may not be rejected, one which, according to classes and kinds of souls, distinguishes between the perfect acts of universal souls, the pure and immaterial acts of divine souls, the efficacious acts of daimonic souls, the great acts of heroic souls, and the mortal acts performed by animals and men.[7]

What distinguished embodied souls was the separation of their *ousiai* and *energeiai*, a hypostatic rupture that condemned them to mortality and separated them from the gods. Theurgy was able to bridge this gap by uniting the *energeia* of mortals with the *energeia* of the gods. Iamblichus explained that each soul began its corporeal life in a fallen and separated state due to the weakened consistency of human souls portrayed by Plato in his metaphor of the demiurgic mixing bowl (*Tim.* 41d). Although every human soul carried the divine ratios (*logoi*) established by the Demiurge, its "measures of coherence" (*metra tēs sunochēs*)[8] were no longer uniformly preserved but were broken apart into divisions of time. Following a suggestion by Proclus, Dillon says that Iamblichus conceived the

---

6. *In Alcib.*, frag. 4, 9–16, Dillon, trans., *Iamblichi Chalcidensis*, 74–75.

7. *Stob.* I, 372, 15–20. This passage employs the fourfold hierarchy typical to the *De Mysteriis*:

Agent	Activity
1. Universal Souls	perfect
Divine Souls	pure and immaterial
2. Daimons	efficacious
3. Heroes	great
4. Human	mortal

8. *Tim.* 41d and *In Tim.*, frag. 82, Dillon, trans., *Iamblichi Chalcidensis*, 194–95.

hierarchy of souls according to their respective allotments of the elements "essence" (*ousia*), "sameness" (*tautotēs*), and "otherness" (*heterotēs*). The distribution of these three elements, respectively, determined the rank of all souls: divine, daimonic, and human, with human souls carrying the greatest proportion of "otherness."[9] Iamblichus believed that inattention to this passage of the *Timaeus* (41d) caused Plotinus and Amelius to miss important distinctions among souls (*Stob.* I, 372, 23–26). Outlining his own position, Iamblichus says:

> Others make a more prudent distinction and insist that the different essences of the soul continually proceed according to a downward sequence of primary, secondary, and tertiary processions— such as one would expect of those who discuss these matters with arguments which are unfamiliar but unshakable. They say that the operations of universal, divine, and immaterial souls are completely realized in their essences, but they will by no means agree that individual souls, *confined as they are to one single form* and divided out among bodies, are immediately identical with their acts.[10]

Like all entities in tertiary procession from the Demiurge, the acts of embodied souls were separated from their essences and completed only within the cycles of generation. Iamblichus says: "In accord with the opinion just espoused the acts of those souls which are self-perfect, uniform, and independent of matter are naturally connected to their powers (*dunameis*), but the acts of imperfect souls, who are divided among parts of the earth, are like plants producing fruit" (*Stob.* I, 373, 10–15). The "plant" in which the soul's actions were brought to fruition was the human body, which gradually manifested the powers of the soul. As Andrew Smith puts it, "the manifestation of the soul in a body is the activity of the soul."[11]

---

9. Dillon, trans., *Iamblichi Chalcidensis*, 378. See also Jean Trouillard, *La Mystagogie de Proclos* (Paris: Les Belles Lettres, 1982), 213.

10. *Stob.* I, 372, 26–373, 8. Cf. Dillon's translation, *Iamblichi Chalcidensis*, 44.

11. Smith, *Porphyry's Place in the Neoplatonic Tradition: A Study in Post-Plotinian Neoplatonism* (The Hague: Martinus Nijhoff, 1974), 14.

Since the body reflected the activity of the soul, it also indicated the kind of soul that animated it.[12] The bodies of celestial souls, for example, were perfectly receptive to their lords and revealed them by their circular activity.[13] These were the self-perfect souls (*autoteleis*) whose actions were realized within their essences. Their *archē* and *telos* were simultaneous. The activity/manifestation of the embodied soul, however, lacked the capacity to receive the powers of the soul at once; they had to be developed over time as the soul gradually bore the fruit of its different psychic powers. Iamblichus describes this progressive animation:

> The powers of the soul and its modes of being are several, and following a measured chronology in which the developing body is appropriately disposed from one period of time to the next, it participates first in a *vegetative* life, then in *sensation*, next in an *appetitive* life, then it participates in the *rational* soul, and finally in the *intellectual* soul. (*Stob.* I, 381, 7–13)

Although the activity of the soul-as-body revealed the soul's essence and powers, it did not define them. Iamblichus emphasized this point in response to Porphyry's questions on the characteristics (*idiomata*) of divine races. In the *De Mysteriis* Iamblichus argued that if one defines the gods or higher races by the receptacles (bodies) that manifest them the ontological hierarchy would be turned upside down (*DM* 10, 12–11, 2). The *energeiai* reveal but do not define the identity of a god:

> For if activities and movements were constitutive of essences they would determine the differences between them. But if, on the contrary, essences generate activities, these essences, being prior to and separate from the effects of the activities, would bestow to movements, activities, and their accidents that which defines them. (*DM* 13, 13–14, 1)

Apart from turning the ontological order upside down, defining

---

12. Following the principle that matter was the index of the spiritual state of the soul.

13. As Aristotle puts it: "for the body whose motion is circular, the place where it ends is also the place where it begins" (*De Caelo* 279b, 4–5).

essences by their activities would place the defining characteristics of incorporeals in their material vehicles, and nothing would distinguish one incorporeal from another apart from its *material* expression. Iamblichus implies that both Plotinus and Porphyry held this view so that, as an ironic correlate to their monopsychist tendencies, they were forced to accept Aristotle's metaphysical position that matter was *principium individuationis*.[14]

Iamblichus considered this a gross misunderstanding and misapplication of the *ousia-dunamis-energeia* method:

> To make bodies principles in determining the specific properties of their own first causes seems terribly out of place (*DM* 23, 16–24, 1).... This argument makes bodies superior to divine races, since they would provide superior causes with their foundation and would impart to them their essential characteristics. (*DM* 24, 15–18)

Iamblichus argued that each divine genre defined itself, and its activity neither exhausted nor determined it. What distinguished divine races was not their material manifestation but their priority and independence with respect to one another:

> If you conceive the unique characteristic [of each divine genre] to be a certain simple state defined in itself as in prior and posterior orders which change entirely and essentially in each genre, this conception of characteristics would be reasonable (*DM* 11, 2–6).... Those of them which are prior are independent of those which are inferior. (*DM* 14, 11–12)

In effect, Iamblichus distinguished divine entities following Aristotle's distinction of Plato's Ideal Numbers and his own Unmoved

---

14. This problem reflects the difficulty of integrating the transcendental psychology of Plato with Aristotle's physics and descriptions of the embodied soul. The Neoplatonists' juxtaposition of Aristotle's technical virtuosity with Plato's teachings pitted the evocative but imprecise imagery of Plato against Aristotle's more articulate physics. This may have caused Platonists to embrace certain Gnostic positions that put a breach between physics and metaphysics, materiality and spirituality. It was precisely this kind of bifurcation that Iamblichus saw in Plotinus's and Porphyry's metaphysics and that he criticized philosophically and sought to correct theurgically.

Movers.[15] According to Aristotle, each was a species unto itself, not under a common genus, and not to be synthesized or combined.[16] Following this mathematical model, Iamblichus tells Porphyry that the correct way to conceive the relations between divine orders is by following a proportional method: "Anyone using proportional methods to determine the analogous sameness in the genres under consideration, i.e., to the many races among the Gods and in turn to the races among *Daimones*, Heroes, and finally Souls, will be able to determine their defining characteristics" (*DM* 14, 15–20).

In Iamblichus's estimation, the human soul was unique because of its radical self-division. Unlike divine souls, the human soul was bound to the generative cycles of its body, yet it projected for itself the mortal life that bound it. Therefore, although the material body defined the soul's characteristics, it did so by proxy, given by the soul when it descended into a body. In each of its incarnations, Iamblichus says the soul projects immortal *logoi* from itself in its descent, and these in turn were combined with mortal lives acquired from the cosmos.[17] Thus, each incarnation produced an entirely new identity.

15. See Philip Merlan's classic treatment of this topic, "Aristotle's Unmoved Movers," *Traditio* 4 (1946): 1–30.

16. The term used by Aristotle is *asumbletoi*, "incombinable," "incomparable" (*Meta.* 1080a, 29) to describe numbers in themselves, prior to their being considered in relation to one another. See *Aristotle's Metaphysics*, 2 vols., text and commentary by W.D. Ross (Oxford: Clarendon Press, 1958), liii and 2:426–27. Merlan argues convincingly that Aristotle identified these "monads" with his unmoved movers and that these were later identified by Saint Thomas with "angels" (9–10). For Thomas's angelology and its background, see Etienne Gilson, *The Philosophy of St. Thomas Aquinas*, trans. Edward Bullough, ed. G.A. Erlington (New York: Dorset Press, 1948), 175–77. The equation of Platonic divine numbers with the angels of medieval Christianity was probably the result of the arithmogonic and theurgic speculations of later Neoplatonists passed on to the West by Muslim philosophers such as Avicenna. In the *Theologoumena Arithmeticae* Iamblichus describes numbers in their "incombinable" essences, as monadic "gods." In the *De Communi Mathematica Scientia* the mathematic expressions of these monads are discussed in their "relations." Since Iamblichus's daimons, angels, and heroes bore the signatures of their presiding deities, the relations of their orders were understood on analogy with the principles they expressed and obeyed.

17. See Iamblichus's description of this process in Simplicius, *In Aristotelis Categorias Commentarium*, in *CAG*, ed. C. Kalbfleisch (Berlin: G. Reimeri, 1907), 8:376, 26–377, 4; cf. *DM* 25, 8–13; 59, 1–8.

As a mean between divine and mortal realms the Iamblichean soul had the unique distinction of being both mortal and immortal. This has led to many difficulties in making sense of Iamblichus's psychology, for depending on the context being discussed the soul could be described with opposite characteristics relative to what it is being compared. Referring to this problem Iamblichus says: "someone might say the soul in bodies is divisible with regard to *Nous*, not because it is only divisible but because compared to the *Nous* it appears to be so, whereas with regard to the divisible essence it appears indivisible."[18]

Although all genres of soul mediated, certain souls did so in a more unified manner than others. The human soul, as we have seen, carried a greater degree of *heterotēs* and therefore suffered a separation unexperienced by other souls. Only in the case of the human soul did its "otherness" (*heterotēs*) bring about a separation in its essence,[19] for only in the case of a human soul did its manifestation produce a *mortal* vehicle. Consequently, the human soul was the lowest of all divine hypostases for below it (e.g., animals and plants) there was no independent or sustained identity.[20]

The diminished status of the human soul is clearly drawn out in the *De Mysteriis* where Iamblichus compares the properties of the highest and lowest classes of souls, that is, the souls of gods and

18. S. Sambursky, *The Concept of Time in Late Neoplatonism*, texts and translation (Jerusalem: Israel Academy of Sciences and Humanities, 1971), 44, 21–26 (translation modified).

19. Cf. Simplicius (Priscianus?), *In Libros Aristotelis de Anima Commentaris*, in *CAG*, ed. M. Hayduck (Berlin: G. Reimeri, 1882), 11–241, 2–20. It is significant that of all the Neoplatonic interpreters of the *Parmenides*, only Iamblichus assigns soul to the fourth hypothesis, putting it under the sway of the "other." See Dillon, trans., *Iamblichi Chalcidensis*, 387–89; see also Proclus, *Théologie platonicienne* (*Th. Pl.*), 5 vols., trans. and ed. H.D. Saffrey and L.G. Westerink (Paris: Les Belles Lettres, 1968–87), 1:lxxv–lxxxix.

20. The technical term to describe the "self-subsistence" or "self-constitution" of the human soul is *authupostaton*, which Iamblichus coined in his treatise on fate (*Stob.* II, 174, 22); cf. also R.T. Wallis, *Neoplatonism* (London: Duckworth, 1972), 129; John Whittaker, "The Historical Background of Proclus's Doctrine of the *AUTHUPOSTATA*," in *Entretiens*, 193–237.

souls of humans,[21] by referring to the *ousia-dunamis-energeia* triad in each class. His distinctions are as follows:[22]

The Gods

ousia: The gods' *existence* is highest, transcendent, and perfect. (*DM* 21, 1–2)

dunamis: The gods have the *power* to do all things at once, uniformly, and in an instant. (*DM* 21, 3)

energeia: The gods *generate and govern* all things without inclining to them. (*DM* 21, 5)

Humans

ousia: The *existence* of souls is lowest, deficient, and imperfect. (*DM* 21, 2)

dunamis: Human souls do not have the *power* to do all things, neither at one time, nor in an instant, nor uniformly. (*DM* 21, 4)

energeia: Souls have the nature to incline and turn toward what they *generate* and *govern*. (*DM* 21, 6–7).

Iamblichus also includes the following distinctions:

21. The "gods" described as one of the "extremes" in Iamblichus's fourfold hierarchy are the *neoi theoi* of the *Timaeus* (41a) and thus part of the creative work of the Demiurge. As such they would be "cosmic gods," but for Iamblichus these encosmic deities were themselves the vehicles through which the "supracosmic gods" (*huperkosmikoi theoi*) revealed themselves. (Cf. *DM* 271, 10–12 for their distinction; *DM* 59, 15–60, 8 for their connection.) Like most Neoplatonists, Iamblichus's use of terms such as *theos* or *psuchē* was not entirely consistent. Plotinus, for example called the human soul the "last god" (*Enn.* IV, 8, 5, 25), and Hierocles referred to human souls as "mortal gods" (*thnetoi theoi*); *Hierocles in Aureum Pythagoreorum Carmen Commentarius*, ed. F. G. Koehler (Stuttgart: Teubner, 1974), 9, 8. In his explanation of the terminology of the "middle genres" Hierocles said that "Daimons," "Heroes," and "Angels" were interchangeable terms depending on the author and the context (*Car. Aur.* 19, 9–27).

22. I have followed the outline of H. D. Saffrey, "Plan des livres I et II du *de Mysteriis* de Jamblique," in *Zetesis Album Amicorum*, ed. E. de Strycker (Antwerp: De Nederlandsche Boekhandel, 1973), 281–95.

The Gods

(a) are the cause of all things. (*DM* 21, 8)
(b) already embrace perfection. (*DM* 21, 10–11)
(c) are superior to every measure and form. (*DM* 21, 4–5)

Humans

(a) are suspended from a cause. (*DM* 21, 8–9)
(b) move from imperfect to perfect. (*DM* 21, 12–13)
(c) are conquered by inclination, habit, and tendency, and take their form from the measures of secondary orders. (*DM* 21, 18–19)

Iamblichus said that the existence of daimons and heroes between these extremes ensured an unbroken continuity between the gods and man. While gods and human souls were distinguished by unity and multiplicity respectively,[23] daimons were "multiplied in unity" (*heni plēthuomenon*; *DM* 19, 12–13), and heroes, while more manifestly divided, still preserved uniformity and continuity in their divisions and motions (*DM* 19, 15–20, 2). Although gods and humans had no characteristics in common, the mediation of daimons and heroes provided communion with the gods. Later in the *De Mysteriis*, perhaps in response to Porphyry's terminology (*DM* 70, 10–12), Iamblichus adds two classes of "angelic" souls between the gods and daimons and two classes of "archontic" souls between heroes and human souls resulting in the following stratification:

1. gods
2. archangels
3. angels
4. daimons
5. heroes
6. archons (sublunary)
7. archons (material)
8. human souls[24]

---

23. The gods are *hēnōmenon* (*DM* 18, 7) and humans are *eis plēthos* (*DM* 18, 15).
24. Cf. *DM* 70, 18–71, 18. For a discussion of these added distinctions see Dillon, trans., *Iamblichi Chalcidensis*, 50–52.

Unlike the system of Plotinus, where the soul could transcend its hypostasis and attain union with the One, Iamblichus fixed the soul in its ontological rank. He allowed it to rise higher than its given class but only through the benevolent will of the gods; regardless of its degree of ascent the soul remained distinctly soul:

> The soul is attached to the Gods with other harmonies of essences and powers than those by which *Daimones* and Heroes are joined to them. And though it possesses an eternity of life and activity similar to, but in a less degree than *Daimones* and Heroes, due to the good will of the Gods and the illumination of light imparted by them the soul often is elevated higher and is lifted up to a greater order, the angelic. Indeed, then it no longer remains within the limits of "soul," but the whole of it is perfected into an angelic soul and an immaculate life. Whence indeed, it seems (*dokein*) that the soul comprehends in itself all manner of essences, activities, ratios, and ideas of every kind. *But if it is necessary to speak the truth, the soul is always limited according to one certain class, but by joining itself to its ruling causes it is sometimes aligned with one group, sometimes with another.* (DM 69, 5–19)

Iamblichus almost allows the soul to embrace all the higher essences like the Plotinian soul. This, however, would give it the characteristics of a god, not a soul (*DM* 28, 18–20); what separated Iamblichus from Plotinus in this regard was his cautionary *dokei* and subsequent explanation.

Each class of soul defined its own activity (Cf. *DM* 11, 2–6; 12, 6–14) and therefore determined the receptacle through which its capacities were expressed. The manifestation of a soul-as-body was itself an activity of the soul, and therefore the kind of body that a soul animated indicated its class. These classes, Iamblichus says, do not change.[25] As lowest of divine beings, the human soul had an unstable and mortal vehicle that alienated it from its own divinity. In embodiment, the soul literally became *other* to itself.

---

25. It should be noted that, for Iamblichus, although human souls cannot rise above their rank neither can they fall below it. As Dillon puts it: "Man was not to be ranked with the gods and angels, but he was not down among the pigs and wolves either" (*Iamblichi Chalcidensis*, 45–46). According to Dillon, Nemesius reported that Iamblichus denied that the soul transmigrated into animals.

7

The Constraints of Embodiment

The soul possesses a double life.

Aristotle's conception of the soul as *entelecheia* of the body may well have influenced Iamblichus more than his Platonic predecessors; the limits of the soul as conceived by Iamblichus were the limits of its mortal body. Yet despite this, Iamblichus did not limit the soul's existence to its corporeal form, and in the *De Anima* he says that sometimes the soul is not in a body: "The soul, of itself, possesses its own actions which, freed from the composite life [soul-as-body] and self-contained, activate the essential powers of the soul: enthusiasms (*enthusiasmoi*), immaterial intuitions (*ahulai noēseis*), and all those spiritual acts which join us to the Gods" (*Stob.* I, 371, 19–24). Iamblichus refers to an independence from the body prior to death, when the soul was "joined to the Gods" (*Stob.* I, 371, 23–24) by divine enthusiasms. Such activities were the concern of theurgic divination, and Iamblichus provides several examples in the *De Mysteriis* to demonstrate their authenticity. His method of proof, as in the *De Anima*, followed the *energeia*-reveals-*ousia* formula applied to various kinds of *enthousiasmos*.

Porphyry had challenged the authenticity of theurgic divination and suggested in his letter to Anebo that divination through dreams did not provide contact with the gods. Iamblichus responded by distinguishing ordinary dreams from those sent by the gods (*theopemptoi*) (*DM* 103, 9). Only the latter were divine and they were superior to contacts made with the gods while awake (*DM* 105, 9–11; cf. Synesius, *De Insomniis* 151, 18–152, 1). Iamblichus explains:

Since the soul possesses a double life, the one with the body and the other separate from all body, when we are awake, for the most part in our ordinary life, we make use of the life in common with the body (except when we are somehow entirely free of it by intuiting and conceiving in pure thought). But in sleep we are completely liberated, freed as it were, from certain bonds closely held on us, and we employ a life separated from generation. At this time, therefore, whether intellectual or divine are the same, or each one exists with its own characteristic, this kind of life is awakened in us and acts according to its nature. (*DM* 106, 4–15)

Iamblichus added that since sleep liberated the soul from the body the presence of the gods was clearer (*saphesteran*) and sharper (*akribesteran*) in dreams than when awake (*DM* 105, 9–11).

Iamblichus applied the *energeia*-reveals-*ousia* formula to more dramatic forms of divination to prove that the miraculous feats of the possessed were, in fact, divine acts and not human, saying:

This is the greatest proof: many are not burned even though fire is applied to them, for the fire does not touch them because of the divine inspiration. And many, though they are burned, do not respond because they are not living the life of a [mortal] creature. And some, while being pierced with spits, and others, while striking their backs with sharp blades, do not feel it. Still others, while stabbing their lower arms with daggers, are completely unaware of it. Their activities (*energeiai*) are in no way human—for the inaccessible things become accessible to those possessed by a God—and they throw themselves into fire, walk through fire, and pass through water just like the priestess at Castabalis.[1] From these examples it is clear that *those inspired by the Gods are not conscious of themselves*; they live neither a human life nor an animal life according to sensation or impulse, but *they have taken in exchange a more divine life* from which they are inspired and perfectly possessed. (*DM* 110, 5–111, 2)

It may be difficult to see how such phenomena met the goals of

---

1. E. des Places notes that according to Strabo (XII, 2, 7; 537 Cas.) the priestesses of Artemis Perasia at Castabalis walked barefoot through burning coals; *Jamblique: Les mystères d'Egypte*, trans. and ed. E. des Places (Paris: Les Belles Lettres, 1966), 104.

Platonic philosophy, but they clearly demonstrated Iamblichus's point that the divine came to the soul from without, and this principle also explained the more subtle possessions experienced in Iamblichus's own life.[2] For example, in discussing theurgic prayer, Iamblichus says: "It [prayer] *quietly* (*erema*) lifts up the habits of our thought and bestows on us the habits of the Gods" (*DM* 239, 5–6), for the activity, life, and habits of the theurgist exemplified the activity and life of the gods. Thus, "the soul . . . takes in exchange (*allattetai*) another life and establishes itself in another order, *entirely giving up its former existence*" (*DM* 270, 17–19).

Iamblichus rejected the possibility that contact with the gods was effected by the soul. He says:

> If, therefore, genuine divination were the liberation of the divine part from the rest of the soul or a separation of the intellect or a sort of attainment—an intensity and effort either of activity or passivity or an acuity and application of thought or a fervor of the intellect—all such things would be awakened by our soul, and it would be correct to assume that divine inspiration (*enthousiasmos*) was a property of the soul. (*DM* 115, 16–116, 4)

Iamblichus explained that if inspiration were awakened by somatic conditions it would derive from the body (*DM* 116, 9–11), and if from the soul-body conjunction it would derive from that common life (*DM* 116, 11–13). He rejected these possibilities: "Inspired action is (derived) neither from the body nor from the soul nor from the two combined, for these do not possess in themselves the cause of divine inspiration; for it is not the nature of superior things to be generated from those which are inferior" (*DM* 116, 14–17).

The upshot of Iamblichus's argument is that of the soul's two activities it was capable of performing only one: the animation of the body as its vehicle (*ochēma*) and instrument (*organon*). The other activity, the inspired acts and intuitions that pertain to the soul's essence (cf. *Stob.* I, 371, 19–21), did not derive from the soul

---

2. Eunapius reports that Iamblichus avoided spectacular displays of power and was accustomed to worship the divine in solitude; Eunapius, *Vita Soph.* 458–59, trans. W.C. Wright, *Philostratus and Eunapius: The Lives of the Sophists* (Cambridge: Harvard University Press, 1921; reprint, 1968), 362–65.

but from the gods who use the soul as *their* vehicle. Iamblichus says: "For the act of divine inspiration is not human, nor does all its authoritative power rest in human members or actions, but these are otherwise disposed, and *the God uses them as his instruments*."[3] Just as the corporeal body was the instrument of the soul and depended on it to receive its "more perfect life" (*DM* 25, 12–13), so the soul was the instrument of the gods and depended on them for its perfection. This is why theurgic activities were ineffable to the soul; they completely transcended its composite life. The activities that joined the soul to the gods were accomplished by the gods themselves, and in a polemical statement that seems clearly directed to the teachings of Plotinus and Porphyry, Iamblichus says:

> Intellectual understanding does *not* connect theurgists with divine beings, for what would prevent those who philosophize theoretically from having theurgic union with the Gods? But this is not true; rather it is the perfect accomplishment of ineffable acts religiously performed and beyond all understanding, and it is the power of ineffable symbols comprehended by the Gods alone that establishes theurgical union. Thus, we don't perform these acts intellectually for then their energy would be intellectual and depend on us, which is not at all true. In fact, these very symbols, by themselves, perform their own work, and the ineffable power of the Gods with which these symbols are charged, itself, recognizes, by itself, its own images. It is not awakened to this by our thinking. (*DM* 96, 13–97, 9)

The actions performed in a theurgic rite were the *erga* of the gods actualized by an embodied soul. Participation in this action depended entirely on the soul's "suitability" (*epitēdeiotēs*)[4] as an *organon* of the gods; from a theurgic perspective, the embodied soul was a receptacle (*hupodochē*) of the god like the other receptacles used in theurgic divination. In the divinatory practice of drawing

---

3. *DM* 115, 3–7. Cf. *DM* 157, 8–15, in divination; 98, 13–15, in all theurgy.

4. *Epitēdeiotēs* was a technical term to describe the mystical or theurgic "capacity" of a soul. Cf. *DM* 125, 5; 29, 1; 105, 1; 127, 9; 233, 1. See Nock's discussion, *Sallustius: Concerning the Gods and the Universe*, ed. with prolegomena and trans. A.D. Nock (Hildesheim: Georg Olms, 1966), xcix, n. 9.

light into the soul (*phōtagōgia*),[5] theurgists used "diaphanous water" (*DM* 134, 2), a "wall on which sacred characters are inscribed" (*DM* 134, 5–6), or "any solid place" (*DM* 134, 8), to enable the soul to receive the light and see the "will of the gods" (*DM* 132, 15). Lest Porphyry misunderstand the purpose of using ritual objects to effect this reception, Iamblichus explained that the sign of genuine theurgy was the manifestation of divine characteristics in the habits of a soul,[6] an explanation that is similar to a theory of embodiment reported by Iamblichus in *De Anima*:

> The Platonists around [Calvenus] Taurus say that souls are sent to earth by the Gods. Some, following the *Timaeus* [39e, 41b] teach that it is for the perfection of the universe, that there be as many living things in the [sensible] world as in the intelligible. Others think the purpose of the soul's descent is to reveal the divine life, for this is the will of the Gods: to be revealed through souls. *For the Gods come forth into bodily appearance and reveal themselves in the pure and faultless life of souls.* (*Stob.* I, 378, 25–379, 6)

As a *receptacle* of the gods, the soul reflected their activity and habits (*DM* 239, 5–6; 176, 10–13). These were symptoms of theurgic exchange, and because of this Iamblichus vigorously condemned any attempt to perform a theurgic invocation for selfish reasons (*DM* 115–16). Although "ineffable symbols" and not "our thinking" established theurgical union (*DM* 97–98), Iamblichus believed that the power of these symbols could not be tapped without the moral and intellectual preparation of the theurgist. For "ineffable acts" to be "perfectly accomplished" they had to be "religiously performed" (*DM* 96, 17–19). In other words although the intellectual effort of the soul was not sufficient to effect a theurgic union, it was a necessary auxiliary (*DM* 98, 8–10).

In his letter to Anebo, Porphyry implied that theurgic rites attempted to manipulate the gods and that theurgists stood on

---

5. *Phōtos agōgia*, the "leading" or "gathering up" of "light" is the rubric under which Iamblichus includes various kinds of divination.

6. *DM* 239, 5–6. Iamblichus maintained that the soul's illumination was not produced by a *mechanical* manipulation of images in mirrors or water (*DM* 94, 3–5; 174, 10–11). Such phenomena were psychic and unworthy of the gods.

magical characters (*charaktēres*) to impose their will on the gods. Iamblichus replied that any attempt to control the gods was the antithesis of theurgy:

> When you say "those who stand on characters" you have put your finger on nothing less than the cause of all evils concerning theurgic invocations. For certain persons, disdaining the entire task of completing their theoretic knowledge about the one who invokes and the overseer,[7] and disregarding the order of the ritual and the most sacred and extensive perseverance in labors over a long period of time, reject sacred laws and prayers and other holy preparations and believe that standing on characters alone is sufficient. Having done this for an hour, they think that a spirit will enter. Such reckless men fail to accomplish anything and are not worthy to be counted among diviners. (*DM* 131, 3–132, 2)

Others, Iamblichus says, were less fortunate:

> All those who are offensive and who awkwardly leap after divine mysteries in a disordered way are not able to associate with the Gods due to the slackness of their energy or deficiency of their power. And on account of certain defilements they are excluded from the presence of pure spirits but are joined to evil spirits and are filled by them with the worst possession. They become wicked and unholy and, being glutted with undisciplined pleasures and filled with evil, they affect habits foreign to the gods. (*DM* 176, 13–177, 4)

The equation of theurgy with *ex opere operato* activity, therefore, must be qualified. Following the Neoplatonic principle that like can only be joined to like, the theurgist had to purify the future vehicle of the god in order to receive its power, for the presence of the god was always in proportion to the purity of its receptacle.

Epitēdeiotēs was the term Iamblichus used to describe the "fitness" or "aptitude" to receive a form. Coined in the second century C.E. to describe the kind of Aristotelian "potency" (*dunamis*) sufficient for

---

7. While the union with the gods was purely theurgical, the preparation for theurgy demanded a *theoretical* knowledge of the gods and ritual procedures; cf. *DM* 267, 5ff.

"actualization" (*energeia*) of a form,[8] *epitēdeiotēs* came to be used by Neoplatonists to account for differences in mystical experience.[9] Just as "dry wood" provided the capacity (*epitēdeiotēs*) for fire to be actualized,[10] so, analogously, the purity of a soul provided the capacity for a god to become manifest. Plotinus accounted for different experiences of souls in the presence of the Intelligible as follows: "One must understand the [degree of] presence as something depending on the fitness (*epitēdeiotēs*) of the recipient" (*Enn.* VI, 4, 11, 3–4), and he compared it to the reception of light in clear or muddy water (9–10). For Iamblichus also, *epitēdeiotēs* described the fitness of a passive element to receive the influence of an active one, regardless of spatial distance or proximity.[11]

Epitēdeiotēs was a component in every theurgy, which is why the mere performance of ritual acts could not join the soul to the gods. Although the gods were everywhere (*DM* 27, 9), their powers could not affect souls that lacked an appropriate receptacle. Only when the vehicle was prepared could divine possession occur. Iamblichus says: "Whenever terrestrial things—which possess their being from the totalities of the Gods—become fit for divine participation they immediately possess, prior to their own essence, the Gods who pre-exist in it" (*DM* 28, 20–29, 3). Consequently, Iamblichus explained that the authority of the oracles at Delphi, Colophon, and Branchidae was not caused by the places themselves but by the careful purification of their oracular vehicles, making them "fit" (*epitē-deiotēs*) to give voice to the god (*DM* 125, 5–127, 9). Similar purifications were necessary for every soul. Iamblichus says, for example,

8. See S. Sambursky, *The Physical World of Late Antiquity* (New York: Basic Books, 1962), 106.

9. See E. R. Dodds's discussion of the theurgic or mystical interpretation of *epitēdeiotēs* by later Neoplatonists; *Proclus, The Elements of Theology*, 2d ed., revised text with intro. trans., and comm. by E. R. Dodds (Oxford: Clarendon Press, 1963), 222–23, cf. 344–45.

10. Sextus Empiricus, *Advers. Mathem.* IX, 243, quoted by Sambursky, *Physical World*, 107.

11. For Iamblichus's discussion of this principle against the view of the Stoics see Simplicius, *In Aristotelis Categorias Commentarium*, in *CAG*, ed. C. Kalbfleisch (Berlin: G. Reimeri, 1907), 8:302, 28–303, 9; quoted in part by Sambursky, *Physical World*, 103–4.

that "the time one spends in prayer nourishes the intuitive mind and greatly *enlarges the soul's receptacles for the Gods.*"[12] The soul itself was a receptacle of the gods, and in Iamblichus's response to Porphyry's questions about famous oracular shrines he makes it clear that it is the purity of the receiving soul—not the geographical place—that allows for divine possessions, including those experienced privately by every theurgist.[13] To equate this "possession" with the spiritualist phenomena of the late nineteenth and early twentieth century, as Dodds has done, is misleading.[14] For the spiritualist was no more a theurgist than was the fourth-century *goēs*, and although all of them share superficial similarities, the purposes of theurgy were altogether different.

12. *DM* 238, 17–239, 1. Iamblichus almost always employs *epitēdeiotēs* in the *De Mysteriis* to describe the soul's "readiness" for divine transformation: 105, 1 to describe conditions of the soul that are "fit" to receive the god; 125, 5 to describe the cleansing of the soul to make it "fit" and 127, 9 explicitly for the reception of a god; 233, 1, the matter sent from the Demiurge is described as "fit" to connect the soul with the gods; in 207, 10–15, however, *epitēdeiotēs* is described in a purely physical way, not theurgic.

13. On Iamblichus's view of public oracles see Polymnia Athanassiadi, "Dreams, Theurgy and Freelance Divination: The Testimony of Iamblichus," *Journal of Roman Studies*, 83 (1993): 123–24.

14. See Dodds, *The Greeks and the Irrational* (Berkeley and Los Angeles: University of California Press, 1951), 297–99; and A. Smith, *Porphyry's Place in the Neoplatonic Tradition: A Study in Post-Plotinian Neoplatonism* (The Hague: Martinus Nijhoff, 1974), 89. Iamblichus's explanation should have been sufficient to deter this interpretation; see *DM* 93, 10–95, 14; esp. 95, 10–12.

8

The Freedom of Immortal Bodies

The aetherial body is...free from centrifugal or centripetal tendencies.

Receiving the gods was not without danger. For Iamblichus, the incorporeal world was just as complex as the corporeal, and one could easily be misled without a discerning guide. Iamblichus is reported by Eunapius, for example, to have exposed a fraudulent séance led by a deceased gladiator posing as the god Apollo (Eunapius, *Vit. Soph.* 473). According to Iamblichus, such phenomena were caused by errors in the theurgic art, "for inferior entities assume the appearance of more venerable orders and pretend to be those entities whose appearance they have adopted and hence they make boastful claims that exceed the power available to them."[1]

Communication with the "other world" would not have been as exotic or unusual for Iamblichus as it might be for moderns who generally deny the existence of spirits, let alone contacting them. Yet a guide was indispensable; not only was he able to determine the imbalances in a soul and the purifications it needed but was also able to determine the deity who possessed the soul:

There are many kinds of divine possession, and divine inspiration is awakened in several ways. Wherefore, there are many different indications of it. On the one hand, the Gods who inspire us are

1. *DM* 91, 12–15. Part of the repertoire of the theurgist was the ability to discern true apparitions and possessions from the false.

different and each produces a different inspiration, and on the other hand, the difference in each mode of enthusiasm produces a different sort of divine appearance. For either the God possesses us, or we become completely the property of the God, or we act in common with him. (*DM* 111, 3–16)

What appears constant among the varieties of divine possession was the manner in which a god joined an embodied soul. Significantly, Iamblichus says their conjunction was effected "circularly" (*en kuklō*):

In dreams:
Sometime an incorporeal and intangible *pneuma encircles those lying down* so that there is no sight of it but its presence is felt by a sensing awareness. It sounds like a rushing wind (*rhoizomenos*) when it enters, permeates everything without any contact, and performs wondrous acts leading to liberation from the passions of the soul and body. (*DM*, 103, 14–104, 4)

In acts of divination:
For if the presence of the fire of the Gods and an ineffable form of light descend on the possessed from outside (*exōthen*), entirely fills and dominates him, and *circularly embraces him from everywhere at once* so that he cannot perform any action proper to his own order, what personal perception or awareness or intuition could occur to someone possessed by the divine fire. (*DM* 113, 8–14)

For the priestess at Delphi:
When the abundantly gathered fire ascending from the mouth of the cave *circularly embraces her on all sides*, she is filled with its divine splendor. (*DM* 126, 11–14)

In his *Timaeus* commentary Iamblichus said that circular activity indicates an assimilation to the *Nous*, "for the intuitive thinking of the soul and the circular motion of bodies imitate noetic activity."[2] An embodied *noēsis* was revealed in the orbits of stars, whose *archē* and *telos* were simultaneous (*DM* 31, 18–32, 7), and this *energeia* was shared by the soul until it "broke the circle" to enter the rectilinear

---

2. *In Tim.*, frag. 49, 15, in Dillon, trans., *Iamblichi Chalcidensis.*

and contrary movements of generated life.[3] The stars were vehicles
of the encosmic gods who themselves were the vehicles of the
hypercosmic gods (*DM* 57, 7–58, 1). The heavenly bodies, therefore,
were visible shrines (*agalmata*)[4] of the demiurgic *Nous*, and to join
these gods the soul had to regain the circular shape of the vehicle
(*ochēma*) it possessed prior to embodiment.[5]

In schematic terms the soul's fall from the *Nous* was equivalent to
its loss of circularity. The correlation of circular motion with the
divine was a recurrent topos in the Platonic dialogues,[6] and Iamblichus said that the entire cosmos was defined by a circular movement (*DM*, 31, 13–32, 7): "The sphere is the only shape that can
include all the elements ... it takes in all shapes ... (and embraces
within itself) secondary and tertiary natures."[7] If an entity had a

---

3. *In Tim.*, frag. 49, 17, in Dillon, trans., *Iamblichi Chalcidensis*, 152–53.

4. Iamblichus uses the term *agalma* (shrine, statue) to describe the stellar manifestations of the gods. These *agalmata*, he implies at *DM* 168, are true icons of the
divine because they are "drawn out of uniform Forms and intelligible Essences"
(168, 4–5) by the Demiurge in the act of creation. *Agalma* is taken from the *Timaeus*
(39e) where it is used to describe the bodies of the gods. See Cornford's discussion of
this term, *Plato's Cosmology: The Timaeus of Plato*, trans. and comm. Francis C.
Cornford (London, 1937; reprint, New York: Bobbs-Merrill, 1959), 99–102.

5. That is, when souls were the "companions" of the gods in the celestial round
described in the *Phaedrus* (248c, 2). In the *DM* (145, 7–9) Iamblichus says that the
god is superior to Necessity and so is the "entire choir of superior beings attached
to him"; cf. *Phaedrus* 248a, 1–3.

6. Cf. Lynne Ballew, *Straight and Circular: A Study of Imagery in Greek Philosophy* (Assen, The Netherlands: Van Gorcum, 1979), 79–107. In the *Timaeus*, for
example, Plato says the head was made spherical in imitation of the divine revolutions. It is the first and "most divine" body of man to which was added a body with
four limbs and length (*Tim.* 44e). In the *Symposium* the fall of man was figuratively
described by Aristophanes as the loss of man's spherical shape (190a–e), and, of
course, the World Soul was a sphere as was every creator god. It is significant that
prior to the splitting of man in Aristophanes' tale his mode of movement was to
"whirl like a cartwheel" with "eight" legs. For a Platonist who recognized the
human soul as a microcosm of the World Soul, the eight-legged circulation of pre-
fallen man might indicate his participation in the World Soul with its "eight" celestial spheres. Note as well, Iamblichus provides "eight" attributes for the sphere in
his encomium to sphericity, and lists "eight" powers of the pre-essential Demiurge
at *DM* 292, 5–18.

7. *In Tim.*, frag. 49, 23–35, Dillon, trans., *Iamblichi Chalcidensis*, 154–55.

spheric body its activities were completed within itself: its *archē* and *telos* were simultaneous (*DM* 31, 13–32, 2). To move out of the sphere to complete one's actions was to fall from the *Nous* and this was the condition of embodied souls.[8]

The circular movements of the encosmic gods were the first and most striking reminder to the embodied soul of its sphericity, and in theurgy, when the soul became the *ochēma* of the god, it regained the spherical form lost in embodiment. This assimilation to celestial bodies was indicated not only by the recovery of the sphere but also by the audible phenomenon that attended this possession: the "rushing sound" (*rhoizos*) that occurred when the soul was circularly possessed. Iamblichus used the term *rhoizos* to describe the sounds emitted by the stars whose intervals served as the bases for theurgical chants and melodies.[9] In *De Vita Pythagorica Liber*[10] Iamblichus attributes the discovery of these sounds to Pythagoras who successfully re-created them in proto-theurgical rites for his disciples (*VP* 35, 24–36, 15). According to Hans Lewy *rhoizos* was a technical term used in late antiquity to describe the sound emitted by the stars;[11] it was also found prominently in the

---

8. Alcmaeon of Croton says that man dies *"because he cannot connect the beginning to the end"* (*Arist. Probl.* 916a, 34); cited by Dodds, *Proclus: The Elements of Theology*, 2d ed., revised text with trans., intro., and comm. E.R. Dodds (Oxford: Clarendon Press, 1963), 219. In his commentary on the categories of Aristotle, Iamblichus says that all contraries of the generated world—even life and death—are present simultaneously in noetic essences; see Simplicius, *In Aristotelis Categorias Commentarium*, in *CAG*, ed. C. Kalbfleisch (Berlin: G. Reimeri, 1907), 8:416, 26f. Cf. P. Hadot's remarks, *Porphyre et Victorinus*, 2 vols. (Paris: Etudes Augustiniennes, 1968), 2:442.

9. *DM* 118, 16–119, 4. Iamblichus refers to stellar motions as "rushing harmonious voices" (*rhoizoumenas enharmonious phōnas*).

10. See two fine translations: *Iamblichus: On the Pythagorean Life*, trans. with notes and commentary by Gillian Clark (Liverpool: Liverpool University Press, 1989), and *Iamblichus: On the Pythagorean Way of Life*, text, translation, and commentary by John Dillon and Jackson Hershbell (Atlanta, Ga.: Scholars Press, 1991). Unless otherwise noted, translations are my own following Deubner's text and pagination, *VP*.

11. Lewy, *Chaldean Oracles and Theurgy*, ed. M. Tardieu (Paris: Etudes Augustiniennes, 1978), 19 n. 46, verse 10; cf. p. 193.

Chaldean Oracles[12] so it is not surprising that Iamblichus marked the moment of divine possession with a sound reserved to celestial bodies (*DM* 104, 1). In ritual possession the theurgist was understood to enter the celestial round and "its most musical harmony" (*VP* 36, 25).

When the soul was divinized it embraced simultaneously the attractions and the repulsions of corporeal life, and this freed it from the physical body. In the *De Anima* Iamblichus says: "Certain souls who are lifted up and freed from generation are liberated with respect to the rest of corporeal life ... [they] have pneumatic vehicles with uniform identity (*autoeides*), and on account of these vehicles can easily accomplish whatever they will."[13] Marcus Aurelius used the same term, *autoeides*, to describe the well-balanced soul: "The sphere of the soul possesses its true form (*sphaira psuchēs autoeides*) when it neither projects itself outside nor shrinks in upon itself, neither expands, nor contracts."[14] Iamblichus employed the image of the sphere to describe the vehicles of celestial souls and also referred to their freedom from inner and outer attractions. He says: "It is acknowledged that the aetherial body is outside of every contrariety, free from every change, completely purified from the possibility of being transformed into something else, and entirely liberated from a centripetal or centrifugal tendency, either because

12. *The Chaldean Oracles*, text, translation, and commentary by Ruth Majercik (Leiden: E. J. Brill, 1989).

13. *Stob.* I, 373, 28–374, 1. *Autoeidesi* is a synonym of monoeidesi to contrast with *polueidos* at 374, 1. As we shall see, this *autoeides ochēma* is created by the Demiurge as the first vehicle of the soul.

14. Marcus Aurelius, 11, 12. See Festugière's comments on this passage, *La Rév.* 3:206 n. 4. It is possible that the *autoeides* was a scribal error of *augoeides* as G. R. S. Mead suggests in *The Doctrine of the Subtle Body in the Western Tradition* (Wheaton, Ill.: Theosophical Publishing House, 1967; originally published 1919), 56–57. Though there is no manuscript evidence to support Mead's conjecture it is not unlikely that in the uncial script *AUGOEIDES* could have been mistaken for *AUTOEIDES*. The only other evidence for *autoeides* is in Alexander of Aphrodisias's commentary, *In Metaphysicam* 791, 8–15, where he explicitly defines the term: *legōn autoeidos to archikon hen* (701, 14–15). For Alexander *autoeidos* is the "ruling One" in which every *eidos* must participate, a different understanding of the term than we see in Iamblichus.

it has neither tendency or *because it is moved circularly*" (*DM* 202, 13–18). To move in a circle was to embrace at once the contraries of embodied life, and the translation of the theurgist to his aetheric body was manifest by his symptoms in the generated world: the *apatheia* and *ataraxia* of a sage whose will revealed the will of the gods (*DM* 21, 2–9).

According to Iamblichus's view of embodiment the recovery of the soul's divine and spheric body was impossible without theurgic ritual, and although *enthousiasmos* was the soul's most appropriate condition it did not ordinarily experience it (*Stob.* I, 371, 17–22). Identification with its corporeal image imprisoned the soul in the contrary tendencies of generated life and separated it from its self. As embodied, the soul was alienated from the *enthousiasmos* proper to it. Plotinus described this inverted condition as the soul's attachment to a part (i.e., its corporeal image) and "separation from the whole" (*Enn.* IV, 8, 4, 16–17; trans. Armstrong). For Plotinus the embodied soul "comes and turns to that one thing battered by the totality of things in every way, and has left the whole and directs the individual part with great difficulty . . . it sinks deep into the individual part. Here the 'moulting' as it is called [*Phaedrus* 248], happens to it and being in the fetters of the body" (*Enn.* IV, 8, 4, 18–25). Yet, for Plotinus, a part of the soul remained free of this condition and continued to enjoy full participation in the *Nous*, though its "shadow," the embodied soul, was not aware of it.[15]

For Plotinus the breach between divine and human souls was bridged by the soul itself. The Plotinian soul has appropriately been compared to a "floating ego"[16] capable of rising by contemplation to its undescended level with the *Nous*. For Iamblichus this was not possible. The gap between divine and human souls was far more than a matter of consciousness. The embodied soul could co-ordinate its somatic and intellectual energies, but these only prepared it

---

15. For a discussion of the "unconscious" presence of the higher soul in the lower for Plotinus, see Andrew Smith, "Unconsciousness and Quasiconsciousness in Plotinus," *Phronesis* 23, no. 3 (1978): 292–301.

16. Ibid., 293.

for theurgic initiation.[17] Of its own power, Iamblichus says, the soul cannot ascend to the gods:

> For if somehow we seem to be capable of doing this it is by partic-
> ipating in and being illuminated by the Gods, and only in this may
> we rejoice in divine activity. Accordingly, the soul does not partic-
> ipate in divine actions through possessing its own virtue and wis-
> dom, yet if such [divine] acts were the province of the soul, either
> every soul would perform them or only the soul which possessed
> the perfection appropriate to it. But, as it is, neither of these are
> sufficiently prepared for this, and *even the perfect soul is imperfect
> with respect to divine activity.* Consequently, theurgic activity is
> different, and the successful accomplishment of divine actions is
> given by the Gods alone. Otherwise it would not at all be necessary
> to worship the Gods, but according to your view divine blessings
> would exist for us of themselves without the performance of rit-
> ual. (*DM* 149, 4–17)

The differences between the soul's "philosophic" ascent as conceived by Plotinus and Porphyry and the "theurgic" ascent of Iamblichus seem striking, yet recent studies have shown an underlying
similarity not only in the goal of their respective ascents but also in
the means to attain it. A. H. Armstrong was the first to note that "it
is possible to develop a theory of theurgy from one side of the
thought of Plotinus,"[18] and he refers to passages in which Plotinus
speaks of union with the One, not as a "rational" event but as something that occurs when the soul is "erotically charged by the One"
and goes "out of its mind" to achieve a mystical union.[19] Andrew
Smith develops this theme in an excellent study of Porphyry[20] that

17. The soul's inversion was outlined in the Platonic dialogues where the transformation of the will is expressed in the form of an "erotic" role-reversal with profound ethical symptoms. See for example Alcibiades' relationship with Socrates,
the divine sage who "knows nothing" (*Symposium* 215e, 4–6; 217c, 7–8).

18. Armstrong, "Tradition, Reason, and Experience in the Thought of Plotinus," in *Plotinian and Christian Studies* (London: Variorum Reprints, 1979), 17:187.
In addition to Armstrong's references, see Plotinus's remarks concerning the ineffability of *henōsis*, which he compares to divine possession; *Enn.* V, 3, 14, 3–13.

19. Armstrong, "Tradition, Reason," 183.

20. Smith, *Porphyry's Place in the Neoplatonic Tradition: A Study in Post-Plotinian Neoplatonism* (The Hague: Martinus Nijhoff, 1974), 83–90.

includes a comparison of the mysticism of Plotinus and Iamblichus. What separated the two Neoplatonists, Smith argues, was not their mystical thinking but their respective use of terms such as *noēsis*, *gnōsis*, and *nous*.[21] Plotinus argued that the soul ascends to the One by means of the erotic presence of the One in the soul, and Iamblichus said the ascent occurs through the beneficent presence of the gods. Smith argues that the differences between Plotinus and Iamblichus were semantic, not substantive, and this view has been corroborated recently by Clemens Zintzen who argues that Iamblichus transformed Plotinus's description of the soul's "noetic impulse" into "theurgic grace," a gift of the gods.[22] Zintzen maintains that Iamblichus translated Plotinus's and Porphyry's description of the soul's "philosophic" ascent into the magical terminology of the Chaldean Oracles and Egyptian cult.[23]

These studies have corrected the facile and once-fashionable distinction that praised Plotinus as the last Hellenic rationalist before Iamblichus corrupted the Platonic school with ritual worship. Having eliminated this false distinction, these authors suggest that what distinguished Iamblichus's theurgical Neoplatonism was his genuine respect for the "magico-religious practices of his times,"[24] which probably resulted from his own "vivid experience of the divine in some ritual."[25] Doubtless, this is true, and Hans Lewy and Friedrich Cremer have demonstrated the profound influence of the Chaldean Oracles on the theurgy of Iamblichus.[26]

The question that has not been addressed, however, is why Iam-

---

21. Ibid., 86–89. Smith's argument follows the methodology of the Neoplatonists themselves who found a uniformity of doctrine underlying the semantic differences of Plato and Aristotle. See H.J. Blumenthal, "Some Platonist Readings of Aristotle," *Cambridge Philological Society Proceedings* 207 (1981): 1.

22. Clemens Zintzen, "Bemerkungen zum Aufstiegsweg der Seele in Jamblichs *De Mysteriis*," *Platonismus und Christentum: Festschrift für Heinrich Dörrie*, ed. H.D. Blume and F. Mann (Münster: Aschendorff, 1983), 319.

23. Ibid.

24. Smith, *Porphyry's Place*, 89.

25. Armstrong, "Tradition, Reason," 187.

26. Lewy, Chaldean Oracles, passim; Cremer, *Die Chaldäischen Orakel*, passim. Although Cremer rightly points out that Platonic teachings underlie both the Chaldean Oracles and the *De Mysteriis*, in some respects he overplays the Chaldean

blichus would have been drawn to ritual practices in the first place. It is, of course, a question that cannot be answered completely, but it is not enough to say that Iamblichus's Platonism was read into the ritual material of the Oracles, or to suggest that this was due to Iamblichus's Syrian background.[27] There were, in any case, as many "magico-religious" practices in Plotinus's Egypt. Apart from saying that it was due to a matter of temperament, which often gives rise to misguided characterizations,[28] I would suggest that the difference between Iamblichus and Plotinus with regard to ritual practices may well have been determined, not by Iamblichus's supposed Oriental background, nor by his attraction to the exotic religious practices of his time, but by the more profound influence of Aristotle's psychology on Iamblichus than on Plotinus.

This influence is reflected in two complementary issues: (1) Iamblichus's view that the soul descends entirely in embodiment, which implicates it within the measures of corporeal existence;[29] and (2) Iamblichus's view—contra that of Plotinus—that when the soul descends into a body it is cut off from the *Nous* and cannot return to the divine of its own power. Iamblichus was more convinced than Plotinus of the underlying agreement (*sumphonia*) between Plato and Aristotle. Therefore, he accepted Aristotle's definition of the soul as *entelecheia* of the body by integrating it with Plato's description of embodiment in the *Timaeus*, and Aristotle's belief that the human soul receives the divine *thurathen* may be seen in Iamblichus's theurgical principle that one's access to the divine

---

influence based solely on Iamblichus's use of Chaldean terminology. Where the *De Mysteriis* clearly contradicts and Chaldean fragments, Cremer's arguments appear to be strained; see 114–15, 122.

27. Following Blumenthal's conjecture, in his "Plutarch's Exposition of the De Anima and the Psychology of Proclus," in *Entretiens*, 27.

28. Iamblichus has been typified as "Oriental," hence only vaguely rational and prone to superstition and emotion; see John H. Smith, *The Death of Classical Paganism* (London: Geoffrey Chapman, 1976), 55–56; Dodds, *The Greeks and the Irrational* (Berkeley and Los Angeles: University of California Press, 1973), 288.

29. As Iamblichus puts it, the embodied soul is "enformed by all the various measures which come from secondary lives" (*DM* 21, 17–22, 1; cf. 18, 16–17).

comes "from without" (*exōthen*).[30] The upside-down status of Plato's embodied soul was, for Iamblichus, the soul described by Aristotle as the entelecheia of the body, cut off from the *Nous*.[31] The re-ascent of the soul to the Good, which Plato described as a dialectical process (*Republic* 511b–c), was replaced by Iamblichus with the practice of ritual theurgy. Yet the *dialektikē*, which Iamblichus dismissed in the *De Mysteriis* as a "mere intellectual exercise" (*DM* 10, 1–9), was not the dialectic of Plato but that of Aristotle, for whom the term indicated mere intellectual jousting and not a practice leading to spiritual transformation.[32]

Iamblichus, like Aristotle, believed that the divine *Nous* was far removed from the soul,[33] and in the *De Mysteriis* he asserted in the strongest terms that the categories of "human" and "divine" were mutually exclusive.[34] Yet, at the same time, Iamblichus believed the human soul was immortal and incapable of losing its divinity. To appreciate these divergent positions is to begin to see the paradox that embodiment presented to Iamblichus and why he embraced

30. Aristotle says: "Reason (*nous*) alone enters in, as an additional factor [to the embodied soul], *from outside*, and it alone is divine" (*De Generatione Animalium* [*GA*] 236b, 28). Iamblichus confirms that contact with the divine must come *exōthen* (*DM* 24, 4; 30, 16–19; 127, 10; 167, 2). Cremer notes, *Die Chaldaïschen Orakel*, 480 n. 95, that this view is "entirely different" from the Plotinian position, which states that the divine comes from within (*endothen*), not from without (*exōthen*); cf. *Enn*. III, 1, 9; IV, 7, 10, 43–52. Cremer's view is only prima facie correct, however, for the *exōthen* that Plotinus denies as a locus of the divine is the sensible other and therefore ontologically subordinate to the soul. In this regard Iamblichus would have agreed (cf. *DM* 171, 5–10), but the *exōthen* that Iamblichus describes as the locus of divine illumination refers to a different sort of "place." Since the divine is beyond the comprehension of the soul, its contact with divine beings must come from something superior to itself, from outside (*exōthen*) its order of existence. Thus, "outside" for Iamblichus refers to an epistemological and ontological beyond and for Plotinus it refers to the sensible external.

31. Aristotle, *GA* 236b, 28; cf. *DM* 148, 12–14.

32. Cf. *Top*. 100a, 18–24; *SE* 165b, 2–4; 172a, 15. For a discussion of the transformation of Plato's anagogic dialectic by Aristotle into an instrument of the rational mind see W.K.C. Guthrie, *A History of Greek Philosophy*, vol. 6, *Aristotle: An Encounter* (New York: Cambridge University Press, 1981), 150–53.

33. *In Tim*. IV, frag. 87, 20–21; in Dillon, trans., *Iamblichi Chalcidensis*, 200–201.

34. Cf. *DM* 171, 11–13 where Iamblichus emphasizes that "human" and "divine" are mutually exclusive terms.

theurgy as the only means to resolve it. On the one hand, because the soul identified with the single form of its corporeal body (*DM* 148, 12–14) and defined itself therein, its salvation could come only from an authoritative "other" (*heteros*) that released it from its false identity and awakened it to its true self (*autos*). From this perspective, the Chaldean Oracles, as important as they were for Iamblichus, simply provided the occasion for a theurgic exchange. Iamblichus was apparently just as impressed with the Egyptian tradition,[35] and Philip Derchain has pointed to the influence of Egyptian rites at Abydos on the theurgy of Abammon (Iamblichus).[36] Yet Iamblichus's adoption of theurgic rites was not merely the result of his following Aristotle's definition of the soul. Theurgy was also an epistemological necessity. For Iamblichus, "knowledge" worked within a dualistic structure: "knowing an 'other' as 'other'" (*DM* 8, 4–6), so it could never engender a union with the divine.

It is on this issue that Iamblichus's theurgical Platonism may be seen as an attempt to resolve philosophical problems left by Plotinus.[37] Plotinus's language concerning union with the One reveals a conflation of mystical impulses that derive from the One itself, with the philosophic language of Platonism. Such a conflation might lead to the rationalization of mystical ascent if the discourse that Plotinus used to describe his union with the One were confused with the experience of that union. As Armstrong says, it would constitute the error of making conceptual idols out of evocative icons,[38] and it was precisely this kind of rationalistic idolatry that Iamblichus perceived

35. After all, the persona that Iamblichus adopts in the *De Mysteriis* is that of an Egyptian priest "Abammon," not a Chaldean. Further, Iamblichus proposes to explain the theology and symbols of the Egyptians (*DM*, books VII–X), not those of the Chaldeans.

36. Philip Derchain, "Pseudo-Jamblique ou Abammon," *Chronique d'Egypt* 38 (1963): 220–26. In addition Armstrong rightly notes that most of the "theurgical" rituals that Iamblichus defends are, in any case, well attested to as "old *Greek* religious practices." Armstrong, "Tradition, Reason," 185. The important point for Iamblichus is that theurgic rites possess an authority and power that transcends human understanding and initiative.

37. J.M.P. Lowry, The Logical Principles of Proclus' *STOICHEIŌSIS THEO-LOGIKĒ As Systematic Ground of the Cosmos* (Amsterdam: Rodopi, 1980), 22–28.

38. For an explanation of Armstrong's use of these terms against the background

in Porphyry's teaching and which he attempted to combat by distinguishing theurgical from philosophical language.

The supposed "irrationalism" of Iamblichean *theourgia*[39] therefore, may well derive from Iamblichus's keener sensitivity for precision in rational discourse. After all, if a discursive statement about the One functioned evocatively[40] rather than descriptively, its conceptual content would be transparent and, in that sense, would function theurgically.[41] It was not its meaning that effected *henōsis* but its ability to transcend meaning,[42] and if the discursive meaning became central its evocative power would be lost.[43] In Platonic terms, the opacity of discursive meanings, however exalted their subject matter, were nothing more than the "shadow language" of Plato's cave (*Rep.* 515). Therefore, Iamblichus's subordination of philosophy to theurgy was simply making explicit a distinction that was already implicit in Plotinus's mysticism but that he failed to work out.[44]

---

of Neoplatonic negative theology see Armstrong, "Negative Theology," *Downside Review* 95 (1977): 188–89.

39. Dodds, "Iamblichus," *Oxford Classical Dictionary*, 2d ed. (Oxford: Oxford University Press, 1970), 538.

40. For a discussion of the "incantative" power of the term *hen* for Neoplatonists, see J. Trouillard, "Un (philosophies de l')" *Encyclopedia Universalis* (Paris, 1968–73), 16:461–63.

41. In precisely the same way that material artifacts in theurgy are not worshiped for their "physical" properties, neither is the discursive icon valued for its conceptual truth or accuracy.

42. One must take care, however, not to confuse the anagogic "negation" of meaning with its mere "privation." For a clear exposition of these terms from Aristotle to the Neoplatonists, see Christian Guérard, "La Théologie négative dans l'apophatisme grec," *Revue des Sciences Philosophiques et Théologiques* 68 (1984): 183–200.

43. Armstrong, "Negative Theology," 188–89.

44. Describing this, Lowry says: "What Iamblichus did was to develop this mystical side of Plotinus more systematically than Plotinus himself had done. . . . [I]t could be argued that Iamblichus, in trying to make sense out of Plotinus, developed philosophical principles which make possible mystical unity with the divine. By doing this he could then be said to have showed that this unity was not primarily philosophical. This should perhaps be the position that any Neoplatonist, especially Plotinus, should have made explicit. There does not seem, to me at least, to be any point in belaboring Iamblichus for being less philosophical than Plotinus. He simply carried the obvious Plotinian philosophical standpoint to its limits and tried to validate it." Lowry, *Logical Principles*, 20–21.

9

The Paradox of Embodiment

That which is immortal in the soul is filled completely with mortality...

T he repercussions of viewing the Platonic soul through Aristotle's doctrine that essences (*ousiai*) are revealed by activities (*energeiai*) have been examined by Carlos Steel in a brilliant monograph on Neoplatonic psychology, *The Changing Self.*[1] Steel outlines Iamblichus's view of the soul by examining the Iamblichean fragments preserved in Priscianus's (Simplicius's?) commentary on Aristotle's *De Anima.*[2] At the outset of his commentary Priscianus says that he "will hold to the truth of the matter as much as possible according to the interpretation of Iamblichus

1. Carlos G. Steel, *The Changing Self: A Study on the Soul in Later Neoplatonism: Iamblichus, Damascius, and Priscianus*, trans. E. Haasl (Brussels: Paleis der Academien, 1978).

2. For the attribution of this commentary to Priscianus rather than to his contemporary, Simplicius, see F. Boussier and Carlos G. Steel, "Priscianus Lydus en de 'In de Anima' van Pseudo(?)-Simplicius," *Tijdschrift voor Filosofie* 34 (1972): 761–822. Ilsetraut Hadot accepts the hypothesis of Boussier and Steel on the basis of the striking similarities between the *De Anima* commentary and Priscianus's *Metaphrasis in Theophrastum*, ed. I. Bywater in *Supplementum Aristotelicum* 1, no. 2 (Berlin, 1886): 1–37, but shows their argument of supposed doctrinal incompatibilities between Simplicius's other works and the *de Anima* commentary to be unfounded; see Hadot, *Le Problème du néoplatonisme alexandrin: Hiéroclès et Simplicius* (Paris: Etudes Augustiniennes, 1978), 193–202. Blumenthal says he shall continue to call the author of the *de Anima* commentary "Simplicius" "as a matter of convenience"; Blumenthal, "The Psychology of (?)Simplicius' Commentary on the *De anima*," in *Soul and the Structure of Being in Late Neoplatonism: Syrianius,*

set out in his teachings on the soul."[3] For Priscianus, Iamblichus was "the best critic of the truth" (*ho aristos tēs alētheias kritēs; DA* 89, 33–37), and his extensive quotations and discussions of Iamblichus's views form the basis of Steel's analysis.

Steel throws light on the disturbing complexity of Iamblichus's psychology. He shows that Iamblichus followed the *energeia-reveals-ousia* formula not only to distinguish incorporeal classes but also to focus on the specific case of the human soul. It led Iamblichus to the conclusion, especially difficult for a Platonist, that because the *energeiai* of embodied souls were mortal and subject to change so their *ousiai*, being the source of this activity, were also mortal and subject to change! Even more problematic was Iamblichus's belief that the soul's separation from the *Nous* also separated the soul from itself and its immortality. Priscianus says:

> If, however, as Iamblichus thinks, a perverse and imperfect activity would not proceed from an essence which is impassive and perfect, *the soul would be, even in its essence, somehow subject to passion.* For, in this view the soul is a mean, not only between divided and undivided, the remaining and the proceeding, the noetic and the irrational, but also between the ungenerated and the generated.[4] ... For on account of its verging outside, the soul simultaneously *remains* as a whole and *proceeds* as a whole, and it is neither entirely involved in, nor free from, either trait. Wherefore, that which is immortal in the soul is filled completely with

---

Proclus, and Simplicius, by H. J. Blumenthal and A. C. Lloyd (Liverpool: Liverpool University Press, 1982), 74; cf. Blumenthal, "Did Iamblichus Write a Commentary on the *De Anima?*" *Hermes* 102 no. 4 (1974): 540–56. I follow Steel in attributing the *de Anima* commentary to Priscianus and will attribute quotations to him.

3. Simplicius (Priscianus?), *In Libros Aristotelis de Anima Commentaria* (*DA*), 1, 18–20, in *CAG* 9, ed. M. Hayduck (Berlin: G. Reimeri, 1882). Steel notes that the last part of this phrase could just as correctly be rendered: "in his own treatise *On the Soul.*" The question of whether or not Iamblichus wrote such a treatise must remain open.

4. *DA* 89, 33–37. Text: εἰ δέ, ὡς τῷ Ἰαμβλίχῳ δοκεῖ, οὐκ ἂν ἐξ ἀπαθοῦς καὶ τελείας οὐσίας διεστραμμένη καὶ ἀτελὴς προΐοι ἐνέργεια, εἴη ἂν παθαινομένη πως καὶ κατ᾽ οὐσίαν· ὡς καὶ ταύτῃ εἶναι μέση οὐ τῶν μεριστῶν μόνον καὶ ἀμερίστων οὐδὲ τῶν μενόντων καὶ προεληλυθότῶν οὐδὲ τῶν νοερῶν καὶ ἀλόγων, ἀλλὰ καὶ τῶν ἀγενήτῶν καὶ γενητῶν.

mortality and no longer remains only immortal. Somehow the ungenerated part of the soul becomes subject to generation just as the undivided part of the soul becomes subject to division.[5]

Ambiguity and paradox defined the very essence of the soul. Again, Priscianus:

> According to Iamblichus, the particular soul embraces both characteristics *equally*, both permanency and change, so that in this way its intermediate position is again preserved; for higher beings are stable, mortal ones are completely changeable. The particular soul, however, which as middle, is divided and multiplied together with the mundane beings, does not only remain permanent but also changes because it lives through so many divisible lives. And not only in its habits, but it changes also in its substance.[6]

These oppositions were triggered by the soul's animation of its body. Since the human soul was "inclined toward the body that it governs" (*DM* 21, 5–7, 16), when it projected its "lower lives" (i.e., the irrational powers of the soul) its *ousia* was broken apart and intertwined with mortal lives.[7] Paraphrasing Iamblichus,[8] Priscianus says: "It is therefore more reasonable and necessary to say that *not only the activity but also the highest essence* of our soul is in some way relaxed, broken up, and has its existence constituted, so to speak, in its descent toward lower lives."[9] While Plotinus and Porphyry also

5. *DA* 90, 20–24. Text: διὰ γὰρ τὴν ἔξω ῥοπὴν ὁμοῦ ὅλη καὶ μένει καὶ πρόεισι, καὶ οὐδέτερον ἔχει παντελῶς οὐδὲ ἀπηλλαγμένον τοῦ λοιποῦ (ὅθεν καὶ τὸ ἀθάνατον αὐτῆς τότε ἀναπίμπλαται τοῦ θνητοῦ κατὰ πᾶν ἑαυτό, καὶ οὐ μένει μόνον ἀθάνατον, καὶ τὸ ἀγένητον γινόμενόν πως τυγχάνει ὄν, ὡς καὶ τὸ ἀμέριστον αὐτῆς μεριζόμενον).

6. Priscianus, *Metaphrasis* 32, 13–19; translation (slightly modified) by Steel, *The Changing Self*, 57.

7. Steel notes that Priscianus uses the term *parathrauōmenos* to describe the "breaking" of the soul's essence when it projects outwardly into a body (*DA* 220, 2–15). This reflects Plato's use of *parathrauō* to describe the "breaking up" of the soul's wings in its descent into a body (*Phaed.* 248d); Steel, *The Changing Self*, 59 n. 24.

8. This passage begins with the phrase: ὡς καὶ τῷ Ἰαμβλίκῳ ἐν τῇ ἰδίᾳ Περὶ ψυχῆς πραγματείᾳ δοκεῖ (*DA* 240, 37–38).

9. *DA* 241, 7–10. Text: εὔλογον ἄρα μᾶλλον δὲ ἀναγκαῖον οὐ τὴν ἐνέργειαν μόνην, ἀλλὰ καὶ τὴν οὐσίαν τῆς ψυχῆς καὶ αὐτὴν τὴν ἀκροτάτην, τῆς ἡμετέρας φημί, διαφορεῖσθαί πως καὶ χαλᾶσθαι καὶ οἷον ὑφιζάνειν ἐν τῇ πρὸς τὰ δεύτερα νεύσει.

maintained that the soul projected its lower powers (*dunameis*) to animate the body and believed that these powers acted as a mean between the *ousia* and the embodied *energeia* of the soul, the essence of the soul was never affected by this projection. Changes may seem to affect the soul, but its rational essence remained untouched. For Plotinus, the diverse activities attributed to the soul were merely accidental and somatic accretions which do not implicate the soul's unfallen *ousia*.[10] For Iamblichus, they do. In embodiment the *ousia*, in fact, becomes *ousiai*, for in accord with the *energeia*-reveals-*ousia* formula, the multiplicity of the *energeiai* and *dunameis* reflect a multiplicity of *ousiai*. Consequently, Iamblichus speaks of the essences (*ousiai*) of the soul,[11] and Priscianus, following him, says: "The definition of these matters is difficult because in truth the *soul is one and many in essence*" (*DA* 14, 7–8).

The soul endured such paradox because of its cosmogonic function as the mean between extremes. Remaining *and* proceeding were essential modes of the soul's existence, and if it were truly to function as a mean its essence could not remain stable and unchanging. The loss of the soul's unity and stability caused it to suffer, but this was the soul's way to participate in the activity of the Demiurge. To deny diversity to the soul would deny its role in cosmogenesis where it bestowed coherence and unity to the chaos and diversity of generated life. However, because it was a *human* soul with weakened measures of coherence, it experienced this demiurgy as a kind of self-alienation and dismemberment. The

---

10. Cf. *Enn.* I, 1, 7, 1–7 where Plotinus says the soul does not descend but extends a "sort of light" (*tis hoios phōs*) to animate a body, and *Enn.* VI, 4, 15, 14–17, where he says the soul does not incarnate but only exudes a "warmth" (*thermasia*) or "illumination" (*ellampsis*) whose "trace" (*ichnos*) animates the composite life. It should be noted that Iamblichus similarly states in the *DM* (35, 8–12) that the soul undergoes no pathos in its embodiment. However, this does not contradict the Iamblichean teachings preserved by Priscianus, for the *pathos* discussed at *DM* 35 is one imposed on the soul from without, as upon perishable creatures. Unlike them, the soul is cause of its own *pathos* as a composite entity (*DM* 35, 11–12), and this agrees with Iamblichus's description of the soul as *autokinēsis* and therefore not subject to the sensible alterations of *poiein/paschein* (*DM* 12, 6–11).

11. *DCMS* 13, 11; 43, 9; see Steel, *The Changing Self*, n. 36.

soul's demiurgic unity, ironically, was available to it only through the act of self-division.

Among the hierarchy of immortal entities, the human soul possessed the greatest degree of "otherness" (*heterotēs*). This caused it to identify with what was other to itself, and the corporeal body became the context of its self-alienation. Priscianus[12] says: "Our soul remains one and is multiplied at the same time in its inclination to the body; it neither remains purely nor is changed entirely, but somehow it both remains and proceeds from itself, and when *it is made other to itself* the sameness with itself is made faint."[13] The soul was self-alienated in embodiment,[14] even to the point of having its existence constituted by its descent to the generated world,[15] yet, as Priscianus explains, "it can never become *entirely* self-alienated or it would cease to be soul."[16] As Steel puts it: "the soul only remains itself because it ceaselessly proceeds from itself and, at the same time, returns to itself."[17]

Iamblichus's definition of the soul was received by his successors in significantly different ways. Proclus, despite following Iamblichus in his teaching that the soul descends entirely in embodiment,[18]

---

12. I have quoted Priscianus here (and elsewhere) as paraphrasing Iamblichus's teaching even where he does not explicitly mention Iamblichus. In the case of the doctrine that the *ousia* of the soul is changed in embodiment one may be sure that Priscianus is, indeed, reporting Iamblichus's position; not only because it is explicitly attributed to Iamblichus elsewhere, but because it was clearly *not* the position adopted by Priscianus himself. Following Proclus, Priscianus believed that the incarnate soul was changed only on the level of its acts, not its essence. See *DA* 19, 16–27 with Steel's translation and discussion, *The Changing Self*, 59.

13. *DA* 223, 28–32. Text: μία γὰρ οὖσα ἡ ψυχὴ ἡμετέρα, ἡ λογική φημι, ἅμα τε μένει μία καὶ πληθύνεται ἐν τῇ πρὸς σῶμα ῥοπῇ, οὔτε μενοῦσα καθαρῶς οὔτε ἐξισταμένη παντελῶς, ἀλλὰ καὶ μένουσά πη καὶ προϊοῦσα ἀφ᾽ ἑαυτῆς καὶ τῷ ἑτεροιοῦσθαι πρὸς ἑαυτὴν ἀμυδροῦσα τὴν πρὸς ἑαυτὴν ταυτότητα.

14. *DA* 223, 26. Text: ...ἀλλοτριωθὲν <δὲ> διὰ τὴν ἔξω ῥοπὴν ἑαυτοῦ.

15. *DA* 241, 9–10. Text: ...καὶ οἷον ὑφιζάνειν ἐν τῇ πρὸς τὰ δεύτερα νεύσει.

16. *DA* 241, 10–11. Text: ...οὐ παντελῶς ἑαυτῆς ἐξισταμένην (οὐδὲ γὰρ ἂν ἔμενεν ἔτι ψυχή).

17. Steel, *The Changing Self*, 66.

18. *Proclus: The Elements of Theology* (*ET*), 2d ed., revised text with trans., intro., and comm. by E.R. Dodds (Oxford: Clarendon Press, 1963), propositions 209–11.

could not accept that the highest part of the soul, its *ousia*, is changed when the soul animated a body. Proclus employed Iamblichus's own principle of mediating terms to argue that the eternal *ousia* of the soul cannot undergo temporal change. Using a triadic division, Proclus placed the human soul between the extremes of (a) that which is eternal in substance and activity; and (b) that which is temporal in substance and activity. The soul, therefore, was (a) and (b), that which is eternal in substance but temporal in activity.[19] Proclus says: "every participated soul has an eternal substance but a temporal activity,"[20] which seems to resolve the tension and contradiction in Iamblichus's view by preserving the *ousia* of the soul from the changes endured in its *energeia*. Yet, in doing this, Proclus splits the soul and returns to the position of Plotinus, for what else is the soul's eternal and unchanging *ousia* if not an undescended soul?

Damascius, on the other hand, accepted Iamblichus's definition of the soul and explained the paradox of change in the soul's *ousia* with a Pythagorean reading of Aristotle's distinction of specific and individual identity. According to Aristotle, perishable entities such as plants and animals possess immortality and identity in their species but not as individuals (*De Anima* 415b, 2–9), for any entity whose essence changes does not remain the same individual. Thus, if the human soul were changed in its essence it would lose its immortal identity. Damascius solved this dilemma by asserting that "the essence of the human soul is the *mean* between that which endures specifically (*kat' eidos*) and that which endures individually (*kat'arithmon*)" (*Dub. et Sol.* II, 263, 12), which is another way of saying that the soul is both mortal and immortal.

According to Damascius, the Platonic definition of the soul as "self-moved" (*autokinēsis*) led directly to the contradictions seen in Iamblichus's position. The soul was *kinēsis* in that its essence was "moved" and endured "change," yet it was *autos* in that the soul "endured" the change, for change itself could have no meaning without a fixed point of reference. Self-change, however, does not mean

---

19. *ET*, props. 106–7; quoted by Steel, *The Changing Self*, 70.
20. *ET*, prop. 191; p. 166, 26–27 (Dodds).

that there are two parts of the soul, a stable element and a moveable element. In the *De Mysteriis* Iamblichus argued that the *autokinēsis* of the soul was "a simple essential movement that subsists from itself and not in relation to another" (*DM* 12, 8–9). Damascius developed this point at length in order to prove that "self-moved" (*autokinēsis*) indicates that "both moved and mover are the same being" (*Dub. et Sol.* II, 263, 12). The soul, he says, "both changes itself and is always being changed, thus, it possesses its being precisely by *always* changing its own essence" (*Dub. et Sol.* II, 263, 12–14).

The preservation of the soul's identity in Damascius's definition is indicated by the word "always" (*aei*). Iamblichus used this term in a technical sense in his *Parmenides* commentary to indicate how Motion (*kinēsis*) and Rest (*stasis*) were combined into one idea (*hen eidos*) at the level of the second hypothesis (*Parm.* 146a).[21] In the human soul Damascius called this combination of *auto-kinēsis*, the *eidos tēs huparxeōs* of the soul, and he again credited Iamblichus for distinguishing between *huparxis*—which is the principle of the soul's determination—and *ousia*, which is its determined essence (*Dub. et Sol.* I, 132, 12–23; cf. I, 312, 4–28). The *eidos tēs huparxeōs* of Damascius and Iamblichus was not conceived as a deeper sub-strate (*ousia*) of the soul but as its *pre-essence*, the presence of the One that revealed itself as *autokinēsis*, self-change. If this *eidos* were simply a higher essence then the changes of the soul would be accidental, not essential. The peculiar characteristic of the human soul, however, was that it preserved its identity "by always changing its own essence."[22]

---

21. Iamblichus says: "So then Motion is permanent (stationary) in the process of being in motion (for it will *always* be in motion), while Rest will be extended in its being at rest (for it in turn will *always* be at rest) inasmuch as Motion will not allow Rest to, as it were, drop off to sleep, while Rest will not permit Motion to 'jump out of its skin.' In this way the notion of 'always' is essentially bound up with both being at rest and being in motion"; see *In Parm.*, frag. 8, 13–16, in Dillon, trans., *Iamblichi Chalcidensis*, 218–19.

22. *DA* 263, 13. According to Iamblichus, the *huparxis* of the soul was the active presence of the One, experienced by the soul in the form of "lights" (*phōta*) (*DM* 117, 2). Pierre Hadot notes that Damascius explains *huparxis* etymologically as *hupo* +

Damascius attempted to explain this change by comparing the soul's aetheric body to a sponge. For Damascius, as for Iamblichus, the soul's sphericity was the sign of its illumination. Damascius says:

> Like a sponge, the soul loses nothing of its being but simply becomes rarefied or densified. Just so does the immortal body of the soul remain individually the same, but sometimes it is made more spherical and sometimes less, sometimes it is filled with divine light and sometimes with the stains of generative acts, and as its life undergoes some essential change so also the soul itself, while remaining what it is, is changed in itself and by itself. (*Dub. et Sol.* II, 255, 7–12)

"Sometimes," Damascius says, "the soul is tied essentially to the Gods, sometimes to mortal creatures" (*Dub. et Sol.* II, 255, 25–26), yet following Iamblichus, Damascius said it never loses its identity as soul. Like the sponge the soul could be filled with divine light and *"established in the essence of the sun"* (*Dub. et Sol.* II, 255, 7), or it could lose the light as well as its spherical shape in the darkness of generative impulses.

Damascius concluded that the soul cannot be split into higher and lower parts. Its *autokinēsis* is, as Iamblichus said, *haplous*, "a simple essential movement" (*DM* 12, 6–9), yet when the soul extends its secondary powers (*deuterai dunameis*) into a corporeal body its essence divides and the soul identifies with its animated parts. Although immortal and divine, the soul becomes a mortal creature.

This last point is of crucial importance and is arguably Iamblichus's raison d'être for theurgy. According to Iamblichus, it was the *entire* soul that changed in embodiment, both its rational and

---

archein, so that *huparxis* was the soul's anterior principle, and therefore not to be included within the order of which it is principle; P. Hadot, "L'Etre et l'Étant dans le Néoplatonisme," *Revue de Théologie et de Philosophie* 2 (1973): 109–13. This follows the principle outlined by Iamblichus in *DCMS* 15, 10–15 where he says that the One and the Many are *principles* of beings and not yet the kind of beings of which they are *archai*.

irrational powers, and, just as significantly, it was the entire soul that remained immortal, both its rational *and* irrational powers. In his *Phaedo* commentary Damascius lists the Platonists who share this position: "Some consider immortality to extend from the rational soul as far as to the irrational soul, among the older are Xenocrates and Speusippus, of the more recent are Iamblichus and Plutarch."[23] Proclus, on the other hand, restricted immortality to the rational soul (*logismos*), which was consistent with his view that only the *energeiai* of souls undergo change (hence mortality), not their *ousiai* (*In Phaed.* 177, 5; trans. Westerink). This was also consistent with Proclus's view that each soul has three vehicles (*ochēmata*): (1) the fleshy vehicle, (2) the pneumatic vehicle, drawn from the planetary elements, and (3) the universal and divine vehicle.[24] For Proclus, as well as for Porphyry, only the divine body was immortal whereas the pneumatic body had a limited immortality relative to its degree of purity; when entirely purified it ceased to exist. Since Porphyry followed Plotinus in his belief that part of the soul was undescended, he held that theurgic rituals were necessary only for cleansing the lower soul and its pneumatic vehicle, for the un-descended soul would need no purification (*De regressu animae* 27, 21–28, 15). Although Proclus says that the soul's *ousia* was unchanged (hence, somehow undescended), he nevertheless followed Iamblichus's view that theurgy was necessary even at the highest levels. This may indicate that he had a different conception of theurgy than Iamblichus, or that his understanding of theurgy was inconsistent with his teachings on the extent of the soul's fall

23. *In Phaed.* 177, 3–5, in L.G. Westerink, trans. and ed. *The Greek Commentaries on Plato's Phaedo*, vol. 2, Damascius (New York: North-Holland, 1977), 106–9. Cf. Blumenthal's discussion, "Some Problems About Body and Soul in Later Pagan Neoplatonism: Do They Follow a Pattern?" in *Platonismus und Christentum: Festschrift für Heinrich Dörrie*, 80–81. It is interesting that Damascius says Plotinus extended immortality "as far as to nature," but Westerink says this should be taken as referring to the immortality of the "World Soul" present in nature; Westerink, *Greek Commentaries*, 107.

24. See *ET*, 319–21. Cf. J. Trouillard, "Réflexions sur *l'OCHĒMA* dans les 'Elements de Théologie de Proclos,'" *Revue des Etudes Grecques* 70 (1957): 102–7.

and the three *ochēmata*.[25] For Iamblichus, the *pneuma* of the soul could be filled with divine light, where it truly became *augoeides* (*DM* 132, 11–13) or darkened by generative affections and lose its sphericity, yet—like Damascius's sponge—it remained the same vehicle.[26]

Iamblichus was reluctant to separate the rational from the irrational parts of the soul: the *logismos* from the *thumos* and *epithumia*. Again, following Aristotle, who rejected Plato's tripartite division of the soul (*Rep.* 435–41), which identified each "part" with a "place" in the body (*Tim.* 69; cf. Aristotle, *De Anima* 414a, 29; 411b, 5), Iamblichus says the soul is a simple essence (*ousia*) with several powers (*dunameis*), and when it incarnates it does so as an integral whole.[27] According to Iamblichus, Plato spoke of the soul ambivalently, sometimes defining it as "essentially tripartite" and sometimes as an "undivided essence of life having many powers and properties in one identity" (see *Stob.* I, 368, 23–369, 2; 369, 1). Although Plato's language varied, Iamblichus believed that Plato understood the soul to be a simple unity with three powers, and the discrepancy with Aristotle on this issue was merely semantic. Iamblichus says: "In

25. For a discussion of Proclus's views on the *ochēmata* and the "parts" of the soul, see Westerink, *Greek Commentaries* 2:108 n. 5; R. T. Wallis, *Neoplatonism* (London: Duckworth, 1972), 108; Dillon, trans., *Iamblichi Chalcidensis*, 373.

26. Ilsetraut Hadot has attempted to make Iamblichus's position agree with that of Proclus by reading an implicit doctrine of "three" *ochēmata* in the *De Mysteriis* and the *De Anima* fragments: (1) the vehicle of the flesh, (2) the pneumatic vehicle "relatively" immortal and subject to fate, and (3) the vehicle of the noetic soul; I. Hadot, *Le problème*, 98–106. Dillon notes, however, that the soul subject to fate (*DM* 269, 1–12) is never described as "mortal, merely that it is subject to Fate" (*Iamblichi Chalcidensis*, 375). Blumenthal is correct, therefore, when he says that Proclus had "two" subtle vehicles and Iamblichus only "one" because Iamblichus held that both the rational *and* irrational parts of the soul were immortal while Proclus granted immortality only to the rational soul; Blumenthal, "Some Problems," 83. I disagree with Blumenthal, however, when he says the theurgical rites relevant to the pneumatic body were the result of Iamblichus's inability to grasp Porphyry's views (84), and his description of theurgy as a "dubious" aid to ascend to the gods is itself dubious since Blumenthal has misconstrued theurgy as "a system for *operating on the gods*" (84; my emphasis).

27. *Stob.* I, 367, 10–17; see Festugière's commentary, *La Rév.* 3:190–91.

short, part differs from power in that part (*meros*) presents to our mind an otherness of essence (*ousias heterotēs*) while power (*dunamis*) suggests a creative or productive distinction in the same subject."[28] For Iamblichus, the soul's *thumos, epithumia,* and *logismos* belonged to one immortal subject, but in embodiment they all verged to the mortal body and were rejoined with the gods only by theurgy.[29]

28. *Stob.* I, 369, 2–4. On Iamblichus believing his position reflected the view of Plato, see *Stob.* I, 367, 12–14.

29. Iamblichus's position may be illustrated in Sallustius's discussion of the three parts/powers of the soul and the virtue associated with each: "The excellence (*aretē*) of reason (*logos*) is wisdom (*phronēsis*), of spirit (*thumos*) courage (*andreia*), of desire (*epithumia*), temperance (*sōphrosunē*), of the whole soul, justice (*dikaiosunē*)." In other words, each aspect of the soul had its proper and necessary function, without which the *entire* soul could never be "just." See A.D. Nock, ed. and trans., *Sallustius, Concerning the Gods and the Universe* (Hildesheim: Georg Olms, 1966), 20, 16–17.

10

Descending to
Apotheosis   *The divine is joined with itself . . .*

I n her classic study, *Le Dualisme chez Platon, le Gnostiques et les Manichéens,*[1] Simone Petrément characterizes dualism as follows: "In religions and philosophies where it appears, dualism seems tied to the belief in a transcendent, to an unknown which is not simply *not yet* known, to an invisible which is not simply *not yet* seen, but to that which essentially goes beyond anything seen and known" (3). Although Iamblichus was not a dualist, this definition is perfectly applicable to his theurgical Platonism. Petrément's thesis is that genuine experiences of transcendence occur beyond one's understanding and that these ruptures in the continuity of consciousness lead naturally to the postulation of a "two-world" cosmology. "To speak of two worlds," she says, "is to speak of total change" (8). Petrément argues convincingly that cosmological dualism is rooted in experiential dualism and that soteriology necessarily precedes cosmology. In this I believe she is correct, but for Iamblichus the dualism that derives from a transcendent rupture: "[when] the soul exchanges one life for another [and] entirely abandons its former existence" (*DM* 270, 17–19), did not produce a cosmological dualism but a psychological one. Iamblichus differed from his Platonic predecessors because he believed the dualism experienced by the soul was caused by its mediating function, linking the oppositions of same and other, unified and divided, immortal and mortal. Iamblichus spoke of the soul's "two lives" (*Stob.* I,

---

1. (Paris: Presses Universitares de France, 1947).

371, 6–8), "two powers" (*Stob.* I, 368, 1–6), and "two activities" (*Stob.* I, 371, 5–8), and in the *De Mysteriis* he cited Hermetic teachings stating that man has "two souls," one subject to fate and the other above fate resting in the noetic world (*DM* 269, 1–270, 12). Yet Iamblichus qualified this description of a noetic and seemingly undescended soul by saying that it was the vehicle of theurgic apotheosis (*DM* 270, 11–12) and thus beyond reach of the embodied soul. The Iamblichean soul had two lives, but because of its embodied condition it could only know one. The higher life received in theurgy was an epistemological impossibility for the embodied soul. Its divine life came from the gods as *other* to the soul even if it expressed the soul's truest identity.

Can Iamblichus's paradoxical psychology still be considered a genuine form of Platonism? Porphyry's letter to Anebo challenged Iamblichus to answer this question, and the *De Mysteriis* was a philosophical apology for a discipline that claimed to transcend philosophy. Yet it was Iamblichus's skill as philosopher that makes his defense of theurgy convincing, for in his reply to Porphyry, Iamblichus used standard Platonic arguments to support the practice of theurgy.[2]

According to Iamblichus, every human soul contained the ineffable presence of the One. By definition this presence was unknowable and would thus satisfy Petrément's demand for the ineffability of an other. This ineffable presence was the functional equivalent of Plotinus's undescended soul, a point Zintzen makes when he says that Iamblichus translated Plotinus's noetics into theurgical terminology.[3] Yet I would argue that the reason for this translation and the difference in their psychologies was due, not only to the greater influence of Aristotle on Iamblichus but more important, to Iamblichus's different understanding of salvation. The psychologies of Plotinus and Iamblichus were coherent with their soteriologies, and

2. B.D. Larsen has demonstrated that Iamblichus's method in the *De Mysteriis* was entirely philosophic and Platonic; see *Jamblique de Chalcis: Exégète et philosophe* (Aarhus: Universitetforlaget, 1972), 165–76.

3. Clemens Zintzen, "Bemerkungen zum Aufstiegsweg der Seele in Jamblichs *De Mysteriis.*" In *Platonismus und Christentum: Festschrift für Heinrich Dörrie*, ed. H.D. Blume and F. Mann (Münster: Aschendorff, 1983), 319.

these, I believe, derived from their attempts to make sense of transcendent experiences. Armstrong distinguishes Plotinus's doctrine of the undescended soul from the Iamblichean view of the soul based on this experiential criterion:

> I believe that Origen, Iamblichus, Augustine, Proclus and the rest who disagreed with Plotinus on this point were aware of and *experienced themselves as one person*. Plotinus, on the other hand, on the strength of his own experience, knew perfectly well that he was two people . . . a rightful inhabitant of the world of pure intelligence . . . [and] here below, body-bound and immersed in earthly concerns and desires.[4]

The "one person" that Iamblichus knew himself to be and that he described in the *De Anima* and the *De Mysteriis* was the completely descended soul identified with its particular mortal body. Indeed, the self-consciousness of any soul was rooted in this identification, and the rigorous limitations that Iamblichus imposed on the soul were not, *pace* Armstrong, necessarily due to his lack of transcendent experiences but from his concern that they be received properly and not confused with "body-bound" matters. Porphyry, for example, had claimed that Plotinus achieved *henōsis* with the One "four" times (*Vita Plot.* 23). This, of course, would have made no sense to Iamblichus, or even to Plotinus, for a *henōsis* that can be enumerated or even known could not be a true *henōsis*. It was precisely this kind of counterfeit spirituality that Iamblichus opposed by distinguishing the human activity of philosophy from the divine activity of theurgy. In one sense, Iamblichus's emphasis on the ineffability of theurgy was not even a theurgical issue, but a philosophical one, to correct the kind of thinking that fails to distinguish between the content of a discursive statement and its evocative and iconic power.[5] That Iamblichus would have questioned the authen-

---

4. Armstrong, "Tradition, Reason and Experience in the Thought of Plotinus," in *Plotinian and Christian Studies* 17 (London: Variorum Reprints, 1979), 189–90; from *Atti del Convegno internationale sul tema: Plotinus e il Neoplatonismo in Oriente e in Occidente* (Rome, 1970).

5. Cf. J.M.P. Lowry, *The Logical Principles of Proclus' STOICHEIŌSIS THEOLOGIKĒ as Systematic Ground of the Cosmos* (Amsterdam: Rodolpi, 1980), 20–21.

ticity of Plotinus's mystical experience is unlikely, but he certainly disagreed with the manner in which Plotinus explained it.[6]

Plotinus retained a Middle Platonic conception of matter as evil. He understood the dualism experienced by the soul to be caused by matter; once cleansed of material accretions, the soul immediately realized its divinity. For Plotinus the soul's division was not essential but accidental, caused by matter and the dualistic cosmos, but for Iamblichus the soul's dividedness was integral to its essence; it could never grasp the undividedness through which it participated in the divine. Therefore, Iamblichus shifted Platonic soteriology from an intellectual to a ritual *askēsis*. What the embodied soul could never know, it could, nevertheless, *perform* in conjunction with the gods. As discursive, however, the mind remained *enantios*, barred from union with the gods.

The goal of theurgy was to awaken the soul to the presence of the One that it bore unknowingly. And, by means of the very images that bound the soul to its generative life, theurgy released the soul from their grip. Theurgic ritual transformed the soul's somatic, emotional, and intellectual identity through "symbols" (*sumbōla*) and "tokens" (*sunthēmata*) that united the soul with the Demiurge (*DM* 97, 4–8; 97, 16–17; 209, 14–19; 65, 6–9; 136, 2–8). However, what the Demiurge contained simultaneously (*DM* 141, 10–13), each soul had to integrate over the course of its life and lives, and because the soul had distributed its powers into generated life, its salvation had to include all the mortal activities with which it was identified. The soul's return to the divine, therefore, demanded that it ritually re-enact cosmogenesis.

Since theurgic symbols transmitted the power of the demiurgic *Nous* they functioned much like the Platonic Forms by enforming matter (*DM* 65, 6–9). Yet because Iamblichus and his successors saw the cosmos as the "most sacred temple of the Demiurge" (*In Tim.* I, 124, 16–22), these Forms also possessed an anagogic power in theurgic ritual. Only then did they function properly as symbols and *sunthēmata*. Describing the relation of theurgic cult to cosmology Iamblichus says:

6. Cf. Lowry, *Logical Principles*, 14–25.

This cult, has it not been intellectually ordained from the beginning according to the sacred laws of the Gods? It imitates the order of the Gods, both the intelligible order and that in heaven. It possesses the eternal measures of beings and wondrous signatures which have been sent down here from the Demiurge and Father of Wholes, through which the inexpressible is revealed through ineffable symbols. (*DM* 65, 3–9)

When the soul activated the power of these symbols their presence in the soul was awakened. Iamblichus tells Porphyry that this occurred, for example, when meaningless (*asēma*; *DM* 254, 15) names of the gods were chanted. As theurgic symbols these names transcended discursive understanding: "Even if they are unknowable to us, this very unknowableness is its most venerable aspect, for *it is too excellent to be divided into knowledge*" (*DM* 255, 17–256, 3). The ineffable names were already present in the soul in the form of an undivided image. Iamblichus says: "We preserve completely in the soul the mystical and ineffable image of the Gods, and through these [names] we lead the soul up to the Gods and, when elevated, we are connected with them as much as possible" (*DM* 255, 17–256, 3).

Chanting the ineffable names awakened corresponding *sunthēmata* in the soul, and Iamblichus says, "these *sunthēmata* themselves do their own work, from themselves, and *without our thinking*" (*DM* 97, 4–5). The embodied soul, as intermediary, was simply the conduit through which the divine will in nature joined the divine will in the soul, a conjunction that transcended discursive consciousness. In practical terms, theurgy matched the images in the soul to their counterparts in nature, and though this demanded effort on the part of the soul, the transformative work was done by the images. Iamblichus says: "It is the divine *sunthēmata* themselves, these are the things which properly awaken the divine will; and thus these *sunthēmata* of the Gods are awakened by the Gods themselves" (*DM* 97, 4–5).

A divine name was the audible *energeia* of the god and when invoked the theurgist entered its power, joining the divine image in his soul to the divine itself: "For the divine, intellectual, and one in us—or if you prefer to call it intelligible—is clearly awakened in prayer, and being awakened, it vehemently yearns for its match and is joined to perfection itself" (*DM* 46, 13–16). Strictly speaking, theurgists did not call down the gods with their prayers; the gods were present already in the invocations (*DM* 47, 6). Iamblichus says: "At the moment of prayer, *the divine itself is literally joined with itself*, and it is united with the spiritual conceptions in prayers *but not as one thing is joined to another*" (*DM* 47, 9–11).

Nevertheless, it is man who prays, and the impulse to prayer was a crucial element in Iamblichus's soteriology. Responding to Porphyry's criticism that man's prayers were impure and unfit to be offered to the divine *Nous*, Iamblichus retorts:

> Not at all! For it is due to this very fact, because we are far inferior to the Gods in power, purity, and everything else, that it is of all things most critical that we do pray to them to the utmost! *For the awareness of our own nothingness, when we compare ourselves to the Gods, makes us turn spontaneously to prayer.* And from our supplication, in a short time we are led up to that One to whom we pray, and from our continual intercourse with it we obtain a likeness to it, and from imperfection we are gradually embraced by divine perfection. (*DM* 47, 13–48, 4)

When the soul fully recognized its nothingness it was stirred to pray, and any presumption that it had the capacity to reach the gods would prevent its occurrence. Before its conjunction with the divine the human soul had to recognize the unbridgeable gulf that separated it from the gods, and the recognition of this limitation was the only genuinely theurgical act that Iamblichus allowed to the soul. Instead of trying to reach the gods by giving them anthropomorphic characteristics (the Gnostics) or by giving divine characteristics to man (Plotinus) (*DM* 65, 16–66, 2), Iamblichus maintained that only when the human soul fully accepted the unflattering reality of its rank, would it spontaneously (*autophuōs*) be drawn to the gods.

Clearly, spontaneous prayer could not derive from discursive deliberation. It was, in fact, the *energeia* of the divine image in the soul yearning for its original. Yet to awaken this divine power the soul had to establish a limit (*to peras*) on its unlimited pretense to know (*to apeiron*). The soul's turn to prayer, in short, was the awakening of its divine *sunthēma*. Iamblichus says: "If one considers that sacred prayers are sent down to men from the Gods themselves and that they are the *sunthēmata* of these very Gods and are known only to the Gods and possess, in a manner, the same power as the Gods, how could anyone justly conceive this sort of prayer to be physical and not divine and intellectual?" (*DM* 48, 5–11). In its unity, the One of the soul was always in a state of prayer, joining itself to itself, yet the soul participated in this union only in moments of theurgy and through the medium of prayer.

Like Plotinus, Iamblichus maintained that the soul's final goal was an ineffable *henōsis* (*DM* 238, 4), yet he was somewhat vague about the divinity with whom the soul unites. Iamblichus said the soul is united with "the Gods" (*hoi theoi*; *DM* 238, 5), with the "universal Demiurge" (*holos demiourgos*; *DM* 292, 7), or even with the "God who transcends thought" (*ho proennooumenos theos*; *DM* 293, 2–3). It should be remembered, however, that the *De Mysteriis* was an apology for ritual theurgy, not a theological treatise, and each ritual was directed to the specific needs of a particular soul. A theurgist, therefore, would not attempt first to ascertain the "highest god" in an abstract sense and then worship it. The highest god for any soul in practical and theurgic terms was the god that ruled the elements that bound it. Therefore, Iamblichus's vagueness concerning divine *henōsis* may simply reflect his theurgic pragmatism. *Henōsis* was always relative to the deity with whom one needed to unite.

Nevertheless, book VIII of the *De Mysteriis* and Iamblichus's commentary on the *Timaeus* suggest that the highest unification for a soul was with the pre-essential (*proousios*) Demiurge,[7] who contained the entire intelligible world.[8] Iamblichus distinguished this primary Demiurge from the secondary Demiurge who managed the

7. *DM* 262, 5; 291, 7. Iamblichus introduced the term *proousios* into Neoplatonism. The use of *pro* instead of *huper*, Trouillard argues, shows that the Iamblichean school was concerned more with the ineffable *foundation* of consciousness (*en deca*) than in extending consciousness into the beyond (*au dela*); see J. Trouillard, "Note sur *PROOUSIOS* et *PRONOIA* chez Proclos," *Revue des Etudes Grecques* 73 (1960): 80–87.

8. See *In Tim.* II, frag. 34, in Dillon, trans., *Iamblichi Chalcidensis*, 136–37, and commentary, 37–38 and 307–9.

generated cosmos. The first Demiurge was an "anterior father,"[9] "cause of all the intelligibles" (*DM* 262, 7–8), and "God of gods" (*DM* 262, 4). Iamblichus calls him the "first God and king" (*DM* 161, 10–11) and identified him with the Egyptian god Ikton, the indivisible one who holds in himself the secondary demiurgic gods Amon and Ptah. In mathematical terms he was simply the "monad from the One" (*DM* 262, 4–5).

Was the One itself beyond the reach of the soul? Strictly speaking, yes. But according to the *Parmenides* the One transcended even itself; strictly speaking, even the One could not be one (*Parmenides* 141d–142). The complexity of this problem was much appreciated by the Neoplatonists. For them "unity" was simply a heuristic term that marked the point of transcendence, and its conceptual meaning was defined only by the particular context from which it was approached.[10] For Iamblichus, beyond the noetic Demiurge was utter ineffability, and it was called "one" only by virtue of its unifying

---

9. *DM* 267, 2–4. In *Jamblique: Les mystères d'Egypt*, des Places translates: "ils (les Egyptians 266, 10) préposant le démiurge au devenir comme un père du démiurge antérieure à celui-ci et distinguent la puissance vivante antérieure au ciel et celle qui est dans le ciel." Scott comments: "According to the reading of the mss. the *propatōr* is *tōn en genesei demiourgos*. But the meaning must have been that the Egyptians recognize a propator distinct from and prior to the *demiourgos tōn en genesei*"; see *Hermetica*, 4 vols., ed. and trans. W. Scott (London: Dawsons, 1968; reprint, Boston: Shambhala, 1985), 4:71. Scott's remark is corroborated by Iamblichus's commentary on the *Sophist* (frag 1, in Dillon, trans. *Iamblichi Chalcidensis*, where he distinguishes three *Demiourgoi*: "the sublunar Demiurge" (1, 1–2), "the heavenly demiurge" (1, 15–16), and the "Father of Demiurges" (1, 18). Dillon explains the fragment: "What we have in this passage is, first, a transcendent Demiurge who sends forth the original creative thoughts; then a heavenly Demiurge, whom one may equate with the *neoi theoi* of the *Timaeus*; and finally our third Demiurge, who presides over generation in the realm of the Moon" (246). The *propatōr* of the *DM* 267, 3 is the "transcendent Demiurge."

10. For an illuminating discussion of the understanding of the "one" in later Neoplatonism, see Trouillard, *La Mystagogie de Proclos* (Paris: Les Belles Lettres, 1982), 94–108. Cf. the discussion following Beierwaltes's essay "Das Problem der Erkenntnis bei Proklos," in *Entretiens*, 186–90. There the notion of *henōsis* and *to en hēmin hen* is discussed in connection with the degree of unity afforded the soul in its *unio mystica*. Beierwaltes, like Trouillard, denies that *henōsis* implies that the soul achieves an "absolute Identität" with the One.

effects, all of which the Demiurge contained. So there was no unification higher than with the pre-essential Father.

Iamblichus maintained that regardless of the degree of the soul's ascent it must always remain soul. Therefore, the soul's conjunction with the divine was never an absolute identity of soul and god but a unification of the will and activity of the soul with the will and activity of the Demiurge. Describing this conjunction Iamblichus says:

> When the theurgic art has united the soul successively to the orders of the universe and to all the divine powers that pervade them, it leads it up to the Creator in his entirety and deposits it there with him, outside of all matter, uniting the soul with the one eternal *Logos*. Specifically, what I mean is this: theurgy joins the soul with the Self-Begotten, Self-Moving, and All-Sustaining Powers, then with the Intellectual Power which arranges the cosmos, with the Anagogic Power leading to Intelligible Truth, with the Self-Perfect and Creative Powers, and with all other demiurgic powers of this God in order that the theurgic soul may be perfectly established in the *activities, thoughts,* and *creations* of these powers. Then, indeed, it establishes the soul in the Creator God in his entirety. And this is the goal of the hieratic ascent according to the Egyptians.[11]

The soul was established in the gods by taking part in their activities, that is to say, in their theurgies, for only by entering the activity of the Demiurge could the soul remain within the eternal logos that held the divine worlds together. Souls who entered this company became "companions of the gods" at which time Iamblichus says, "the aetheric and luminous pneuma, which surrounds the soul, is divested of all generative impulses" (*DM* 239, 9–11).

Iamblichus explicitly rejected the idea that the soul achieves an absolute union with the divine. In the *De Anima* he contrasted the view of the Ancients (i.e., theurgists),[12] who denied absolute

---

11. *DM* 292, 5–18. W. Scott suggests that the eight Powers mentioned by Iamblichus (Abammon) refer to specific Egyptian gods and the order of initiation among Egyptian priests. See Scott, ed. and trans. *Hermetica*, 4:97–99.

12. *Presbuteroi* (*Stob.* I, 458, 6); *palaioi*, (458, 18).

unification, with the view of Numenius (and by implication Plotinus), who affirmed it. Iamblichus says:

> Numenius appears to maintain that there is *unification and identity without distinction* of the soul with its principles, but the Ancients maintain that the soul is *united while remaining distinct as an essence*. Numenius compares it to a "resolution" (*analusis*) but the Ancients to an "association" (*suntaxis*) and while the former used the terms "unification with no distinction of parts," the latter say it is a "unification *with* distinction of parts." (*Stob.* I, 458, 3–8)

This forms part of Iamblichus's explanation of the rewards given to the purified soul after death. It is germane because theurgy, like death, separated the soul from its embodied identity and caused it to experience post-mortem purifications and rewards.[13] Therefore, Iamblichus's description of liberated souls in the *De Anima* concurs with his description of theurgic souls in the *De Mysteriis*. Like theurgists, divinized souls after death share in the creation and preservation of the cosmos. Contrasting the more theurgic view of the Ancients with the Platonists, Iamblichus says:

> According to the Ancients, the souls freed from generation *co-administer* the cosmos with the Gods, but according to the Platonists they contemplate their divine hierarchy. And in the same way, according to the Ancients, liberated souls *create the cosmos together with the angels*, but according to the Platonists they *accompany them* in the circular journey. (*Stob.* I, 458, 17–21)

---

13. That theurgy may be seen to culminate in a kind of "voluntary death" is implied in Proclus's remark that "in the most mystic of all consecrations (*en tē mustikōtatē tōn teletōn*) the theurgists order the whole body to be buried except for the head" (*Th. Pl.* IV, 30, 19, trans. and ed. H.D. Saffrey and L.G. Westerink [Paris: Les Belles Lettres, 1981]). See Saffrey's discussion of this passage, 135–36; and Hans Lewy, *Chaldean Oracles and Theurgy*, ed. M. Tardieu (Paris: Etudes Augustiniennes, 1978), 204–7. Damascius, in his catalogue of "deaths," refers to a "supernatural (*huperphuēs*) death by dissolution of the elements, in other words, the deaths which many theurgists have died" (*In Phaed.* II, 149, 7–8). This form of "voluntary death" (*hekousious thanatos*) Damascius calls "setting the soul free in the most divine way" (149, 12–13); See *In Phaed.* II, trans. L.G. Westerink, in *The Greek Commentaries on Plato's Phaedo*, vol. 2: *Damascius* (New York: North-Holland, 1977), 368–69.

Theurgic *henōsis* was not a beatific repose but an active embodiment and beneficent sharing of beatitude in cosmogenesis. After all, unification in the will of the Demiurge was a unification in the divine generosity (*aphthonos; Tim.* 29e) that creates the cosmos. To remain above with the Demiurge, souls had to descend demiurgically in the act of creation.

When the soul was liberated it joined the circulation of angels and archangels "united in mind"[14] with the Demiurge. The soul performed its cosmogonic round in the luminous and spheric body gained after a life of theurgic purification. Yet this final body of the soul was identical to its first body created in the beginning by the Demiurge. To become a "companion" (*sunopados*) of the gods (*Phaedrus* 248c), the soul had to re-enter its first *ochēma* at the moment of creation. According to Iamblichus, this vehicle was a microcosm, "produced from the entire aether . . . which possesses a generative power."[15] Yet its recovery demanded a laborious reharmonizing of the "numerous pegs" (*puknoi gomphoi; Tim.* 43a, 4) that bound the soul to its body. It is significant that Iamblichus equates these bonds with the "reason-principles of Nature" (*hoi phusikoi logoi*);[16] "binding" is an accurate description of the soul's unknowing bestowal of divine *logoi* to the world. In theurgy these *logoi* were ritually realigned with their divine principles and the soul was translated to its luminous *ochēma* as if to its "first birth" (*prōtē genesis*).[17] The soul's ascent to the rank of an angel was therefore experienced as a descent into its first vehicle at the moment of creation. This was consistent with the Neoplatonic paradox that the return (*epistrophē*) to the One manifests the procession (*prohodos*) of Ideas from the One. Only temporal experience and discursive

---

14. For Iamblichus the term *homonoētikos* describes the noetic concord that is the culmination of all theurgy (*DM* 294, 5). Cosmologically, it is also the term that describes the perfect concord of demiurgic powers in the orders of creation (*DM* 23, 5), as well as the condition of the human soul when it has been assimilated to these powers (*Stob.* I, 456, 24).

15. *In Tim.* IV, frag. 84, 4–5, in Dillon, *Iamblichi Chalcidensis,* 196–97.

16. *In Tim.* IV, frag. 86, 5, in Dillon, *Iamblichi Chalcidensis,* 198–99.

17. *In Tim.* IV, frag. 85, 3, in Dillon, *Iamblichi Chalcidensis,* 198–99. Cf. *Tim.* 41de.

thought separated the procession from the return.[18] Theurgy over-
came this and allowed the soul to return to the gods by embodying
the eternal measures (*metra aidia*) which continually proceed from
them (*DM* 65, 6).

The noetic simultaneity of *prohodos* and *epistrophē* was also
reflected in the salvation of the soul although it was extended over
time:

> From their first descent God sent souls here in order that they
> might return again to him. Therefore there isn't any change [in the
> divine will] on account of this sort of [theurgic] ascent, nor do the
> descents and ascents of souls oppose each other. For just as in the
> entire cosmos generation and this world below are conjoined with
> the Intellectual Essence, so in the order of souls, *their concern for
> generated lives is in concord with their liberation from generation.*
> (*DM* 272, 10–15)

The embodiment of the soul and its concern for generated lives was
a fall only so long as the soul failed to limit (*to peras*) its ceaseless
attraction to external phenomena (*to apeiron*).[19] As the soul was
initiated into the eternal measures of the cosmos, its fall was transformed into theophany, revealing a demiurgic concern for genesis.

Iamblichus and the later Platonists rejected the notion of static
perfection as an idol of the discursive mind. Their negative theology

---

18. Henry Duméry discusses this aspect of Neoplatonic metaphysics in H.
Duméry, *The Problem of God in Philosophy of Religion* (Evanston: Northwestern
University Press, 1964), 96–97.

19. For Iamblichus each soul is stamped with the ineffable principles of *peras*
and *apeiron*. Metaphysically the latter is responsible for procession *from* the One
and the former for return *to* the One. The uneducated soul described by Plato
(*Tim.* 44) and the uninitiated soul described by Iamblichus are dominated by the
principle of *apeiron*, for they have not yet learned to limit their powers in accord
with the divine economy of the cosmos. In the *Philebus*, where *peras* and *apeiron*
are investigated as cosmogonic powers, Plato puns on the homonym *apeiron*,
which also means an "inexperienced one." (*Phil.* 17e). The embodied soul, therefore, may properly participate in the demiurgic mixing of the principles *peras-
apeiron* (*Phil.* 26cd) only when, through the experience of its embodiment, it discovers its limits. For Iamblichus, the education/initiation of the soul was necessarily its homologization to the demiurgic mixing of these principles, which Plato
called the *genesis eis ousian* (*Phil.* 26d8).

demanded that even the terms "one" and "good," should not be taken descriptively but symbolically; that is to say, by virtue of their beneficial and unifying effects. As Trouillard puts it: "La bonté caractérise la cause, *non parce qu'elle possède le bien, mais parce qu' elle la crée.*"[20] In the same way, the highest condition for souls was not their enjoyment of divine status, but their bestowal of divine measurements in cosmogenesis. This made *theourgia* superior to the highest forms of *theōria*, and from this perspective even the descent of souls into bodies was an expression of the same informing activity though it came at the cost of the soul's beatitude.[21] For although embodiment broke the soul's connection with the gods, theurgy recovered it through a mimesis of divine action.

---

20. Trouillard, "La Joie de quitter le ciel," *Diotima* 11 (1983): 190.
21. See Trouillard, "La joie," 191–92, and *La Mystagogie*, 219.

11

Eros and the One of the Soul

There is another principle of the soul...

Iamblichus's doctrine of the "one of the soul" provided important theoretical support for the practice of theurgy. Because the soul carried the presence of the One it had the capacity to rise above itself, be homologized to the cosmos and united with its divine cause. The fact that the soul possessed correspondences to the entire cosmos meant that, like the cosmos, it possessed a principle that preceded its multiplicity. Iamblichus called this principle "the one of the soul" (*to hen tēs psuchēs*), and he identified it with the "helmsman" (*kubernētēs*) of the *Phaedrus* who unites the soul with the Intelligibles in its celestial circuit.[1]

In his *Phaedrus* commentary Iamblichus described this helmsman as "an entity more perfect than the charioteer,"[2] yet in his *Timaeus* commentary he says that the "charioteer [not the helmsman] is the highest element in us."[3] The discrepancy in the two statements may reflect the difference for Iamblichus between the henological and ontological orders. As a being in the hierarchy of souls, man's highest element was certainly *logismos*, the rational faculty, but Iamblichus

---

1. Dillon notes that in the phrase *psuchēs kubernete monō theatē nō* (*Phaedrus* 247c, 7–8) the *nō* was not in the Platonic text used by Iamblichus and, if it were, he would have had to explain it away; Dillon, trans., *Iamblichi Chalcidensis*, 253; cf. frag. 6, pp. 96–97.
  2. *In Phaedrum*, frag. 6, 5–6; Dillon, trans., *Iamblichi Chalcidensis*, 96–97.
  3. *In Tim.* IV, frag. 87, 23–24; Dillon, trans., *Iamblichi Chalcidensis*, 200–201.

distinguished between an entity's being (*ousia*) and its *huparxis*. Damascius explains this distinction etymologically:

> [*Huparxis*], as the word (*hupo* + *archein*) itself indicates, signifies the first principle of every hypostasis. It is, as it were, a sort of foundation or substructure previously established *for the structure as a whole and for each part.* . . . *Huparxis* is the simplicity anterior to all things. . . . It is the One itself, which pre-exists beyond all things and is the cause of every *ousia* but is not yet itself *ousia*.[4]

Considered essentially, the charioteer/*logismos* was indeed the soul's highest faculty, but *pre*-essentially the helmsman/*huparxis* or "one of the soul" was its highest element. Strictly speaking, the "one of the soul" was not part of the soul but was present to it in a pre-essential way, just as the One was present to all hypostases as their pre-essential cause.[5]

Iamblichus explains that the helmsman is called a "spectator" (*theatē*) of the supercelestial realm, "not to signify that it directs its gaze on this object of intellection as being other than it (*kath' heterotēta*), but that it is united with it (*henoutai autō*) and appreciates it on that level . . . for it is the essential nature of the "one of the soul" to be united with the Gods."[6] Theurgy was the embodied realization of this union, for in theurgy the "one of the soul" united with the hypercosmic gods just as the "helmsman" joined the disembodied soul to the supercelestial realm. Iamblichus said the soul was capable of this unification "[because] there subsists in its very essence an innate knowledge (*emphutos gnōsis*) of the Gods" (*DM 7*, 13–14). Iamblichus admits that he uses the term *gnōsis* inexactly, for the highest aspect of the soul could not possibly "know" the gods any more than the helmsman could "see" them. Defining this innate knowledge, Iamblichus says:

---

4. Damascius, *Dub. et Sol.* I, ed. C.A. Ruelle (Paris: 1889; reprint, Brussels: Culture et Civilisation, 1964). Translated from the Greek by P. Hadot, "L'Etre et L'Etant dans le Néoplatonisme," *Revue de Théologie et de Philosophie* (1973): 110–11. The same principle was articulated already by Iamblichus in the *DCMS* 15, 6–14.

5. Cf. the *proousios patēr* of *DM* 262, 6.

6. *In Phaedrum*, frag. 6, 2–6, in Dillon, trans., *Iamblichi Chalcidensis*, 96–97.

[It] subsists in our very essence, is superior to all judgment and choice, and exists prior to reason and demonstration. From the beginning it is united to its proper cause and is established with the soul's essential desire (*ephesis*) for the Good. *But if one must speak the truth, contact with the divine is not knowledge.* For knowledge is separated [from its object] by otherness. But, prior to the act of knowing another as being, itself, "other," there exists a spontaneous [. . .] uniform conjunction suspended from the Gods.[7]

It is a contact, Iamblichus says, established by the gods, and the soul's very existence depended on it, "for we are enveloped in it, even more, we are filled by it, and our existence itself we possess by "knowing" (*eidenai*) the Gods" (*DM* 8, 11–13). This essence-making knowledge, like the gaze of the helmsman, is not of one to another; it is a unifying contact. And since the "principles (*archai*) of reason and life" (*DM* 9, 6) can never be grasped by the orders they establish, it is through the soul's preconceptual contact with the gods that it sees and knows them.

Des Places has noted the influence of Plato's *Phaedrus* on the *De Mysteriis* and points to Iamblichus's direct borrowing of words and phrases.[8] In his explanation of the soul's innate knowledge of the gods Iamblichus says: "Indeed, it seems (*eoiketō dē*) that with the eternal companions of the Gods is fitted an inborn (*sumphutos*) perception of their Lords" (*DM* 9, 10–11). The terms *eoiketō dē* and *sumphutos* were also used by Plato in his description of souls who are joined to the gods in their celestial round (*Phaedrus* 246a, 5), and though (unlike Iamblichus) Plato used *sumphutos* to describe the

---

7. *DM* 7, 14–8, 6. I find A. Smith's explanation of *emphutos gnōsis* (7, 14) as "still divided" (see *Porphyry's Place in the Neoplatonic World: A Study in Post-Plotinian Neoplatonism* [The Hague: Martinus Nijhoff, 1974], 85–86) and therefore subordinate to the *sumplokē*, which is uniform (*monoeidēs*; 8, 5) to be unconvincing. Iamblichus begins his explanation of human contact with the gods with the term *gnōsis* probably because it was the term Porphyry used in his question (10, 2), and in any case, Iamblichus clearly distinguishes it from human *gnōsis* and explicitly denies its dividedness since he equates the *emphutos gnōsis tōn theōn* with the *sumplokē*. Iamblichus, therefore, defines two kinds of gnosis: divine and human (10, 1–6) and explicitly states that the *gnōsis/eidēsis* of divine things is *monoeidēs* (10, 8).

8. *Oracles Chaldaïques*, 42 n. 2

unity of the vehicle and rider and not their contact with the super-celestial realm, Iamblichus's use of the terms *sumphutos* (9, 11) and *emphutos* (7, 14) in this context suggests that he imagined theurgical unification against the background of the *Phaedrus*.[9]

Iamblichus's use of terms, however, must be understood in context. For example, although Iamblichus denies that *noēsis* is sufficient to reach the divine he also says that souls join the gods by *noēsis*: "It is by pure and blameless intuitions (*noēseis*) that are received out of eternity from the Gods that the soul is joined to them" (*DM* 9, 16–18). Iamblichus's reference to *noēsis, gnōsis*, or *eidēsis* to describe contact with the gods should not be confused with human modes of understanding. These terms were used as metaphors to describe the soul's pre-essential contact with the gods, and Iamblichus always qualified them as innate (*emphutos*), natural (*sumphutos*), uniform (*monoeidēs*), or pure (*katharos*) to distinguish them from human understanding.

Since the *noēsis* of the gods had no "otherness" in the separated manner of human knowledge, their "pure intuitions" (*katharai noēseis*) necessarily transcended the soul. Theurgic *noēsis* was, in fact, the act of a god knowing itself through the activity and the medium of the soul, not vice versa. *Noēsis*, in fact, was not conceptual, and Iamblichus maintained that noetic contacts with the gods were more erotic than intellectual. In his *Parmenides* commentary he says: "The Intelligible is held before the mind, not as knowable (*hōs gnōston*), but as desirable (*hōs epheton*), and the mind is filled by this, not with knowledge, but with the being and every intelligible perfection."[10]

The "one of the soul" was anterior to the soul's hypostasis. As *archē* of the soul's being and consciousness, it was pre-essential and

9. Trouillard has demonstrated the influence of the *Phaedrus* on the theurgy of Proclus. See, *L'Un et l'âme selon Proclos* (Paris: Les Belles Lettres, 1972), esp. 171–89.

10. Damascius, *Dub. et Sol.* I, 154, 9–11. In the same section (70), Damascius lists nine ways in which the *noēton* cannot be grasped by the soul (151, 18–23), again attributing this to the "great Iamblichus"; cf. Dillon's translation of this passage, *In Parm.*, frag. 2A, in *Iamblichi Chalcidensis*, 208–9, and commentary, 389–91. Cf. *DM* 239, 8–9, where Iamblichus says that theurgic prayer stimulates the growth of the "divine eros" in the soul.

pre-noetic, completely inaccessible to understanding. Although the soul could not consciously know the gods or even its own divinity, it was nevertheless drawn to them by its innate *gnōsis* and desire (*ephesis*). Theurgy successfully embodied this desire in proportion to the soul's capacity to homologize itself to the cosmos. Graphically put, the soul's vertical ascent was determined by its horizontal extension and its co-ordination of the many attractions of embodied life. According to Damascius, Iamblichus believed that "the ascent to the One is not possible unless the soul co-ordinates itself to the All and, with the All, moves itself toward the universal principle of all things" (*Dub. et Sol.* I, 79, 12–14). According to Pythagorean teachings, the One manifested itself as a co-ordinated multiplicity: a Whole, and similarly, the "one in the soul" manifested itself when the soul ritually co-ordinated its multiplicity into a whole, imitating "the anterior and commanding principle *which contains in and around itself otherness and multiplicity*" (*DM* 59, 13–15). In its co-ordination of parts the soul was lifted out of the contraries of embodied life[11] and entered the unity that preceded its embodied existence.

Iamblichus referred to the "one of the soul" differently depending on the context, and his inconsistency suggests that he was not concerned about the term he used so long as it conveyed the idea of an anteriority pre-established with the gods. Responding to Porphyry's question on prayer, Iamblichus used the terms *hen*, *theios*, *noeros*, and *noētos* to describe the divine element in the soul (*DM* 46, 13–15). In a discussion of divination, Iamblichus explained that prophecy was caused by this "one principle" and he made a rigorous distinction between theurgic divination (*to theion mantikēs eidos*; *DM* 64,

---

11. P. Hadot, citing Simplicius, *In Categ.* 116, 25–30, says that for Iamblichus and other Neoplatonists, categories that are opposed in the sensible world are contained uniformly in the intelligible world. See Hadot, 2 vols. (Paris: Etudes Augustiniennes, 1968), *Porphyre et Victorinus*, 442. The Iamblichean fragment preserved by Simplicius (*In Categ.* 116, 25–118, 15) reveals Iamblichus's application of the Aristotelian categories *kata analogian* (116, 26) to the entire noetic realm as well as to celestial divinities such as stars and planets. B. D. Larsen comments on the above-mentioned fragment and shows its relation to the "Pythagorean" Aristotle of Iamblichus; see Larsen, *Jamblique de Chalcis: Exégète et philosophe* (Aarhus: Universitetsforlaget, 1972), 243, 260–62.

16–17) and the varieties of human divination. The latter, Iamblichus says, are "false and deceptive" (*DM* 165, 2–3), in contrast to theurgic divination which is "one, divine, and unmixed" (*DM* 164, 18–19). He says: "The divine kind [of divination] must be uniformly comprehended according to one measure and order (*hen logos kai mia taxis*) and according to one intelligible and immutable truth" (*DM* 165, 4–6). True divination was not a natural gift, "but a certain divine good which is pre-established as *more ancient than our nature*" (*DM* 165, 18–19; cf. *Stob.* II, 174, 15–16). This "certain divine good" stood in precisely the same relation to man as the "one of the soul" and Iamblichus maintained that it came to the soul from outside: "It is necessary to contend vigorously against anyone who says that divination originates from us" (*DM* 166, 14–15). Divine *mantikē* came to the soul "from without" (*exōthen*; *DM* 167, 2), just as the Aristotelian *nous* came to the soul "from without" (GA 736b, 28). Even the soul's "innate knowledge" of the gods had to come to it from without for due to its anteriority it was "more ancient" (*presbutera*) and therefore inaccessible to the soul.

That this more ancient principle remained outside the soul was a point on which Iamblichus was unwilling to compromise. One might suppose that since the soul enjoyed a degree of union with the gods between incarnations it could sustain this connection subliminally or, as Plotinus seems to suggest, "unconsciously,"[12] but Iamblichus's view of the descent of the soul and his distinction of incorporeal hypostases did not allow for this. The embodied soul was incapable of returning to the gods of its own power and needed their aid to reach them. This "otherness" of the divine principle was consistent with Iamblichus's psychology. Because of the inversion of the soul its *autos* was recovered only by ritually embracing the *heteros*, and although the objects employed in theurgy appeared as "other," it was through them that the soul's external inclinations were united with their celestial archetypes. By ritually unifying its

---

12. For a discussion of the "unconscious" presence of the higher soul in the lower in Plotinus see A. Smith, "Unconsciousness and Quasiconsciousness in Plotinus," *Phronesis* 23, no. 3 (1978): 292–301.

own multiplicity the soul entered the activity of the One and penetrated to its own pre-essential *archē*.[13] Of this principle Iamblichus
says:

> But *there is another principle (archē) of the soul,* superior to all
> nature and knowledge, by which we are able to be unified with the
> Gods, transcend the mundane order, and participate in the eternal
> life and activity of the supercelestial Gods. . . . The soul is then
> entirely separated from those things which bind it to the generated
> world and it flies from the inferior and exchanges one life for
> another. It gives itself to another order, having entirely abandoned
> its former existence. (*DM* 270, 8–19)

Iamblichus believed that the unifying principle that transformed
the soul in theurgy was the same principle that held the cosmos
together as its universal *philia* or *erōs* (*DM* 211, 3–6): "There is a single
friendship (*philia*) which contains all things and produces this unifying bond (*sundesmos*) by means of an ineffable communion" (*DM*
211, 16–18). The unifying power of *philia* defined the steps of theurgic
ascent at the same time as it revealed the cosmogonic procession. In
short, *philia* sustained both the cosmos and every act of theurgy.
Consequently, Iamblichus argued that the effective agent in theurgy
was *philia* or, speaking Platonically, that *erōs* drew the soul back to
the gods (cf. *DM* 239, 6–13). Although the heavenly cycles described
in the *Phaedrus* and the *Timaeus* were the goal to which a Platonist
aspired, it was erotic madness that brought him there. According to
the Chaldean Oracles, Eros was the first god born of the Paternal
Father;[14] Eros co-ordinated the Ideas in the intelligible world[15] and,
proceeding with them, knitted the cosmos together in a unified
bond.[16] In a word, the will of the Demiurge was revealed as Eros:

13. Dillon notes that it is only "through the Circuit of the Same within it" that
the embodied soul, with the aid of theurgy, is allowed to rise above the material
world; Dillon, trans., *Iamblichi Chalcidensis*, 342.

14. *Chaldean Oracles* (*CO*), frag. 42, trans. Ruth Majercik (Leiden: E.J. Brill,
1989), 64–65, 159–60. Cf. Hans Lewy, *Chaldean Oracles and Theurgy*, ed. M. Tardieu
(Paris: Etudes Augustiniennes, 1978), 126–28; also cf. des Places, *Oracles chaldaïques*
(Paris: Les Belles Lettres, 1971), 77–78.

15. *CO*, frag. 42, trans. Majercik.

16. *CO*, frag. 44, trans. Majercik, 66–67. Cf. Lewy, *Chaldean Oracles*, 126–28; des
Places, *Oracles chaldaïques*, 77.

For after he conceived his works, the Self-generated Paternal Mind sowed the bond of love, heavy with fire, into all things . . . in order that the All might continue to love for an infinite time and that the things woven by the intellectual light of the Father might not collapse. . . . [It is] with this Love (*erōs*) that the elements of the world remain on course.[17]

According to the Oracles the Demiurge filled each soul with a "deep eros" (*erōs bathus*) to draw it back to the gods.[18]

The deep eros of the Oracles, like the innate *gnōsis* or essential desire (*ephesis*) of the *De Mysteriis* (*DM* 7, 14; 8, 2), was present in the soul but anterior to consciousness. It was the desire that drew the soul down into a mortal body and led it back to its immortal *ochēma*. The theurgist received this eros from the gods, and returned it to them in the form of a ritualized cosmos (cf. *DM* 210, 3–4; 211, 3–10). Embodiment was simply the pivot through which the eros of the Demiurge returned to itself.

In this light, the embodiment of the soul and the tension caused by its separation from divinity was not a fall or an error but the sine qua non to stimulate the circulation of Eros. For only in the embodied soul, in its self-alienation and inversion, could the divine genuinely experience separation, and consequently, an *erōs* for itself.[19] In the *Timaeus* Plato says that without the descent of souls into mortal bodies the universe would remain incomplete (41b, 8–9). Thus, theurgy saved the soul *and* the cosmos, for without the embodiment of the soul and its inversion (*anatropē*), the divine could never yearn for itself, Eros would never arise as the "firstborn god," and the cosmos would never come to exist. For a theurgist, his experience in a

17. *CO*, frag. 39, trans. Majercik, 62–65. For the will of the Demiurge being equivalent to the *erōs* of the Oracles, see Friedrich W. Cremer, *Die Chaldäischen Orakel und Jamblich de Mysteriis* (Meisenheim am Glan: Anton Hain, 1969), 117–19.

18. *CO*, frag. 43, trans. Majercik, 64–65. Cf. Lewy, *Chaldean Oracles*, 126–28; des Places, *Oracles chaldaïques*, 78.

19. For a discussion of the cosmogonic role of Eros in later Neoplatonism, see Stephen Gersh, *KINĒSIS AKINĒTOS: A Study of Spiritual Motion in the Philosophy of Proclus* (Leiden: E.J. Brill, 1973), app. I: "*ERŌS* as a Cosmic Process," 123–27. F. Cremer explains Eros as a theurgic virtue according to the Oracles; Cremer, *Die Chaldäischen Orakel*, 139–43.

corporeal form was the linchpin of the cosmos: embodiment was a creative and sacramental act.

That the soul's embodiment was the ultimate *sunthēma* of its ascent remains an insoluble logical paradox, but appropriately, for the lover it is a commonplace experience. In the erotic dialectic discussed by Plato in the *Symposium* (200–202), the separation of the lover from the beloved was the sine qua non of their attraction and unification,[20] and in Iamblichean theurgy the *sunthēma* had the same function as the beloved (*erōmenon*) in Plato's erotic ascent. Both were sensible objects drawn from the elements to which the soul was bound, and both deified the soul through an act of creation.[21] Theurgy, therefore, may be seen as the ritual elaboration of both the Platonic doctrines of *erōs* and *anamnēsis*.

It is perhaps appropriate to conclude Iamblichus's vision of the embodied soul with a hagiographical image of Iamblichus himself. In the *Lives of the Philosophers*, Eunapius reports that when Iamblichus journeyed to the baths of Gadara with his disciples he acceded to their demands to demonstrate his power. Eunapius says:

> There were two hot springs smaller than the others but prettier, and he [Iamblichus] bade his disciples ask the natives of the place by what names they used to be called in ancient times. When they had done his bidding they said: "There is no question about it, this spring is called *Erōs*, and the name of the one next to it is *Anterōs*."[22]

20. J. Trouillard explains the unifying activity of Eros in the soul as "the active presence of the One in us," and as much dependent on our "procession" as on our "return"; see Trouillard, "Sur un pluriel de Plotin et de Proclus," *Association Guillaume Budé* 4 (1958): 90.

21. In the *Symposium* Diotima defines the *praxis* and *ergon* of love: "To love," she says, "is to bring forth upon the beautiful both in body and in soul" (206b, 7–8). "The act of creation (*hē gennēsis*)," she adds, "is the one deathless (*athanaton*) and eternal (*aeigenes*) element in our mortality" (206e, 7–8). In the *Phaedrus*, Plato says the *erastēs* "would offer sacrifice to his beloved *as to a holy image of deity*" (251a, 6–7); and at 253a he says the divine habits that the soul receives from the deity who possesses him are attributed to the beloved upon whom he pours out his love. See J. Trouillard's discussion of this passage in *L'Un et L'âme*, 180–84.

22. Wright suggests the two Erotes of Themistius's fable (304d) as a possible source for the names of these springs. Considering the profound similarity in the function of Platonic *erōmenoi* and theurgic *sunthēmata*, it is more likely that

He at once touched the water with his hand—he happened to be sitting on the ledge of the spring where the overflow runs off—and uttering a brief summons, he called forth a boy from the depth of the spring. He was white-skinned and of medium height, his locks were golden and his back and breast shone; and he exactly resembled one who was bathing or had just bathed. His disciples were overwhelmed with amazement, but Iamblichus said, "Let us go to the next spring," and he rose and led the way, with a thoughtful air. Then he went through the same performance there also and summoned another Eros like the first in all respects, except that his hair was darker and fell loose in the sun. Both the boys embraced Iamblichus and clung to him *as though he were genuinely their father.* He restored them to their proper places and went away after his bath, reverenced by his pupils.[23]

We need not concern ourselves about the veracity of this fabulous tale to appreciate its iconic truth. Perhaps no better image for the theurgist could be portrayed than this: Iamblichus himself, seated by an overflowing stream, invokes its *Erōs* and having called it out, joins it—through his own body—to its responsive *Anterōs*. All theurgy did the same: situated in the stream of generation, the theurgist invoked the *erōs* of this stream to awaken the *anterōs* hidden in his soul; in the hieratic moment of joining the divine to the divine the theurgist himself became a creator. Yet it was only by virtue of his embodiment and alienation from the gods that he was able to fulfill this task.[24] In the theurgic *act* of an embodied soul, Eros was allowed to join itself and regenerate the bonds that unite the cosmos.

Eunapius borrowed his terms from the *Phaedrus* (255d) where Plato describes the yearning of the beloved for his lover: "And when the other is beside him, he shares his respite from anguish, and when he is absent, he likewise shares his longing and being longed for, *since he possesses a counter-love (anterōs) which is the image of love (erōs)*." See *Philostratus and Eunapius: The Lives of the Sophists*, trans. W.C. Wright (Cambridge: Harvard University Press, 1921; reprint, 1968).

23. Eunapius, *Lives of the Sophists*, trans. W.C. Wright, 369–71.

24. Iamblichus discusses the "double role" of the theurgist in two passages, *DM* 184, 1–8; 246, 16–247, 2.

III

The Liturgy of the Cosmos

12

Cult and
Cosmos *God is the leader of these things...*

I amblichus believed that theurgy was entirely compatible with
Plato's teachings on the soul and that it provided a practical
solution to the problem of embodiment. Yet Iamblichus's apology for theurgy did more than address the philosophical problem of
the soul's embodiment; more generally, it provided a defense of religious ritual against well-known arguments brought forward by Porphyry in his letter to Anebo and his treatise *On the Abstinence of
Animal Food*. Far from being a mere *propaideia* to philosophy, Iamblichus argued that the concrete performance of ritual was the culmination of one's philosophical development. Theurgy tied soteriology to cosmogony and allowed the soul to share in both.

Up to this point Iamblichus's Platonism has been considered
with respect to his metaphysical positions. In Part I, matter and
embodiment were examined and absolved of the pejorative conno-
tations given to them by Iamblichus's predecessors. In Part II, the
embodied soul was examined, the most problematic aspect of Iamblichus's metaphysics. Yet Iamblichus's paradoxical definition of the
soul as "self-change" is crucial for a proper understanding of Platonic theurgy. The anatropic condition of the embodied soul was
tied to the mysteries of creation and salvation. Far from being
denied, the inversion of the soul was seen by Iamblichus to be necessary to complete the cosmogonic cycle, and embodied experience,
progressively incorporated by theurgic activity, put the soul in place
despite the prima facie fact of its being out of place, i.e., *anatropē*.

Iamblichus's metaphysical solutions to the problems of matter
and the embodiment of the soul form an essential background to

his theory of theurgy. Yet without ritual performance they would remain, by his own definition, discursive fantasies cut off from the divine. Therefore, we must examine the rituals themselves: although theurgy may be described theoretically as a soteriological and cosmogonic practice, it must be seen specifically how this was understood and accomplished. Since this is the question Iamblichus himself was challenged to answer, we can do no better than (1) follow Iamblichus's explanation of the correspondence that exists between the cosmos and the cult; (2) consider the significance of this correspondence for man in finding and performing an appropriate ritual; and (3) examine in detail how the rites exemplify this correspondence and fulfill a theurgic function. In sum, the question to be answered is how Iamblichus understood ritual to be simultaneously soteric and cosmogonic, and consequently, how the stages of cosmogony were reflected in the theurgic cult.

In his letter to Anebo, Porphyry accused theurgists of believing that the gods "were especially enticed by the vapors of animal sacrifice" (*DM* 212, 2–3), and Iamblichus responds by laying out the principle of all theurgic sacrifice: "The best of all beginnings is the one which demonstrates that the law of sacrifices (*thesmos tōn thusiōn*) is connected with the order of the gods (*taxis tōn theōn*)" (*DM* 217, 3–5). In *On the Abstinence of Animal Food* Porphyry had argued that the "gods" worshiped in blood sacrifices were not gods at all, but daimons counterfeiting as gods. That daimons were the immediate objects of worship was a point with which Iamblichus agreed, for it followed the hierarchical law that man must approach the gods through the mediation of daimons. However, Iamblichus disagreed with Porphyry's description of these entities. While both acknowledged that daimons were invisible beings with pneumatic bodies, Porphyry contended that their bodies were perishable and nourished by the vapors of blood sacrifice. Iamblichus categorically denied it: "For although *Daimones* possess a kind of body which some believe is nourished by sacrifices, this body is unchangeable, impassive, luminous, and without needs, so that nothing flows from it and, in addition, it does not need anything outside to flow into it" (*DM* 212, 3–7). As a class daimons were ontologically superior to man and revealed the invisible powers of the gods. Iamblichus says:

"they bring into manifest activity the invisible good of the Gods, reveal what is ineffable in them, shape what is formless into forms, and render what is beyond all measure into visible ratios" (*DM* 16, 17–17, 4). In short, daimons were agents of the Demiurge in his cosmogonic activity. Understandably, for Porphyry, the agents of a desacralized cosmos could not be considered superior to man. Therefore, his estimation of daimons as perishable and perverse demons was a correlate to his view of the cosmos as a topsy-turvy realm from which souls must escape, a point not missed by Iamblichus who accused Porphyry of holding unreasonable views, saying: "It is not possible that the Creator has generously provided ready nourishment for animals in the sea and on earth, but has made the beings superior to us [i.e. daimons] in want of it" (*DM* 212, 15–18). To believe, as Porphyry did, that daimons depended on man for their sustenance contradicted the rational order of the cosmos. Thus, Iamblichus argues:

> Why don't those who say this simply turn the entire hierarchy of things upside down, making us more powerful and in a better class? For if they make us responsible for nourishing and fulfilling *Daimones* we would be above them in the order of causes. For every order receives its perfection and nourishment from the order that generates it. One can see this even in the generation of visible things, and it is also seen among cosmic entities; in fact, earthly things are nourished by the celestial. And this becomes especially clear among the invisible causes. For Soul is perfected by Intellect, and Nature by Soul, and other things similarly are nourished by their causes. And since it is impossible for us to be the ruling causes of *Daimones*, for the same reason we could not be the causes of their nourishment. (*DM* 213, 8–214, 3)

Iamblichus's position on the question of sacrifice and daimons was based on his understanding of the "order of the gods" (*taxis tōn theōn*). Although his criticism of Porphyry on the question of daimons exemplifies only one instance where he found himself at odds with his former teacher, the issue typifies Iamblichus's more general critique of Porphyry's soteriology. Iamblichus continually referred to the hierarchical order of the cosmos to correct Porphyry's misunderstandings of theurgy, so to understand theurgic ritual we must understand the order of the Iamblichean gods, the *archai* of his cosmos.

Iamblichus divided superior beings (*hoi kreittones*) into four distinct classes: gods, daimones, heroes, and pure souls. As discussed previously, the extreme classes, gods and souls, were unified and divided respectively; whereas daimons and heroes served as media connecting the extremes. Iamblichus imagined the gods at the top and souls at the bottom of an ontological scale, with daimons in the second rank "suspended far below the gods" (*DM* 16, 13–14). Heroes, situated below daimons, were adjacent to souls but superior to them in virtue, beauty, magnitude, and other goods (*DM* 16, 8–10). Due to Porphyry's questions about daimons, Iamblichus devoted more attention to explaining their function.

Significantly, their task was cosmogonic. Daimons were the agents of *prohodos*. They obeyed the "beneficent will of the gods" (*DM* 16, 15–17) and revealed the divine and invisible good. Insofar as daimons served the processional impulse of the gods they were responsible, as well, for binding souls to bodies (*DM* 67, 15–68, 1). In their extrovertive function, daimons produced growth in plants and preserved animal species (including human) through the sex drive and other instincts. In this sense daimons might seem opposed to the soul's desire to free itself from material attachments. Yet Iamblichus never forgets that it is the gods and the Demiurge who send the daimons forth. Therefore, man had to understand how to work with these demiurgic functions, not to reject or oppose them. As Iamblichus asserts: "I say, therefore, that *Daimones* are produced by the generative and demiurgic powers of the Gods in the most extreme culmination of the [cosmogonic] procession and the last distribution of parts" (*DM* 67, 3–6). The daimons of Iamblichus may be likened to "laws of nature."[1] As guardians of the generated realm, daimons blindly performed their tasks, and souls prospered or not depending on their judicious use of these powers. Heroes, on the other hand, performed a soteriological function and guided

1. For a development of this idea in the context of Egyptian rites and symbols see Philip Derchain, *Le Papyrus Salt 825* (*B.M. 10051*): *Rituel pour la conservation de la vie en Egypte* (Brussels: Paleis der Academien, 1965), 3–21.

souls in their spiritual integration. Iamblichus says: "But Heroes are produced according to the *logoi* of life in divine beings, and the first and perfect measures of souls are completed and defined by Heroes" (*DM* 67, 6–9). Typical to Iamblichus's method, he distinguished daimons and heroes in the same manner that he distinguished gods and souls: by their essence (*ousia*), power (*dunamis*), and activity (*energeia*). "For," Iamblichus says, "being generated from different causes, the essence of one is different from the essence of the other" (*DM* 67, 10–11). His distinctions are as follows:

> *ousia*: The essence of *Daimones* is fit for bringing about final effects; it is perfective of mundane natures and gives completion to the providential care that oversees each generated being. But the essence of Heroes is vital and rational and is the leader of souls. (*DM* 67, 11–15)

> *dunamis*: With respect to their powers, those of *Daimones* must be defined as fecundating, for they oversee nature and the binding of souls into bodies; but to Heroes one must assign powers that are vivifying, that lead men, and are liberated from generation. (*DM* 67, 15–68, 2)

> *energeia*: It follows that the activities of these classes should be defined. The actions of *Daimones* should be defined as more mundane and more widely extended in the deeds they bring to completion; but the actions of Heroes are less pervasive and are concerned with the orderly arrangement of souls. (*DM* 68, 3–7)

According to these definitions the function of daimons was cosmogonic. Acting centrifugally, they carried the generative will of the Demiurge into its most minute and particular expressions. The function of heroes, by contrast, was convertive. As agents of *epistrophē* they guided the soul's daimonic drives into divine measures.

Viewed statically, daimons and heroes were in conflict, the former binding souls to bodies and the latter aiding in their release. In this light it is understandable how the daimons of the Platonic tradition became the demons of the Gnostic and Christian worlds. For Iamblichus, however, both daimons and heroes acted in conjunction and obedience to the divine will (*DM* 70, 5). They completed the circuit of divine life that descends continually into sensible expression while remaining rooted in the Forms. Thus, Iamblichus says:

> these mediating classes complete the universal bond between Gods and souls, they effect an indissoluble connection between them, and they bind together one continuum extending from the highest to the lowest. They make the communion of universal beings indivisible and provide an excellent blend and proportionate mixing for all. They allow the procession (*prohodos*) to pass from more excellent to inferior natures, and they equally facilitate the ascent (*anagogē*) from inferior to superior natures. They insert order and measures of the communication descending from more excellent natures, [they allow for] its reception into imperfect beings, and they make all things mutually agreeable and in harmony with each other, receiving from on high, from the Gods, the causes of all these things. (*DM* 17, 8–20)

The continuity (*sunecheia*) and kinship (*sungeneia*) of the cosmos were essential to Iamblichus's theory of theurgy. Based on the principle that there was an unbroken continuity throughout the cosmos (*DM* 20, 5), Iamblichus could defend rites that used material objects. Theoretically, any object could connect the human soul with the gods because the entire world was their *energeia* and therefore manifested their presence. As Iamblichus put it, the gods were "present immaterially within material things" (*DM* 232, 15–16), and therefore theurgists invoked the gods in accord with their different expressions (*DM* 30, 13).

Porphyry challenged this view and asked how theurgists can invoke subterranean and terrestrial deities if the gods dwell only in the heavens (*DM* 29, 17–19). Repeating Thales' well-known dictum, Iamblichus replied: "To begin with, it is not true that the Gods dwell only in heaven, for all things are full of the Gods" (*DM* 30, 1–3; cf. *DM* 27, 8–10). Each god's authority was allotted to a different region of the cosmos: heaven, earth, sacred cities, sacred places, or certain sacred groves or statues (*DM* 30, 14–16), yet the gods themselves were not affected by these allotments for

> the divine illuminates all these externally (*exōthen*) just as the sun externally (*exōthen*) illuminates all things with its rays. Therefore, just as light envelops things illuminated by it, so does the power of

the Gods externally embrace those natures that partake of it. And just as natural light is undividedly present in the air . . . so also the light of the Gods shines separately (*chōristōs*), and though it remains firmly established in itself it proceeds through all existing beings. (*DM* 30, 16–31, 6)

Although the light of the gods was indivisible (*DM* 31, 6–10), the world was divided and therefore their light was received in different ways.

Yet the light itself is everywhere and entirely one and it is indivisible in all things that are able to participate in it. By its perfect power it fulfills everything, and by virtue of its unlimited and causal transcendence it brings all things to completion in itself. Everywhere it is united to itself and joins last things to their principles. (*DM* 31, 13–18)

The gods were revealed by their participants aetherially (*aitheriōs*), aerially (*aeriōs*), aquatically (*enhudriōs*), etc. (*DM* 33, 8–9), and theurgists invoked the gods accordingly (*DM* 33, 9–11).

Attempting to find contradictions in Iamblichus's Platonism, Porphyry asked how theurgists could worship the gods as sun, moon, and other heavenly *bodies* if the gods were incorporeal (*DM* 50, 14–17). To which Iamblichus replies: "Indeed, we maintain that the celestial Gods are not contained by bodies but that they contain bodies in their divine lives and activities (*energeiai*)" (*DM* 50, 17–51, 2). The celestial gods *contained* their bodies, and since all gods were defined by unity their activities were also unified. As we have seen, the only body that exemplifies unified action is the sphere, so the bodies of the gods were spheres, the geometric complement to their unity. Yet heavenly spheres were not bodies in the ordinary sense for they were perfect *energeiai* of gods. Quite literally they were the divine acts (*theia erga*) or theurgies of the gods. Like the theurgic actions performed by human souls, the celestial bodies "imitate the sameness of the Gods with an eternal motion, in accord with the same principles and similarly toward the same end, according to one ratio (*heis logos*) and one order (*mia taxis*)" (*DM* 51, 16–52, 2). According to Iamblichus, the bodies of the celestial gods were "entirely similar," "united," and "uniform" (*DM* 52, 6–8) so that,

153

despite their embodiment, "the visible Gods in the heavens are all, in a certain sense, incorporeal" (*DM* 52, 17–18).

Because the body of a visible god was totally under the control of its soul and guiding *Nous*, its noetic character was iconically revealed as a sphere and, like other *sunthēmata*, it served as a mean between the corporeal and the incorporeal.

According to Iamblichus, incorporeal gods existed above their celestial counterparts. In a lost treatise entitled *On the Gods* Iamblichus distinguished these two classes of deities as "cosmic" (*perikosmioi*) and "hyper-cosmic" (*huperkosmioi*) (*DM* 271, 11), and in his discussion of sacrifices and gods in the *De Mysteriis* he referred to these gods respectively as "material" and "immaterial":

> In the first place, we maintain that among the Gods some are material and others immaterial. The material Gods are those that contain matter within themselves and give it order, but the entirely immaterial Gods are removed from matter and transcend it. (*DM* 217, 4–8)

The material gods were the celestial deities, and though Iamblichus distinguished them from the "incorporeal" (*asōmatoi*) and "intelligible" (*noētoi*) gods (*DM* 57, 7–8), all the gods were united. The different allotments—whether material or immaterial—simply reflected the contexts in which they communicated the will of the Paternal Demiurge. In response to Porphyry's question about the relation of corporeal to incorporeal gods, Iamblichus says:

> Since the Gods ride upon celestial spheres while remaining incorporeal, intelligible, and united, they continue to possess their principles in the intelligible realm, and while contemplating their own divine forms they govern the entire heaven according to one infinite activity. And if, while being in the heavens separately (*chōristōs*), they lead the eternal revolutions through their will alone, they remain themselves, unmixed with the sensible order and co-existing with the intelligible Gods. (*DM* 57, 7–14)

Like light that remains "firmly established in itself" (*DM* 31, 5), the celestial gods remained in the intelligible realm yet served as principles for their "visible statues," the celestial spheres (*DM* 57, 18). In turn, the celestial gods generated sublunary existences which also remained in "continuity" (*sunecheia*) with the intelligible gods "according to one union" (*kata mian henōsin*) (*DM* 58, 3–4). The dominant characteristic of the gods was unity, their activity was unifying, and thus, although the One was present everywhere (*DM* 58, 7), it was most evident among the gods. The material gods were therefore united with the immaterial gods through their common characteristic of "unity." Iamblichus says:

> In the case of the Gods, their order exists in the union of them all: their primary and secondary genres and all natures generated from them co-exist together in unity. The beginning, the middle, and the end co-exist according to the One itself, so as regards the Gods one ought not to seek from whence the One comes to them. For whatever the Being itself is in them, this Being of theirs *is* the One. And according to this principle, the secondary Gods remain in the One of the primary Gods while the primary Gods give to the secondary the unity proceeding from themselves. All of them together possess the communion of an indissoluble connection. (*DM* 59, 15–60, 8)

Despite this unity at the level of the gods, the soul could reach the immaterial level only first by passing through the material gods. In fact, the characteristics of these two orders may have been determined by their effects on souls. For example, Iamblichus said that the soul's liberation from fate was effected by the hypercosmic gods (*DM* 271, 11–12). Unfortunately, his explanation of these gods has been lost, but Damascius says that his description of the liberated gods (*apolutoi theoi*) was based on Iamblichean teachings so we will follow his explanation.

Damascius says that according to "Orpheus" and "the theurgists" (*Dub. et Sub.* II, 214, 8) each order of the gods was determined and guided by the order immediately prior to it. Thus, the summit of any order was rooted in the order above it and guided it from there. Concerning the liberated gods, Damascius says:

> Thus, the liberated (*apolutoi*) Gods should be conceived as the last of the hypercosmic (*huperkosmioi*) Gods and as exercising providential attention over the world. Therefore, [we ask], do these liberated Gods occupy the highest point among the encosmic

155

(*enkosmioi*) Gods, and are they to be counted among them with respect to their characteristics, or are the liberated Gods not only encosmic but also reveal a hypercosmic nature? Accordingly, and with respect to their proper species, one ought to classify them as the mean (*mesotēs*) of these [i.e., the hyper- and encosmic gods]. We maintain that the liberated Gods are those that exercise a providential attention over the cosmos but are neither held in its nature nor completed within its order. (*Dub. et Sol.* II, 214, 8–15)

Under the reign of Kronos, the "liberated Demiurge" (*apolutos demiourgos*; *Dub. et Sol.* II, 214, 22), the gods ruled in Plato's Golden Age (*Dub. et Sol.* II, 214, 17–19), guiding the world from above with noetic and providential care. As the *mesotēs* between encosmic and hypercosmic gods, the liberated gods were in contact with both worlds. Damascius continues:

> Indeed, their position according to their half-related status reveals more clearly how they occupy the middle rank among the Gods. For at the same time that their status of being "related" (*to kata schesin*) is proper to the encosmic Gods, their status of being "unrelated" (*to ascheton*) is proper to the hypercosmic Gods. For [their] nature is one but [also] double since they project a single life which is both encosmic *and* hypercosmic. (*Dub. et Sol.* II, 215, 4–6)

Damascius applied the law of mean terms to create an intermediary class of gods, and since he attributed these teachings to Iamblichus it is safe to assume that Iamblichus's material and immaterial gods would have been joined in the same way. Iamblichus said that the liberation of souls was effected by the hypercosmic gods, but to fulfill a liberating function Damascius reminds us that these gods must somehow have been *in* the cosmos: how else could they lead souls out of it? The difference between the material and immaterial gods therefore, like the difference between fate and providence, cannot be separated from the soul's experience of them.[2] The mediating class (or function) of "liberated" gods reflected the soul's experience of the liberating presence of immaterial gods in the material order

---

2. In the same way that Iamblichus says that "fate is providence" so the material gods, in one sense, *are* the immaterial gods; cf. *Stob.* II, 174, 5–7.

and further, since the soul's experience was triadic,[3] the order of the gods was also assumed to be triadic.[4] Just as the spherical bodies of celestial gods mediated between the corporeal and incorporeal realms, the liberated gods mediated between the encosmic and hypercosmic realms, their identity and position being relative to the context in which they were experienced (see Diagram 1, below).

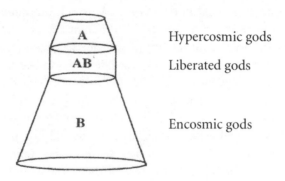

Hypercosmic gods

Liberated gods

Encosmic gods

Diagram 1. The liberated gods, AB, allow the hypercosmic gods, A, to manifest themselves as cosmic gods, and they allow the encosmic gods, B, to participate in the hypercosmic gods.

The division of the gods into hypercosmic (A), encosmic (B), and liberated (AB) is an extension of Iamblichus's "law of mean terms" to the divine classes.[5] Since Iamblichus assumed the law of the

3. That is, the soul *experienced* the hypostasis of the liberated gods and thus identified with the mean term embracing two divine orders: immaterial and material.

4. Personal experience must always be taken into account to understand the abstract schemas of the Neoplatonists. As A.C. Lloyd puts it: "The hypostases are experiences; they are types of consciousness. . . . It follows that the element of personal experience is needed to complement the non-empirical philosophical system. The two together constitute Neoplatonism"; *The Anatomy of Neoplatonism* (Oxford: Clarendon Press, 1990), 126.

5. See Dodd's discussion of the influence of this Iamblichean principle on Platonic tradition in *ET*, xxi–xxii.

mean distinguished the classes of the gods, the *archai* of his universe, it necessarily distinguished lower levels of manifestation. With the law of the mean Iamblichus connected the extremes of any opposition, including that between gods and men.

In his letter to Anebo, Porphyry understandably had asked why theurgists subordinated invisible daimons to visible gods (*DM* 61, 12–15). Iamblichus replied that the visible gods were "united" (*sunhēmmenoi*; *DM* 61, 17) with the intelligible gods because their very Form (unity) was held in common (*DM* 61, 18) but daimons were far removed from unity and had a different essence (*DM* 62, 1). With respect to the invisibility of the noetic gods and daimons, Iamblichus said that although both daimons and the noetic gods were invisible (*aphaneis*), significant differences separated them. Daimons were merely invisible to the senses, but the gods were invisible to "rational knowledge" and "material intelligence" (*DM* 62, 5–7). For Iamblichus, whatever was invisible to the intellect because of its transcendence was certainly higher than what was merely invisible to sight. In the case of the celestial gods, although they were empirically visible, they remained invisible to the grasp of the mind. Iamblichus says:

> What then? Are the invisible Gods, by virtue of being invisible, any greater than the visible Gods? Not at all! For the divine wherever it is and whatever allotment it has, possesses the same power and dominion over its subordinates. Accordingly, even if it is visible it rules in the same way over invisible *Daimones*, and if it exists in the earth, it still rules over the *Daimones* of the air. For neither the place of reception nor a part of the world can produce any change in the authority of the Gods. (*DM* 62, 10–63, 1)

Gods and daimons were also distinguished by their dominions. The dominion of the gods was universal while that of daimons was divided into parts (*DM* 63, 5–10), and the gods were "entirely independent" (*pantelōs kechōrismenoi*; *DM* 63, 14–15) of the bodies they commanded while daimons were not separated (*achōristoi*) from the things they ruled (*DM* 63, 12–13). As Iamblichus put it:

> Generally, the divine is leader and stands over the order of beings, but the daimonic nature is attendant and willingly receives what-

ever the Gods instruct them to do, and they work out manually the things which the Gods conceive, wish, and command intellectually. Surely this is why the Gods are free from the powers that verge into generation, but *Daimones* are not completely free of them. (*DM* 64, 2–9)

Consequently, every god manifested itself through its attendant daimons, who were in *sumpatheia* with animate life while the god remained entirely independent (*chōristōs*).

Since the order of the gods and of each god was triadic, the structure of the universe and of every ontological order necessarily reflected this triune principle. The Pythagorean influence on Iamblichus is particularly evident in the role of the triad, which was central to Pythagorean worship. In *De Caelo* Aristotle reports:

It is just as the Pythagoreans say, the whole world and all things in it are summed up in the *triad*; for end, middle, and beginning give the number of the whole and their number is the triad. Hence it is that we have taken this number from nature, as if it were one of her laws, and *make use of it even in the worship of the gods.*[6]

More specifically, the triadic rule was reflected in each ontological class. For example, Iamblichus distinguished three kinds of daimons: (1) those who help the gods reward theurgists for their sacred labors (*DM* 181, 8–13); (2) those who preside over judgments as the agents of justice, aiding good men and punishing the evil (*DM* 181, 13–19); and (3) those who are without reason (*alogistos*) or judgment (*akritos*), are allotted one power, and preside over a single natural function (*DM* 182, 1–4). Of this third group Iamblichus says:

Just as the function of a knife is "to cut" and to do nothing else it is the same in the case of the spirits distributed into the cosmos.... Indeed, in the case of certain invisible spirits each receives but one power, and by nature it performs only this one task that has been ordained for it. (*DM* 182, 4–13)

This last class of daimons was irrational, blindly preserving the order of nature and corporeal life. They manifested in the rhythms

---

6. Aristotle, *De Caelo* 268a, 11–17, in *Aristotle*, vol. 6, *On the Heavens*, trans. W. K. C. Guthrie (Cambridge: Harvard University Press, 1939; 1971).

of somatic life: the diastole and systole of the heart, the rhythm of breath, the digestion of food, and the consistency of the nervous system. In the psychic life they were instincts of preservation, sustaining the hungers and drives that preserve individuals and society. The task of each soul, therefore, was to engage these daimons in a way that "imitates the Demiurge," to act "justly" and in obedience to the laws of the creator gods (*Tim.* 41c). If the soul succeeded in this it was lifted to the level of the gods. Since these laws were as much biological as ethical, the labors of the embodied soul included eating justly, exercising justly, sleeping and waking justly, as well as behaving justly toward other human beings and the ruling gods: in short, labors that made up the Pythagorean *bios* as conceived by Iamblichus in *De Vita Pythagorica*.

The Chaldean Oracles reflect the same Pythagorean influence and one fragment reads: "For in every world shines a *triad*, ruled by a monad."[7] While the One ruled transcendentally over all triads, its immanent activity took the form of *philia*, a term Iamblichus borrowed from the Pythagoreans.[8] Cosmologically, *philia*, like the Chaldean *erōs*, was the power that bound all things to all. Theologically, *philia* unified the triads of the gods, and since the gods ruled all theurgies, each theurgic rite was an expression of the *philia* that governed the cosmos and "[binds] the Gods to men . . . through learned worship" (VP 123, 7–9). This *philia* was conveyed to humanity in rituals that both embodied and reflected the divine order. Iamblichus says:

> Is not every sacred ritual legislated intellectually from first principles according to the laws of the Gods? *For each rite imitates the order of the Gods*, both the intelligible and the celestial, and each possesses the eternal measures of beings and the wondrous symbols which have been sent here by the Demiurge, the Father of all things." (*DM* 65, 3–7)

Every rite had its beginning and end in the gods; man was the performer, not the initiator, for "it is not possible for any of the divine

---

7. The *CO*, frag. 27, p. 59; cf. des Places, ed., *Oracles chaldaïques* (Paris: Les Belles Lettres, 1971), 73.

8. See Iamblichus's discussion in *VP* 123, 7–21.

actions to be performed in a sacred manner without one of the Superior Beings present to oversee and complete the sacred acts" (*DM* 144, 1–3). Since the human soul was the lowest divinity and, in its embodied and anatropic state, was incapable of reaching the gods, it could neither invent nor initiate a theurgic rite. On this point Iamblichus was clear:

> If these things were only human customs and received their authority from our legal institutions one might say that the worship of the Gods was the invention of our ideas. But in fact God is the leader of these things, the one who is invoked in the sacrifices and a great number of Gods and angels surround him. And each nation on earth is allotted a certain common guardian by him, and every temple is similarly allotted its particular overseer. (*DM* 236, 1–8)

13

Ritual and the Human Hierarchy

Even the perfect soul is imperfect when compared with divine action.

Theurgic rites reflected the order of the gods and therefore played a role in cosmogenesis, but since human souls performed the rites their differences influenced the form and intensity of their theurgies. Given the variety of human beings it would be impossible to see how theurgic ritual mirrors cosmogony unless one first understands how Iamblichus conceived these differences. Not surprisingly, he divides human souls into three classes distinguished by their purposes for descending into bodies.

According to Iamblichus, the purpose for the descent of the soul was revealed in its embodiment and this determined the kind of theurgy appropriate for it. Following the principles of continuity, filiation, and the rule that "like can only be joined to like" each soul was fit to perform a specific kind of ritual. For Iamblichus's description of the descents of souls we must return to the *De Anima*.

It is significant that Iamblichus begins his review with the teachings of the Platonist Calvenus Taurus, who maintained that the Demiurge sent souls to earth to complete the cosmos (*Stob.* I, 378, 25–28) and, more specifically, to reveal the life of the gods in the pure and faultless life of souls (*Stob.* I, 379, 2–6). This view is consistent with Iamblichus's own explanation for the descent of souls. Since souls were the lowest of the superior kinds they were the last mediators of immortality to the mortal world. The common purpose of each soul's descent was cosmogonic and revelatory, but since souls were seeded into the ranks of different gods, the nature of their manifestations differed. In addition, because embodiment itself was anatropic, it caused each soul to experience alienation and lose the continuity it possessed with the gods. Therefore, to the degree that each soul lost its original filiation with its god and divine community, it had to undergo corresponding degrees of correction. In accord with this, Iamblichus described the descent of souls first as being voluntary or involuntary: "According to another division, some modes of descent are conceived to be voluntary, either when the soul chooses to govern terrestrial things, or when it is persuaded to do so by the Superior Kinds. But other descents are involuntary, when the soul is forcibly dragged to what is inferior" (*Stob.* I, 379, 6–10). The causes for these different modes of descent were the different purposes of embodiment. Iamblichus continues:

> I think that inasmuch as there are different purposes for the soul's descent this creates differences in the manner of descent. For if the soul descends for the salvation, purification, and perfection of the things in this world then it descends purely. But if the soul is turned toward the body for the sake of exercising and correcting its habits, the descent is not entirely without passion nor is the soul, in itself, released and liberated. And if the soul descends as if being dragged down here for punishment and judgment, the descent is forced. (*Stob.* I, 380, 6–14)

Contrary to the view of Porphyry, Iamblichus did not believe that apotheosis resulted in the soul's escape from the cosmos. The perfectly purified soul continued to "descend," not for the sake of punishment or correcting psychic imbalances, but for the benefit of others, revealing through its own perfection the perfection of the gods.[1] The descent of a purified soul may not have severed its connection with divine beings (*ta ekei*), yet it had to descend.[2] As Olympiodorus says, following Iamblichus: "Indeed, Plato does not

---

1. Dillon aptly compares the descended soul of the theurgist (i.e., a purified soul) to the *bodhisattva* of Mahayana Buddhism who takes on a body for the benefit of his fellow beings. See Dillon, *Iamblichi Chalcidensis*, 243.

2. Dillon, *Iamblichi Chalcidensis*, 243.

allow the souls of theurgists to remain always in the intelligible world, but even they descend into generation, concerning which the oracle says: '[to] the angelic order.'"[3]

Dillon suggests that the epithet *theios* given by Neoplatonists to Plato and Pythagoras, and later to Iamblichus himself, may be explained in part by this doctrine of divine incarnation: the belief that angelic souls took on human bodies for the salvation of the race. Such a soul, in the estimation of the Neoplatonists, was *theios*.

Before examining the impact of these views on Iamblichus's theory of ritual practice, their apparent conflict with the Platonic doctrine of embodiment must be taken into account. For if a divine soul did not lose contact with the gods, as Iamblichus seems to suggest, it would be spared the trauma of birth and the experience of *anatropē* described in the *Timaeus*, but I do not think this was Iamblichus's point. To cite the words of the Athenian stranger in the *Laws*: "This much I know—that no creature is ever born in possession of that intellect (*nous*), or that amount of intellect that properly belongs to it when fully developed" (672b). The context, appropriately, is the condition of newborn children, and what may be inferred is that even a perfect soul would have to pass through stages of growth and accommodate itself to a mortal body and the generated world. This may have led to the theory of "progressive animation" that Iamblichus discussed in the *De Anima* (*Stob.* I, 381, 7–13).

If *anatropē* was experienced by every embodied soul, then theurgic rituals would have been necessary for even the purest. Yet, because of the high purpose of its descent, when a divine soul entered the human condition, it may have been born into a family where it could receive the pedagogy proper to a vehicle of the gods.[4] As embodied, the soul would still be anatropic—identified with an individual self—but in the case of a pure descent the inversion of

---

3. Olympiodorus, *Olympiodori Philosophi in Platonis Phaedonem Commentaria*, ed. W. Norvin (Leipzig, 1913; reprint Hildesheim: Georg Olms, 1958), 64, 2–5.

4. One such family was that of Julian the Chaldean who prayed to the Paternal Demiurge that his son be given the soul of an archangel. According to Psellus, this son, "Julian the Theurgist," received the soul of Plato himself; see Hans Lewy, *Chaldean Oracles and Theurgy*, ed. M. Tardieu (Paris: Etudes Augustiniennes, 1978), 223–24 n. 195.

the soul would never become deviant.[5] Its *anatropē* would never become habitual, making it actively *enantios*: opposed to itself and to the Whole. On the contrary, its anatropism would function as a pivot through which the soul could manifest the cosmogonic principle of *philia*, joining the parts with the Whole. Although no extant work of Iamblichus takes up this problem specifically, I would argue on Iamblichean principles that each individual consciousness, even that of a perfect soul, would be seen as deficient simply because it was human. As Iamblichus says: "*Even the perfect soul is imperfect when compared with divine action*" (*DM* 149, 11–12). For soteriological reasons the perfect soul would have to become human in any case in order to experience *anatropē* and mediate the human realm with the angelic.[6] Like the liberated gods who held a middle rank and lived a double life: encosmic and hypercosmic, the theurgist also held a middle rank and lived a double life: human and divine.[7]

Theurgic apotheosis was not a flight to the gods. As human, the soul remained anatropic, embedded in the natural cosmos and human society; but to the degree that the soul embodied the divine measures of the gods it sustained a direct connection with them. The gods, Iamblichus says, were everywhere (*DM* 30, 1–3; 27, 8–10), but they could be received only by a vehicle that had been properly prepared. Thus, speaking for all theurgists, Iamblichus says: "Let us not disdain to say this also, that we often have occasion to perform rituals for the sake of genuine bodily needs, to the Gods who oversee the body, and to their good *Daimones*" (*DM* 221, 1–4). The reverence paid by theurgists to the gods that ruled over physical nature was an expression of their confidence in *philia*. This comprehensive force extended from the unity of the gods to the divisions of the sensible world, but to experience *philia* the soul had to know the grade of the cosmos to which it was attached so that it could honor its tutelary gods and daimons. To prescribe the appropriate ritual

5. That is to say, when *heteros* permanently assumes the role of *autos*.

6. Dillon says Iamblichus's *bodhisattva* doctrine was in conflict with the myth of the soul's descent in the *Phaedrus* but in accord with the role of philosopher in the *Republic* returning to the cave; *Iamblichi Chalcidensis*, 243.

7. Iamblichus described this double life of the theurgist in the *De Mysteriis* 184, 1–13; 246, 16–247, 5.

for a soul the theurgist needed to be able to "read" the nature of its *energeia*, for this revealed the mode of its descent and, consequently, the purpose (*telos*) for its embodiment.

The purpose for the embodiment and descent of souls was reflected in their bodies and lives: the manifesting *energeia* of their souls.[8] Distinguishing the three grades of souls in the *De Mysteriis*, Iamblichus says:

> According to another division,[9] the great herd[10] of humanity is subject to nature, is governed by natural powers, and looks downward towards the works of nature;[11] it fulfills the administration of fate, and accepts for itself the order of things which are brought to completion by fate. It makes use of practical reasoning all the time and only concerning things in nature. But there are a small number who, using a certain power of the mind that surpasses nature, are released from nature and are led to the separate and unmixed *Nous*, and at once they become superior to the powers of nature. And there are others who are between these, placed about the *media* between nature and the pure *Nous*. Some of them follow both [i.e., the separate *Nous* and nature], others pursue a life mixed from these, and others are liberated from inferior natures and pass on to better things. (*DM* 223, 10–224, 6)

Iamblichus distinguished three types of souls: (1) the great herd who follow nature and fate; (2) those who have risen to the divine

8. This triad of (1) "purposes" (*tele*); (2) "modes" (*tropoi*); and (3) "bodies" (*sōmata*), function in a manner corresponding to the *ousia-dunamis-energeia* triad that Iamblichus uses to distinguish classes among incorporeals (see Chapter 6). In both cases, the body, the living *energeia* of the soul, revealed the *tropos* of its descent (just as *energeia* reveals its *dunamis*) and this, in turn, allows the theurgist to identify the *telos* for that soul's embodiment.

9. The following division concludes that begun in book V, 15 where Iamblichus distinguished two modes of worship appropriate to two different conditions of the soul: when it is purely noetic, with the intelligible gods, and when it is in a body. In the division quoted here he developed this into three modes.

10. This phrase, *hē pollē agelē*, was probably drawn from the *CO*, frag. 153; 107, 198; cf. des Places, ed., trans., and comm., *Oracles chaldaïques* (Paris: Les Belles Lettres, 1971), 103.

11. Cf. *DCMS* 18, 9–13, where the embodied soul "falls out" of the natural order, and *DM* 21, 6–7, which describes the soul's inclination toward the phenomena of nature.

Nous above nature and fate; and (3) those who are between the two extremes. To each type of soul there was a corresponding mode of worship. Iamblichus continues:

> Therefore, since these distinctions have been made, what follows should be most obvious. Souls governed by the nature of the universe, leading lives according to their own personal nature and using the powers of nature, should perform their worship in a manner adapted to nature and to the corporeal things moved by nature. In their worship they should employ places, climates, matter and the powers of matter, bodies and their characteristics and qualities, movements and what follows movements, and changes of the things in generation, along with other things associated with these in their acts of reverence to the gods, and especially in the part that pertains to performing sacrifice.
>
> Other souls, living according to the *Nous* alone and the life of the *Nous*, and liberated from the bonds of nature, should concern themselves in all parts of theurgy with the intellectual and incorporeal law of the hieratic art.
>
> Other souls, the media between these, should labor along different paths of holiness according to the differences of their intermediate position, either by participating in both modes of ritual worship, or by separating themselves from one mode, or by accepting both of these as a foundation for more honorable things—for without them the transcendent goods would never be reached. (*DM* 224, 7–225, 10)

The objects sacrificed to the gods had a direct affinity with them. Iamblichus says: "Whenever we worship the Gods who rule over the soul and nature it is not out of place to offer natural powers to them, nor is it despicable to consecrate to them bodies under the rule of nature, for all the works of nature serve the Gods and contribute to their government" (*DM* 226, 3–9). To the gods who presided over particular places, the things produced in those places were the appropriate sacrifices (*DM* 234, 1–2). Iamblichus says: "For always, to creators their own works are especially pleasing, and to those beings who are primarily the causes for producing certain things, those very things are primarily dear to them" (*DM* 235, 3–5). Such creations, Iamblichus says, may be "animals" (*zōa tina*), "plants" (*phuta*) (*DM* 235, 6) or other earthly products that contribute to the administration of the gods. These creations united embodied souls with the universal *philia*. As Iamblichus put it, "they preserve the power of the communion between Gods and men" (*DM* 235, 11–12).

Material creations were the proper elements to sacrifice in the theurgies of souls bound to material concerns. Through the consecration of these elements souls brought themselves into accord with the gods who ruled them; that is, with the material and encosmic deities. All souls began theurgic disciplines with sacrifices to these gods to establish a foundation for more comprehensive forms of worship, and the material gods themselves presided over these offerings. Iamblichus explains:

> According to the art of the priests it is necessary to begin sacred rites from the material Gods. For the ascent to the immaterial Gods will not otherwise take place. The material Gods, therefore, are in communion with matter in as much as they preside over it. Hence they rule over material phenomena: (i.e., division, collision, impact, reaction, change, generation, and corruption of all material bodies).
>
> If anyone wishes to worship these Gods theurgically, [that is to say,] in the manner in which they naturally exist and have been allotted their rule, one ought to render to them a material form of worship. For in this way we may be led into complete familiarity with all these Gods, and in worship we offer what is appropriately related to them. In the sacrifices, therefore, dead bodies and things deprived of life, the blood of animals, the consumption of victims, their diverse changes and destruction, and in short, the breakdown of the matter offered to the Gods is fitting—not for the Gods themselves—but with respect to the matter over which they preside. For although the Gods are pre-eminently separate (*chōristoi*) from matter they are nevertheless present to it. And though they contain matter by virtue of an immaterial power, they co-exist with it. (*DM* 217, 8–218, 12)

Elsewhere, Iamblichus described the benefits of animal and blood sacrifices. In the case of expiatory sacrifices to appease the "anger of the gods" (*DM* 43, 2), he explained that the "anger" did not come from the gods but from the soul's "turning away from their beneficent care" (*DM* 43, 4–5). The purpose of the sacrificial rite was to turn the soul's attention back to the gods and the higher order. The expiation did not affect the gods but souls, converting them to the divine order. Iamblichus says: "If anyone believes that deserting the guardian care [of the gods] leads to a sort of automatic injury, the appeal to Superior Beings by means of sacrifice *serves to remind us again of their beneficent care*, removes the privation [of their presence], and is entirely pure and inflexible" (*DM* 44, 5–10). Animal sacrifice and the burning of victims portrayed how the soul's impurities were consumed in its apotheosis. Iamblichus chided Porphyry for ignoring this symbolic (and theurgic) dimension of fire (*DM* 214, 5–6, 216, 9–10):

> Your question betrays an ignorance concerning the offering of sacrifices by means of fire, for it is the greater power of fire to consume, destroy, and assimilate matter to itself but not to be assimilated to matter, and fire lifts up the offering to the divine, heavenly, and immaterial Fire instead of drawing it down to matter and generation. (*DM* 214, 5–10)

The power of fire to destroy and assimilate matter was a ritual anticipation of the soul's assimilation to the gods. Iamblichus says:

> For Superior Beings, those for whom the breakdown of matter through fire is dear, are impassive, and they render us impassive. Whatever exists within us is made similar to the Gods just as fire assimilates all solid and resistant substances to luminous and attenuated bodies. And by means of sacrifices and the fire of the sacrificial offering, we are led up to the Fire of the Gods just as [we see] in the ascent of fire to the Fire invoked and in the drawing up of gravitating and resistant things to divine and heavenly natures. (*DM* 214, 17–215, 7)

In effect, the drama of blood sacrifice was a mnemonic rite to remind the soul of its fiery origin. One can imagine how the sounds, smells, and colors of an animal sacrifice would hold the attention of the worshiper; for Iamblichus, one's absorption in the rite was the sine qua non to awaken the divine *sunthēma* in the soul. As he says, "the fire of our sacrifice imitates the divine *Fire*" (*DM* 215, 19), which "liberates" (*DM* 216, 5) the soul from the bonds of matter, "assimilates" (*DM* 216, 5) it to the gods, and makes it fit to participate in their *philia* (*DM* 216, 6).

The offering and consumption of a victim was vicariously the sacrifice of the soul, yet to achieve the desired familiarity (*oikeōsis*) with the gods of the sacrificed elements, the worshiper had to be similar to the elements offered. His communion with the gods depended on his connaturality (*sungeneia*) with the elements. Material theurgy often called for the consumption of life and blood, which may signify that for the "great herd" of humanity, embodied for punishment (*dikē*) and judgment (*krisis*) (*Stob.* I, 380, 12–13) the ritual suffering of matter effected their own. The "middle class" of souls who descended to "exercise" and "correct" (*Stob.* I, 380, 10) their habits also participated in material worship that accelerated their spiritual progress. Iamblichus says: "The law of sacrifices for this use therefore will be necessarily corporeal-formed, some sacrifices cutting off what is superfluous in our souls, others filling us to the degree that we are deficient, and others leading into symmetry and order that in us which is offensively disordered" (*DM* 221, 13–17). Still other "sacred operations" (*DM* 221, 19) fulfilled the practical needs of human existence such as the health and well-being of the body (*DM* 222, 1–2), and these rites were also offered to the material gods who preside over such things.

Since the soul offered the gods things connatural to them, Iamblichus explained that there was also a completely immaterial mode of worship directed to the immaterial gods: "Whenever we take it upon ourselves to honor those Gods who are uniform in themselves, it is appropriate to celebrate them with liberated honors. Intellectual gifts and things of incorporeal life are fitting for these beings. As much virtue and wisdom that the soul has is offered, any perfection, and all the goods that are in the soul" (*DM* 226, 9–14). Theurgists who performed this kind of rite were "entirely purified" and very rare (*DM* 219, 14–15). Indeed, Iamblichus says to participate in the gods in this manner was "the rarest of all things" (*to panton spaniotaton*; *DM* 228, 2–3), and the *De Mysteriis* provides little information on the theurgy practiced by these souls.[12] Undoubt-

---

12. Iamblichus says that it would not be appropriate to discuss this kind of theurgy with those who are beginning sacred operations or even with those who have reached the intermediate stage (*DM* 228, 6–12).

edly, these were the *bodhisattvas* to whom Dillon refers, the perfect souls who descended into bodies for the salvation of others (*Stob.* I, 380, 8). Since they were already in perfect harmony with the gods who ruled the material cosmos they had no need to perform material worship. Nevertheless, because of the weakness of the human soul, their noetic perfection could not manifest immediately, and material forms of worship would have been necessary during their years of maturation. Such practices established the proper "foundation" (*hupothesis*; *DM* 225, 8–11) for the immaterial worship of hypercosmic gods.

Finally, to the intermediate gods, who were both encosmic and hypercosmic, a twofold kind of worship was appropriate. Iamblichus says: "And in truth, to the intermediary Gods, who are leaders of intermediate blessings, sometimes two-fold offerings are adapted, sometimes a common gift to both, or such gifts that are detached from what is inferior and connected with more elevated natures, or generally, in one of the modes of worship that fills the mean position between extremes" (*DM* 226, 14–20).

To sum up, Iamblichus affirmed a tripartite anthropology determined by the three purposes (*telē*) for the descent of souls into bodies: (1) to save, purify and protect the cosmos; (2) to correct and exercise their character; or (3) to undergo punishment and judgment. These divisions correspond to Iamblichus's tripartite theology where gods are distinguished as: (1) hypercosmic; (2) hypercosmic and encosmic; and (3) encosmic. To each class of gods a corresponding mode of worship was assigned, drawn from the elements over which it ruled. Since encosmic gods were responsible for the material order they received material offerings, hypercosmic gods received noetic gifts, and the intermediate gods received both, or a mixture, or one in favor of the other. The divisions of the gods in their cosmogonic procession, therefore, had corresponding expressions in worship. Since there were three classes of human souls, each performed the worship appropriate to its type and to the occasion for the worship. The "great herd" of humanity worshiped the material gods with material offerings, the extremely rare noetic souls worshiped the immaterial gods with noetic gifts, and the intermediate souls worshiped the intermediate gods with twofold gifts. The correspondence between Iamblichus's theology, psychology, and ritual worship may be portrayed in Table 1.

Table 1

Souls	Purposes for Embodiment	Rituals	Gods
1. noetic	to save, perfect, and purify generated life	completely immaterial and noetic	hypercosmic/ immaterial
2. intermediate	to exercise and correct moral habits	immaterial and material	intermediate: joining encosmic to hypercosmic
3. material	for judgment and punishment	material	encosmic/material

14

Ritual as Cosmogony

The omission, even of few things, subverts the entire effect of worship.

To divide theurgists into three groups corresponding to three levels of the cosmos suggests a static structure, with each soul assigned a specific rank to worship a specific class of gods fixed in its rank. Although this schema is not inaccurate it overlooks the vitality of the structure, the dynamic character of theurgy as the unifying *energeia* of the gods. Cosmogonically theurgic action was *philia*, the demiurgic weaving of opposites (cf. *In Nic.* 73, 1–5), and it should be remembered that theurgic rites were performances that initiated human souls into the activity of the gods.

In the previous chapter I argued that every sacrifice had to meet two criteria of fitness (*prosēkon*): the sacrifice had to be connatural (*sungenes*) both with the soul who offered it and with the god who received it. The sacrifice, therefore, served as a mean to awaken the *philia* between the god and the soul. The affinity of the theurgist with his offering and its connection to the god allowed him to enter the god's *energeia* when the sacrifice was properly performed. Through sacrifice the soul tapped the power of the ruling god whether the offering was an animal, a plant, a song, or a virtue, and these sacrifices were not extraneous to the will of the gods but direct expressions of their own activity. For Iamblichus, theurgy was fundamentally dynamic, for the *philia* that sustained both cosmos and sacrifice was seen, ultimately, as the *erōs* of the One, proceeding from, and returning to, itself.

Theurgic sacrifice was also dynamic from the perspective of an individual soul; in its worship each soul gradually moved from material to immaterial gods. Following the Aristotelian principle

173

that the first in ontology was last in generation, the human soul proceeded to the intelligible gods by first accommodating itself to the material gods; only when the soul had integrated itself with material powers could its immaterial principles become active.[1] The soul's ascent to the noetic Father followed an unbroken continuum and any attempt to worship the Father directly and without intermediaries was bound to fail. Iamblichus explains that "for people not yet liberated from the fate of the material world and the communion tied up with bodies, unless a corresponding sort of worship is offered, they will utterly fail to attain immaterial or material blessings" (*DM* 219, 18–220, 5). Although the immaterial gods contained (*perichein*) the material gods and were the ultimate source of material blessings, their goods had to be mediated by the material gods and their daimons. Iamblichus says: "it must not be allowed for anyone to say that the immaterial Gods provide their gifts with their attention immediately bound up in the affairs of human life" (*DM* 222, 9–13).

The worship of the material gods fulfilled the order of fate (*DM* 223, 13–15), which allowed the soul to experience its laws as providential and liberating.[2] Since the material gods were revealed by daimons, material rites necessarily worked with daimonic orders, and since these same daimons ruled over bodily instincts and passions, the rituals that established the proper measures for associating with them also stabilized the passions of the soul. Somatic life was ritually sewn into the cosmogonic *philia*, but to attain this affiliation the theurgist had to awaken all the powers in his soul through their correspondences in the cosmos. Iamblichus says: "The theurgists know

---

1. This progress through the orders of the gods is reflected in the psychological progress within the orders of the soul itself; just as the immaterial gods were present, but hidden, in the material gods, so the soul's circle of the "same" was present in the circle(s) of the "other" but remained inactive until the soul balanced them (*Tim.* 37ab). Cf. the soul's relation to the two horses of the *Phaedrus* (247ab). For Iamblichus, this rectification was possible only by theurgy. See Dillon's comments, *Iamblichi Chalcidensis*, 341–42.

2. See Iamblichus's identification of fate and providence in his letter to Macedonius; *Stob.* II, 173, 26–174, 27.

that the omission, even of insignificant things, subverts the entire effect of worship; just as in a musical scale, if one string is broken the whole scale becomes inharmonious and out of tune."[3]

To deny any power its honor would deny to one's soul the divinization of its corresponding element. Thus Iamblichus says:

> He who has not distributed to all [these powers] what is fitting and in accord with the appropriate honor that each is worthy to receive, will depart imperfect and deprived of participation in the Gods. But he who celebrates all these powers and offers to each gifts that are pleasing and honors that are as similar to them as possible, will always remain secure and infallible since he has properly completed, perfect and whole, the receptacle of the divine choir. (*DM* 228, 19–229, 7)

The "receptacle of the divine choir" was the soul itself whose task it was to receive all the gifts of the gods (*DM* 55–56). In Aristotelian terms, this reception transformed the soul from a cosmos in potentiality (*en dunamei*) to a cosmos in actuality (*en energeia*). Since the cosmos was collectively the *energeiai* of the gods, the human soul, in effect, assimilated itself to the gods by ritually enacting their *energeiai*; first, however, the soul had to co-ordinate its passions with material daimons. The affections that enslaved the soul to daimons had to be purified and aligned with *sunthēmata* in nature before the soul could reach the simpler and more unified levels of the gods. Without this collaboration with daimons the soul lacked the foundation necessary to homologize itself to the material gods.[4]

Noetic worship was useless without this foundation. Yet, in the view of Iamblichus, such premature noetic worship was being encouraged in Platonic schools, and Porphyry, his chief rival, was a

---

3. *DM* 230, 2–6. Repeating the same principle, Simplicius says: "Just as in the case of a word, if letters are left off or added on the form of the word is lost, so with divine works and words, if anything is left off, or added on, or mixed up, the divine illumination will not take place"; Simplicius, *Commentarius in Enchiridion Epicteti*, ed. L. Deubner (Paris, 1842), 94, 42–46.

4. Philo of Alexandria, faced with a similar challenge (i.e., to justify the traditional Jewish cult in the face of philosophic critique) argued that without the fulfillment of the material cult the soul would lack a *foundation* for spiritual initiations; see *De Mig. Abr.* 89; 92–93; 96.

prime example of one who attempted to short-circuit the material gods and daimons. Although Porphyry had spoken of his *henōsis* with the One, he was subject to severe bouts of depression, even to the point of suicide. Such emotions would suggest that Porphyry neglected to honor the god and daimons associated with his depression and thus failed to homologize himself to the material gods, gatekeepers of the immaterial gods and true union with the One. From a theurgical perspective, Porphyry lacked a foundation, the security (*asphalēs*) and infallibility (*aptaistos*; *DM* 229, 5–6), that came from properly completing the "receptacle" of the divine choir. From Iamblichus's perspective Porphyry's *henōsis* had to have been false: if someone were still dominated by worldly passions (e.g., suicidal depression), he could not presume to pass beyond the material gods.[5] Iamblichus says:

> For if we ourselves are in the world, are contained as individual parts in the whole of the universe, are brought into existence primarily through it, are perfected by all the powers in it, are constituted by its elements, and receive from it our share of life and nature, if this is the case, it is not allowed for us to pass beyond the cosmos and the encosmic orders. (*DM* 227, 6–13)

The soul could not rise to the paternal Demiurge alone.[6] To reach the One, the soul had to be assimilated to the Whole, and this was accomplished only by honoring "all the gods." Though Iamblichus admits that noetic theurgy worshiped the "One, at the summit of the whole multitude of gods" (*DM* 230, 15–16), the direct worship of the One came only "at the very end of life and to very few" (*DM* 230, 18–231, 1). In the *De Mysteriis* Iamblichus did not reveal the details of this elevated form of theurgy (*DM* 231, 2–5) except to say that its method of worship corresponded to the simplicity of its object, the One. Although noetic theurgy made no use of material objects, it

---

5. Apart from the fact that it is self-contradictory to know one has experienced an *ineffable* union.

6. Cf. Iamblichus's remarks preserved in Damascius, *In Philebum* 227, 3–7; in L.G. Westerink, trans. and ed., *Lectures on the Philebus* (Amsterdam: North-Holland, 1959), 106–7.

would not have been opposed to material theurgies; the One was as present to sublunary natures as it was to the hypercosmic gods. The theurgist who performed noetic worship consequently honored the multitude of encosmic orders contained in the One. In fact, the One was never reached directly—by seeking unity—but by unified activity that imitated the *energeia* of the One: the manifesting cosmos. Iamblichus explains:

> [J]ust as a cosmos is gathered into one congregation out of many orders, so also the completion of sacrifices—to be faultless and whole—must be connected to the entire order of Superior Beings. And if, indeed, this order is numerous, all-perfect, and united in several ranks, it is necessary that *the sacred rite also should imitate its variety* by attaching itself to all the powers. Therefore, in accord with this, and with respect to the great variety of beings around us, it is not allowed to be joined with the divine causes that preside over these powers from a certain part (*meros*) that they contain, nor to ascend imperfectly to their first causes. (*DM* 231, 6–17)

In contrast to Porphyry, Iamblichus felt that souls must participate directly, and theurgically, in the material cosmos. For Iamblichus, cosmogenesis was *the* divine activity and the material cosmos, including its daimons, was a theophany. To participate in this activity required simply that the ritual and the gods invoked in the rite be appropriate (*prosēkon*) to the soul that performed the sacrifice. As Iamblichus says: "Each man attends to his sacrifice according to what he is, not according to what he is not; therefore the sacrifice should not surpass the proper measure of the one who performs the worship."[7]

There is no simpler or more comprehensive expression of theurgy's pragmatism. The theurgic cure for any disturbance in the soul had to be adapted to the nature of the illness. When this concerned

---

7. *DM* 220, 6–9. I follow the emendation by Gale and Sicherl of *thusias* for *hosias*. The *ousias* preserved in book V was probably a copyist's error due to the similarity of omicron and theta in the uncial script. The *hosias* preserved in M, therefore, represents a subsequent attempt to emend the error of *ousias*. See *Jamblique: Les Mystères d'Egypt*, trans. and ed. E. des Places (Paris: Les Belles Lettres, 1966), 170.

exaggerated affections or disturbances the god and daimons who had jurisdiction over that condition had to be placated. Theurgy simply attempted to balance the disturbed element of the soul by restoring it to the lord of that element, and to effect this the soul focused on a ritual object connatural (*sungenēs*) to itself and to the ruling god. Explaining this method, Iamblichus says:

> The law of religious worship distributes similars to things obviously similar (*ta homoia . . . tois homoiois*) and extends through all things from the highest to the lowest, assigning incorporeals to incorporeals, but bodies to bodies, and to each of these classes (it distributes) things that are proportionate to their natures [*DM* 227, 16–228, 2]. . . . *Indeed, when the divine causes and the human preparations resembling them are united in one and the same act, the accomplishment of the sacrifice achieves all things and bestows great blessings.* (*DM* 232, 6–9)

The objects of the rite varied depending on the soul and the god invoked, but if the objects were offered properly they worked in the same way—through the *sungeneia* that existed between the soul and its sacrifice and the *sungeneia* between the sacrifice and the god. Because the soul employed animals, plants, and other objects to enter the *energeiai* of the gods, one might assume that theurgists believed the objects themselves effected the soul's unification. Porphyry suggested that this was what theurgists believed, making them no better than sorcerers. Iamblichus disagreed with the assumption: "It is better to assign as the cause [of the power in sacrifices] the intimacy (*philia*), familiarity (*oikeiōsis*), and united relationship (*schesis sundetikē*) of creators toward their creations and of generators toward things generated" (*DM* 209, 11–14). Iamblichus maintained that the sacrifice of a material object released the will of the Demiurge by means of the intermediate orders and the preparation of the soul:

> Therefore, with this common principle [i.e., the universal *philia*] leading us, whenever we take a certain animal or any of the plants of the earth that preserve intact and pure the will of its maker, by means of this intermediary then, we appropriately move the demiurgic cause which presides over this undefiled. But since these

causes are numerous, some, like the *Daimones*, are immediately engaged, [but] others, like the divine causes [Gods], are situated above these, and even further above these is the one most venerable and leading cause, and in conjunction with the perfect sacrifice, all these causes are moved. (*DM* 209, 14–210, 4)

The ritual objects awakened corresponding *sunthēmata* in the soul, and for each soul its unification was proportionate to its level of existence. Thus, a noetically received union communicated a more intense awareness of the One than a union received through material objects. Yet the *philia* was the same, and the noetic theurgist would not have disdained material sacrifices for he already comprehended them through a vital identification with their *energeiai* (cf. *DM* 8, 3–6). Again, in theurgy the soul did not escape from generation but assimilated itself to the demiurgy of the world. As the "inspired" Socrates explains in the *Cratylus* (411e), *noēsis* comes from *neou* + *hesis*, the soul longing for the new and generating world. "Ugliness" (*aiskron*), by contrast, was "the obstacle to the flow" (416a), from which it may be inferred that the soul's resistance to generation is what alienated it from beauty and divinity, not the flow of generation itself (see *Tim.* 43d).

The initial *anatropē* that the soul suffered in birth was caused, not by the flow of generation—for the flow was theophany—but by the soul's incapacity to receive the flow. Theurgy enhanced the soul's receptivity and drew it into deeper resonance with the demiurgic will. Ultimately the soul's individual identity was restructured so that the anatropic self became a pivot for the gods to experience mortality. The theurgist became a living *sunthēma*, a vehicle of the gods. The theurgic progress of the soul from the sublunar realm to the cosmic and hypercosmic gods may be exemplified in Diagrams 2 and 3.

The apotheosis of the soul has been divided into three stages: A and A. 1 represent the soul at the beginning of theurgic disciplines using material *sunthēmata* connected to the orders of the encosmic gods. B and B. 1 represent the middle stage of worship using intermediate rites tied to the intermediate (or liberating) gods. C and C. 1 represent the noetic worship of a wholly purified soul directed to

the hypercosmic gods. A, B, and C, from above, show how the disorder and imperfections of the anatropic soul were replaced at each
stage by the divine order of the World Soul. Beginning with material rites the soul used material *sunthēmata* as a foundation (A) for
intermediate rites and intermediate *sunthēmata* (B), and these, in
turn, supported the complete alignment of the soul into the order
of the World Soul in the final state (C). A.1, B.1, and C.1 (side
view), show how this movement to the principle of the soul also
effected its ascent up the axis of cosmogenesis. At birth the cosmogonic procession from unity was experienced by the anatropic soul
as brute necessity and the laws of fate (broken lines). In A.1 as the
soul assimilated itself to the encosmic gods (indicated by the solid
ascending lines) the continuity of the encosmic order was realized
and fate began to appear as providence (solid descending lines). In
B.1 the same transformation occurred, as errant necessity and fate
were seen as the will of the paternal *Nous*. Finally in C.1 the circulation of the procession and return became continuous and unbroken, but this was not realized until the soul completely integrated
itself to the divine will. The reward of the soul's *anagōgē* to the
paternal *Nous* was realized in its active participation in the procession from the *Nous* to the hypercosmic, cosmic, and sublunary
worlds, ensuring that the "parts" the soul had purified remained
properly situated within their "causes." In the soul's coadministra-
ting—with the encosmic gods—the extension of daimons into the
last things, it helped to ensure that these extensions remained in
their causes. This was the cosmogonic weaving of *apeiron* into *peras*,
and it was accomplished by each soul in its material, intermediate,
and noetic theurgies.

In each mode of worship the gods were mediated to the soul by
means of *sunthēmata*, and though Iamblichus did not provide a ritual taxonomy he referred to objects that may be distinguished heu-
ristically as material, noetic, and intermediate *sunthēmata*. Since
theurgy was more a practical therapy than a philosophic system,
this division of *sunthēmata* is based on therapeutic appropriations,
not on metaphysical essences. A *sunthēma* may be defined as material when it divinizes the material powers of the soul, intermediate
when it divinizes the soul's intermediate powers, and noetic when it

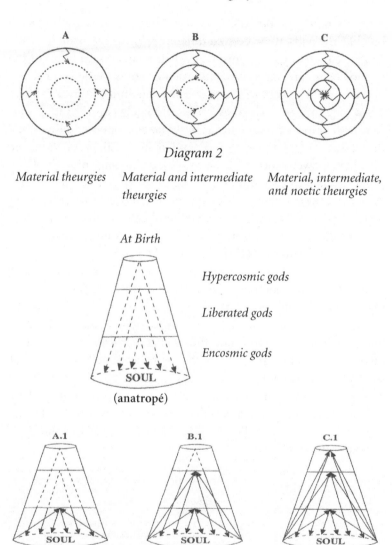

Diagram 2

Material theurgies   Material and intermediate   Material, intermediate,
                      theurgies   and noetic theurgies

At Birth

Hypercosmic gods

Liberated gods

Encosmic gods

SOUL

(anatropé)

A.1   B.1   C.1

SOUL   SOUL   SOUL

Diagram 3   (apotheosis)

The broken lines represent the soul's experience of fate.

The ascending lines represent the theurgic *epistrophē* of the soul to the One.

The solid descending lines represent the transformation of fate into the soul's co-operation with the Demiurge.

divinizes its noetic powers. All *sunthēmata* were essentially divine but, like the gods, they received different allotments cosmologically and were therefore distinguished by their recipients. In terms of the previous diagram, all *sunthēmata* oriented souls to the vertical axis of the cone. In view of their common divinity but contextual differences they may be defined as "proportionately equivalent." Therefore, if the ratio 1:2 represents a *sunthēma* appropriate to divinize a noetic soul, for a more divided and materialistic soul the same divinizing power/ratio would be employed in a range of multiplicity proportionate to that soul, say 16:32. In other words, for the *sunthēma* to draw a soul into the demiurgic will it had to affect that soul on its level of existence. This is what Iamblichus means when he says "the sacrifice should not surpass the proper measure of the soul who performs the worship" (*DM* 221, 8–9). The *sunthēma* affected the soul in its world of experience, whether this was entirely material or noetic. Therefore, noetic *sunthēmata* would not be effective in moving a material soul to the vertical axis. On the contrary, if the soul's intellect served anatropic desires, its movement would not be axial but peripheral to appropriate the noetic *sunthēma* as an idea to inflate its self-importance.[8] Iamblichus believed that this kind of conceptual spirituality threatened the integrity of the Platonic school. Theurgy guaranteed that the soul's *anagōgē* could not be "rationalized"; the *sunthēmata* that released the will of the Demiurge and effected the soul's ascent functioned at a level that preceded all conceptualization.

8. Such "prizes" would be the equivalent of the false rewards sought by the keen-eyed prisoners of the "cave" in the *Republic* (516cd).

15

Material
Sunthēmata

Immaterial beings are present in material natures immaterially.

Iamblichus used the terms *sunthēma, sumbolon,* and *sēmeia,* to describe respectively the theurgic "token," "symbol," or "sign" that divinized the soul. Iamblichus's use of the term *sunthēma* probably derived from the Chaldean Oracles where it was synonymous with *sumbolon.* In fragment 108 of the Oracles, the *sumbōla* are said to be "sown . . . throughout the cosmos" by the Paternal Demiurge,[1] and Ruth Majercik explains that these symbols "can be equated with the Platonic Forms" (*CO,* 182). The *sunthēmata* of the Oracles had a cosmogonic role like the Forms of Middle Platonism. Both functioned as dynamic powers enforming the cosmos, and both were considered the "thoughts of the Father."[2] From Oracle fragments 2 and 109 it is clear that the *sunthēmata* were also anagogic, for when the soul "remembers the pure, paternal token (*sunthēma*)," it returned to the paternal *Nous.*[3] In the Chaldean system and the *De Mysteriis* the *sunthēmata* were distributed simultaneously into the cosmos and into every soul by the Demiurge.

Iamblichus discussed *sunthēmata* in a cosmogonic context three

---

1. *CO,* frag. 108, p. 91.
2. For the Middle Platonic interpretation of the Forms as the "thoughts" of the Demiurge see Philo, *De opif.* 4, 17–20; 44, 129–130; cf. Albinus, *Didasc.* 9, 1–2. Also, see the discussion by John Dillon, *The Middle Platonists* (London: Duckworth, 1977), 55.
3. *CO,* Frag. 109, 91. Frag. 2 states to reach the Intelligible "you must cast into your imagination the entire token (*sunthēma*) of the triad" (49). See Majercik's commentary, 141.

times in the *De Mysteriis*. In *DM* 65–66 Iamblichus says that each theurgic rite engaged the "eternal measures" (*metra . . . aidia*) and "wondrous deposits" (*enthēmata thaumasta*) sent by the Demiurge to our world (*DM* 65, 6–8), and through them "the inexpressible is expressed through ineffable symbols" (*DM* 65, 8–9). This describes a cosmogonic and hieratic function of *sunthēmata*. In an explanation of augury Iamblichus makes the hieratic and cosmogonic connection even more explicit. He says that the gods use the cosmogonic power of daimons to reveal their will through natural signs (*DM* 135, 8–10). He explains:

> The Gods produce signs (*sēmeia*) by means of nature which serves them in the work of generation, nature as a whole and individual natures specifically, or by means of the generative *Daimones* who, presiding over the elements of the cosmos, particular bodies, animals, and everything in the world, easily produce the phenomena in whatever way seems good to the Gods. They reveal the intentions of the God symbolically (*sumbolikōs*) (*DM* 135, 14–136, 3)

Quoting Heraclitus, Iamblichus says this is the oracular mode: "neither speaking, nor concealing, but *signifying*" (*DM* 136, 4–5) and suggests that this was also the cosmogonic mode. He continues: "Therefore, just as the Gods create all things by means of images and signify all things in the same way through *sunthēmata*, in the same way the Gods stir up our understanding to a greater sharpness by the same means" (*DM* 136, 6–10).

Finally, Iamblichus says the Egyptians imitated the nature of the universe and the creation of the gods through their use of noetic images (*eikones*) (*DM* 249, 14–250, 7). For Iamblichus, the Egyptian cult served as a model for theurgy because of its imitation of cosmogenesis. The hieroglyphic symbols were images of creative powers, the same powers that effected the soul's return to the gods. The *eikones* of the Egyptian cult, like the *sunthēmata* of theurgy, performed a cosmogonic function. Iamblichus uses the verb "to impress" (*apotupein*) to describe Egyptian cosmogenesis,[4] following

---

4. At *DM* 65, 10, to reveal the Forms in images; at 135, 5, to stamp out the character of the Demiurge; and again at 250, 5, to reveal the Forms in images.

Plato, who says the Demiurge perfected the world by "impressing (*apotupoumenos*) living creatures according to the nature of the paradigm" (*Tim.* 39e, 6–7). For Iamblichus the living *eikones* impressed by the Demiurge were simultaneously cosmogonic and anagogic.

The *sunthēmata* and *sumbōla* of theurgy functioned in a manner similar to Plato's Forms in that both revealed the divine order. According to Plato, however, only the Form of Beauty is sensibly revealed, and therefore it is Beauty that instigates man's *anamnēsis* of the gods (*Phaedrus* 250, b–d). Significantly, in Proclus's theory of prayer, where he purports to explain the view of Iamblichus (*In Tim.* I, 209, 11), *sunthēmata* are described as

> the material causes (*hulikai aitiai*; *In Tim.* I, 213, 16) [of prayer], implanted in the essences of souls by the Demiurge for their recollection (*anamnēsis*) of the Gods who made them and of other [divine] things. (*In Tim.* I, 213, 16–18)

Common to Beauty and to theurgic *sunthēmata* was the *erōs* that initiated the soul's divinization. In Chapter 13, I suggested that the *erōmenoi* of the *Symposium* and the *sunthēmata* of theurgy were functionally equivalent. Both revealed divinity to the soul at its level of attraction, and both initiated its ascent to the gods. If *sunthēmata* may be equated with the Forms of Plato, they should especially be associated with the Form of Beauty for, like Beauty, *sunthēmata* were revealed to the senses and through the sanctification of the senses the *sunthēmata*—like expressions of Beauty—gradually led the soul back to the highest level as the soul elevated its *erōs* for the Good.

Posing the question of what relation theurgic *sunthēmata* have to the Platonic Forms, Andrew Smith acknowledges their similarity but distinguishes the *sunthēmata* and *sumbōla* by noting that they "*perfect* the cosmos rather than simply *enform* it."[5] Smith explains that for Proclus the *sunthēmata* tend to express more the anagogic

---

5. Smith cites Proclus *In Tim.* I, 161, 10; see Smith, *Porphyry's Place in the Neoplatonic Tradition: A Study in Post-Plotinian Neoplatonism* (The Hague: Martinus Nijhoff, 1974), 107 n.11.

than emanative power of the Forms, and he says this distinction is also present in the *De Mysteriis* where Iamblichus asserts the "analogy" but not identity between the *sunthēmata* and the Forms (*Porphyry's Place*, 107 n. 11).

Smith's distinction is correct, yet it may be developed further. Since Iamblichus asserts that questions may be discussed in a philosophical, theological, or theurgical manner, it is possible to see the cosmological description of the Forms as proper to a philosophic discourse while an anagogic description would stress the theurgic function of the Forms as *sunthēmata*. In other words, although every soul was created by the Demiurge with "harmonic ratios" (*logoi harmonikoi*) (*In Tim.* I, 4, 32), and "divine symbols" (*sumbōla theia*; *In Tim.* I, 4, 32–33), the former were active in all souls by virtue of cosmogenesis while the latter remained inactive until awakened in theurgy. Thus, when the *logoi* that constitute the soul's essence were ritually appropriated and awakened in the life of the soul, these *logoi* could then be called *sumbōla* or *sunthēmata*.

Friedrich Cremer argues that theurgic *sunthēmata* were charged with demiurgic will, and he contends that Iamblichus's source for this understanding was the Chaldean Oracles.[6] Cremer's first point is indisputable, but I believe he exaggerates Iamblichus's dependence on the Oracles for this teaching. The notion of the "beneficent (*aphthonos*) will" of the Demiurge was already described by Plato in the *Timaeus* (29e) as the primary cause for creation. This was a Platonic topos and had been developed by Middle Platonists in their description of the Forms as the "thoughts" of the Father. In the hieratic discourse of the Oracles these "thoughts" were translated into *sunthēmata* and *sumbōla*, charged with divine will. Iamblichus says that despite the variety of these symbols the Demiurge contains them all undividedly: "he contains the signs within himself, has comprehended them in unity, and creates them from himself *according* to one will" (*DM* 141, 11–13).

If the generosity of the Platonic Demiurge was the cause for creation, it follows that this will was immanent throughout his

---

6. Cremer, *Die Chaldaïschen Orakel und Jamblich de Mysteriis* (Meisenheim am Glan: Anton Hain, 1969), 106–11.

creation. As Proclus put it, the world was *contained* within his will (cf. *In Tim.* I, 209, 13–210, 4). When the Platonic Forms were transformed by Middle Platonists into the "thoughts" of the Creator and these, in turn, were understood to be "powers" extending into the cosmos, it was perhaps inevitable that these demiurgic powers would be "discovered" in their manifest expressions and adapted in some manner to benefit embodied souls. Theurgy and the doctrine of divine *sunthēmata* was the practical culmination of this development, and it is one that Iamblichus believed to be entirely Platonic.

The hieratic function of *sunthēmata* in the noetic, material, and intermediate realms reinforced the connection between the highest and lowest levels and communicated the demiurgic will to every part of the world where the soul was bound. Iamblichus says: "The abundance of power of the highest beings has the nature always to transcend everything in this world, and yet this power is immanent in everything equally without impediment. According to this principle, therefore, first beings illuminate the last, and immaterial beings are present in material natures, immaterially" (*DM* 232, 11–16). In his explanation of prayer Proclus repeats this principle almost verbatim. He says that although the procession from the gods is carefully graded, the gods contain everything "directly" (*autothen*; *In Tim.* I, 209, 17–18): "for the divine is separate from nothing, but is present equally (*ex isou*) to all" (*In Tim.* I, 209, 19–20). Hieratic Neoplatonists believed that *sunthēmata* had a twofold function. They remained "equally" (*ex isou*) in the gods because they were all "vertically" rooted in their causal power, yet each also had a "horizontal" identity in its respective order in the cosmos (*In Tim.* I, 210, 12–20). Since each god had a specific cosmic function, its *sunthēmata* bore its identifying marks in their respective (horizontal) realms of expression and possessed a special intimacy with others marked by the same god.

In *On the Hieratic Art* Proclus explains that the relationship between the *sunthēmata* tied to the same deity was not based on natural power but on the degree of participation in their ruling god. For example, in the case of lions and cocks, which are both solar animals, Proclus says:

Indeed, it is amazing how things that are lesser in natural power and size are fearful to those greater than them in both attributes. For they say the lion draws back from the cock. The cause for this may not be grasped from the physical senses but from intuitive observation and from the differences among the causes. For the symbol of solar qualities is certainly more actively present in the cock [than in the lion].[7]

The "things below," Iamblichus says, are connected to "divine causes," yet, as Proclus explains, the relationship between sensible symbols was determined by the degree of "verticularity" that each actualized. This would explain Iamblichus's hierarchy of human souls: the more active the god in a soul, the higher the soul's spiritual rank. In addition, human souls under a hermetic, solar, or lunar order had a special affinity for the plants, animals, and stones associated respectively with Hermes, Helios, or Selene (*In Tim.* I, 210). As cause of a specific order, the god contained all its symbols and the theurgist had to re-create the entire collection in his ritual. Therefore, theurgists observed the natural properties of things in order to identify their gods and to gather the appropriate objects when invoking a specific deity. Proclus says: "Hence, in the mixture of many things the theurgists united the aforementioned [divine] emanations and made the unity derived from many things resemble that unity which is whole prior to the many" (*CMAG* VI, 150, 28–30). Without this collection of things, each of which "bears a certain characteristic of the god" (*CMAG* VI, 150, 27), Proclus says the theurgist could not invoke him. This follows Iamblichus's teaching that one must honor all the powers or the gods will not be reached (*DM* 228, 19–229, 7). One could not ascend to the undivided deity through only one of its parts or divisions.

The fragmentation of material souls required a corresponding multiplicity in their worship. Material souls had to gather a multitude of objects to represent and contain their own dividedness. To consecrate a statue, worshipers collected various objects through which they could invoke the deity. The statue was a mean that func-

---

7. Proclus, *Peri tes kath' Hellenas Hieratikēs Technēs* [On the hieratic art of the Greeks], in *CMAG*, 6:150, 5–10.

tioned both as a projection of the soul's powers and as an image of the powers of the god revealed in single coherent form.[8] To ensure the effectiveness of the rite the objects had to be fitting (*prosēkon*) to the god invoked and to the material attachment of the soul. These collections formed "receptacles" (*hupodochai*) for the gods and Iamblichus says that theurgists created them with "stones" (*lithoi*), "herbs" (*botanai*), "animals" (*zōa*), "aromatics" (*arōmata*), and other sanctified objects (*DM* 233, 9–12) that possessed intimate affiliations with the gods invoked. These material objects were necessary for worship and therefore Iamblichus warns Porphyry that

> one ought not to despise all matter, only matter that is estranged from the Gods, for matter that is related to them should be chosen since it is able to be in harmony with the shrines built to the Gods, the erecting of statues, and also with the holy acts of sacrifices. For there is no other way that places on earth or men who dwell in them might receive participation in the Superior Beings unless a foundation of this kind is first established.[9]

The objects and shapes used to erect a temple or consecrate a statue had to possess *sunthēmata* of the god invoked or theurgic contact would not be effected. In addition to the objects listed above Iamblichus refers to the use of "batons" (*rabdoi*), "pebbles" (*psephidia*; *DM* 141, 14), and "incense" (*aroma*; *DM* 233, 13–16) to awaken corresponding *sunthēmata* in the soul, and a form of theurgic divination called "light-gathering" (*phōtagōgia*) employed "water" (*hudor*; *DM* 134, 2–3) and "walls" (*toichoi*; *DM* 134, 2–7) as media for light. Iamblichus's most extensive discussion of a material *sunthēma* concerned the vernal rites of erecting phalli whose worship introduced man to cosmogonic action. He says: "Speaking of particular things, we say that the erection of phalli is a *sunthēma*

8. For a discussion of the telestic branch of theurgy that awakens the "divine statue" in the soul see Pierre Boyance, "Théurgie et téléstique néoplatoniciennes," *Revue de L'Histoire des Religions* 147 (1955): 189–209.

9. DM 233, 17–234, 7. Proclus maintained that theurgic statues revealed the properties of the gods through their shapes, signs, postures, and expressions; Proclus, *A Commentary on the First Book of Euclid's Elements*, trans. with introduction and notes by Glenn R. Morrow (Princeton: Princeton University Press, 1970), 110–11.

of generative power, and we believe this act calls out for the fecundation of the cosmos. Hence, most are offered in the spring, precisely when the entire cosmos receives from the Gods the germination of the whole natural world" (*DM* 38, 14–39, 3). The obscenities uttered during this rite also had a psychagogic function. Iamblichus continues:

> In my view the obscene words spoken indicate the privation of beauty in matter and of the antecedent state of deformity in things about to be brought into cosmic order. The entities in need of being ordered yearn [for it] proportionately more as they despise more the ugliness in themselves. Again, therefore, they pursue the causes of the forms and of beauty after they have learned about ugliness from the uttering of obscenities. The execution of base actions is averted, yet by means of verbal expressions the knowledge of it is revealed, and they turn their desire to the opposite [of what is base]. (*DM* 39, 3–13)

Iamblichus employed Aristotle's theory of catharsis to explain the psychological effects of phallus rituals (*DM* 39, 14–40, 8), for he believed that the experience of the embodied soul was vicariously portrayed in the rite. Estranged from its own divinity, the soul—like chaotic matter—was deprived of beauty, and the obscenities shouted in the ritual allowed the soul to recognize its ugliness apart from the divine. This recognition awakened the soul's desire (*ephesis*) for the divine, and the erect phallus—as *sunthēma*—was an image of that desire.[10]

The participant in the rite did not literally worship a phallus but the divine power of fecundation. In other words, the erect phallus functioned as an intermediary to the divine, a *sunthēma* of the god. As Julian explains in his *Letter to a Priest*: "Our fathers established images and altars, and the maintenance of undying fire, and all such things, in a word, as symbols of the abundant presence of the Gods, not that we may regard these things as Gods, but that we

---

10. The recognition of one's "ugliness," like the recognition of one's "nothingness" (*oudeneia*) in prayer (*DM* 47, 17), caused the soul to yearn more intensely for the divine.

may worship the Gods through them (*di' autōn*)."[11] The horizontal sympathy that the soul shared with a symbol became the foundation through which its vertical power was received, and any ritual that stopped at the horizontal level of *sumpatheia* and did not "preserve the analogy with divine creation" (*DM* 168, 13–16) was not theurgy at all, but sorcery (*goēteia*). Theurgic activity was always—in *analogia*—cosmogonic activity, and Iamblichus condemned sorcery specifically because it did not share in the creative generosity of the gods: "If some of those [sorcerers] who perform invocations make use of natural or corporeal powers of the universe, the influence (*dōsis*)[12] of the energy, in itself, is involuntary and without evil, but he who uses it perverts the influence to a contrary purpose and to base things" (*DM* 193, 15–18). Although the influence of the material gods was universal and worked on the principle of like to like (*di' homoiotēta*; *DM* 193, 18–19), the sorcerer "directs this gift toward base things according to his will and contrary to justice" (*DM* 194, 1–2). Iamblichus continues:

> The influence [from the Gods] causes things that are furthest apart to move together according to the one harmony of the cosmos, but if someone who understands this tries to draw certain parts of the universe to other parts in a perverse way the parts are in no way the cause of the perversion but the audacity of men and their transgression of the order in the cosmos, perverting things which are beautiful and lawful. (*DM* 194, 2–7)

The perversity of the sorcerer returned to himself:

> If anyone takes the things that contribute properly to the perfection of the universe and diverts them to another purpose and illegitimately achieves something, the damage from what he has evilly used will fall on him personally. (*DM* 182, 13–16)

---

11. Julian, *Letter to a Priest* 292ab, in *The Works of the Emperor Julian*, 3 vols., ed. W. C. Wright (Cambridge: Harvard University Press, 1969); cf. 294c: "When we look at the images of the god, let us not indeed think they are stones or wood, but neither let us think they are the gods themselves."

12. *dōsis*, "influence" or "gift," refers to the beneficent emanations that come to man from the gods; cf. *DM* 29, 13–15.

16

Intermediate Sunthēmata— Seeing and Hearing the Gods

Sounds and melodies are conse-crated to each one of the Gods…

B ecause intermediate souls performed a combination of noetic and material rites, they necessarily employed material *sunthē-mata*. Indeed, material *sunthēmata* would not have been inappropriate for purely noetic souls either since material rites were guided by the same gods and, by *analogia*, in the same way as noetic rites. Nevertheless, there are forms of worship discussed in the *De Mysteriis* that exhibit less material characteristics than those discussed previously, and for heuristic purposes the objects used in these rites will be designated as "intermediate *sunthēmata*." These were the visible and audible *sunthēmata* that Iamblichus described in the *De Mysteriis* as hieratic characters, symbols, names, and musical compositions. Although the designation "intermediate" is my own, I believe the distinction is consistent with Iamblichus's thought. Following Iamblichus's principle that the law of worship derived from the order of the gods, the visible and audible symbols mediated between immaterial and material realms just as liberated gods mediated between the hypercosmic and encosmic realms. Incantations and hieroglyphics did not draw directly from the material order like plants, animals, or stones, yet neither were they wholly immaterial. They were intermediate and remained material to the degree that they had a sensible expression.

It is important not to misunderstand this distinction. It does not mean that the unity of the gods was less present in a stone because it was materially more dense. Iamblichus's division of *sunthēmata* was based on the needs of souls, not on the degree of divinity in the ritual objects. A soul already justified with material daimons and encosmic gods, for example, still had to sanctify its dianoetic capacities. For such a soul, following the homeopathic principle described in Chapter 4, the cure for its disorder was found in the disordered elements themselves, and this called for *sunthēmata* more akin to dianoetic activity. In short, the symbolic vehicle for a soul's purification had to be suited to the specific needs of that soul, and if the soul was ready for contact with the intermediate gods, it called for rites and *sunthēmata* of an intermediate order.

Iamblichus speaks of diviners who invoke the gods with "characters" (*charaktēres*) sketched on the ground and says that they should follow a carefully prescribed order of worship (*DM* 129, 14–131). Further, in his explanation of divinization effected through the medium of light (*phōtagōgia*), Iamblichus says that theurgic contact may be awakened when light is cast on a wall prepared "with sacred inscriptions of characters" (*DM* 134, 4–6). Although he does not describe these characters in any detail, Proclus, in his commentary on the *Timaeus*, says the chi (X) (*Tim.* 36b) was the "character" (*charactēr*) or "shape" (*schēma*) most evocative for recollecting the divinization of the world and our souls (*In Tim.* II, 247, 14–29). The *charactēres* mentioned by Iamblichus probably included this X and other symbols that corresponded to the planetary gods.[1] Subsequent Arabic Hermeticists describe such planetary "characters" and claimed that their science derived from theurgists.[2]

Iamblichus provides an explicit account of visible *sunthēmata* in his exegesis of Egyptian symbols. He explains that since Egyptian symbols originate with the gods, they cannot be understood discur-

1. See Dodds, *The Greeks and the Irrational* (Berkeley and Los Angeles: University of California Press, 1951), 292; cf. F Dornsieff, *Das Alphabet in Mystik und Magie*, 2d ed. (Leipzig: B.G. Teubner, 1925), 35.

2. See, for example, the writings of Ibn Wahshiya, *The Long-Desired Knowledge of Secret Alphabets Finally Revealed*, in *La Magie arabe traditionnelle*, ed. René Alleau, introduction and notes by Sylvain Matton (Paris: Retz, 1977), 132–241.

sively or in terms of human imagination. Here Iamblichus follows Plotinus who praised the Egyptians for having developed a mode of communication superior to discursive thought. For Plotinus the "images" (*agalmata*) engraved on the walls of Egyptian temples "manifest the non-discursiveness of the intelligible world" (*Enn.* V, 8, 6, 8–9), and he compared them to the "spectacles" viewed by the gods, i.e., to the divine Forms, real and not imagined (*Enn.* V, 8, 5, 20–25).

Fig. 1. The sun god as a child seated on the primeval lotus (first century B.C.E.)

The first Egyptian symbol Iamblichus describes is a god seated on a lotus (see Fig. 1).[3] Iamblichus begins with the "mud" (*ilus*) in which the lotus was rooted. For Iamblichus "mud" represented matter and all that is corporeal, nutritive, generated, and subject to change (*DM* 250, 17–251, 3). Mud was the "primordial cause" (*archēgon aition*; *DM* 251, 5) of the elements and was therefore pre-established as their "foundation" (*puthmen*) (*DM* 251, 5). The god of generation, however, wholly transcended his material powers. He was "immaterial" (*ahulos*), "incorporeal" (*asōmatos*), "supernatural" (*huperphuēs*), and "ungenerated" (*agennētos*; 251, 8–9). This god "contains all things" (*DM* 251, 11–12) though he remains "separate" (*chōristos*; *DM* 251, 14) and elevated above the mundane elements. This condition, Iamblichus says, is represented by his being seated on a lotus that separates him from the "mud." The lotus, therefore, functioned as the intermediary between the transcendent god and the material world, and Iamblichus says its circularity represented the god's intellectual empire for the circle was the image of the *Nous* (*DM* 252, 2–6).

3. See Erik Hornung, *Conceptions of God in Ancient Egypt: The One and the Many*, trans. John Baines (Ithaca: Cornell University Press, 1982), 145–46, 271 fig. 16.

Iamblichus's exegesis of this symbol outlines the itinerary of the embodied soul. Material and corporeal concerns were first balanced to establish a proper foundation (mud); the soul's intellectual capa-

Fig. 2.

cities were then rectified (made circular) to create a receptacle sufficient to seat (i.e., activate) the anterior presence of the god. The hieroglyph symbolically portrayed the entire cycle of embodiment.

The second Egyptian symbol discussed by Iamblichus portrays a god sailing in a barge (see Fig. 2),[4] which represented the god that guides the material world while remaining *chōristos* (*DM* 252, 13). He identifies this god with the sun, Helios: "Thus, *Hēlios, being separate, governs the tiller of the entire cosmos*" (*DM* 252, 15–16). The sun played a central role in the theurgic cult. For Iamblichus, its light-giving power was far more than a conceptual analogue of the noetic Demiurge, it was a *sunthēma* of the One itself. The importance of Helios in the Neoplatonism of Emperor Julian testifies to its importance in the Iamblichean school, and the solar motif also reappears in Iamblichus's remarks on audible symbols.

The visible "characters" of the planetary gods invoked in theurgic ritual had their audible counterparts. Consider, for example, the following rules for composing theurgic hymns:

> 1. Find out what powers and effects any particular star has in itself, what positions and aspects, and what these remove and produce. And insert these into the meanings of our lyrics, detesting what the stars remove and approving what they produce.

---

4. S.G.F. Brandon, *Man and God in Art and Ritual* (New York: Scribner, 1975), 144, fig. 178 "Atum-Re in solar boat."

2. Consider which star chiefly rules which place and man. Then observe what modes these regions and persons generally use, so that you may apply similar ones, together with the meaning first mentioned, to the word which you wish to offer to these same stars.

3. The daily positions and aspects of the stars are to be noticed; then investigate to what speech, songs, movements, dances, moral behavior and actions most men are usually incited under those aspects, so that you may make every effort to imitate these in your songs, which will agree with the similar disposition of the heavens and enable you to receive a similar influx from them.[5]

These principles for invoking the gods were written by Marsilio Ficino, the fifteenth-century leader of the Platonic Academy in Florence. Following Iamblichus, he says that his invocations were not attempts to compel the gods[6] but to allow men to "imitate them" and share in their divine activity.[7]

Ficino reports that his celestial music derived from "the Ancients," among whom he includes Iamblichus,[8] and though Ficino's explanation of the effects of these rites differs somewhat from that of Iamblichus,[9] their principles were nearly identical. Consider, for example, Iamblichus's description of the divinizing effects of theurgic music. Refuting Porphyry's suggestion that theurgic hymns worked on the passions, he says:

5. Ficino, *Opera Omnia*, 2 vols. (Basel, 1576; reprint, Turin, 1962), 562–63; translated by D. P. Walker, *Spiritual and Demonic Magic from Ficino to Campanella* (London: Warburg Institute, University of London, 1958; Liechtenstein: Klaus Reprint, 1976), 17.

6. Walker, *Spiritual and Demonic Magic*, 42.

7. Ficino, *Opera Omnia*, 562; cf. Walker, *Spiritual and Demonic Magic*, 16–17; cf. *Marsilio Ficino: The Book of Life*, trans. Charles Boer (Irving, Tex.: Spring Publications, 1980), 160–61.

8. Boer, trans. *Marsilio Ficino*, 150ff.

9. Ficino, unlike Iamblichus, says these rites have an effect only on the human soul. Faced with the charge of attempting to compel angels or, worse yet for Ficino, "demons," he argues that the rites change only the soul by accommodating it to the divine powers. Iamblichus says nearly the same, but because for him theurgy is not merely psychological he says that what is awakened in the rites is not the soul, but the "one in the soul," which, collectively, are the various *sunthēmata*.

Rather, we say that sounds and melodies are consecrated to each of the Gods in a proper way and that a natural alliance (*sungeneia*) has been suitably allotted to these [planetary] Gods according to the particular orders and powers of each, the motions of the universe itself, and the harmonious whirring sounds emitted by their motions. Then, by means of such melodies adapted to the Gods, their divinity becomes present (for there is nothing at all to stop it). So, whatever happens to possess a likeness to the Gods directly participates in them; a perfect possession immediately takes place and the [experience of] being filled with the essence and power of a Higher Being. (*DM* 118, 6–119, 9)

Iamblichus emphasizes that although this possession manifested through bodily organs and emotions, it was not caused by somatic conditions. He says:

It is not that the body and soul are in sympathy with each other and are together affected by the melodies. Rather, because *the inspiration of the Gods is not separate from the divine harmony, and since it has been adapted to it from the beginning*, it is participated by it in the appropriate measures. And the awakening of this inspiration as well as its ceasing occurs in accordance with each order of the Gods. (*DM* 119, 9–15)

The divine inspiration (*epinoia*) or possession (*katochē*) could not occur unless the soul already possessed measures that corresponded "horizontally" to the audible melodies and "vertically" to their inaudible principles. Musical theurgy was a form of *anamnēsis* that awakened the soul to its celestial identity with the gods. It was not, Iamblichus argues, a way to purge the soul of psychological or somatic disorders,[10] for it affected the soul at a level that preceded its embodiment. Musical theurgy came from the gods and gave the soul direct contact with them. Iamblichus says:

Indeed, before the soul gave itself to the body, it heard the divine harmony plainly. Therefore, after it departs into a body and hears the sort of melodies that especially preserve the trace of the divine harmony, it welcomes these and recollects (*anamimnēsketai*) the divine harmony from them. It is drawn to this, makes itself at

---

10. An explanation adopted by Dodds, *The Greeks and the Irrational*, 79, 98.

home with it, and partakes of it as much as possible. (*DM* 120, 7–14)

According to Iamblichus, Pythagoras was the first composer of this anagogic music. Pythagoras's special gifts[11] allowed him to "thread his intellect into the divine harmony of the stars" (*VP* 36, 18) where he was "assimilated to the heavens" (*VP* 37, 10–11), heard its ineffable harmony, and re-created its audible "traces" for the disciples of his school.

The sacred names and incantations used in theurgic invocations also originated from the gods, and Iamblichus says the Egyptian prophet Bitys revealed "the name of the god that pervades the entire cosmos" (*DM* 268, 2–3). This recalls Chaldean fragment 37 where the Paternal *Nous* "sounded forth (*rhoizein*)" the multiform Ideas. The term *rhoizos*, "whirring" or "rushing," was used by Iamblichus to describe the sound of the divine harmony (*DM* 119, 3), and Chaldean fragment 146 uses the same term. It speaks of "formless fire, from which a voice (*phonē*) is sent forth . . . a sumptuous light (*phōs*) rushing (*rhoizaion*) like a spiral round the earth."[12] For the soul to make its ascent to the gods the Oracles say that it had to recover the audible *sumbōla* sent from the Father by giving them expression, through "speaking a word."[13]

For Iamblichus the god whose "name" pervaded the cosmos was Helios, yet because the recipients of "the undivided gift of the god" (*DM* 253, 14) were themselves divided, they received and expressed it in different ways. Iamblichus says:

11. *VP* 36, 17–18. Iamblichus refers to a "certain ineffable divinity" (*arrhētos tis theiotēs*).

12. *CO*, Frag. 146, 105.

13. *CO*, Frag. 109; 158–59a. In his commentary on the *Alcibiades* Proclus says: "The secret names of the gods have filled the whole world, as the theurgists say; and not only this world, but also all the powers above it . . . since the 'mediating name that leaps into the boundless worlds' has received this function. The gods, then, have filled the whole world both with themselves and with their names"; *Commentary on the First Alcibiades of Plato*, ed. L.G. Westerink (Amsterdam: North-Holland, 1954), 150, 10–15; trans. W. O'Neill (1965, 1971), 99. Proclus adds that this "naming power" is perversely reflected in every man's desire to have the world impressed with his own "name" and power (150, 8–10).

These multiform powers are received from *Hēlios* according to the unique movements of the recipients, and because of this, the symbolic teaching means to show that God remains one through the multitude of his gifts and through the diversity of powers he proves his one power. Hence, this doctrine says God remains one and the same and it assumes that his changes of form and shifting aspects occur in the recipients. (*DM* 253, 15–254, 3)

Iamblichus refers here to the movement of the sun through the signs of the zodiac. They exist, he says, through receiving the "powers descending from *Hēlios*."[14] Man's prayers must therefore be presented to Helios through the many zodiacal *schēmata* that the god assumes. Iamblichus says: "The Egyptians employ these sorts of prayers to *Hēlios* not only in their visions but also in their more ordinary prayers that have this same kind of meaning, and they are offered to God according to this symbolic mystagogy" (*DM* 254, 6–10).

The names used in these prayers were *sunthēmata* of the gods and they functioned in the same manner as stone, plant, or musical *sunthēmata*. Iamblichus explains that despite the prima facie meaning of the term, invocations do not, in fact, "invoke" the gods or call them down. On the contrary, they "evoke" the divine *sunthēmata* lying in the human soul:

> It does not, as the name [*prosklēsis*; *DM* 42, 6] seems to indicate, incline the intellect of the Gods to men, but according to the truth itself—as it means to teach—*the invocation makes the intelligence of men fit to participate in the Gods*, elevates it to the Gods, and harmonizes it with them through orderly persuasion. Whence, indeed, the names of the Gods are adapted to sacred concerns, and with the other divine *sunthēmata* they are anagogic and have the power to unite these invocations to the Gods. (*DM* 42, 9–17)

Iamblichus says the names of the gods were impressed on souls before birth and that theurgic chants awakened them. As Trouillard puts it, "le nom prononcé devient, pour ainsi dire, le symbole efficace

---

14. *DM* 253, 6. In the same way Iamblichus says human souls exist by virtue of gazing on (receiving) the gods (*DM* 8, 13–14).

d'un vertu divine."[15] The "names" of the gods, in effect, defined transforming experiences in the soul. Paraphrasing Proclus, Trouillard writes:

> Les dieux, comme Zeus, Poseidon ou Hermès, personnifient des théophanies qui sort des révélations diverses de la même divinité. Celle-ci, étant au-dela de la lumière elle-même, se devoilera sous des aspects divers par autant de systèmes expressifs dont chacun sera présidé par un dieu. Les noms des dieux ne sort pas des attributs divines proprement dits, mais *les modes selon lesquels l'efficacité divine retentit en nous.*[16]

In his *Timaeus* commentary Iamblichus said the paternal Demiurge (the hidden sun) contained the intelligible (i.e., hypercosmic) realm, just as Helios contained the encosmic powers of the zodiac. Their power was transmitted in theurgic invocations by awakening the corresponding Helios/Demiurge in the soul. Since "naming," "thinking," and "creating" were one and the same activity for the gods,[17] theurgic naming allowed souls to experience the thinking/ creating of the gods. Theurgic naming was equivalent to primordial demiurgy, articulating the powers of the paternal Father through his audible *sunthēmata*.[18] By reciting the *agalmata* of the gods the theurgist was assimilated to their order and the silence that contained them (cf. Proclus, *In Crat.* 32, 18–25; 59, 1–8).

---

15. J. Trouillard, "Âme et esprit selon Proclos," *Revue des Etudes Augustiniennes* 1 (1959): 11.

16. Ibid., 10.

17. *In Crat.* 33, 7–13; *In Platonis Cratylum Commentaria*, ed. G. Pasquali (Leipzig: Teubner, 1908).

18. Cf. J. Trouillard, "L'Activité onomastique selon Proclos," *Entretiens*, 250.

17

Intermediate
Sunthēmata—
Naming the
Gods

We Egyptians do not use words,
but sounds...

O
ne might assume, with Porphyry, that since "names" fall
within the order of discourse they would have discursive
meanings, so he asked why theurgists recited "names without meaning" (*ta asēma onomata*; DM 254, 15). Iamblichus replied
contentiously that such names "are not meaningless" (*ta de ouk
estin asēma*; DM 254, 16) even if they are "unknowable" (*agnōsta*) to
us: "to the Gods, however, they are all meaningful, but not in a way
that can be described, or in a manner that is significant or indicative to men through their imaginations" (*DM* 254, 18–255, 3). These
names, he continues, were revealed through the intellect of the gods
or remained completely ineffable (*aphthengtos*) and intelligibly
united with them (*DM* 255, 4–6). Therefore, Iamblichus says:

> It is necessary to remove all conceptions and logical deductions
> from divine names, and to remove as well the physical imitations
> of the voice naturally akin to the things in nature. Rather, it is the
> symbolic character of divine resemblance, intellectual and divine,
> that must be accepted in the case of divine names. [*DM* 255, 6–
> 11] ... even if it is unknowable to us, *this very thing is its most ven-*
> *erable aspect.* (*DM* 255, 11–13)

If divine names, like other names, were conceptually knowable
they would possess the same properties as human thoughts; Por-

phyry's interest in their "meaning," therefore, was characteristically anthropocentric and misguided. It was equivalent to seeing herbal *sunthēmata* as food, or mineral *sunthēmata* as building material. In short, Porphyry was caught up in the horizontal expression of the nominal *sunthēmata*, and since he saw no meaning in the names, he questioned their value. For Iamblichus, however, their ineffability was their "most venerable" (*to semnotaton*) aspect because it awakened the ineffable presence of the divine in the soul. Thinking, by itself, could not achieve this. As Iamblichus says:

> Whence indeed, the divine causes are not called into activity prompted by our thoughts. Rather our thoughts and all the noble dispositions of the soul, as well as our purity, should be considered as auxiliary causes, but the things that truly excite the divine will are the divine *sunthēmata* themselves. And so the causes from the Gods are activated by the Gods themselves, who accept nothing for themselves from their inferiors as cause of their own proper activity. (*DM* 97, 11–19)

Sunthēmata were the "wild cards" in Iamblichus's cosmological deck. They revealed the presence of the gods at any grade of reality since each grade was sustained directly (*autothen*) by them. Yet the ascent of each soul was gradual, and at its particular level of attachment only an encounter with a *sunthēma* from that level allowed the soul to proceed.

With respect to the names used in theurgy Porphyry also asked why the priests prefer barbarian names over "our own." For this Iamblichus says there is a "mystical reason" (*mustikos logos*) (*DM* 256, 5–6): "Because the Gods have taught us that concerning the sacred races such as the Egyptians and Assyrians their entire language is adapted to sacred concerns, and on account of this we believe that it is necessary for us to address the Gods in a language which is connatural (*sungeneia*) to them" (*DM* 256, 6–9). Iamblichus maintained that the Egyptians and Assyrians received the names of the gods through divine revelation, kept them intact and thus connected with the gods who sent them.

Iamblichus opposed Porphyry's suggestion that sacred names could be translated, as if their conceptual meanings were indepen-

dent of their phonetic expressions. This view overlooked the theurgic and "vertical" dimension of the *sunthēmata*. Iamblichus says:

> The situation is not as you have supposed. For if it were according
> to convention (*kata sunthēkēn*) that names were established, it
> would make no difference whether some names were used instead
> of others. But if they are tied to the nature of reality those names
> which are more adapted to it would no doubt be more pleasing to
> the Gods. Indeed, from this, as is reasonable, the language of
> sacred races are preferred over those of other men. (*DM* 257, 3–10)

The translation of "sacred names" would be ineffectual, "for even if
it were possible to translate them, they would no longer hold the
same power" (*DM* 257, 13–15).

The translation of divine names was a much-debated topic in
antiquity, and while the question cannot be treated here in detail it
is worth noting that Iamblichus's *mustikos logos* was shared by Origen, for whom Hebrew was the sacred language, "not concerned
with ordinary, created things, but with a certain mysterious divine
science that is related to the Creator of the universe."[1] And in the
Corpus Hermeticum "Asclepius" warns King Ammon not to translate Egyptian mysteries into Greek:

> For the Greeks, O King, who make logical demonstrations, use
> words emptied of power, and this very activity is what constitutes
> their philosophy, a mere noise of words. But we [Egyptians] do
> not [so much] use "words" (*logoi*), but "sounds" (*phōnai*) which
> are full of effects.[2]

Fragment 150 of the *Chaldean Oracles* puts it very simply: "Do not
change the *nomina barbara*."[3]

In a critical essay on the question of translation Claire Préaux
explains the underlying issue of the debate. "The attitude of religious
communities with regard to translation," she says, "is conditioned by
the degree of rationality that they admit in the relations between

---

1. Origen, *Contra Celsum* (I, 24), trans. Henry Chadwick (New York: Cambridge University Press, 1953; reprint, 1980), 24.
2. *CH* XVI, 2; Nock and Festugière, *Corpus Hermeticum*, 4 vols., trans. A.-J. Festugière, ed. A.D. Nock (Paris: Les Belles Lettres, 1954–60; reprint, 1972–83), 232.
3. *CO*, 107.

man and the divine."[4] Because of the limits of embodiment, Iamblichus allowed human rationality only a small role in these relations. By contrast, Porphyry—with his doctrine of the undescended soul— believed that the exercise of rationality allowed the soul direct access to the divine. Préaux concludes by suggesting that the nontranslators' view of human existence was pessimistic, but in this she fails to see the cosmological affirmation that underlies it, at least in Iamblichus's case. She also overlooks the cosmological pessimism in the translators' view, implied in their devaluation of the sensible expression of the word. For if one adopts the translators' view that the sound of a sacred name is not significant or powerful apart from its conceptual meaning, then the sound as such would be superfluous, and the sensible aspect of the word could be disregarded in favor of its inaudible *logos*. For Iamblichus, however, to deny the value of the god's audible expression would dismiss the *energeia* of the god, and in principle it would deny the value of the entire sensible cosmos as the *energeia* of the Demiurge.[5] The names of the gods were individual theophanies in the same way that the cosmos was the universal theophany, and since both preceded man's conceptual understanding Iamblichus says they should not be changed according to conceptual criteria (*DM* 259, 1–5). Out of the same respect that Iamblichus held for the cosmos as the sensible expression of the Demiurge, he honored the audible manifestations of the gods. The sacred names were "bodies" of the gods that should not be violated by translation.

In contrast to Iamblichus, Proclus believed that several nations possessed divine names, among whom he includes Egyptians, Chaldeans, Indians, and Greeks.[6] Proclus maintains: "Even though God may be called by the Greeks *Briareus* under the influence of the Gods, and is called in another way by the Chaldeans, it must be

---

4. Claire Préaux, "De la Grèce classique à l'Egypte hellénistique: Traduire ou ne pas traduire," *Chronique d'Egypte* 42 (1967): 369–83.

5. As Trouillard explains in his discussion of the Neoplatonic understanding of the revelatory power of the "spoken word": "Mais il ne faut pas oublier qu'un être supérieur ne contient pas en acte les déterminations qui procèdent de lui. En s'exprimant et en se manifestant, il fait de nouveau. Il ne se redouble pas." "L'Activite onomastique selon Proclos," in *Entretiens*, 254.

6. Proclus, *In Cratylum* 32, 5.

understood that each of these names is the offspring of the Gods and signifies the same essence."[7]

The difference between Proclus and Iamblichus on this issue depends on how much emphasis is given to Proclus's phrase: "under the influence of the gods" (*para tōn theōn*). If taken in a strong sense, it puts Proclus in the same camp as Iamblichus with respect to theurgic principles, for it implies that the name Briareus was divinely received by the Greeks, that is to say, in the same manner that the Assyrians and Egyptians received their divine names "having mixed them with their own language" (*DM* 256, 11–13). Iamblichus never argued that there was only one sacred language—after all, this would contradict his own principles by giving universal power to a particular *qua* particular. He argued, rather, that the names of the gods were determined by the gods themselves and established as inviolate. Proclus, for his part, never argued that divine names were changed or even translated; he simply asserted an equivalence between the Greek and the barbarian names of the gods. Where the two clearly part company was in their estimation of the Greeks. The Athenian *diodochos* allowed for a theurgy of names native to the Hellenes while the Syrian Iamblichus polemicized against the Greeks as proponents of undisciplined speculation.[8]

In this regard, Iamblichus followed the Hermetic teachings of the Asclepius tractate and emphasized the stability of the Egyptians against the instability of the Greeks. Because the names used in Egyptian prayers remained unchanged, they were still charged with the unchanging power of the gods. The Greeks, however, lost the power of their prayers through continual innovations.

The contrast is twofold. In general, throughout the *De Mysteriis* Iamblichus contrasted the stability and goodness of the gods with the instability and perversity of men (cf. *DM* 146, 10–12; 144, 12–14; 284, 19–285, 2); more specifically, he opposed sacred races, who humbly preserve rituals given by the gods, to the Greeks and others

7. Ibid., 32, 9–12.

8. Trouillard also points out that for Proclus the *onoma* is distinguished from *phōnē* because the latter functions as *hulē* and the former as *eidos*. "L'activité onomastique," 252–54.

who presumed a creative license about sacred matters. In this regard the Egyptians functioned for Iamblichus as a racial *sunthēma*, and he upbraided Porphyry for thinking that he might be singling them out arbitrarily. There was nothing about the Egyptian language *qua* Egyptian, that made it sacred (i.e., viewed "horizontally" in comparison with other languages), but rather it was because "the Egyptians were the first human beings to be allotted participation in the Gods" (*DM* 258, 3–5), and sustained this connection in their language. It was due to this divine ("vertical") dimension that Iamblichus honored their rituals and language.[9]

Neither Iamblichus nor any of his Platonic successors provide concrete examples of how names, sounds, or musical incantations were used in theurgic rites. There is a great wealth of evidence from nontheurgical circles, however, to suggest that theurgists used the *asēma onomata* according to Pythagorean cosmological theories and a spiritualization of the rules of grammar. In Demetrius's first-century book *On Elocution* he reports: "In Egypt, the priests, when singing hymns in praise of the gods, employ the seven vowels (*phōnetai*), which they utter in due succession."[10] The report is tantalizing but only suggestive. More theoretical evidence for the liturgical chanting of the vowels by theurgists is given by Nicomachus of Gerasa who explains that each of the seven spheres is associated with a tone and a vowel. Nicomachus says:

> Indeed, the tones of the seven spheres, each of which by nature produces a particular sound, are the sources of the nomenclature of the vowels. These are described as unspeakable (*arrhēta*) in themselves and in all their combinations by wise men, since the tone in this context performs a role analogous to that of the monad in number, the point in geometry, and the letter in grammar. However, when they are combined with the materiality of the

9. *Laws* 656d–657b. B. D. Larsen rightly explains that in antiquity it was the common conviction that Greek philosophy derived from Egyptian wisdom. Larsen says that in the role of Abammon, Iamblichus represents Egyptian wisdom answering the questions posed by Greek philosophy, represented by Porphyry. Larsen, *Jamblique de Chalcis: Exégète et philosophie* (Aarhus: Universitetsforlaget, 1972), 150–54.

10. *Demetrius: On Style*, 71, trans. W. Rhys Roberts (Cambridge: Cambridge University Press, 1902), 104, 23–27.

consonants, just as soul is combined with body, and harmony with strings, (the one producing a creature (*zōon*), the other notes and melodies), they have potencies which are efficacious and perfective of divine things. [Thus whenever the *theourgoi* are conducting such acts as worship they make invocations symbolically with hissing, clucking, and inarticulate and discordant sounds].[11]

Hans Lewy suggests that Proclus substituted *theourgoi* for another term or simply added the last sentence, since theurgists were unknown in the first half of the second century c.e.[12] Nevertheless, Nicomachus's association of vowel sounds, the seven spheres, and their power to effect divine things when uttered anticipated the principles of theurgy if not its nomenclature, and Iamblichus was undoubtedly familiar with this teaching. In the *Theology of Numbers*, attributed to Iamblichus, the author describes the attributes of the heptad:

> Seven is also called "voice"[13] because the seven elementary sounds [vowels] exist not only in the human voice but also in the instrumental, the cosmic, and, in short, the *consonant* voice, and not only because of the single and primary sounds emitted from the seven stars—as we have learned—but also because the first scale of the musicians is a heptachord.[14]

---

11. Nicomachus, *Harmonikon Enchiridion*, in C. von Jan, *Musici Scriptores Graeci* (Leipzig, 1895; reprint, Hildesheim, 1962). Gersh, *From Iamblichus to Eriguiena: An Investigation of the Prehistory and Evolution of the Pseudo-Dionysian Tradition* (Leiden: E. J. Brill, 1978), 295.

12. Lewy, *Chaldean Oracles and Theurgy*, ed. M. Tardieu (Paris: Etudes Augustiniennes, 1978), 250 n. 83; cited by Gersh, *An Investigation*, 295.

13. I follow Meurs's addition in the apparatus of *phone de* after *dierei* of line 13.

14. *TA* 71, 13–18. Text: ὅτι οὐ μόνον τῆς ἀνθρωπίνης φωνῆς ἀλλὰ καὶ ὀργανικῆς καὶ κοσμικῆς καὶ ἁπλῶς ἐναρμονίου φωνῆς ζ′ ὑπάρχει τὰ στοιχειώδη φθέγματα, οὐ μόνον παρὰ τὸ ὑπὸ τῶν ζ′ ἀστέρων ἀφίεσθαι μόνα καὶ πρώτιστα, ὡς ἐμάθομεν, ἀλλ' ὅτι καὶ τὸ πρῶτον διάγραμμα παρὰ τοῖς μουσικοῖς ἑπτάχορδον ὑπέπεσεν. [Iamblichus], *Theologumena Arithmeticae*, ed. V. de Falco, 1922; ed. with additions and correction, V. Klein (Stuttgart: Teubner, 1975). Note here Iamblichus's distinction of three kinds of voice: (1) of the spheres: *musica mundana*; (2) of man's body and soul: *musica humana*; and (3) of instruments: *musica instrumentalis*, a distinction that has been attributed to Boethius. Cf. D. P. Walker, *Spiritual and Demonic Magic from Ficino to Campanella* (London: Warburg Institute, University of London, 1958; reprint, Liechtenstein: Klaus Reprint 1976), 14.

Iamblichus cites the authority of Ostanes and Zoroaster to explain the connection of the heptad with planetary angels. The Babylonians, Iamblichus says, call the stars "herds" (*agelai*) because they move together in circles and act as "bonds" (*sundesmoi*) and "collections" (*sunagogai*) of physical ratios. (*TA* 57, 2–3). Since the administration of these ratios was an "angelic" function, Iamblichus notes that with the addition of a *g* these "herds" (*agelai*) were called "angels" (*aggeloi/angeloi*), by the Babylonian priests (*TA* 57, 5). He continues:

> Hence, in a similar way, they call the stars and *Daimones* that rule over each of these herds "Angels" and "Archangels," and these are seven in number. So, according to the truest etymology the hebdomad is called *angelia*.[15]

Iamblichus says the heptad is also called the "Guardian" (*phulakitis*) because the seven starry spheres guard the universe and rule over it with "continuous and everlasting permanence" (*TA* 57, 12).

Iamblichus believed that the seven vowels were connatural (*sungenia*) with the seven planetary gods, and certain Gnostic writings suggest that one-to-one correlations were ritually developed. For example, Valentinus's disciple Marcus associated the vowels with heavenly spheres as follows:

a	first heaven
e	second heaven
ē	third heaven
i	fourth heaven
o	fifth heaven
y	sixth heaven
ō	seventh heaven[16]

---

15. *TA* 57, 6–9. Text: διὸ καὶ τοὺς καθ' ἑκάστην τούτων τῶν ἀγελῶν ἐξάρχοντας ἀστέρας καὶ δαίμονας ὁμοίως ἀγγέλους καὶ ἀρχαγγέλους προσαγορεύεσθαι, οἵπερ εἰσὶν ἑπτὰ τὸν ἀριθμόν, ὥστε ἀγγελία κατὰ τοῦτο ἐτυμώτατα ἡ ἑβδομάς.

16. Irenaeus, *Adv. haerses*, 1, I. C, XIV, P. G., t. VII, col. 610; cited in C. E. Ruelle, "Alphabet vocalique des gnostiques," *Dictionnaire d' archéologie chrétienne et de liturgie* (Paris: Letouzey et Ane, 1907), 1:1268–88.

Ruelle provides examples from the magical papyrus of Leiden that demonstrate how these vowels were used in invocations. The papyrus reads:

> I invoke you Lord, with a chanted hymn, I sing your holy prayer: *A E Ē I O Y Ō Ō Ō*.[17] Your name made up of seven letters in harmony with the seven sounds which have voices (*phōnai*) corresponding to the 28 lights of the moon ("Le chant," 40).

There are numerous other examples of vocalic invocations in the Greek Magical Papyri.[18] The so-called *Mithras Lithurgy* as well as certain Hermetic tractates provide examples of theurgic-like invocations that were certainly known to Iamblichus. This prevalence of *voces mysticae* in the rites of late antique sorcerers probably played a significant role in Iamblichus's defense of theurgy in the *De Mysteriis*. For, as Dodds pointed out, the techniques of the sorcerer and the theurgist would have been indistinguishable to the uninitiated,[19] so Iamblichus had to explain theurgy in a way that was entirely consonant with Platonic philosophy. The *hieratikē technē* of the later Platonists had to be distinguished from sorcery (*DM* 161, 10–16). After all, Iamblichus employed the craft and material of sorcerers, the *asēma onomata* for example, and he probably shared their cosmological assumptions, but in theurgy the purpose of the rite was never to manipulate the gods or call them down. On the contrary, theurgic invocations called souls up to experience the gods.

In a discussion of theurgy's relation to Gnosticism, Birger Pearson suggests that Iamblichus's theories of theurgy might profitably be applied to certain Gnostic texts.[20] Pearson has already shown the

17. Ruelle, "Le Chant des sept voyelles grecques," *Revue des Etudes Grecques* 2 (1889): 40.

18. See Hans Dieter Betz, ed., *The Greek Magical Papyri, Including the Demotic Spells*, vol. 1 (Chicago: University of Chicago Press, 1986).

19. E.R. Dodds, "Supernormal Phenomena in Classical Antiquity," in Dodds, *The Ancient Concept of Progress and Other Essays on Greek Literature and Belief* (Oxford: Clarendon Press, 1973), 200–201.

20. Birger A. Pearson, "Theurgic Tendencies in Gnosticism and Iamblichus' Conception of Theurgy," in *Gnosticism and Neoplatonism*, ed. R.T. Wallis and Jay Bregman (Norfolk, Va.: International Society for Neoplatonic Studies, 1992): 253–75.

decidedly Platonic flavor in some later forms of Gnosticism;[21] so, he argues, there is reason to suspect that certain Gnostics shared the theoretical presuppositions of the Neoplatonists.[22] Since the Gnostics did not provide a theoretical framework to explain their rites and Iamblichus did not provide concrete ritual data, Pearson's study is useful for both scholars of Gnosticism and later Neoplatonism.

Pearson suggests that some Gnostic rites effected the soul's salvation through a simultaneous ascent and descent achieved by chanting the *nomina barbara* and unintelligible vowels. He explains the Gnostic chants with a passage from the *De Mysteriis* where Iamblichus maintains that anagogic rites fulfilled divine law since the purpose of the soul's descent was to reascend.[23]

Since the ascent of the soul was integrally tied to the descent of the gods in cosmogenesis, when the soul chanted the names and vowels associated with the gods it entered their *energeia*. Because the names were divinizing the soul ascended, yet insofar as the soul chanted the names, it descended with them into the sensible world. Since these sounds were the *agalmata* of the gods, when the soul chanted them, it imitated the activity and the will of the Demiurge in creation. In this sense the theurgist did bring the gods down into the world, but he did so at their command and to fulfill their will. This clearly would distinguish theurgy from sorcery, for a theurgic incantation preserved the transcendence and ineffability of the gods while making the soul an embodiment or actualization of their will. Since the soul itself could never grasp or initiate theurgy, the incantation, strictly speaking, was accomplished by the god, yet it freed the soul by allowing it to actively experience what it could never conceptually understand.

Again, theurgical Platonism may be seen as Iamblichus's practical application of Pythagorean theory. Following the rule that first principles contained and yet remained hidden in their pluralities,

21. Pearson, "Gnosticism as Platonism: With Special Reference to Marsanes (NHC 10, 1)," *Harvard Theological Review 77* (1984): 55–72. Pearson, "The Tractate *Marsanes* (NHC X) and the Platonic Tradition," in *Gnosis: Festschrift für Hans Jonas*, ed. Barbara Aland (Göttingen: Vandenhoeck and Ruprecht, 1978), 373–84.

22. Pearson, "Theurgic Tendencies."

23. Ibid.; Pearson quotes from the *DM* 272, 8–12.

the theurgist reached the primordial silence of the One only by embracing the plurality of sounds. Just as the monad was present in multiplicity monadically, preexisting silence was present in the seven sounds silently, and the theurgist entered this silence by chanting/containing the sounds that proceed from it.

In an incantation the theurgist became a citizen of two worlds. On the one hand, he joined the gods through his assimilation to the Demiurge; on the other, he remained mortal due, in part, to the expression of the demiurgic will. Insofar as the theurgist became divine, he commanded the daimons who served the gods, yet he did not command them as a man but as one of the gods. Discussing this double nature of the theurgist Iamblichus says: "According to this distinction, therefore, as is proper, [the theurgist] invokes as his superiors the powers from the universe since the one making the invocation is a man and, on the other hand, he commands them since, somehow, by means of the ineffable symbols, he is invested with the hieratic shape of the Gods" (*DM* 184, 8–13).

18

Noetic
Sunthēmata—
Mathematics
and the Soul

*The soul contains in itself the
sum-total of mathematical reality.*

In the *De Mysteriis*, Iamblichus says he will not discuss noetic
forms of worship; but to pursue the division of *sunthēmata* into
material, intermediate, and noetic categories, I would argue that
the soul's noetic powers would have to be transformed by noetic
objects, and that these would have been best exemplified in numbers. An implicit arithmetic influence is evident already in the intermediate *sunthēmata*, for a numerical framework determines the
composition of theurgic incantations and melodies. Since Iamblichus was a Pythagorean, it seems likely that he would have given
mathematics a central role in the highest form of worship.

That mathematical objects made up the *sunthēmata* of noetic
worship is a supposition that may easily be misunderstood. Iamblichus never states this explicitly, which might be enough to dismiss
the conjecture. I believe, however, that the context of Iamblichus's
thought as demonstrated in relevant citations will bear the supposition out. Far more problematic is our tendency to presume that in
noetic or mathematic theurgy Iamblichus's genuinely Platonic (i.e.,
"rational") teachings may be discerned. In this light, recent studies
of theurgy have argued that the material and intermediate forms of
worship represent Iamblichus's "concession" to the intellectual inad-
equacies of the common man, his effort to save Platonism by creating a salvific cult to rival the increasing popularity of Christianity. In

212

two recent studies, Andrew Smith and Anne Sheppard argue that there was, in fact, a "higher" form of theurgy free from the sinister elements of animal sacrifice, the chanting of *nomina barbara*, and other superstitions. With a more sympathetic approach to Neoplatonic theurgy, they have attempted to save it from the accusations of irrationality by E. R. Dodds and others by dividing theurgy into high and low forms, the former being appropriate for genuinely spiritual and Platonic souls, the latter for the uneducated.[1] Such efforts to render theurgy more intelligible and acceptable to our norms of rationality, however, succeed only in obfuscating the problem.

Our norms of rationality are not the norms of the Neoplatonists. On this issue Jean Trouillard says:

> Dans notre Occident le rationalisme et le primat de la technologie ont tellement imprégné notre mentalité qu'ils sont le plus souvent inconscients. D'ou la difficulté d'entrer dans des pensées comme celle de Proclus, *aussi longtemps que nous tentons de lui appliquer nos modèles d'intelligibilité.*[2]

Trouillard argues here that our belief in the univocity of reason prevents us from grasping the mystagogy of the later Neoplatonists (223). Although they valued clarity and coherence of thought, it was never an end in itself. Yet it is difficult for us to realize that "rational thought" did not have the same value for "Platonists" as it does in our age where reason and mathematics form the bases of our worldview. One must grant to Trouillard the credit for recognizing this. He says: "il faut revenir *à la thèse capitale du néoplatonisme selon laquelle la pensée n'est pas la valeur suprême. Elle est une médiation* entre la dispersion du sensible et la pure coincidence mystique" (83; my emphasis). The function of reason for the Neoplatonists was simply to reveal "*l'Ineffable qui l'habite*" (*La mystagogie*, 233), and

1. For a discussion of recent interpretations of theurgy, particularly those that divide it into "higher" and "lower" forms, see Gregory Shaw, "Rituals of Unification in the Neoplatonism of Iamblichus," *Traditio* 41 (1985): 1–28; A. Smith, *Porphyry's Place*, 32–99; and Anne Shepard, "Proclus' Attiude to Theurgy," *Classical Quarterly* 32 (1982): 212–24.

2. Trouillard, *La Mystagogie de Proclus* (Paris: Les Belles Lettres, 1982), 12 (my emphasis).

rational thought was simply one mode of activity through which a superior intelligence guided and sustained the soul throughout its embodiment.

If mathematic elements functioned for Iamblichus as *sunthēmata* it was not because of their "horizontal" expression as rational formulas. Their intelligibility alone did not make them theurgic but their capacity to create noetic rhythms capable of receiving the gods. Their horizontal expression as intellectual formulas was no more theurgic than the horizontal expression of stones, animals, or songs. Taken as ends in themselves, mathematical formulas were as much obstacles to the soul as the crudest form of fetish worship or passionate obsession. If, as I shall argue, mathematic elements made up the *sunthēmata* of noetic theurgy, they must be understood as ritual objects and according to the same principles as the other *sunthēmata*, "not that we may regard those things as Gods, but that we may worship the Gods *through* them."[3] Despite the cognitive content of mathematics their theurgic function was to transform the soul, not "teach" it.[4]

The importance of mathematics in the Platonic dialogues is unquestioned today. What is unclear, however, as it was even to Plato's students, is the role that mathematics played in their spiritual discipline and how it related to the soul.[5] Mathematic elements are fully evident in the *Timaeus* where the Demiurge creates the World Soul out of geometric, harmonic, and arithmetic proportions. The entire passage from 35a to 35b is based on the *tetraktus*,

3. Julian, *Letter to a Priest* 293ab, in *The Works of the Emperor Julian*, 3 vols., trans. W.C. Wright (Cambridge: Harvard University Press, 1969), 2: 308–9.

4. Cf. Aristotle's remark that the "mysteries" did not teach the soul anything, but made it experience something; Synesius, *Dion* 10, 48a. Similarly, mathematic rituals were not learned or taught but "performed" to effect a transformation of the soul; cf. Aristotle, *Metaphysics* 1051a, 29–31.

5. Aristoxenus's well-known report on Plato's lecture "On the Good" shows how paradoxical and disturbing his listeners found the identification of the "One" and the "Good." The variety of reports on what Plato meant by his mathematizing of the Forms suggests that Plato himself never made this clear to his students or that his explanations allowed for a variety of interpretations; see Aristoxenus, *Elements of Harmony*, II, 30–1, Meibom; see J.N. Findlay, *Plato: The Written and Unwritten Dialogues* (London: Routledge and Kegan Paul, 1974), appendix I, 413.

the Pythagorean symbol for cosmogenesis.[6] Mathematics was central to the educational program of Platonists and each teacher developed his own interpretation of the numerical proportions of the World Soul described by Plato.

In Iamblichus's commentary on the *Timaeus* 35b, for example, he posits that the seven numbers that divide the World Soul—1, 2, 3, 4, 9, 8, 27—had metaphysical functions. Sameness and unity were under the monad, procession under the dyad, and return under the triad. The tetrad functioned as a mean, communicating the primary order to its secondary manifestation, the ennead functioned as a "new monad," the ogdoad as dyadic procession, and the *eikosiheptad* (27) exemplified the power of return. According to Iamblichus the tetrad held the pivotal position of the *mean*. He says: "The Tetrad, being in the middle, through being a square, has the quality of remaining stable; on account of its being even times even, (it has) the quality of proceeding; and through being filled with all the ratios from the monad, (it has) the property of returning. And these are symbols of divine and ineffable things."[7] There were, however, a variety of opinions in the later Academy as to how the soul was defined with regard to the mathematicals.

In the *De Anima* Iamblichus reviews the opinions of those who identified the soul as a "mathematical essence." He lists three positions:

1. *Soul as geometric figure*:
Now, one kind of mathematical essence is the figure (*to schēma*), being the limit of extension and the extension itself. The Platonist Severus defined the soul in these very terms, while Speusippus defined it as the form of that which is extended in all directions. (*Stob*. I, 364, 2–5)

2. *Soul as number*:
Number, therefore, is still another kind of mathematical essence. Indeed, some Pythagoreans find that number without any qualification is a fitting description of the soul: Xenocrates, as "self-

6. Francis M. Cornford, trans. and comm., *Plato's Cosmology: The Timaeus of Plato* (London, 1937; reprint, New York: Bobbs-Merrill, 1959), 66–72.
7. Dillon, *Iamblichi Chalchidensis*, frag. 53, 21–24.

moved" [number]; Moderatus the Pythagorean, as containing [numerical] ratios. (*Stob.* I, 364, 8–11)

3. *Soul as harmony*:

Let us now consider harmony, not that seated in the body, but the mathematical harmony. This latter harmony, in a word, somehow brings things which are disjointed into proportion and connection, and Moderatus equates the soul with this. (*Stob.* I, 364, 19–23)

It is clear that Platonic and Pythagorean philosophers identified the soul with different branches of the mathematicals, and in the *De Anima* Iamblichus leaves the issue unresolved. In his treatise *On General Mathematical Science*, however, he takes up the problem again and attempts to solve it.

It would not be reasonable to posit the soul as being just one class of the mathematicals.... Therefore, the soul, should not be defined either as [1] idea of the all-extended [Speusippus], or as [2] self-moved number [Xenocrates], or as [3] harmony of (numerical) ratios [Moderatus], or as anything else of this kind specifically, but rather, all these should be intertwined together. For if the soul is a numerable idea and subsists according to the numbers containing harmony, all the symmetries of the mathematical order ought to be subsumed together under the soul along with all the mathematical proportions. On account of this, then, the soul coexists together with the geometric, arithmetic and harmonic proportions, so that by analogy the soul is identical with [all] mathematical ratios; it has a certain connaturality (*sungenia*) with the *archai* of existing things; it lays hold of all reality and has the capacity to resemble all things.[8].... To sum up the whole doctrine, we think the soul exists in ratios common with all mathematicals, possessing, on the one hand, the power of discerning them, and on the other hand, the power of generating and producing the incor-

---

8. *DCMS* 40, 12–41, 3. Text: Ἕν μὲν οὖν γένος τῶν ἐν τοῖς μαθήμασιν [τῶν] ὄντων οὐκ ἄν τις αὐτὴν εὐλόγως θείη κατὰ τὴν τοιαύτην ἐπιβολὴν τῆς θεωρίας· μεριστὴ γὰρ ἂν οὕτω γένοιτο ἡ περὶ τῆς μαθηματικῆς οὐσίας γνῶσις. διόπερ οὔτε ἰδέαν τοῦ πάντῃ διαστατοῦ οὔτε ἀριθμὸν αὐτοκίνητον οὔτε ἁρμονίαν ἐν λόγοις ὑφεστῶσαν οὔτε ἄλλο οὐδὲν τοιοῦτο κατ᾽ ἰδίαν ἀφοριστέον περὶ αὐτῆς, κοινῇ δὲ συμπλέκειν

poreal measures themselves, and with these measures the soul has the capacity to fit together the generation and completion of forms in matter by means of images, proceeding from the invisible to the visible, and joining together the things outside with those inside. In view of all this, in brief, the definition of the soul contains in itself the sum-total of mathematical reality.[9]

For Iamblichus, the soul was identified with *all* branches of the mathematicals together, a position that Philip Merlan summed up aptly: "he who says 'soul' expresses mathematics in its fulness";[10] this is particularly so when soul bestows mathematical measures on the material realm.[11]

There is nothing explicitly theurgical in this view of the soul and mathematics. Nevertheless, Iamblichus's description of the soul joining the "inside" with the "outside" by means of mathematical images, parallels the function of ritual *sunthēmata*. While it would be incorrect to conflate theurgy with mathematics, the structural analogy between them is striking, particularly where Iamblichus compares mathematical exercises to a kind of Platonic *anamnēsis*. He says:

πάντα ἄξιον, ὡς τῆς ψυχῆς καὶ ἰδέας οὔσης ἀριθμίου καὶ κατ᾽ ἀριθμοὺς ἁρμονίαν περιέχοντας ὑφεστώσης, πάσας τε συμμετρίας κοινῶς, ὅσαι ποτέ εἰσιν ὑπὸ τὴν μαθηματικήν, ὑπὸ ταύτην ὑποτακτέον, τάς τε ἀναλογίας ὅλας ὑπ᾽ αὐτὴν θετέον. διὰ δὴ τοῦτο γεωμετρικῇ τε ὁμοῦ καὶ ἀρθμητικῇ καὶ ἁρμονικῇ ἀνὰ λογίᾳ συνυπάρχει, ὅθεν δὴ καὶ λόγοις τοῖς κατ᾽ ἀναλογίαν ἡ αὐτή ἐστι, ταῖς τε ἀρχαῖς τῶν ὄντων ἔχει τινὰ συγγένειαν καὶ πάντων ἐφάπτεται τῶν ὄντων καὶ πρὸς πάντα ὁμοιοῦσθαι δύναται. I depended on Merlan's translation of this passage and his commentary: Philip Merlan, *From Platonism to Neoplatonism*, 2d ed. (The Hague: Martinus Nijhoff, 1960), 18–20.

9. *DCMS* 41, 24–42, 6. Text: ἵνα δὲ συνέλωμεν τὴν ὅλην δόξαν, ἐν λόγοις κοινοῖς πάντων τῶν μαθημάτων τὴν ψυχὴν νοοῦμεν οὖσαν, ἔχουσαν μὲν τὸ κριτικὸν αὐτῶν, ἔχουσαν δὲ καὶ τὸ γεννητικόν τε καὶ ποιητικόν αὐτῶν τῶν ἀσωμάτων μέτρων, οἷς καὶ τὴν γενεσιουργίαν δύναταί τις προσαρμόζειν τῶν ἐνύλων εἰδῶν τήν τε δι᾽ εἰκόνων ἀπεργασίαν, ἐκ τῶν ἀφανῶν εἰς τὸ φανερὸν προϊοῦσαν, συνάπτουσάν τε τὰ ἔξω τοῖς εἴσω. κατὰ γὰρ πάντα ταῦτα, ὡς συλλήβδην εἰπεῖν, ὁ τῆς ψυχῆς λόγος περιέχει ἀφ᾽ ἑαυτοῦ τὴν ὅλην τῶν μαθημάτων συμπλήρωσιν.

10. Merlan, *From Platonism to Neoplatonism*, 18.

11. While I agree with Merlan's characterization of the soul and numbers, B.D. Larsen argues that Merlan mistakenly interprets Iamblichus in chapters 9 and 10 of the *DCMS* as identifying the soul with mathematicals as such. Larsen contends that

The soul is raised up to the objects of knowledge from without (*exōthen*), and while it receives from things other [than itself] the beginning of its recollection (*anamnēsis*), it projects (*proballein*) this beginning from itself. This activity is not stable according to one energy—as is the case with the *Nous*—but in movement the soul proceeds out of itself and into itself. Nor, in this, is the soul complete, as is the *Nous*, but in continually seeking and finding the soul proceeds from a lack of knowledge to a fulness thereof. It is divided equally between the limit (*peras*) and the unlimited (*apeiron*). Wherefore, the soul continually advances from the unlimited to being defined and transforms itself for the reception of mathematical figures.[12]

This transformation was more than intellectual because mathematics permeated the soul's entire life (*DCMS* 69, 18–23). In strictly Platonic terms, the soul was a mathematical entity (*Tim.* 34–36; 43–44) and its immortal *ochēma* was also designed according to mathematical ratios. Iamblichus's view of mathematical images as living *logoi* of the *Nous* shares little with our understanding of numbers as

---

this led Merlan to posit two contrasting views in the *DCMS* with respect to the soul and mathematicals. In chapters 3 and 4 Iamblichus clearly does not classify soul and mathematicals under the same genus, while in chapters 9 and 10 he does (see Merlan, *From Platonism to Neoplatonism*, 11–33). The contradiction, according to Merlan, was due to Iamblichus's practice of compiling diverse sources without attempting to make them cohere (151). Larsen, on the other hand, argues that there is no contradiction and that Merlan failed to see that in chapters 3 and 4 Iamblichus spoke "des principes et du domaine ontologique de la mathématique," but in chapters 9 and 10 he spoke of the "application" of numbers as principles of movement, principles bestowed upon living beings by the soul. It is in this latter sense, Larsen argues, that Iamblichus said the soul comprises all the mathematicals and he concludes, "il n'est pas justifié de contester l'unité du livre." B. D. Larsen, *Jamblique de Chalcis: Exégète et philosophe* (Aarhus: Universitetsforlaget, 1972), 125–29.

12. *DCMS* 43, 19–44, 3. Text: ἔξωθεν δὲ διεγείρεται πρὸς τὰς εἰδήσεις, καὶ δεχό-μενον παρ᾽ ἄλλων τὴν ἀρχὴν τῆς ἀναμνήσεως, οὕτως αὐτὴν ἀφ᾽ ἑαυτοῦ προβάλλει· σταθερόν τε οὐκ ἔστι κατὰ μίαν ἐνέργειαν, ὥσπερ τὸ τοῦ νοῦ, ἀλλ᾽ ἐν κινήσει μᾶλλον πρόεισιν ἀφ᾽ ἑαυτοῦ καὶ εἰς ἑαυτό. ἀλλ᾽ οὐδὲ πλῆρές ἐστιν ἑαυτοῦ, ὥσπερ τὸ νοερόν, ἐν δὲ τῷ ζητεῖν καὶ εὑρίσκειν ἀεὶ ἀπό τινος κενώσεως τοῦ γιγνώσκειν εἰς πλήρωσιν αὐτοῦ προέρχεται. πέρατός τε καὶ ἀπειρίας ὁμοίως ἐν μέσῳ διείληπται· ὅθεν ἀπὸ τοῦ ἀπείρου ἐπὶ τὸ ὁρίζεσθαι ἀεὶ προχωρεῖ, καὶ ἐπὶ τὸ μεταλαμβάνειν τῶν μαθηματικῶν εἰδῶν μεθίσταται.

intellectual abstractions.[13] For Pythagoreans the study of numbers was a religious exercise. Iamblichus says that "if we wish to study mathematics in a Pythagorean manner, we ought to pursue zealously its God-inspired, anagogic, cathartic and initiatory process."[14] Hardly the prerequisites of mathematicians today! The requirements for a Pythagorean mathematician were far more demanding, for Pythagoreans accepted only those who were willing "to share their entire life with the community" (*DCMS* 74, 23–26).

For Iamblichus, mathematics revealed divine mysteries. Specifically, he maintained that mathematics recapitulated the soul's descent and return, and since the soul was a mathematical entity, the performance of mathematical disciplines allowed it to see this process clearly. The soul's mental projection of mathematic images initiated a ritual activity that effected the soul's return to its true self (*autos*) if the *mathēsis* was performed in a Pythagorean manner. As Proclus put it, in the performance of mathematics "the soul becomes at the same time seeing and seen."[15]

Mathematical activity exemplifies the Iamblichean standard for every theurgic apotheosis: that the embodied and self-alienated soul recover its identity (*autos*) by immersion in the other (*heteros*). The divinizing "other" was encountered in a theurgic rite, and each rite had to be appropriate to the condition of the soul who performed it; that is, to its degree and manner of self-alienation. Just as the material powers of the soul were divinized through material sacrifices, and the intermediate powers were divinized by visual or audible images, so the noetic powers of the soul were divinized through the mental imagery of mathematic objects. In each case, the "weight" of the rite was proportionate to the "weight" of the soul's self-alienation; otherwise it would not have the proper effect. And

13. Iamblichus argues that *ta mathēmatika* are not drawn out of sensible things by abstraction (*kata aphairesin*) but descend directly from the Forms which also give them their appearance in our imagination; *DCMS* 34, 7–12.

14. *DCMS* 69, 26–29. Text: εἰ δὴ βουλοίμεθα Πυθαγορικῶς μαθηματικὴν ἀσκεῖν, τὴν ἔνθεον αὐτῆς ὁδὸν καὶ ἀναγωγὸν καὶ καθαρτικὴν καὶ τελεσιουργὸν μεταδιώκειν σπουδῇ προσήκει.

15. Proclus, *In Euclidem* 141; cited by J. Trouillard, "La Puissance secrète du nombre chez Proclos," *Revue de Philosophie Ancienne* 1 (1983): 234.

in each case the soul was made divine through its imitation of the cosmogonic cycle: it went out of itself in a ritually controlled manner to return to the god within.

The structural similarity of *mathēmatikē* to theurgy is not the only reason to suppose that mathematic elements made up the noetic *sunthēmata*. Iamblichus's portrayal of the Pythagorean *bios* in *De Vita Pythagorica* suggests a direct correlation between ritual worship and mathematic disciplines. Iamblichus says that Pythagoras learned his mysteries from "barbarians," in particular the Egyptians, in whose temples he spent twenty-two years, "studying astronomy and geometry, and being initiated in all the mystic rites of the Gods."[16] During his tenure with the Babylonians, Pythagoras was instructed by the Magi, "where he was educated thoroughly in their solemn rites, learned perfect worship of the Gods with them, and reached the highest point in knowledge of numbers, justice, and other mathematical disciplines."[17] These mathematical initiations were passed down by Pythagoras in symbolic and enigmatic forms yet, Iamblichus says, these enigmas were designed to illuminate those philosophers whose genius surpassed human understanding (*huper anthropinen epinoian*; VP 59, 27–60, 1; chap. 103).

The fact that Iamblichus's portrayal of Pythagoras reflects the ideal life as conceived by Iamblichus more than it does a history of Pythagoras,[18] makes it all the more useful for understanding Iamblichus's theurgical agenda and the role of mathematics in ritual. The Iamblichean Pythagoras was primarily a revealer of mysteries. Iamblichus says: "Pythagoras proclaimed the purificatory rites of the Gods and what are called 'mystic initiations' (*teletai*), and he

---

16. *VP* 13, 8–11, chap. 19, in *De Vita Pythagorica Liber*, ed. L. Deubner (1937); ed. with additions and corrections by U. Klein (Stuttgart: Teubner, 1975). The translation, modified slightly, is that of John Dillon and Jackson Hershbell, *Iamblichus: On the Pythagorean Way of Life* (Atlanta, Ga.: Scholars Press, 1991). Unless otherwise noted, translations are my own and pagination from Deubner and Klein's edition of *De Vita Pythagorica*.

17. *VP* 13, 14–16; chap. 19; translation, slightly modified, by Dillon and Hershbell, *Iamblichus: On the Pythagorean Way of Life*.

18. See J. A. Philip, "The Biographical Tradition—Pythagoras," *American Philosophical Association Transactions and Proceedings* (1959): 185–94.

had most accurate knowledge of these things. Moreover, the Pythagoreans say that he made a *synthesis of divine philosophy and the worship of the Gods.*"[19] The synthesis of philosophy and ritual worship was precisely the agenda that Iamblichus took upon himself. He attempted to integrate the *theia philosophia* of the Platonic tradition with the *therapeia* of the gods that he, like Pythagoras, learned from the barbarian priests of Egypt and Chaldea.

The result of this synthesis, as read into the life of Pythagoras, was a thoroughgoing application of numbers to worship. Libations were to be made three times; Apollo delivered oracles from a tripod because the *trias* was the first number; Aphrodite received sacrifices on the sixth day, and Herakles on the eighth day of the month (*VP* 86, 1–8; chap. 154). Temples were to be entered on the right but departed from the left because the "right" (*dexion*) was the principle of the "odd number" and divine, while the "left" (*aristeron*) was a symbol of the "even number" and of what dissolves (*VP* 88, 3–6; chap. 156). Iamblichus also reports that Pythagoras taught the Scythian Abaris "physiology" and "theology," which included a new form of divination. He says: "Instead of divination through the examination of sacrificed animals he taught Abaris divination through numbers, believing this to be purer, more divine, and more akin to the heavenly numbers of the Gods" (*VP* 54, 22–25; chap. 93). Abaris must have been spiritually ready for this teaching or Pythagoras would not have revealed it (*VP* 54, 24–26; chap. 93) for Pythagorean (i.e., theurgic) pedagogy required that each person perform only the kind of worship appropriate to his "nature" (*phusis*) and "power" (*dunamis*; *VP* 54, 28; chap. 93).

Iamblichus says that Pythagoras did not want to diminish Abaris's desire for the truth but taught him that instead of divining through blood sacrifices he could more securely discover the divine will through arithmetic science (*VP* 83, 9–18; chap. 147). By means of it the soul was able to bring the mind into resonance with the numbers of the World Soul. Iamblichus says the mathematical mysteries (*mathēmatikoi orgiasmoi*) of the Pythagoreans purified the

---

19. *VP* 85, 7–15; chap. 151; translation, slightly modified, by Dillon and Hershbell, *Iamblichus: On the Pythagorean Way of Life.*

mind and allowed it to participate in the gods (*VP* 122, 17–20; chap. 228). The purpose of Pythagorean "divination" (*mantikē*) was not to predict the future but to discern and obey the will of the gods (*VP* 78, 6; chap. 138). For some in the Pythagorean community, blood sacrifice was the appropriate means for this, for others, the performance of mathematic mysteries.[20] Indeed, as Walter Burkert suggests, there may have been a hidden connection between the mathematical *tetraktus* and the *triktus*, the altar of blood sacrifice. Burkert explains:

> The *tetraktys*, "a tetrad" made up of unequal members, is a cryptic formula, only comprehensible to the initiated. The word inevitably reminds of *triktys*, the "triad" of different sacrificial animals. Is the sacrificial art of the seer, involving the shedding of blood, superseded by a "higher," bloodless secret?[21]

For Iamblichus, the answer was clearly yes. The Pythagorean *bios*, which in large part was the theurgical bios, defined a continuity of worship extending from blood sacrifice to the sacrifice of numbers. In a passage from Pythagoras's *On the Gods*, Iamblichus says the "eternal essence of number" was praised as the "most providential principle of the universe, of heaven, earth and the intermediate nature."[22] He concludes: "By means of these same numbers Pythagoras created a marvelous divination and worship of the Gods according to the numbers that are most especially allied to them" (*VP* 83, 5–7; chap. 147).

---

20. *VP* 84, 19–21; chap. 150. While Pythagoras and his contemplative disciples did not sacrifice animals, "he ordered the *Acusmatikoi* and *Politikoi* [his exoteric disciples] to sacrifice animals such as the cock, lamb, or some other newly born animal—but not frequently, and not to sacrifice oxen."

21. Walter Burkert, *Lore and Science in Ancient Pythagoreanism*, trans. Edwin Minar Jr. (Cambridge: Harvard University Press, 1972), 187.

22. *VP* 82, 19–83, 1; chap. 146; translation, slightly modified, by Dillon and Hershbell, *Iamblichus: On the Pythagorean Way of Life*.

19

Noetic
Sunthēmata—
The Theurgy
of Numbers   *A man of this kind is above all law.*

I f, as I have argued, mathematics formed an essential part of the
worship of the gods, Iamblichus left no practical guide for its
theurgic use. Proclus and Damascius provide the only references
to a theurgy of numbers and even they give little concrete detail. In
Platonic Theology IV where Proclus discusses the anagogic power of
numbers he says:

> The unifying numbers, in themselves, are unknowable. For they
> are more ancient than Beings and more unified than Forms, and
> since they are the generators of Forms they exist prior to those
> beings we call "intelligibles" (*noēta*). The most august of theurgies
> demonstrate this, since they make use of numbers capable of act-
> ing ineffably, and by means of them, they effect the greatest and
> most ineffable of operations.[1]

Proclus explains that unifying numbers are "monadic" and have
two aspects: (1) as the numerical Forms of triad, pentad, heptad;
and (2) as unities or principles of these Forms. Thus, Proclus
says, "each of them is one and many."[2] What Proclus means may

---

1. Proclus, *Théologie platonicienne* (*Th. Pl.*) IV, 100, 21–101, 4, trans. and ed.
H.D. Saffrey and L.G. Westerink (Paris: Les Belles Lettres, 1980).
2. Ibid., 101, 8–11.

be explained by reference to Nicomachus's distinction[3] between "conventional" numbers, which are man's invention (e.g., $\iota' = 10$, κ' = 20, and $\omega' = 800$) and "natural" numbers, which are more "primitive" and are expressed graphically, the number bearing an intrinsic relationship to its shape. Thus, for example:

$$1 = a \qquad 2 = aa \qquad 3 = aaa \qquad 4 = aaaa^4$$

With regard to the formal and henadic aspects of numbers the triad as henad would be imagined as 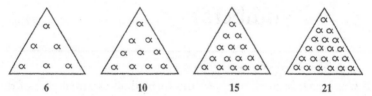 (i.e., the unified triad, or triad in potential), and the actualized triad as followed by all the subsequent "triadic" numbers.

(i.e., numbers which are "graphically" triangular). The same holds for the pentad which, as unified, is 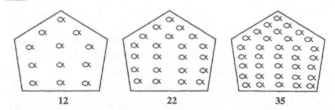 but in actualized form is and so on.[5]

Although Proclus does not say how theurgical numbers were employed, he refers to them as the temporal measures of the cosmos and speaks of the power of Time to perfect souls:[6] "Time

3. It may be of interest to note that Proclus considered himself to be the reincarnation of Nicomachus. See Marinus, *Vita Procli* 28, ed. J.F. Boissonade (Leipzig, 1814). Latin translation with Greek text by Portus, in *In Platonis Theologiam* (Hamburg, 1618; reprint, Frankfurt am Main, 1960).

4. Nicomachus, *Nicomachus of Gerasa: Introduction to Arithmetic* II, 6, 2. trans. M.L. D'Ooge (New York: Macmillan, 1926).

5. Cf. ibid., II, 8, 1–10, 1.

6. *Th. Pl.* IV, 102, 4–5.

proceeds according to number, and by number it measures the existence of all souls."[7] Given the fact that the proportions of Time—revealed in the heavens—were identical with the numerical proportions of the soul, the regulation of ritual *energeia* with heavenly *energeia* would tie the numbers of the soul to their ineffable unities. By performing rituals at precise times and in accord with appropriate constellations, the soul would be united with the gods.[8] Iamblichus seems to suggest this mode of theurgy in the *De Mysteriis* when he discusses Egyptian astrology:

> The Egyptians do not simply contemplate these things theoretically, but by means of sacred theurgy they report that they ascend to higher and more universal realms, superior to fate, even up to the Creator God, using neither matter nor employing anything else at all *except the observation of the critical moment*. (*DM* 267, 6–12)

In his *Platonic Theology* I, Proclus reports that the Pythagoreans made use of mathematics "for the recollection (*anamnēsis*) of divine principles"[9] and "consecrated numbers and geometric shapes to the gods."[10] In his *Commentary on Euclid* Proclus describes the "rhythmic choruses of the heavenly bodies" (*In Euclidem* 137, 13) that trace out copies of the "Intellectual Forms" (*In Euclidem*, 137, 16). He says:

> Transcending all these forms are the perfect, uniform, unknowable and incomprehensible figures of the Gods (*schemata tōn theōn*), which, being mounted on the intellectual figures, impose unifying limits upon all figures, holding all things together in their unifying boundaries. Theurgy, having represented their properties in the statues of the Gods, has amplified them in various ways. (*In Euclidem*, 138, 5–12)

To each god, he concludes, there are appropriate symbols and shapes

---

7. Ibid., 102, 4–5. In attributing to "time" such powers Proclus followed Iamblichus; see *In. Tim.*, frag. 63 and commentary, in Dillon, *Iamblichi Chalcidencis*, 172–75; 345–47.

8. This would be the theurgic fulfillment of Platonic *paideia* as outlined in the *Timaeus* 90b–d.

9. *Th. Pl.* I, 20, 8–10, trans. and ed. Saffrey and Westerink (1968).

10. Ibid. 20, 11. In his commentary on Euclid's *Elements*, Proclus attributes this teaching to Philolaos (*In Euclidem* 173–74).

(*In Euclidem*, 138, 21–22). One may assume, therefore, that each god was associated with a geometric figure that appeared in the heavens "at critical moments," and that these figures (constellations?) were employed at such times in some form of theurgic worship.

An extensive citation from Damascius supports this. In his discussion of the "figure" (*schēma*) of the One-Being of the *Parmenides* (145b, 3), after explaining that each of the gods has a shape, he says:

> For why did the Pythagoreans consecrate to one God the circle, to another the triangle, to another the square, and to each of the others another rectilinear figure as well as their mixtures, as the semicircle to the Dioscouroi? Philolaos, who was wise in these matters, oftentimes assigned to one same God one or another figure in accord with one or another property of that God. *In general terms it is certain that the circular figure is common to all the intellectual Gods qua intellectual, while the different rectilinear figures are the properties of each respectively in accord with their particular properties of numbers, angles and sides.* For example, the triangle is the property of Athena and the square of Hermes—as Philolaos has already said. And of the square, one angle is the property of Rhea, another of Hera, and the other angles are associated with other deities.[11] And this is the complete theological definition of figures. (*Dub. et Sol.* II [261], 127, 7–17)

Damascius adds that not all sacred figures need be enclosed and cites the helix which he also accepts as a "figure" (*Dub. et Sol.*, 127–20–21). His second example of an unenclosed figure is that of the Egyptian god "Tet" represented as a vertical line with three, or four, horizontal lines, depending on the local cult:[12] 手. The inhabitants of Gaza, he says, consecrate this same figure (with one more horizontal line) to Zeus (*Dub. et Sol.* II, 128, 1–2): 丰.

---

11. In his commentary on Euclid, Proclus also cites Philolaos as the authority for attributing goddesses to the angles of the square. He says that since the square is associated with earth, its "angles" are tied to the life-giving goddesses: Rhea, Hestia, and Demeter (*In Euclidem* 173, 11–21).

12. Ibid., 128. See Chaignet's reference to an article by Maspero who says that "tet" was a vulgarization of "ded" who was represented in Mendes and later in Heliopolis where Osiris was also designated by the "tet": See *Damascius: Dub. et Sol.* 2:344.

Damascius concludes, citing the authority of the Oracles, that since the gods often reveal themselves in a single curved line, and since every line has a beginning, a middle, and an end, each of these may also be considered a "figure" (*Dub. et Sol.* II, 128, 3–7).

Sources are too few and fragmentary to reconstruct a coherent system of mathematic symbols employed in theurgy. In any case, given its practical and therapeutic purposes, the possibility that a coherent systematization ever existed should probably be ruled out. On the basis of the evidence, however, it may be inferred that the geometric figures of the gods functioned as contemplative icons, perhaps like the geometric mandalas of yogic disciplines. The comparison is intriguing, particularly in consideration of the mandala's function. According to Mircea Eliade: "the mandala is at once an image of the universe and a theophany—the cosmic creation being, of course, a manifestation of the divinity. But the mandala also serves as a 'receptacle' for the gods. In Vedic India the gods descended into the altar—which proves the continuity between the tantric liturgy and the traditional cult."[13] The continuity asserted by Eliade seems to be the same kind of continuity that Burkert suspected between the sacrificial *triktus* and the mathematical *tetraktus*. Both demonstrate the transformation of cults of blood sacrifice into mathematical forms that served the same function: to provide a receptacle (*hupodochē*) to receive and worship the gods.[14]

In the case of *sriyantra* mandala of tantric worship the feminine

13. Mircea Eliade, *Yoga: Immortality and Freedom* (Princeton: Princeton University Press, 1958; reprint, 1969), 220.

14. Though the structural comparison between tantra and theurgy should not be pressed too far, the similarities between the two are striking. Tantra, like theurgy, may be defined as that which provides continuity or unfolding of divine gnosis (Eliade, *Yoga*, 200), and it was introduced to India in the fourth century C.E. with the argument that ritual practice was the only mode of worship capable of saving man in this age. Tantra incorporated aboriginal Indian elements as well as alien features, which led Eliade to suggest that it may have been introduced to India from "the great Western mysteriosophic current" (202). According to Eliade, the Buddhist tantras are divided into four classes which, like theurgy, are related "to the principal human types and temperaments" (201). As in Neoplatonic theurgy, these classes are graded and proceed from the more material and overt forms of ritual practices/persons, to the more spiritual and interior.

or differentiated aspects of the cosmos were represented by triangles with their apex down: ▽ the masculine or undifferentiated aspect, was represented by triangles with apex up: △ and the two were intertwined: ✡

In theurgic "mandalas" the principles were the same but represented differently. Proclus reports that rectilinear angles proceed from the (masculine) principle of the Limit (*to peras*) and

> produce the one right angle, ruled by equality and similarity to every other right angle; [they are] determinate and fixed in nature, admitting neither of growth nor of diminution: ⌐ (*In Euclidem* 132, 9–12).

From the (feminine) principle of the Unlimited (*to apeiron*) come acute and obtuse angles that are subject to variations of more and less (*In Euclidem* 132, 9–12): ◣, ◿ . The right angles, Proclus continues, are associated with the hypercosmic gods whereas the acute and obtuse angles are associated with the encosmic gods. The latter lead the soul down into generation while the former, remaining present in the latter as their principles, provide to the soul a connection with the gods above fate (*In Euclidem* 132–34). Since the soul contains all the mathematicals, the geometric figures that it consecrates, draws, and visualizes would schematize the entire process of its separation from, and return to the gods.

In the *De Mysteriis* Iamblichus discusses the ritual use of number only incidentally in order to distinguish ritual objects that are in physical *sumpatheia* with one another, from the gods who are the causes of those sympathies. As causes, the gods were unaffected by the sympathies enjoined in the rites. The latter, Iamblichus says, served only to reveal, not affect, the divine principles. Others, however, believed that the benefits of sacrifice were caused by the objects employed in the rite. Iamblichus refutes this view by referring to the belief that numerical sympathies *caused* the benefits of sacrifice: "The same absurd conclusions occur if some of those among us [i.e., Egyptian priests], attribute the effect (of the sacrifice) to numbers—since the "sixty" associated with the crocodile is related to *Hēlios*" (*DM* 208, 7–9). Iamblichus refers to the Egyptian belief that the crocodile lays sixty eggs and lives sixty years, the number associated with the heavenly cycle of the sun. Because of this, some believed that rites involving the crocodile would command the presence of the sun god through their common numerical identity.[15]

Although Iamblichus denied that the sympathy of crocodile and sun with the number "sixty" could effect the presence of the sun god, his refutation did not rule out the possibility that numbers were used in theurgy as a kind of organizational system through which rituals could be designed and performed. Dominic O'Meara's study of Iamblichus's Pythagorean texts, including the fragments preserved by Psellus: *On Physical Number* and *On Ethical and Theological Arithmetic*, supports this idea.[16] In *On Physical Number* Iamblichus explained that all things in nature not only were determined by number but were the concrete manifestations of number, including the stars, animals, plants, and stones. This also included all the rhythms of life: cycles of disease, reproduction, growth, and death. In short, the variety and vitality of nature was simply the concrete manifestation of numerical powers. Iamblichus distinguished intelligible numbers (*noētoi arithmoi*)[17] from mathematical numbers (*mathēmatikoi arithmoi*)[18] and then discussed natural numbers (*phusikoi arithmoi*), those involved directly in the shaping of matter. He says:

15. For the association of the crocodile with the number "60," see Aristotle, *Historia Animalium*, trans. A.L. Peck (Cambridge: Harvard University Press, 1963), 558a, 15–18; *Plutarch's Moralia*, vol. 5: *De Iside et Osiride*, trans. F.C. Babbitt (Cambridge: Harvard University Press, 1969), para. 75, 381 b–c; Clement of Alexandria, *The Stromata*, trans. A.C. Coxe, in *The Ante-Nicene Fathers*, vol. 2: *Fathers of the Second Century* (Grand Rapids, Mich.: Eerdmans, 1979), bk. 5, 7.

16. Dominic J. O'Meara, *Pythagoras Revived: Mathematics and Philosophy in Late Antiquity* (Oxford: Clarendon Press, 1989). O'Meara initially published the fragments from Psellus in "New Fragments From Iamblichus' *Collection of Pythagorean Doctrines*," *American Journal of Philology* 102 (1981): 26–40.

17. These would be the ineffable henads. Iamblichus describes them as "the highest and first." *On Phys. Numb.* 6; O'Meara, *Pythagoras Revived*, 219.

18. These are numbers "seen in common precepts"; *On Phys. Numb.* 6–7; O'Meara, *Pythagoras Revived*, 219.

Physical number is found in the lowest things, things generated and divided in bodies. For the principles mixed in bodies, both in animals and plants, are physical numbers (*phusikoi arithmoi*), for each of these is born, grows, and dies at determined times. And the philosopher should fit the appropriate numbers to the causes in nature.

And since form (*eidos*) is, in nature, the first and most important cause (for the being of all depends on it), thus such numbers as provide being to nature and are essential, these are connatural (*homophuēs*) with forms.[19]

Iamblichus later identified odd numbers specifically as form-giving and even numbers as "appropriate to matter,"[20] with their mixture creating the physical world. Even the human being was made of two numbers:

For since animals are made up of soul and body, the Pythagoreans say soul and body are not produced from the same number, but soul from cubic number [6 x 6 x 6 = 216],[21] and body from the irregular volume (*bōmiskos*) [5 x 6 x 7 = 210].[22]

The fact that *bōmiskos* also described the shape of a sacrificial altar was a coincidence unlikely to have been missed by Iamblichus. It brings to mind Burkert's connection between the *triktus* of blood sacrifice and the Pythagorean *tetraktus*, yet it also points to something distinctively and paradoxically Iamblichean. For, although the theurgist's physical body effected his separation from the gods, it was also the sacrifical altar (*bōmiskos*) by which he returned to them.

Iamblichus did not think that discursive conceptions of numbers and letters could influence the gods, but he firmly believed that cosmogonic and natural numbers were their *energeia*. Therefore, Iamblichus was careful to distinguish conventional numbers from the natural and theurgic. Evidence of Iamblichus's caution is seen in his

---

19. *On Phys. Numb.* 7–16; O'Meara, *Pythagoras Revived*, 219.
20. O'Meara, *Pythagoras Revived*, 30.
21. Iamblichus later provides these numbers in his explanation of the *arithmos kubikos* and *arithmos bōmiskos*. Both were volumes, the former with all sides equal, the latter with all sides unequal; O'Meara, *Pythagoras Revived*, 49–58.
22. Ibid. 47–49; translation by O'Meara slightly modified.

refutation of the numero-logical and grammatical theories of Amelius.[23] Amelius theorized that since there were four elements (*stoicheia*) in the cosmos[24] and four elements (*stoicheia*) in the word "soul" (ψυχή), the soul must be the "sum of number or the geometrical number" on the grounds that Plato said all geometric proportions exist among the four elements.[25] According to Iamblichus this theory derived from human imagination and convention, not from divine inspiration. Amelius's "proof" was that if one took the "extremes" of ψυχή, i.e., ψ and η, and substituted for ψ (= 700) its root, i.e., ζ (= 7), one had, as a result, ζη, or ζῇ = "the soul lives" (Proclus, *In Tim*. II, 275, 24–26). Such theorizing was rejected by Iamblichus:

> For after all, "Body" (*sōma*) is composed of the same number of letters, and even "Non-Being" (*mē on*) itself; so that then Non-Being (*mē on*) would be the sum of number. And you could find many other words made up of the same number of letters, words for things base and even mutually contradictory, all of which it is surely not correct to mix and jumble up together.[26]

In response to Amelius's other conjectures concerning the "shape" of numbers, Iamblichus says:

> Secondly, it is not safe to base any theories on the letters themselves; for these are conventional (*thesei*), and their shapes have changed between ancient times and the present. . . .
> Thirdly, reduction of the Soul to the root numbers [i.e., ψ = 700 to ζ = 7] and wasting one's time on them transfers the speculation from one set of numbers to another; for the number seven in the units is not the same as that in the tens or that in the hundreds.[27]

---

23. The theory refuted is actually that of Theodorus, as Proclus reports, but Dillon suggests that Amelius may have shared the same theories and that Iamblichus wanted to avoid refuting Theodorus, his own pupil, so refutes Amelius; see Dillon, *Iamblichi Chalcidensis*, 338.

24. These would have been the fire/air/water/earth described in the *Timaeus* (32bd).

25. The Greek word *stoicheia* meant "element" of language as well as element of the natural world.

26. *In Tim*., frag. 57, 9–15, Dillon, *Iamblichi Chalcidensis*, 166–67.

27. *In Tim*., frag. 57, 15–22, Dillon, *Iamblichi Chalcidensis*, 166–67.

Dillon explains that Iamblichus was criticizing the practice of "gematria," where each letter of the Hebrew or Greek alphabet was assigned a numerical value. In this theory, when the sums of the letters of two different words were equivalent they were considered en rapport.[28] For Iamblichus, however, this kind of "hidden connection" was contrived and only a caricature of the true continuity and *philia* of existing things. Since numerical systems based on letters were merely "conventional" (*thesei*) and not "natural" (*phusei*), they could not provide the basis for theurgic ritual. If theurgists employed an arithmetic system to conduct theurgies, it would not have been based on an artificial gematria for this would contradict Iamblichus's rule that superior orders cannot be moved by their inferiors.[29] To invoke the gods, one had to employ *their* speech as revealed in the cosmos and in their numerical powers.

Although Iamblichus denied that the discursive use of numbers was theurgic, he knew that as a numerical entity the soul eventually had to undergo a numerical transformation. Since all mathematical images ultimately had their "foundation" (*epereismos*) in the Forms (*DCMS* 34, 9) to imagine them—even discursively—was to enform one's *phantasia* with their noetic *energeiai*. Since these images were intrinsically connected to the *noēta*, if the soul had the capacity to coordinate its *phantasia* with these mathematic images it could create a subtle receptacle to embody them. Just as material souls were united with material gods through material *sunthēmata*, noetic souls were united with the immaterial *Nous* through mathematical *sunthēmata*. This form of theurgy might initially have been a discursive exercise: mathematic visualizations, but at a certain point the visualizations would spontaneously become visions empowered by the gods. This lifted the soul's discursive energies into the numbers of the heavens described in the *Timaeus*, and the soul surrendered its false "unity" to the unifying action of the One. Noetic theurgy, therefore, penetrated to the core of the soul's inversion, for

---

28. Dillon, *Iamblichi Chalcidensis*, 338–39. In this case Amelius (Theodorus) appears to be using an even more simplified gematria.

29. For a discussion of this problem in later Neoplatonism and Iamblichus, see Stephen Gersh, *From Iamblichus to Eriugena* (Leiden: E. J. Brill, 1978), 297-304.

the objectified unity of the soul—its self-identity—was the fore-most obstacle that barred it from sharing in the objectifying unity of the One. Yet, paradoxically, this alienation was the sine qua non for the soul's theurgy and participation in cosmogony.[30]

It is possible that mathematics did not make up what Iamblichus calls "the simple and incorporeal form of worship purified from all generation" (*DM* 219, 8–9). Although I have argued that *ta mathē-matika* were the "intellectual offerings adapted to the hypercosmic gods" (*DM* 226, 9–10) I may be wrong. Iamblichus himself says the "summit" of hieratic worship was attained only rarely and that souls who reach it were beyond the limits of his discourse (whether he means book V alone, or possibly all of the *De Mysteriis* is unclear). He says: "Our present discourse, however, does not ordain laws for a man of this kind *for he is above all law*, but to those in need of a certain law it introduces this kind of legislation" (*DM* 231, 2–5). The noetic theurgist was "above all law" (*kreitōn pantos nomou*). Does this mean that such souls have left behind the rituals of the common man, as an "enlightened society" frees itself from the superstitions of a darker (and more ritualistic) age? This is how the enlightened scholar sympathetic to Iamblichus might read this passage. "Here," he would argue, "here is the Plotinian dimension of Iamblichus's theurgy!" Leaving to the side what a Plotinus might say, I would argue that the most elevated theurgist was "above the law" not because he knew better or had graduated beyond such superstitions. In light of Iamblichus's view of cosmology, he was above the law because he was above its effects, having become their living embodiment.[31] After all, since the laws of ritual reflected the order of the gods, a divinized soul would have been assimilated to

---

30. A paradox reflected in the fact that its alienation was a false unity rooted in the body, the altar-shaped (*bōmiskos*) number.

31. The relation between *nomos* and *thesmos* for the later Neoplatonists is anal-ogous to that between *heimarmenē* and *pronoia*. Both sustain the order of things as "law," yet nomos has to do with the soul's relations in the generated realm and *thes-mos* with its preexisting divine ratios. For a discussion of their distinction, see Ronald Hathaway, *Hierarchy and the Definition of Order in the Letters of Pseudo-Dionysius* (The Hague: Martinus Nijhoff, 1969), 38–46.

that order and hence to the laws (*nomoi*) of hieratic worship. He was no longer under the law because he *was* the law.[32]

We might reconsider the notion of a mathematic system for Iamblichean theurgy through the image of the theurgist as an embodiment of divine law. According to Iamblichus, all theurgic ritual, by definition, was rooted in ancient tradition; it could not be concocted to suit one's mood or personal desires. Theurgic rites, in fact, appear to have been traditional acts of worship practiced for centuries in the Mediterranean world. The oldest and most conservative people, the Egyptians, were seen by Iamblichus as exemplary because of their preservation of god-inspired rites that were enactments of their myths.

Iamblichus was by no means intellectually naive; he was a leading figure in the most learned circles of his time. Yet he rejected the anthropocentric "demythologizing" of Porphyry and defended the sanctity and power of the ancient rites—regardless of our ability to explain them. Nevertheless, it seems that Iamblichus did embrace an underlying paradigm for these myths and rites, a master myth outlined by Plato and the Pythagorean interpreters of his dialogues. The cosmogonic myth of the *Timaeus* demanded great intellectual skill of its interpreters, yet for Iamblichus this Platonic myth sustained a vital connection to the most primitive myths and rituals: Egyptian, Chaldean, Assyrian, and other ancient traditions of the Mediterranean. If there was a mathematical model of Iamblichean theurgy it would have been a Pythagorean schema reflecting the creative tensions of the One and the Many. These tensions, Iamblichus believed, were portrayed in the traditions of ancient and holy people, in their art, dance, sacrifice, and prayers, and would have been discovered as mathematical only after the fact of their cultural embodiment.[33]

---

32. Philo of Alexandria, faced with the same challenge as Iamblichus—to justify the practice of traditional rituals according to Platonic principles—produced very similar arguments. For Philo, although the Patriarchs lived prior to the written law they had no need of it for they were, like the noetic theurgists, "living laws" (*empsuchoi nomoi*). See Philo, *De Abrahamo*, 4-6; Samuel Sandmel, *Philo of Alexandria* (New York: Oxford University Press, 1979), 57.

33. Following the Aristotelian rule, adopted by Iamblichus, that what is first in ontology is last in generation.

Mathematical proportions simply outlined the intensity and valences of ritual patterns already established in nature and cult. Perhaps when a theurgist ritually embodied the numbers of a tradition he could translate this vital mathematics into other traditions. This may have put him "above all law" and free from the specific requirements of any tradition, yet since the theurgist became an embodiment of the law, it is more likely that he would have been subject to all traditions that preserved the divine *arithmoi*, for in them he would have recognized and experienced divine authority.

I believe that Pythagorean mathematics made up the *sunthēmata* employed in noetic worship because they exemplify both the transcendence and immanence common to theurgic *sunthēmata* and because their exercise expressed the dynamics seen in all theurgy. Perhaps the most suggestive confluence of mathematics and theurgy may be seen in the enigmatic warning from the Chaldean Oracles: "Do not deepen the plane" (*mēde bathunēs to epipedon*).[34]

Hans Lewy explains this warning by referring to the Pythagorean theory of cosmogenesis described as the unfolding of dimensions from point to line to plane to volume, with the pyramid as the first body:[35] "•", "●——●", " △ ", " ◁▷ "; i.e., the *tetraktus*: ⦂∴⦂ According to Lewy, the oracle warns the soul to remain in the "plane," the triad. As he explains: "The number three is in the Oracles the measure of the noetic and therefore the purport of the Oracular warning is that the mortal should not "materialize" his mental substance by extension into the realm of the somatic."[36]

Assuming that Lewy's analysis is correct, the question remains: How was the soul to avoid its fall into matter? How does the soul remain in the plane? The obvious response: "by not descending into volume," may be correct, but it is insufficient and, if accepted prima facie, it would lead to a distortion of one of the central principles of theurgy. To eschew embodiment and the descent into volume

---

34. *CO*, frag. 104, 88.

35. Hans Lewy, *Chaldean Oracles and Theurgy*, ed. M. Tardieu (Paris: Etudes Augustiniennes, 1978), 394–96.

36. Ibid., 396. Cf. the remarks of R. Merkelbach cited by des Places, ed. *Oracles Chaldaïques* (Paris: Les Belles Lettres, 1971), 176 n. 1.

would leave the *tetraktus* unfinished, unexpressed, and imperfect. To disdain the corporeal *qua* corporeal would alienate the soul from the activity of the gods who will to reveal themselves in their geometrizing descent into the world.[37] To avoid the body *tout court* was a gnostic or dualist answer to the oracular warning. The theurgic answer, however, not only preserved the soul in the plane while completing the volume; I would argue that it kept the soul in the plane *only* by completing the volume. An examination of this paradox should reveal how thoroughly the Pythagorean teachings influenced Iamblichus, and how, today, they may still throw light on Neoplatonic theurgy.

From the beginning of this study I have argued that theurgy was cosmogonic activity, a mimesis of the gods in creation. Correlate to this axiom is the view that the ascent of the soul in theurgy was realized as a cosmogonic descent, that procession and return were not opposed to one another but that the soul's return confirmed the divinity of its procession. Strictly speaking, this means that procession and return cannot be separated, either temporally or spatially, except in discursive thought.[38]

Theurgy, however, was not a conceptual enterprise. "It is not thinking that connects theurgists to the gods . . . but ineffable acts" (*DM* 96, 13–19). Therefore, only a hieratic performance was able to give the soul "the ineffable power of the gods" (*hē arrhētos dunamis tōn theōn*; *DM* 96, 19-97, 2). This *arrhētos dunamis* could not be grasped or explained, and in that sense it was irrational (*alogos*). Yet it was an *alogos* power that generated *logos*, and in this sense it bears a profound similarity to the Pythagorean solution to the "scandal" of the irrational diagonal. Burkert maintains that prior to 460 B.C.E. "Pythagoreans" had discovered that the diagonal of a square with the side of "1" has an irrational value and therefore

37. That demiurgy was conceived by later Platonists as a "geometric" activity; see Plutarch, *Quest. Conviv.,* VIII, 3.

38. For a discussion of this principle in later Neoplatonism, see Annick Charles-Saget, *L'architecture du divin: Mathématique et philosophie chez Plotin et Proclus* (Paris: Les Belles Lettres, 1982), 313.

cannot be defined arithmetically.[39] Nevertheless, it becomes defined when it is geometrically *performed*, which means that the irrational becomes rational when it functions as a generative power. In the same way, a corresponding irrational power was understood to exist in the soul,[40] a power that remained ineffable until it was revealed in theurgic performance: the "ineffable acts." The supposed "irrationality" of the theurgic rite, therefore, was consistent with the mathematic solution to the problem of incommensurate lines within the "unit square" and "unit cube."[41] Like the irrational diagonal, the ineffable power of the gods was *alogos* with respect to discrete (arithmetic) reasoning yet became the source for a *logos* revealed in embodied (geometric) action.

Henri Joly argues that the geometric solution to the arithmetic problem of the irrational shifted the Hellenic philosophic tradition to an entirely new epistemological foundation, one that demanded an integration of *epistemē* with an elevated sense of *technē*.[42] In the parlance of the later Neoplatonists, this would be the *hieratikē technē*, anterior to conceptual reflection yet capable of being performed by the soul.[43] Against the background to this problem in the Pythagorean tradition, the theurgic solution to the warning of the Chaldean Oracles may support my hypothesis that noetic theurgies

39. Walter Burkert, *Lore and Science in Ancient Pythagoreanism*, trans. Edwin L. Minar Jr. (Cambridge: Harvard University Press, 1972), 447–56.

40. For a detailed investigation of the presence of the irrational diagonal in the soul based on the *Timaeus* (36), see Konrad Gaiser, *Platons Ungeschriebene Lehre* (Stuttgart: Ernst Klett), "Die Speile als Begrenzung des Korpers," 59–60.

41. A "unit square" and "unit cube" have all sides equal to 1. In the square the diagonal has a value of $\sqrt{2}$; in the cube the diagonal that traverses the volume has a value of $\sqrt{3}$.

42. Henri Joly, *Le Renversement platonicien: Logos, épistémé, polis* (Paris: J. Vrin, 1974), 271.

43. Walter Burkert discusses the double sense of the term "irrational" (*arrhētos*) in the Pythagorean tradition and notes von Fritz's hypothesis that Hippasus's "betrayal of the secret of the irrational" had to do with his revelation of the sacred dodecahedron, made up of regular pentagons with "incommensurate" diagonals of the value *phi* which came to be known as the Golden Section. Walter Burkert, *Lore and Science*, 458–63. Paul Friedländer (*Plato*, 2, *The Dialogues: First Period*, trans. Hans Meyerhoff [New York: Bollingen Foundation, 1964], p.283) describes the moment of recollection in the *Meno* (82a–85b) as being concerned with secrets of

were, indeed, mathematic rituals. In any case, the Pythagorean principles will help to explain the raison d'être of theurgic rites.

In the geometric unfolding of the *tetraktus*, each dimension functioned as the principle (*archē*) and limit (*peras*) of the dimension that it contained and of which it was the boundary (*horos*). The "point" was the limit of the "line," the "line" was the limit of the "plane," and the "plane" was the limit of the "volume." In each stage the limit was "outside" and therefore "contained" what it limited. Damascius explains this process of dimensional unfolding in his *Parmenides* commentary:

> The point (*sēmeion*), insofar as it limits, contains; it limits the length (*mekos*) without depth[44] and contains it either from both extremes or only one, but it does not contain the whole length in itself—not entirely in itself—as a part is contained in a whole, or a figure in the limit which encloses it but as something limited is contained in a limit. *For the Limit is always outside what is limited*, as is the Unlimited, but the Unlimited is outside infinitely, while the Limit is outside only once. . . . Thus, the body (*sōma*) is within the surface (*epiphania*), the surface is within the line (*grammē*), and the line is within the point, but not (literally) "in" it. (*Dub. et Sol.* II, 121, 13-21)

Damascius's use of the terms "within" (*eisō*) and "in" (*en*) in the last sentence points to an important distinction between ontological containment, when subordinate entities are contained "within"

---

the irrational: "Now we are suddenly lifted up into the sphere of that ultimate reality which, according to the *Republic*, culminates in what is 'beyond being,' i.e., in the 'ineffable.' Is it an accident, or is it rather a signpost pointing toward those heights that the geometrical task of doubling a square contains the problem of the irrational, i.e., again the 'ineffable' (*arrhētos*)?" For Plato's discussion of the "irrational" as a problem of central importance see *Laws* 819d–20b; *Epinomis* 990c–91a; *Theatetus* 147de; compare also *Republic* 534d and note the interesting contrast between an education *tō logō* and *tō ergō*.

44. Damascius's terms are taken from Euclid's *Elements*. For example, definition 2 reads: "A line is a length without depth"; *Euclid: The Thirteen Books of the Elements,* trans., intro., and comm. Sir Thomas Heath (New York: Dover, 1956), 1:158. For the Neoplatonists, Euclid's geometric definitions described the soul's spiritual generation and ancestry.

their primaries, and empirical containment, when an object is spatially contained in another.

Now, in order for a volume to become manifest it must be limited by a plane; the plane, in turn, must be limited by a line; and the line must be limited by a point. Iamblichus says that a line should not be conceived as a "collection of many points"[45] because the point *qua* point is of a different order—it is the *archē* of the line and, strictly speaking, has no dimension at all. The transition from point to line occurs only when a fundamental change takes place in the orientation of the point, to be precise: when it begins to *flow*. "The geometricians," Iamblichus says, "maintain that the line is the 'flow' (*rhusis*) of the point."[46] To use the example of a cubic volume, the process may be exemplified as follows:

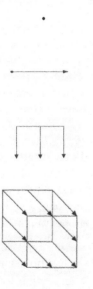

1. The point as principle of all expression. [No dimension.]

2. The point realizes its limiting power in the manifestation of the line. [The point *flows* into the line.]

3. The line realizes its limiting power in the manifestation of the plane. [The line *flows* into the plane.]

4. The plane realizes its limiting power in the manifestation of the volume. [The plane *flows* into the volume.]

To return to the oracular warning, in the case of the human soul the Oracle states: "Do not deepen the plane"; that is, remain at the

---

45. *In Nic.* 57, 18. Text: οὐδὲ γάρ ἐστιν ἡ γραμμὴ πλειόνων σύνθεσις σημείων.

46. *In Nic.* 57, 8. Text: ῥύσιν φασὶν εἶναι οἱ γεωμέτραι τὴν γραμμήν; cf. Aristotle, *De Anima* 409a, 4–6.

third level of descent and do not fall into a body, the volume. The theurgical solution to the warning now may be understood: the principal understanding of theurgy is that for the soul to remain a plane and free of volume it must *act* as a plane. That is to say, it must bestow limit to volume: it must descend (i.e., flow) into a body and rule it as its limit and *archē*.

In each successive degree of the *tetraktus* the superior dimension becomes the principle (*archē*) of the subsequent level and manifests its specific logos in its descent. Descent in itself was not wrong so long as it was measured. After all, the genesis of the world was the result of the descent of divine powers. Therefore, from a theurgical perspective, what the Oracle warned against was not descent in itself, but an unmeasured descent. Contrasting these two notions of descent in his analysis of the *Laws* (894a) Konrad Gaiser says:

> To be precise, it is necessary to distinguish two different possibili-
> ties in that which concerns the passage from an anterior dimen-
> sion to a posterior dimension. It is clear that one may speak of
> "genesis" if—when a dimension is extended to pass into
> another—the original dimension produces its effect *by imposing a
> form*, by playing the role of a limit (*peras*). But there exists another
> way, a completely different sort of movement between dimen-
> sions, which is produced following the *loss of the regulating limita-
> tion*. When a singular being is detached from the connection it had
> with the Superior dimension of being (its *eidos*), it loses its unify-
> ing form and is totally dissolved in the subordinate dimension. In
> the case of such a descent, it is no longer a matter of genesis but of
> the downfall of that which exists, thus, of a passage to non-being,
> of a "corruption" (*phthora*).[47]

The misunderstanding of theurgy by modern scholars may be explained by these two notions of "descent." Theurgy has too often been judged as an example of the latter kind, as a loss of rationality and corruption of the soul. In light of Iamblichus's Pythagorean

---

47. Konrad Gaiser, *Platons Ungeschriebene Lehre*, 188; quoted by Remi Brague, *Le Restant: Supplément aux commentaires du Ménon de Platon* (Paris: Les Belles Lettres, 1978), 101. Brague discusses this principle at some length in his chapter 4, 100–105.

principles, however, theurgy was the means for the soul to participate in "genesis" at the highest possible level.

In the cosmos conceived by Iamblichus one acted with the Demiurge or against him. The theurgist, of course, did the former. He
embraced the Unlimited (*to apeiron*) in his descent/embodiment by
assuming the role of the Limit (*to peras*). If he avoided this responsibility he forfeited his role as Limit and was condemned to an inferior dimension and the ignominy of having limits imposed on him
by others: that is, by daimons who preserve the orders of genesis. In
short, only by flowing into *apeiron* could the theurgist remain *peras*.
Only by measuring himself into matter could he participate directly
in the immaterial forms. If, as the Platonists maintained,[48] "god is
always doing geometry" (*aei gēometrei ho theos*), then the theurgists
were his instruments.

---

48. For this notion, see Plutarch, *Moralia* VIII, 718b–720c: "Question 2: What
Plato meant by saying that God is always doing geometry."

20

The *Sunthēma* of the Sun

*The theologians call the sun
"Fire, channel of Fire . . . and
dispenser of Fire."*
— The Chaldean Oracles

The two kinds of descent outlined in the previous chapter may help shed light on Iamblichus's distinction in the *De Anima* between souls who voluntarily and involuntarily enter bodies. Iamblichus subdivided the former group into souls who were (a) already free and entered the corporeal realm to preserve it and (b) those who were imperfect but were working toward perfection (*Stob.* I, 380, 6–14). The descent of this latter type of soul was neither entirely a corruption nor a creative participation in genesis though it was moving toward the latter. The great majority of souls, however, were embodied involuntarily and were completely verged toward *to apeiron*. Nevertheless, in Iamblichus's estimation, even these souls could participate in cosmogenesis if they limited their passions with material theurgies. The material rites laid the foundation for the soul's final exchange of a life shaped by the *perata* of daimons, for a life bestowing *peras* upon *apeiron*, like the gods. The divinity appropriate to the soul guided each rite, and as the soul became increasingly aligned with cosmogonic measures, so did its awareness of the gods.

The most marked transition in the progress of the soul was the rare moment that it received a god as a guardian to replace its personal (*oikeios*) daimon (*DM* 280, 17–281, 1). In book IX of the *De Mysteriis* Iamblichus describes this transition in response to Porphyry's question about discerning the "Lord of one's nativity" (*DM* 278, 15–19). While Iamblichus did not reject the validity of *mathēmatikē* (i.e., the "calculation" of astrological nativities) as a divine science, he said that it had been distorted by mortal conceptions

(*DM* 277, 14–18). Iamblichus explained that one's guardian daimon cannot be determined simply by finding the "Lord of the geniture"[1] for the guardian is distributed to the soul through all aspects of its astrological portrait (*DM* 280, 2–6). Iamblichus maintained that the soul's daimon was "more ancient" than the nativity and therefore could not be discovered by astrological calculations or identified with a particular section of the heavens. He says:

> If we must to reveal to you the truth concerning one's personal *Daimōn* we must say that he is not distributed to us from one part of the heavens nor from any of the visible planets but from the entire cosmos—its multi-faceted life and its multi-form body— through which the soul descends into generation. And a certain individual allotment is imparted to us, allotted to each of our aspects, according to an individual jurisdiction.[2] This *Daimōn*, therefore, is established in the paradigm even before souls descend into generation. And when the soul selects him as its leader the *Daimōn* immediately attends to his task of fulfilling the lives of the soul, and he binds the soul to the body when it descends. (*DM* 280, 1–13)

The ruling daimon mixed the soul's immortal *logoi* with the mortal lives received from the body in order to meet the particular demands of its incarnation.[3] The daimon served as coordinator of the soul's descent into the material world.

The task of each soul was to align itself and its activities with its

---

1. *DM* 278, 16. Astrology describes the "ruler" as follows: "The Lord of the Geniture would be precisely termed the Ruler of the Figure meaning that planet having the most dignities, either Essential [i.e., being situated in a sign amicable to its properties] or Accidental [i.e., in positive relation to other planets]." Nicholas Devore, *Encyclopedia of Astrology* (New York: Philosophical Library, 1947), 246. Usually the planet on the ascendant of one's horoscope—if it is well-aspected— would be considered the "ruler" of one's nativity. Thus, if the sign Leo is on the eastern horizon at one's birth then the planet associated with it, the sun, if well-aspected, would be considered the Lord of one's nativity. If Sagittarius were ascending then a well-aspected Jupiter would be one's "Lord," etc.

2. This is the process of the soul's "taking on attributes" (*prosthēkē*) in its descent into the physical cosmos.

3. See Iamblichus's description of the soul's descent in Simplicius, *In Aristotelis Categorias Commentarium* ed. C. Kalbfleisch (Berlin: Reimeri, 1907), 374, 31–34.

ruling god, and when this was achieved the guardian daimon gave way to a higher guide. Iamblichus continues:

> [T]he *Daimōn* oversees the composite life of the soul [and body] and the individual life of the soul; and all that we think, we conceive due to the principles he has implanted in us. We do the things that he suggests to our mind, and he continues to govern human beings until, by means of sacred theurgy, the time comes that we are entrusted with a God as guardian and leader of the soul. For then the *Daimōn* either yields to the superior entity or hands over his jurisdiction to him or subjoins himself to him as a co-collaborator or in some other way ministers to him as to his Lord. (*DM* 280, 13–281, 4)

This was a privilege reserved for very few souls. The great majority were best served simply by fulfilling the dictates of their guardian daimons.[4] It should be noted that despite Iamblichus's occasional references to "evil" daimons, there was no evil daimon competing for control of the soul. Iamblichus explicitly states that the soul has only one ruling daimon and that he is good (*DM* 282, 1–5). To fulfill the charges of its guardian, however, the soul first had to recognize him and then develop a rapport. Recognition of the daimon was not gained by artificial means or human effort but was given directly and theurgically by the Lord of daimons (*DM* 283, 18–19). Iamblichus says:

> The invocation of these guardian *Daimones* is effected through their one ruler God who, from the beginning, distributed individual *Daimones* to every soul, and in the sacred rites he reveals the individual *Daimōn* to each soul according to his own will. For, in the theurgic hierarchy, subordinate entities are always invoked by their superiors. Consequently, in the case of *Daimones*, one universal leader of those who are charged to rule over generation dispatches individual *Daimons* to every entity. And, when the familiar *Daimōn* appears to each soul, then he reveals his particular mode of worship as well as his name, and he also teaches the particular manner of invoking him. (*DM* 283, 19–284, 10)

---

4. This is a standard Platonic teaching. In the *Timaeus* 90a–c Plato says that only by constantly "worshiping" the daimon who dwells with us can man partake of immortality.

In each embodiment, the daimon acted on behalf of the god until its "limits" (*ta perata*) had been realized by the soul. The soul's freedom from the daimon—like its freedom from the "law"—was determined, paradoxically, by its degree of identity with it. The daimon was not left behind but was, as it were, digested and incorporated by the theurgist. In addition, insofar as daimons served a processional and dividing function in cosmology, the graduation to a god as overseer indicated that the soul was no longer identified with a "particular" self. When the soul became resonant with the ratios of the World Soul, it began to live for the entire world, and since daimons had jurisdiction over parts, not wholes, the soul then received a god for its leader.

The personal daimon revealed himself to the theurgist and taught him how to stay in contact, but to recognize one's daimon demanded an ability to discriminate among the appearances (*phasmata*) of invisible entities. In book II, chapters 3–9 of the *De Mysteriis* Iamblichus provides a diagnostic guide of the entities that appear in theurgic worship. Porphyry had asked how theurgists were able to distinguish among gods, archangels, angels, daimons, archons, and souls (*DM* 70, 10–82), and Iamblichus provided an exhaustive answer. He distinguished among the appearances of (1) gods, (2) archangels, (3) angels, (4) daimons, (5) heroes, (6) sublunary archons, (7) material archons, and (8) souls according to the *ousia*, *dunamis*, and *energeia* of each class. Iamblichus examined twenty different visionary qualities whose manifestations were diminished in each succeeding ontological class. Examining first the "uniformity" of appearances, then their "beneficence," "immutability," "beauty," etc., Iamblichus concluded with a discussion of the "benefits" provided to souls by each class. H. D. Saffrey provides an excellent outline of these chapters,[5] and Friedrich Cremer has covered the same ground to demonstrate the influence of the Chaldean Oracles.[6]

5. Saffrey, "Plan des Livres I et II du *de Mysteriis* de Jamblique," *Zetesis Album Amicorum*, ed. E. de Strycker (Antwerp: de Nederlandsche Boekhandel, 1973), 281–95.

6. Cremer, "Die gottliche Epiphanie (de myst. II, 3-9)," in *Die Chaldaïschen Orakel und Jamblich de Mysteriis* (Meisenheim am Glan: Anton Hain, 1969), 37–91.

Following the Iamblichean principle that *energeia* reveals *ousia*, the appearances of invisible entities were the *energeiai* that revealed their sources, the *ousiai*. In terms of human experience, however, the rank of the divinity that appeared depended on the soul's receptive capacity (the *epitēdeiotēs* discussed in Chapter 7). Iamblichus, in fact, seems to suggest that the soul actually contributed something to the appearance of the deity. Speaking of the "benefits" (*dōra*) that come to souls from the appearance of a god, he says:

> [T]he presence of the Gods gives us health of body, virtue of soul and purity of mind. In short, it elevates everything in us to its proper principle. It annihilates what is cold and destructive in us, *it increases our heat* and causes it to become more powerful and dominant. It makes everything in the soul consonant with the Nous; it causes a light to shine with intelligible harmony, and it reveals the incorporeal as corporeal to the eyes of the soul by means of the eyes of the body.[7]

Iamblichus's reference to corporeal vision as the means to see the incorporeal points to imagination as the medium of theophanies. By means of images the "eyes of the soul" (*hoi tēs psuchēs ophthalmoi*) clothed the gods in an interior space. Clearly, a contribution on the part of the soul was necessary to reveal what was invisible, and Proclus explains that it was the soul's "body of light" (*augoeides sōma*). He says:

> The Gods themselves are incorporeal, but since those who see them possess bodies, the visions which issue from the Gods to worthy recipients possess a certain quality from the Gods who send them but also have something connatural (*sungenēs*) with those who see them. This is why the Gods are seen yet not seen at all. *In fact, those who see the Gods witness them in the luminous garments of their souls* (*augoeidē tōn psuchōn periblemata*). The point is, they are often seen when the eyes are shut. Therefore, since the visions are extended and appear in this different kind of "atmosphere" they are connatural with those who see them. However,

---

7. *DM* 81, 13-82, 2; cf. Proclus's "Fire-Song," lines 8–9, discussed by Lewy, *Chaldean Oracles and Theurgy*, ed. M. Tardieu (Paris: Etudes Augustiniennes, 1978), 491–93.

because visions emit divine light, possess effectiveness, and portray the powers of the Gods through their visible symbols, they remain in contact with the Gods who send them. This is why the ineffable symbols of the Gods are expressed in images and are projected sometimes in one form, sometimes in another. (*In Remp*. I, 39, 5–17)

In summary, Proclus adds:

Each God is formless (*amorphotos*) even if he is seen with a form. For the form is not in him but comes from him due to the incapacity of the viewer to see the formless without a form; rather, according to his nature he sees by means of forms.[8]

The psychic organ that received the divine light was the pneumatic or luminous body. In his treatise *On Dreams* (*De Insomniis*) Synesius identified this body with the "imagination" (*to phantastikon*; 136a, 1) and described it as the soul's "first vehicle" (*to prōton ochēma*; 137a, 2). It was within this imaginal body that the soul experienced its most profound illuminations. The imaginal body, however, should not be confused with ordinary imagination. Iamblichus distinguished not only the "god-sent" dreams from the "human" (*DM* 103, 2–10) but also the "divine appearances" given by the gods from the images concocted by man.[9] The former possessed transformative power while the latter were merely reflections of embodied life. Just as the horizontal expressions of *sunthēmata* were distinguished from their vertical or divine dimension, so with the imagination. On the horizontal level *phantasia* was merely the play of the discursive mind, but if properly purified and trained, the vertical dimension that sustained it could be awakened. The imaginal body of the ordinary person, however, was "diseased" (Synesius, *De Insomniis*, 136d, 1) and until purified it could not serve as a vehicle for the god.

---

8. Proclus, In Remp. I, 39, 28–40, 4. My translation of this passage is adapted from the translation of Jean Trouillard, *La Mystagogie de Proclos* (Paris: Les Belles Lettres, 1982), 42.

9. The *phasmata* of *DM*, book II, chaps. 3–9, are divine as are the visions described in *DM* 132, 11–15, but human imaginations are rejected as being non-theurgical (see *DM* 287, 1–3).

In reply to Porphyry's questions about lights seen in divination Iamblichus explains the role of *phantasia* and catalogues, under the rubric of *phōtagōgia*, the various methods used to illuminate it. He explains:

> The entire kind of divination that you describe, while of many kinds, is contained in a single power which may be called "drawing in the light" (*phōtos agōgē*). This power illuminates with divine light the aetherial and luminous vehicle surrounding the soul, from which divine visions (*phantasiai theiai*) take possession of our imaginative faculty being moved by the will of the Gods. For the entire life of the soul and all its powers, when directed by the Gods, are moved however the Lords of the soul wish.
>
> And this occurs in two ways, either when the Gods are present with the soul, or when they shine into the soul a certain advance light coming from themselves. In each case, the divine presence or the illumination, they are transcendent [to the soul]. The attention and discursive power of the soul follow what takes place [cf. *DM* 104, 11] since the divine light does not touch them, but the imaginative faculty (*to phantastikon*) is divinely inspired because it is lifted into modes of imagination that come from the Gods, not from itself, and it is utterly removed from what is ordinarily human.[10]

The Neoplatonic doctrine of the imaginal body and its role in theurgic ascent exemplifies what Mircea Eliade has called a "mystical physiology." In his well-known study on yoga Eliade explains that the descriptions of such "physiologies" are "not conceptualizations, but images expressing transmundane experiences."[11] It is in this sense that Iamblichus's doctrine of the soul's pneumatic or aetherial body must be understood, for he used physiological terms to describe experiences that transcend the physical realm. In effect, Iamblichus used "the eyes of the body" to awaken "the eyes of the soul."

---

10. *DM* 132, 9–133, 9. Compare this mode of divination with that described at *DM* 117, 1–9 where the discursive mind is unaware of what takes place. In both cases, the cause for the divine inspiration is "the lights which come down from the Gods" (*DM* 117, 2).

11. Mircea Eliade, *Yoga: Immortality and Freedom*, trans. Willard Trask (Princeton: Princeton University Press, 1969), 289.

The similarities between the doctrines of the subtle body in later Neoplatonism and the yoga traditions are suggestive, particularly with respect to the role of "heat" as it relates to "breath" and the "channels" of the soul's mystical body in yogic and theurgic practices.[12] Iamblichus says the presence of the god heats the soul and effects a visual theophany. The divine heating occurred within the soul's "mystical" body, yet the fact that this body was called pneumatic (*pneumatikos*), as well as aetheric (*aitherodes*) and luminous (*augoeides*; DM 239, 9–11) suggests that physical breath (*pneuma*) played a role in this heating and incandescence. Breath may have been the means through which the soul was translated to its mystical body and, once established there, homologized to the cosmos and Creator. Evidence from the *Chaldean Oracles* supports this. In fragment 130, the soul established in god is said to "breathe in the flowering flames that descend from the Father,"[13] and fragment 124 speaks of liberated souls who are "thrust out" [of their bodies] (*exōstēres*) by "inhaling" (*anapnooi*; trans. Majercik, 97). Psellus explains that this was not effected by the soul but by divine powers who "cause the soul to breathe far from the weariness and oppression of the body."[14] It is possible that Iamblichus's legendary ability to levitate in prayer[15] had its origins in these breathing techniques and that the story of his "levitation" (which he laughed off),[16] may

12. A careful comparison cannot be developed here except to point to the terms and their functions in the respective spiritual practices. "Heat" (*tapas*/yoga : *thermon*/theurgy) is awakened by, or directly related to, the "breath" (*prana*/yoga : *pneuma*/theurgy). When sufficiently heated, it flows up the "channels" (*nadis*/yoga : *ochetai*/theurgy) of the mystical body to divinize the soul. It may be possible also to compare the fiery goddess Hecate, invoked by theurgists, with the goddess Kundalini, invoked by yogins, since both were responsible for the salvation or punishment of souls depending on their purity and preparation for the encounter.

13. *CO*, 98–99.

14. Psellus, PM 1144c, 8–9; Appendice 1: Michel Psellus, *Commentaire des Oracles Chaldaïques*, in E. des Places, *Oracles Chaldaïques* (Paris: Les Belles Lettres, 1971), 181.

15. Iamblichus was reported by his servants to levitate more than 10 cubits and to take on a golden hue when praying; Eunapius, *Philostratus and Eunapius: The Lives of the Sophists* (458), trans. W.C. Wright (Cambridge: Harvard University Press, 1921; 1968), 364–65.

16. Ibid., 365.

have derived from a misinterpretation of the phenomenon that occurred when the theurgist coordinated his breath and visualization. For example, the Mithras Liturgy states: "Draw in breath from the [sun's] rays, drawing in three times as much as you can, and *you will see yourself lifted up* and ascending to the height so that you seem to be in midair."[17]

The key to these pneumatic exercises was the belief that the soul's aetheric body was directly connected with the sun, the source of light. It should be borne in mind that the radiance of this body was related, not only to the physical sun, but also to its hidden source. Plato's reference to the sun as the image of the Good in the *Republic* (509b, 2–10) profoundly influenced the Neoplatonists who saw the physical sun as revealer of the divine *Nous*. In a cosmology where nature was seen as a theophany of the gods it would be inconsistent if the sun did not play a central role in soteriological rites. Julian says that Helios was surrounded by the "fifth body" (*pempton sōma*) with its summit being the rays of the sun,[18] and Iamblichus identified this "fifth body" with aether (*TA*, 34, 13), the same aether that made up the soul's subtle body. Thus, through its aetheric vehicle the embodied soul participated in the aetheric body of the sun in varying degrees of intensity. According to the *Chaldean Oracles* the leader god of each soul was identified with one of the solar rays, and fragment 110 says that the soul must discover its "ray" (*ochetos*) and perform the proper ritual in order to make its ascent. Fragment 123 says that the soul is relieved by *heated breath*, pointing again to the connection of breath and the sun. In the *De Anima* Iamblichus says that according to the Ancients (i.e., theurgists), souls are purified by all the visible gods "and of them all most especially by the sun."[19]

The connections between light, fire, the pneumatic body, and physical breath were also described in the *De Mysteriis* where Iam-

17. *The Mithras Liturgy* (PGM IV, 538–41), trans. Marvin Meyer, in *The Greek Magical Papyri in Translation*, ed. Hans Dieter Betz (Chicago: University of Chicago Press, 1986), 1:48.

18. Julian, *Oration IV: Hymn to King Helios* (132c), in *The Works of the Emperor Julian*, trans. W. C. Wright (Cambridge: Harvard University Press, 1969), 1:358–59.

19. *Stob.* I, 455, 2.

blichus measures the degrees of divine light by their effects on breath. He says:

> Indeed, with respect to the subtlety of light, the Gods irradiate it to such a fine degree that the eyes of the body cannot receive it, and *they undergo the same experience as fish when they are lifted up out of turbid and thick fluid into subtle and diaphanous air.* In fact, those who contemplate the divine fire are not able to inhale the subtlety of it; *they appear to fall into a swoon, to all appearances, and are cut off from their natural breath.* (*DM* 86, 5–14)

This passage suggests some form of trance in which the theurgist's breath was completely stopped. Such phenomena are not uncommon in yogic practices and Iamblichus may be describing the theurgic equivalent of yogic *turiya*, a "cateleptic" condition where the breath appears to stop.[20] On the other hand, Iamblichus may simply be pointing out that when the human soul entered the subtlety of divine light it began to breathe, in Psellus's terms, "far from the weariness and oppression of the body" (*PG* 1144c, 8–9). To "breathe," that is to say, to "live" with the gods, the soul could not continue to breath/live in an ordinary way. One could "inhale the sun's rays" only with an *augoeides sōma*, a solar body. Iamblichus adds that the light emitted by the archangels was also too rarefied for the soul to inhale but notes that the presence of angels produced a mixture of air that theurgists were capable of breathing (*DM* 86, 13–18). Since Iamblichus believed that human souls were able to live no higher than the rank of angels (*DM* 69, 12–14), perhaps this passage simply reiterates that position, employing "breath" as the index of the soul's "life."

Iamblichus's description of the soul's inability to endure the atmosphere of the gods is also reminiscent of Plato's *Phaedo*. There, Socrates tells Simmias that humanity lives in the "hollows of the earth," the "dregs of the starry aether," unable or unwilling to emerge to the true surface of the world (109c):

> We are too feeble and sluggish to make our way out to the upper limit of the air. If someone could reach to the summit, or put on

---

20. Eliade, *Yoga*, 57.

wings and fly aloft, when he put up his head he would see the world above, *just as fishes see our world when they put their heads out of the sea.* And if his nature were able to bear the sight, he would recognize that that is the true heaven and the true light and the true earth. (109c)

For Platonists the mythic geography of the *Phaedo* was a map of the soul. It was possible for the soul to live in resonance with divine ratios, suspended in perfect equilibrium (109c) on a "true earth" (110b, 5) "as pure as the starry heavens in which it lies" (109b, 9); or the soul might live in the "dregs of that aether" (109c, 2), in anatropic dissonance, alternately attracted and repelled by the flux and reflux of sensible matter.

The theurgist emerged from this perversity and heaviness to behold the true heaven, true light, and true earth and live in direct contact with the divine causes. He achieved this condition by means of *sunthēmata* that purified his luminous body and translated him to the divine. Since the luminous vehicle (*augoeides ochēma*) was solar in origin, when it was purified it returned to the sun. Damascius explains that the theurgist was made divine "when the radiant vehicle journeys upward to the sun . . . when we are established in the soul of the sun" (*Dub. et Sol.* II, 255, 17–18).

It is almost certain that the cultic expression of theurgy centered on the worship of the sun. Julian says that his devotion to Helios was perfected through the teachings of Iamblichus, and his *Hymn to the Mother of the Gods*[21] testifies to the importance of the sun in the apotheosis of the human soul. The drama of Attis was the drama of the human soul in its descent into generation. Like human souls, Attis was the lowest of divine beings, and although he was "as pure as the Milky Way" (171a) he was troubled by passion when he joined with matter. Like human souls, Attis entered the generated world "following the will of the gods" (171b), but this obedience came at the cost of his equanimity. The descent, in other words, was a sacrifice willed by the gods and performed by Attis, and his subsequent "castration" symbolized the completion of his mission. In meta-

---

21. Julian, *Oration V: Hymn to the Mother of the Gods*, trans. W.C. Wright, in *Works*, 1:439–503.

physical terms, the castration of Attis represented the limiting of the soul's unlimited propensity, the bestowal of *peras* upon *apeiron*, which is the act of demiurgy and theurgy par excellence. The apotheosis of Attis, significantly, was effected by Helios. Julian says: "After bringing a halt to his unlimited procession, Attis brought this chaos into order through his sympathy with the cycle of the equinox since the great *Hēlios* controls the most perfect measure of his motion within due limits" (171c). The myth portrayed this demiurgy as an ongoing activity, for the cycle of Attis did not happen in the past, nor was it ever finished. Thus, Julian says: "And never did this happen, except in the manner that it happens *now* . . . for Attis *always* yearns for generation, and he is *always* cutting short the unlimited through the limited cause of the Forms" (171d).

The role of souls as suggested in the myth of Attis was demiurgic, but once embodied—and souls were *always* entering bodies—their divine measures had to be received from without. The sun, therefore, was the initiator in the recollection and return of souls. In his manifestation as physical light and chief among encosmic gods Helios served as administrator for the cult of "material" souls, yet in his noetic expression Helios's invisible rays defined the mathematic ratios invoked in the cult of noetic souls.[22] "[For] *Hēlios*," say the Pythagoreans, "is the great geometer and arithmetician."[23] Julian explains the role of the sun as follows:

> Consider this clearly: *Hēlios*, by his vivifying and marvelous heat, draws up all things from the earth and calls them forth and makes them grow, separating, I believe, corporeal things to their highest degree of tenuity, and he makes things light that naturally would sink. These things should be taken as sure signs of his unseen powers. For if among corporeal things he can effect this through his corporeal heat, how would he not draw and lead upwards the souls of the blessed by means of the invisible, wholly incorporeal, and divinely pure essence established in his rays? (172b)

22. Cf. *Epinomis* 977ab. For a discussion of the cult of the sun in the Platonic tradition see H.D. Saffrey, "La Dévotion de Proclus au Soleil," *Institut de Philosophie (et Science Morale) Annales* (Brussels, 1984): 73–86.

23. Hippolytus, *Adv. haer.* VI 2.28; quoted by C.J. de Vogel, *Pythagoras and Early Pythagoreanism* (Assen: Van Gorcum, 1966), 201.

For Julian the worship of Helios was a theurgical mystery. He continues:

> If I should also touch on the ineffable mystagogy (*hē arrhēte myst-agōgia*) which the Chaldean, divinely frenzied, celebrated to the God of the Seven Rays—he who lifts up the souls of men through himself—I would be describing unknowable things, indeed, entirely unknowable for the vulgar, but quite familiar to the blessed theurgists. (172d–173a)

Julian's religiosity should not be taken as a sure index of Iamblichus's views; certainly not with the same confidence that one may draw from Proclus, Simplicius, or Damascius.[24] Nevertheless, the role of the sun, or rather, the *sunthēma* of the sun, as symbol of the noetic fire and Demiurge, was almost certainly the central mystery of Neoplatonic theurgy. Proclus worshiped the sun three times a day, at rising, noon, and setting.[25] In his *Timaeus* commentary he spoke of the demiurgic powers of the hidden sun described in the Oracles: "The truer sun measures the All together with Time, truly being . . . 'Time of Time'"[26] and in his *Parmenides* commentary he says: "[The sun is] the analogue of the One, established in it secretly and inseparably" (1045, 6–9).

In the later Roman Empire the sun became increasingly important not only as a god appropriated for the emperor cult but also in the most spiritual worship. Tractate XIII of the *Corpus Hermeticum* suggests that the sun played a key role in the highest mysteries, and the Hermetic apotheosis exemplifies several theurgic characteristics. Tat, the disciple of Hermes, learned to "regenerate" his soul and complete the *tetraktus* of intelligent generation (i.e., the "measured descent" described in Chapter 19). At this point, Hermes tells him:

---

24. There was understandably a greater tendency to dogmatism and theological uniformity in the Neoplatonism of a political figure like Julian than in spiritual teachers like Iamblichus and Proclus. For an excellent discussion of this issue see A.H. Armstrong, "The Way and the Ways: Religious Tolerance and Intolerance in the Fourth Century A.D.," *Vigiliae Christianae* 38 (1984); esp. 6.

25. Marinus, *Vita Procli*, 22; cited in Saffrey, "La Dévotion," 73.

26. See *CO*, frag. 185, 117.

"You now know, my child, the way of regeneration. When the Decad comes into being, my child, your spiritual birth has been established" (*CH* X, 10; 204, 21–24). Tat replies:

> Being stabilized by the God, O Father, I visualize for myself, *not with the vision of the eyes but through the Powers, in intelligible activity.* I am in heaven, in earth, in water, in air. I am in animals, in plants, in the womb, before the womb, after the womb, every-where! (*CH* XIII, 11; 205, 3–7)

Hermes explains to Tat that by completing the decad he has entered into contact with the One since "the Decad is in the One, and the One is in the Decad" (*CH* XIII, 12). The decad was the Pythagorean symbol of the actualized *tetraktus*, the manifestation of all principles in the cosmos. Having been reborn into this "body," Tat sees himself in all things, an experience amenable to a theurgical interpretation for, according to Iamblichus, the soul may return to the One only if it has been homologized to the All. The soul must first "see itself in all things" before it enters the immortal body measured by the gods. At the culmination of his ascent Tat asks for the final mystery and Hermes, significantly, does not explain it—the divine powers perform the mystery *through* him. They sing a mystery oriented to the sun. Hermes instructs Tat to "bow down at the setting and rising of the sun" (*CH* XIII, 16, 207, 11–12) and sing a hymn to the "intelligible light" (*to noēton phōs*; *CH* XIII, 18, 208, 5) to celebrate the union of the will of the soul with the will of the Demiurge. Hermes sings to the Creator: "The Powers that are in me sing these things; they chant out the universe. They complete your will, your plan as it proceeds from you and returns to you as the [completed] universe. Receive from all existing things the spiritual sacrifice" (*CH* XIII, 19, 208, 13–16).

Whether or not the authors of this Hermetic tractate formed part of a "theurgic" community, or any community at all is a question that will not be addressed, yet the motifs involved—(1) Pythagorean mysticism; (2) homologization to the cosmos as a means of release; (3) participation in demiurgy; and (4) the central role of the sun in the ritual act—were all characteristics of theurgy as conceived by Iamblichus. The evidence suggests that theurgic mysteries were solar mysteries, for the goal of all *mantikē* and theurgic ritual was "the ascent to the intelligible Fire" (*DM* 179, 9–12) and theurgists, Iamblichus says, "are true athletes of the Fire" (*DM* 92, 13–14).

IV

Toward a
Universal
Platonism

21

The Platonizing of Popular Religion

There are two kinds of madness, one resulting from human illness, the other from a divine disruption of our codes of conduct.
                    —Phaedrus (265a)

D ivination (*mantikē*) in the late antique world was the art of bird watchers, gut-gazers, dream interpreters, trance mediums, and others to predict the future and determine the will of the gods. Divinational practices were an integral part of the Greco-Roman world and provided Iamblichus with striking, yet universally recognized evidence that divine powers exist beyond the human soul. In the *De Mysteriis* the phenomena of *mantikē* became the *exempla* of theurgy, furnishing Iamblichus's hieratic Platonism with a familiarity that it did not yet possess. At the same time, by arguing for the philosophical legitimacy of divinational rites—under the rubric of theurgy—Iamblichus provided a theoretical justification for well-known religious practices of the Greco-Roman world.

Iamblichus's interpretation of *mantikē* was perfectly orthodox for a Platonist, since Plato himself had already pointed to a connection between divine madness (*theia mania*) and divination (*mantikē*; *Phaedrus* 244a–c). For Plato, "man's greatest blessings come by way of madness, indeed of madness that is heaven-sent" (*Phaedrus* 244a, 6–8), and Iamblichus maintained that since divination came from the gods it was "divine work," hence, *theourgia*. The theurgical interpretation of divination, therefore, represents Iamblichus's attempt to flesh out the suggestions about divine madness (*theia*

259

mania) in the *Phaedrus*. For Platonists, the dramatic change of consciousness seen in trance diviners and rhapsodists would have vividly exemplified the kind of transformation sought for in the soul. Plotinus, for example, referred to the phenomenon of the *mantis* to describe the soul's contact with the One:

> But just as those who have a god within them (*enthousiōntes*) and are in the grip of divine possession may know this much, that they have something greater in them, even if they do not know what; and from the ways in which they are moved, and the things they say, get a certain awareness of the god who moves them, though these are not the same as the mover; so we seem to be disposed towards the One.[1]

However, what served Plotinus as an evocative comparison and Plato as a suggestive etymology became, for Iamblichus, the principal example of his theurgical program. One cannot fail to recognize the influence of the *Phaedrus* on the *De Mysteriis*, particularly Plato's statement that *mania*, like theurgy, comes from the gods and reasoning from men (*Phaedrus* 244d, 3–5). Cast against the background of this dialogue, Porphyry becomes the "merely clever" man of the *Phaedrus* while Iamblichus/Abammon assumes the role of the "wise" spokesman for theurgy, the *theia mania* of the fourth century (*Phaedrus* 245c, 1–2).

According to Iamblichus, whenever a soul was touched by the gods it entered the condition of a *mantis*, and just as a traditional *mantis* exchanged ordinary consciousness for a divine possession, so Iamblichus believed that each transformation of the soul was a theurgic exchange, a *theia mantikē*. In effect, Iamblichus generalized the specific phenomenon of the *mantis* or the *enthousiastēs* to describe theurgic transformations and he required in turn that the traditional oracles at Delphi, Colophon, and Branchidae fit his interpretive criteria for theurgy (see *DM* 123, 11–127, 11).

True divination, according to Iamblichus, was equivalent to divinization, making the soul divine, and knowledge of the future

---

1. Plotinus, *Enn.* V, 3, 14, 9–14, trans. A.H. Armstrong (Cambridge: Harvard University Press, 1966–68).

was merely a secondary consequence of ascending to the *archē* of temporal events. Iamblichus argued that theurgical divination should be carefully distinguished from inductive techniques aimed at making predictions or diagnosing illnesses,[2] and he also distinguished it from the natural prescience of animals to predict earthquakes or rain. Such presentiments arose from a sympathy with natural elements or from acute sense perception, but they were fallible and did not have the same function as divine *mantikē* (*DM* 162, 16–163, 11). Iamblichus admitted that human souls, like animals, receive impressions of coming events—what today would be called ESP—but he maintained that this was divination of a second order and fell short of divine stability and truth. Most significant, it did not transform the soul. "This intuitive faculty," Iamblichus says, "has nothing in it that is truly blessed" (*DM* 288, 18–19). As a consequence of having appropriated the phenomenon of *mantikē* into his theurgical program, any aspect of popular divination that did not meet Iamblichus's criteria for theurgy was not considered true divination.

According to Iamblichus, the function of divination was the deification of the soul:

> Divine *mantikē* alone *unites us with the Gods*, for it genuinely gives us a share of the divine life, has a share in prognosis and divine intuitions, and *makes us truly divine*. It truly bestows the Good on us, because the most blessed intuition of the Gods is filled with all the good things. (*DM* 289, 3–8)

The divinatory elements and techniques might be modified according to the needs of the time and the soul, but the divine function of *mantikē* remained constant:

> There is one correct definition and principle for all forms of divination and it has nothing to do with irresponsibly divining the future with things that lack foreknowledge. Rather, it is to view from [the perspective] of the Gods—who contain in themselves the limits of the entire knowledge of reality—the divination allotted throughout the whole world and all the lives defined in it. This

---

2. *DM* 288, 9–11; 163, 11–13. Iamblichus, again, follows Plato; cf. *Phaedrus* 244cd; *Republic* 516d.

cause is primordial and eminently universal, possessing in a primary way (*protōs*) what it bestows to its participants. Certainly, it possesses the truth necessary for divination and anticipates the essence and cause of events from which it necessarily and accurately yields foreknowledge. Let us take this kind of principle universally as the cause for all divination and from which we may scientifically discover all its species. (*DM* 101, 15–102, 11)

The foreknowledge (*prognōsis*) given in divination was not knowledge of particular events. It was, rather, an immediate knowing, "possessing in a primary way (*protōs*)" things that happen serially in time. Like the *noēsis* of the gods, this primary knowing was unreflective and therefore was not "knowledge" in a discursive sense.[3] It lifted the soul from particular knowing to the level of the gods where all events, past and future, were simultaneously contained. Theurgic prognosis was literally a *pro* + *gnōsis*, an ascent to the *archē* of knowing and thus, to that which *precedes* knowing. Yet, as the *archē* of knowledge, prognosis contained all its species, so the information received in divination, although accurate, was merely incidental to the soul's ascent to the *archē*. Knowledge of the future was not an essential characteristic of theurgic *mantikē*. Iamblichus says: "Whenever it is necessary for the soul to exercise virtue, and ignorance of the future contributes to this, *the Gods conceal the things that will happen* in order to make the soul better" (*DM* 289, 17–290, 1). Divine *mantikē* did not serve human desires; it existed solely "for the sake of the salvation and ascent of souls" (*DM* 290, 2–3). Nor was *mantikē* an "artifice or invention useful for the conduct of life" (*DM* 100, 5–6). "It is not a human work at all," Iamblichus says, "but divine and supernatural and sent down to us from heaven" (*DM* 100, 6–8).

The differences between Porphyry and Iamblichus are most clearly defined on the topic of divination, for both used the phenomenon to distinguish their forms of Platonism. Porphyry defined the piety of the philosopher by contrasting it with the false wisdom

3. For "knowledge is separated [from its object] by otherness. But *prior to the act of knowing* another as being itself 'other' there exists a spontaneous . . . uniform conjunction suspended from the Gods" (*DM* 8, 4–6).

of the diviner. He says: "The philosopher . . . is detached from exterior things . . . and has no need of diviners or the entrails of animals. *For the goods about which divinations are concerned are the very things from which the philosopher strives to detach himself.*"[4] In his letter to Anebo, Porphyry maintained that the dramatic effects observed in divination were not indicative of the soul's exaltation but of diseases caused by "black bile, drunkenness or the fury of mad dogs" (*DM* 158, 7–10). Porphyry said that the *ekstasis* that threw the soul out of discursive awareness was a degenerative phenomenon and that the "not-knowing" condition of the *mantis* indicated a privation of knowledge, not an ascent to its principle. The issue is significant, for if theurgy translated the soul to an ineffable possession, what would distinguish this from a derangement and loss of intelligence? Indeed, this issue continues to lie at the heart of current debates over the value of theurgy in the history of Platonism. Iamblichus recognized its importance and responded by distinguishing two kinds of ecstasy:[5]

> From the beginning, it is necessary to divide ecstasy into two species: one is turned toward the inferior [and the other reaches up to the superior];[6] one is filled with foolishness and delirium, but the other imparts goods more honorable than human wisdom. One degenerates to a disorderly, confused and material movement, but the other gives itself to the cause that rules over the very order of the cosmos. The former deviates from understanding because it is deprived of knowledge, but the latter because it is attached to beings that transcend all human understanding. The former is unstable, the latter unchangeable; the first is counter to nature (*para phusin*), the latter is beyond nature (*huper phusin*); the former makes the soul descend, the latter raises it up; and while

4. *De Abst.* II, 52, 2–4; in *Porphyre: De l'abstinence*, text, translation, and introduction by Jean Bouffartique and Michel Patillon (Paris: Les Belles Lettres, 1977).

5. The distinctions that follow elaborate upon the distinction already made by Plato in the *Phaedrus*. "There are two kinds of madness," Socrates says, "one resulting from human illness, the other from a divine disruption of our codes of conduct" (*Phaedrus* 265a, 9–11).

6. I follow the conjecture of Westerink for the lacuna that precedes *kai* (*DM* 158, 12). See the apparatus of des Places's text and translation of *Jamblique: Les mystères d'Egypte* (Paris: Les Belles Lettres, 1966), 133.

the former entirely separates the soul from participation in the divine, the latter connects the soul with the divine. (*DM* 158, 10–159, 6)

These contrasts are crucial for understanding Iamblichus's defense of theurgy and they represent his clearest refutation of the implications of sorcery raised by Porphyry and those of "irrationalism" brought by modern scholars. To an untutored observer a deranged ecstasy *para phusin* might appear the same as a divine ecstasy *huper phusin*, but they were fundamentally opposed, and the *De Mysteriis* represents Iamblichus's attempt to clarify this opposition. In a subsequent passage he makes the same kind of distinction with respect to *phantasia*, contrasting the imagination stirred up by diseases with divine imaginations (*theiai phantasiai*; *DM* 160, 9–11) sent by the gods. Iamblichus's criterion for determining whether the ecstasy was divine or deranged was whether or not it had a beneficial and stabilizing effect on the soul.

It is significant that Plotinus used the term *ekstasis* only once in a positive sense and even then, Armstrong says, the manuscript may be in error.[7] *Ekstasis*, the "standing outside oneself," would not have played a part in the spiritual discipline of one whose soul was already equivalent to the *Nous*. For Plotinus and Porphyry, *ekstasis* could only be a degenerative act, falling out of one's true self, which was equivalent to falling away from the divine *Nous* itself.[8] Hence, Porphyry saw mantic phenomenon as a derangement and loss of the "sacred sobriety of the gods" (*DM* 160, 7). In contrast, because of his embodied psychology, Iamblichus believed that "standing outside oneself" was altogether necessary for the salvation of the soul. The human "sobriety" extolled by Porphyry was simply not enough; Iamblichus tells him: "You should in no way regard human sobriety as comparable to divine sobriety" (*DM* 160, 6–8). Theurgic *ekstasis* was Iamblichus's answer to Plato's *theia mania*, and he saw the doctrine of the complete descent of the soul as its correlate.

7. *Enn.* VI, 9, 11, 22–25. See Armstrong's note, *Plotinus*, trans. A.H. Armstrong (Cambridge: Harvard University Press, 1988), 7:242–43.

8. *De Abst.* I, 29, 4; in *Porphyre: De l'abstinence*, text, trans., and intro. Bouffartique and Patillon.

Because of the soul's hypostatic disjuncture from the gods, *ekstasis* was a sine qua non for apotheosis. The gods came to the soul from without, *exōthen*, and to attain a divine life the soul had to undergo an ecstatic transformation and "exchange." Every theurgist had to become a *mantis*.

Conclusion

For my part I would rather receive
one letter from Iamblichus than
possess all the gold of Lydia.
—Pseudo-Julian

What was it about Iamblichus that attracted the respect
and veneration of Platonic thinkers from the fourth century to the Renaissance? Why did the emperor Julian
regard Iamblichus as the equal to Plato? And why did a student
describe Iamblichus as the "great glory," "universal blessing," and
"savior"[1] of the Hellenic world? The slavish cheerleading of an
enthusiast? Why then did later Platonists like Proclus and Damascius give Iamblichus's teachings more authority than even the
teachings of Plotinus? Was Iamblichus's influence due simply to the
"loss of nerve" among late antique intellectuals—as many would
have us believe—or did he, perhaps, outline a compelling and comprehensive vision of a world that we no longer understand?

In light of the pressures confronting Platonists in the fourth century, Iamblichus's unknown student may have been correct to see
his teacher as the *sōter* of the Hellenic world. Under the leadership
of Plotinus and Porphyry, the influence of Platonism had receded to
an intellectual elite that was becoming increasingly alienated from
the common man. Following the social and economic changes of
the third and fourth centuries, the loyalties of the latter were being
drawn away from the traditional cults of old Hellenism, and
increasing numbers of people were adopting new identities as participants in the *mustēria* of Christ. This was certainly true in the
Antioch of Iamblichus's time, and although pagan philosophers
were still respected, their authority was gradually being transferred

1. An anonymous student of Iamblichus; in *The Works of the Emperor Julian*,
trans. W.C. Wright (Cambridge: Harvard University Press, 1980), *Apocryphal Let-
ter(s)* 76, 449bc; 78, 418d.

266

to Christian bishops who offered salvation to all regardless of their social or intellectual class.[2]

It would be tempting, but incorrect, to see Iamblichus's soteriological praxis as a reaction to this state of affairs, as his attempt to accommodate Platonism to the changing times. It is tempting because Iamblichus's theurgic reinterpretation of Platonism fulfilled the requirements of popular religion while preserving the esoteric disciplines of a privileged few. The former aspect has usually drawn attention, but it is the latter that is of greater importance. In one sense theurgy was the logical correlate to the law of arithmogonic procession; namely, that the higher and more unified a principle, the more extensive or more piercing (*drimutera*)[3] its effects. Because theurgy provided a more direct and simplified participation in the One, it had a wider circle of application and was as available to the common man as to the intellectual. Rather than falling outside the circumference of Platonism—as many have suggested—theurgy penetrated to a deeper center, one that extended the boundaries of the Platonic world. To say that Iamblichus *preserved* the esoteric disciplines of the Platonic school, however, is not quite correct, for in his estimation those disciplines had already been lost or distorted by his predecessors.

Iamblichus broke away from the teachings of Porphyry and Plotinus in order to reestablish—in theurgical Platonism—what he believed to be the true teachings of Plato and Pythagoras. Iamblichus thought that he had inherited a kind of gnosticized Platonism from Porphyry, with its attendant consequences: (1) a cosmological dualism with matter viewed as evil; (2) the human soul equated with the World Soul and the *Nous*; and (3) a desacralized and demonic cosmos from which the soul, in Porphyry's view, should seek its permanent escape. The impact of these views on popular audiences may or may not have been significant, but it was far more important to Iamblichus that they were mistaken and therefore incapable of leading souls to a genuine transformation and apotheosis.

---

2. Peter Brown, *The World of Late Antiquity* (London: Harcourt Brace Jovanovich, 1971), 60–96.

3. *In Alc.*, Frag. 8, 8; in Dillon, *Iamblichi Chalcidensis*, commentary, 236–38.

In a manner that was traditionally Platonic, Iamblichus turned to the "Egyptians" and the "Chaldeans"—that is, to barbarian wise-men—for the authority to change the direction of his philosophical tradition. The degree to which theurgy reflects genuine Egyptian cult practices may be significant,[4] but it is not the central issue. At issue is Iamblichus's belief in a sacred tradition. Only a tradition received from the gods could play the role of authoritative "other" to the fallen soul and fallen society. Deference to Egyptian wisdom in this sense was already a topos in the Platonic dialogues where "Egypt" func-tioned as an ideal culture against which Plato measured his own.[5] The role of Plato *redivivus*, as seen in the Chaldean Oracles, cannot be underestimated either as an important influence on Iamblichus's development of theurgic Platonism. As divine *logia*, the Oracles also functioned as an authoritative "other" capable of saving the soul.

The influence of Pythagorean thought on Iamblichus was per-haps most critical, as it provided him with the conceptual frame-work and the theoretic justification for the practice of theurgy. Although Iamblichus was an advocate of conserving traditional pagan religions, he discovered in Pythagoreanism a revolutionary method to identify himself with the "old ways." Using Pythagorean cosmological principles as his standard, Iamblichus discovered theurgical dimensions in a variety of religious practices. While each cultural embodiment of the gods was unique in its myths and ritu-als—and therefore untranslatable by man—each possessed a com-mon theurgic power. As a theurgist, and one who had coordinated himself with the numbers of creation, Iamblichus had the ability to become unified with the gods in a variety of cultural guises. The cult simply had to meet his Pythagorean standards, one being that the soul's apotheosis was the result of its homologization to the *arithmoi* of the World Soul. These unchanging mathematical pro-portions were the constants in the shifting valencies of Iamblichean theurgy. Plato too had spoken of a "great power of geometric equal-

---

4. See for example Derchain's essay, "Pseudo-Jamblique ou Abammon?" *Chro-nique d'Egypt* 76 (1973): 220–26.

5. See Henri Joly, "Platon égyptologue," *Revue philosophique de la France et de l'Etranger* 2 (1982): 255–66.

ity amongst gods and men" (*Gorgias* 508bc) and for Iamblichus the *arithmoi*, in their theological, mathematical, or material expression were the invisible foundation of every theurgy.

The most distinctive cosmological feature in theurgy was the central position given to the sun. For Iamblichus, Helios played the key role in the apotheosis of the soul: first awakening it through the senses and then leading it noetically to the eternal *arithmoi*. As Plato says in the *Timaeus*: "God lit a fire which we now call the sun . . . that it might give light to the whole of heaven, and that animals, as many as nature intended, might participate in *number*" (*Tim.* 38bc). And as choreographer of the heavens, the sun led souls into their mathematical bodies. The *Epinomis* says: "But this is the greatest boon of all, if a man will accept his *gift of number* and let his mind wander freely over the whole heavenly circuit" (977b).

Like Plato, Iamblichus attempted to uphold the "old ways" of traditional religions by reinterpreting them according to a cosmological and arithmetic schema. Yet, even more than Plato, Iamblichus preserved these schemas in their own cultural expressions, believing that the power of these rites could never be explained intellectually; they had to be enacted and embodied. In this, particularly, Iamblichus differed from his Platonic predecessors, especially where it concerned the capacity of the human intellect.

The role of the intellect in the soul's salvation was a recurring motif within the *De Mysteriis*. While Plotinus allowed that each soul already contained the *Nous* but was "unconscious" of it, Iamblichus made the unconscious presence of the *Nous* and the One radically distinct, ontologically other, and therefore inaccessible despite all efforts of the soul. To reach the superior hypostases the soul needed the aid of superior entities and these were received from without (*exōthen*).

One consequence of Iamblichus's embodied psychology was that to reach the gods *all* the energies engaged in the soul's descent had to be ritually reengaged and transformed into theurgic receptacles: a world ritualized into the *energeiai* of the gods. In one sense, the differences between Plotinus and Iamblichus might seem insignificant since the Iamblichean gods (like Plotinus's undescended soul) were always present and available to any soul able to receive them.

However, because the Iamblichean soul was anatropic it was unable to receive this aid, which is why the Egyptian/Chaldean element becomes important. For Iamblichus, the only way the soul could receive the gods was by preparing the proper receptacles, the knowledge of which was preserved by the priests of sacred races like the Egyptians and Chaldeans. According to Iamblichus, their mystagogy was a reflection of cosmogony, and their receptacles of the gods recapitulated the act of creation. Apotheosis was realized only through the soul's mimesis of cosmogony, and therefore an "escape" from the cosmos apart from a more causal and responsible involvement in it not only was undesirable, it was impossible. Such a notion could arise only from an exaggerated sense of personal importance, and an escape of this kind did not result in freedom but in bondage to an anatropic fantasy.

Iamblichus argued that theurgy provided everyone, regardless of intellectual training, a way of returning to the gods by preparing their receptacles, however crude or subtle these needed to be. A soteriological cult of this kind might easily degenerate into a form of fetish worship if the ritual receptacles (the *sunthēmata*) became objects of veneration in themselves. This may account for Iamblichus's harsh condemnation of the "image makers" who attend to the dregs of matter rather than to divine causes (*DM* 171, 5–18). Iamblichus reserved some of his most severe criticism for these men, no doubt because the integrity of theurgy was vulnerable to the degenerative worship they encouraged. Conversely, a sterile intellectuality that abstracts itself from nature was the weakness to which Plotinus's model was vulnerable, and Iamblichus criticizes this attitude throughout the *De Mysteriis* as a form of intellectual hubris.

At the conclusion of the *De Mysteriis* Iamblichus sums up the goals of Egyptian theurgy, claiming that "theurgists do not address the divine *Nous* over trifling matters but only concerning things that pertain to the purification, liberation, and salvation of the soul" (*DM* 293, 5–8). From the theurgies performed by "material" souls with heavier *sunthēmata* to those performed by "noetic" souls in the more subtle vehicles of mathematic images, the purpose of every theurgic ritual was the purification (*katharsis*), liberation (*apolusis*), and salvation (*sōtēria*) of the soul. Iamblichus's complaint to Porphyry is as relevant today as it was when Iamblichus wrote his apology for theurgy. He says: "One should not introduce mistakes when making a true judgment of reality, for in the case of other sciences or arts we do not judge their works based on distortions that occur in them" (*DM* 92, 4–7). I believe that Iamblichean theurgy and the ritual practices of the later Neoplatonists have suffered from just this kind of misunderstanding. Because theurgy has erroneously been portrayed as an attempt to manipulate the gods it has been dismissed as a debased and superstitious form of Platonism. It was nothing of the kind. Rather, Iamblichus's prestige in his own and subsequent eras was due to his success in creating—like his fictional Pythagoras—a synthesis of worship and divine philosophy. In theurgy the highest thought of Platonic philosophy was fully integrated with common religious practices, and the immaterial gods were connected to the lowest sublunary daimons: in sum, heaven was joined to earth through the common mathematical structures of Pythagorean science. The Pythagorean solutions that mediated the One and the Many were translated by Iamblichus to the tensions pulling at the fourth century; the result was a comprehensive vision of a cosmos connected everywhere by numbers and accessible to anyone who ritually embodied them. This theurgical vision shaped the thinking of later Platonists such as Syrianus, Proclus, and Damascius, and its influence also extended beyond Platonic circles and may well be reflected in the sacramental theology of Christian thinkers. Indeed, the Church, with its ecclesiastical embodiment of the divine hierarchy, its initiations, and its belief in salvation through sacramental acts, may have fulfilled the theurgical program of Iamblichus in a manner that was never concretely realized by Platonists. In a sense that has yet to be examined, the Church may well have become the reliquary of the hieratic vision and practices of the later Platonists.[6]

6. See James Miller, *Measures of Wisdom: The Cosmic Dance in Classical Antiquity* (Toronto: University of Toronto Press, 1986) for an excellent description of theurgical principles enacted in the liturgy of the sixth-century Orthodox church (pp. 515–17). One important difference between Platonic and Christian (pseudo-Dionysian) theurgy, however, is that for Christians their *ekklēsia* replaces the physical cosmos of the Platonists; it is a theurgy in some sense opposed to the cosmos, an idea entirely at odds with Iamblichean theurgy.

Even if theurgy were limited to Platonic circles, its significance would call for a more careful examination than it has received. It is my hope that this study has made some contribution to that end.

Select Bibliography

PRIMARY SOURCES

Anonymous Prolegomena to Platonic Philosophy. Introduction, text, and translation by L.G. Westerink. Amsterdam: North-Holland, 1962.

Aristotle. *Aristotle.* Vol. 6, *On The Heavens.* Translation by W.K.C. Guthrie. Loeb Classical Library. Cambridge: Harvard University Press, 1939; 1971.

———. *Aristotle's Metaphysics.* 2 vols. Text, introduction, and commentary by W.D. Ross. Oxford: Clarendon Press, 1958.

The Chaldean Oracles. Text, translation, and commentary by Ruth Majercik. Leiden: E.J. Brill, 1989.

Corpus Hermeticum. 4 vols. Trans. A.-J. Festugière. Ed. A.D. Nock. Paris: Les Belles Lettres, 1954–60; reprint, 1972–83.

Damascius. *Dubitationes et solutiones de primis principiis in Platonis Parmenidem.* 2 vols. Edited by C.A. Ruelle. Paris, 1889. Reprint, Brussels: Culture et Civilisation, 1964. French translation in 3 volumes by A.-Ed. Chaignet. Paris, 1898. Reprint, Brussels: Culture et Civilization, 1964.

———. *In Phaedonem.* In *The Greek Commentaries on Plato's Phaedo,* Vol. 2: *Damascius.* Translated and edited by L.G. Westerink. New York: North-Holland, 1977.

———. *Lectures on the Philebus.* Translated and edited by L.G. Westerink. Amsterdam: North-Holland, 1959.

———. *Traité des premiers principes.* 3 vols. Text established by L.G. Westerink. Translation by J. Combes. Paris: Les Belles Lettres, 1986–91.

Demetrius. *Demetrius: On Style.* Translated by W. Rhys Roberts. Cambridge: Cambridge University Press, 1902.

Dionysius the Pseudo-Aréopagite. *Oeuvres complètes du Pseudo-Denys l'Aréopagite.* Translation, preface, and notes by Maurice Gandillac. Paris: Aubier Editions Montaigne, 1943.

Euclid. *Euclid.* Vol. 1, *The Thirteen Books of the Elements.* 2d ed. Translated with introduction and commentary by Sir Thomas Heath. New York: Dover, 1956.

Eunapius. *See* Philostratus and Eunapius.

Ficino, Marsilio. *Opera Omnia.* 2 vols. Basel, 1576; reprint, Turin, 1962.

Hermetica. 4 vols. Edited and translated by W. Scott. London: Dawsons, 1968; reprint, Boston: Shambhala, 1985.

Hierocles. *Hierocles in Aureum Pythagoreorum Carmen Commentarius.* Edited by F. G. Koehler. Stuttgart: Teubner, 1974.

Iamblichus. *De Anima.* Translation and commentary by A.-J. Festugière. In *La Révélation d'Hermès Trismégiste,* appendix 1, 3:177–248. Paris: Gabalda, 1953.

———. *De Communi Mathematia Scientia Liber.* Edited by N. Festa, 1891. Edited with additions and corrections by U. Klein. Stuttgart: Teubner, 1975.

———. *De Vita Pythagorica Liber.* Edited by L. Deubner, 1937. Edited with additions and corrections by U. Klein. Stuttgart: Teubner, 1975.

———. *Iamblichi Chalcidensis: In Platonis Dialogos Commentariorum Fragmenta.* Translated and edited by John Dillon. Leiden: E. J. Brill, 1973.

———. *Iamblichi: De Vita Pythagorica.* Edited by A. Nauck. Amsterdam: Hakkert, 1965.

———. Index to *De Mysteriis Liber.* Pp. 294–328. Edited by G. Parthey. Berlin, 1857.

———. *Iamblichus: On the Pythagorean Life.* Translated with notes and introduction by Gillian Clark. Liverpool: Liverpool University Press, 1989.

———. *Iamblichus: On the Pythagorean Way of Life.* Text, translation, and notes by John Dillon and Jackson Hershbell. Atlanta, Ga.: Scholars Press, 1991.

———. *In Nicomachi Arithmeticam Introductionem.* Edited by H. Pistelli, 1894. Edited with additions and corrections by U. Klein. Stuttgart: Teubner, 1975.

———. *Jamblique de Chalcis: Exégète et philosophe. Appendice: Testimonia et Fragmenta Exegetica.* Collected by B. D. Larsen. Aarhus: Universitetsforlaget, 1972.

———. *Jamblique: Les Mystères d'Egypte.* Translated and edited by E. des Places. Paris: Les Belles Lettres, 1966.

———. *On the Mysteries of the Egyptians, Chaldeans, and Assyrians.* 2d ed. Translated by Thomas Taylor. London: Bertram Dobell, 1895.

———. *Protrepticus.* Edited by H. Pistelli, 1888; reprint, 1967. Stuttgart: Teubner, 1975.

———. [Iamblichus] *Theologumena Arithmeticae.* Edited by V. de Falco, 1922. Edited with additions and corrections by U. Klein. Stuttgart: Teubner, 1975.

————. *The Theology of Arithmetic.* Translated by Robin Waterfield. Grand Rapids, Mich.: Phanes, 1988.

————. [Jamblichus]. *Über die Geheimlehren: Die Mysterien der Ägypte Chaldäer und Assyrer.* Translated by Thomas Hopfner. Leipzig, 1922. Reprint, Schwarzenburg: Ansata-Verlag, 1978.

Jamblichus. *See* Iamblichus.

Julian. *The Works of the Emperor Julian.* 3 vols. Translated by W.C. Wright. Loeb Classical Library. Cambridge: Harvard University Press, 1969.

Marinus. *Vita Procli.* Edited by J.F. Boissonade. Leipzig, 1814. Latin translated with Greek text by Portus. In *In Platonis Theologiam.* Hamburg, 1618; reprint, Frankfurt am Main, 1960.

The Mithras Liturgy (*PGM* IV, 538–41). Translated by Marvin Meyer. In *The Greek Magical Papyri in Translation.* Edited by Hans Dieter Betz. Chicago: University of Chicago, 1986.

Nemesius. *De Natura Hominis.* C. Matthaei. Magdeburg, 1802.

Nicomachus. *Harmonikon Enchiridion.* In C. von Jan, *Musici Scriptores Graeci.* Leipzig, 1895; reprint, Hildesheim, 1962.

————. *Nicomachus Geraseni Pythagorei: Intoductionis Arithmeticae.* Edited by R. Hoche. Lipsae: Teubner, 1866.

————. *Nicomachus of Gerasa: Introduction to Arithmetic.* 3 vols. Translated by M.L. D'Ooge, with Studies in Greek Arithmetic by F.E. Robbins and L.C. Karpinski. New York: Macmillan, 1926.

Numenius. *Fragments.* Translated and edited by E. des Places. Paris: Les Belles Lettres, 1973.

Olympiodorus. *Olympiodori Philosophi In Platonis Phaedonem Commentaria.* Edited by W. Norvin. Leipzig: Teubner, 1913.

Oracles chaldaïques. Edited with translation and commentary by E. des Places. Paris: Les Belles Lettres, 1971.

Origen. *Origen: Contra Celsum.* Translated with introduction and notes by Henry Chadwick. New York: Cambridge University Press, 1953; reprint, 1980.

Philostratus and Eunapius. *Philostratus and Eunapius: The Lives of the Sophists.* Translated by W.C. Wright. Loeb Classical Library. Cambridge: Harvard University Press, 1921; reprint, 1968.

Plato. *Plato.* Vol. 9, *Timaeus, Critias, Cleitophon, Menexenus, Epistles.* Translated by R.G. Bury. Loeb Classical Library. Cambridge: Harvard University Press, 1929; 1981.

————. *Plato.* Vols. 10 and 11, *The Laws.* Translated by R.G. Bury. Loeb Classical Library. Cambridge: Harvard University Press, 1926; 1984.

————. *Plato: Symposium*. Edited by K. J. Dover. New York: Cambridge University Press, 1980.

————. *Platonis Opera*. Vol. 2. Edited by J. Burnet. Oxford: Clarendon Press, 1979.

————. *Plato's Cosmology: The Timaeus of Plato*. Translation and commentary by Francis M. Cornford. London, 1937. Reprint, New York: Bobbs-Merrill, 1959.

Plotinus. *Plotinus*. 6 books in 7 volumes. Translated by A. H. Armstrong. Loeb Classical Library. Cambridge: Harvard University Press, 1966–88.

Plutarch. *Moralia*. Vol. 13, *Plutarch: On the Generation of the Soul*. Edited by Harold Cherniss. Loeb Classical Library. Cambridge: Harvard University Press, 1976.

Porphyry. *Porphyre: De l'abstinence*. 2 vols. Text and translation by Jean Bouffartigue and Michel Patillon. Paris: Les Belles Lettres, 1977.

————. *Porphyre: Vie de Pythagore, Lettre à Marcella*. Text and translation by E. des Places. Paris: Les Belles Lettres, 1982.

————. *Porphyrii: Sententiae Ad Intelligibilia Ducentes*. Edited by E. Lamberz. Leipzig: Teubner, 1975.

————. *Porphyry On Abstinence from Animal Food*. Translated by Thomas Taylor, 1823. Edited and introduced by E. Wynne-Tyson. New York: Barnes and Noble, 1965.

Priscianus Lydus, *Metaphrasis in Theophrastum*. Edited by I. Bywater. In *Supplementum Aristoteliuim*, I, 2:1–37. Berlin: 1886.

Proclus. *Commentarium in Platonis Parmenidem*. 2d ed. Edited by V. Cousin. Paris, 1864. Reprint, Hildesheim: Georg Olms, 1961.

————. *A Commentary on the First Book of Euclid's Elements*. Translated with an introduction by Glenn R. Morrow. Princeton: Princeton University Press, 1970.

————. *Commentary on the First Alcibiades of Plato*. Edited by L. G. Westerink. Amsterdam: North-Holland, 1954. English translation by W. O'Neill. The Hague: Martinus Nijhoff, 1965; reprint, 1971.

————. *In Platonis Cratylum Commentaria*. Edited by G. Pasquali. Leipzig: Teubner, 1908.

————. *In Platonis Rempublicam Commentaria*. Edited by G. Kroll. 2 vols. Leipzig, 1903–6.

————. *In Platonis Timaeum Commentari*. 3 vols. Edited by E. Diehl. Leipzig, 1903–6. Reprint, Amsterdam: Hakkert, 1965. French translation in 5 volumes by A.-J. Festugière. Paris: J. Vrin, 1966–68.

————. *Peri tes kath' Hellenas Hieratikōs Technēs* [On the hieratic art].

Edited by J. Bidez. In *Catalogue des manuscrits alchimiques grecs*, 6:139–51. Brussels: Maurice Lamertin, 1928.

———. *Procli Diadochi in Platonis Cratylum Commentaria*. Edited by G. Pasquali. Lipsiae: Teubner, 1908.

———. *Proclos: Eléments de Théologie*. Translation, introduction, and notes by J. Trouillard. Paris: Aubier, 1965.

———. *Proclus: The Elements of Theology*. 2d ed. Revised text with translation, introduction, and commentary by E. R. Dodds. Oxford: Clarendon Press, 1963.

———. *Proclus: Trois études sur la providence*. Vol. 3, *De l'existence du mal*. Edited by D. Isaac. Paris: Les Belles Lettres, 1982.

———. *Théologie platonicienne*. 5 vols. Translated and edited by H. D. Saffrey and L. G. Westerink. Paris: Les Belles Lettres, 1968–87.

Sallustius. *Sallustius: Concerning the Gods and the Universe*. Edited with prolegomena and translated by A. D. Nock. Hildesheim: Georg Olms, 1966.

Simplicius, *Commentarius in Enchiridion Epicteti*, ed. L. Deubner, Paris, 1842.

Simplicius. *In Aristotelis Categorias Commentarium*. Edited by C. Kalbfleisch. *CAG*, vol. 8. Berlin: G. Reimeri, 1907.

———. *In Libros Aristotelis de Anima Commentaria*. Edited by M. Hayduck. *CAG*, vol. 11. Berlin: G. Reimeri, 1882.

Stobaeus. *Stobaeus: Anthologium*. 4 vols. Edited by C. Wachsmuth and O. Hense. Berlin: Weidmanns, 1958.

Theo Smyrnaeus. *Theonis Smyrnaei: Expositio Rerum Mathematicarum ad Legendum Platonem Utilium*. Edited by E. Hiller. Leipzig: Teubner, 1878.

Secondary Sources

Alleau, René, ed. *La Magie arabe traditionnelle*. Introduction and notes by Sylvain Matton. Paris: Retz, 1977.

Armstrong, A. H. "The Apprehension of Divinity in the Self and Cosmos in Plotinus." In *The Significance of Neoplatonism*, edited by R. B. Harris, 187–97. Norfolk, Va.: International Society for Neoplatonic Studies, 1976.

———. *Classical Mediterranean Spirituality*. New York: Crossroad, 1986.

———. "The Escape of the One: An Investigation of Some Possibilities of Apophatic Theology Imperfectly Realized in the West." *Studia Patristica* 13:77–89. Berlin, 1975.

————. "Gnosis and Greek Philosophy." In *Gnosis: Festschrift für Hans Jonas*, edited by B. Aland et al., 87–124. Göttingen: Vandenhoeck S. Ruprecht, 1978.

————. "Iamblichus and Egypt." *Etudes Philosophiques* 2–3 (1987): 179–88.

————. "Man in the Cosmos: A Study of Some Differences between Pagan Neoplatonism and Christianity." In *Romanitas et Christianitas*, edited by W. den Boer et al., 5–14. London: North-Holland, 1973.

————. "Negative Theology." *Downside Review* 95 (1977): 176–89.

————. *Plotinian and Christian Studies* 17. London: Variorum Reprints, 1979.

————. "The Self-Definition of Christianity in Relation to Later Platonism." In *Jewish and Christian Self-Definition*, edited by E. P. Sanders, 74–99, 228–36. London: SCM Press, 1980.

————. "Tradition, Reason, and Experience in the Thought of Plotinus." In *Plotinian and Christian Studies*, chap. 17, 171–94. London: Variorum Reprints, 1979.

————. "The Way and the Ways: Religious Tolerance in the Fourth Century A.D." *Vigiliae Christianae* 38 (1984): 1–17.

————. ed. *The Cambridge History of Later Greek and Early Medieval Philosophy*. Cambridge: Cambridge University Press, 1967.

Athanassiadi, Polymnia. "Dreams, Theurgy and Freelance Divination: The Testimony of Iamblichus." *Journal of Roman Studies* 83 (1993): 115–30.

————. "Persecution and Response in Late Paganism: The Evidence of Damascius." *Journal of Hellenic Studies* 113 (1993): 1–29.

Ballew, Lynne. *Straight and Circular: A Study of Imagery in Greek Philosophy*. Assen, The Netherlands: Van Gorcum, 1979.

Barnes, T. D. "A Correspondent of Iamblichus." *Greek, Roman, and Byzantine Studies* 19 (1979): 99–106.

Bäumker, Clemens. *Das Problem der Materie in der Griechischen Philosophie*. Frankfurt am Main: Minerva, 1963. (Originally published 1890)

Bebek, Borna. *The Third City: Philosophy at War with Positivism*. Boston: Routledge and Kegan Paul, 1982.

Beierwaltes, Werner. "Das Problem der Erkenntnis bei Proklos." In *Entretiens sur l'antiquité classique*, vol. 21: *De Jamblique à Proclus*, 153–92. Geneva: Fondation Hardt, 1975.

Betz, Hans Dieter, ed. *The Greek Magical Papyri, Including the Demotic Spells*. Vol. 1. Chicago: University of Chicago Press, 1986.

Bidez, J. *Catalogue des manuscrits alchimiques grecs*. Vol. 6. Brussels: Maurice Lamertin, 1928.

———. *Eos, ou Platon et l'orient*. Brussels: M. Hayez, 1945. Reprint, New York: AMS Press, 1979.

———. "La liturgie des mystères chez les Néo-platoniciennes." *Académie Royale des Sciences* 5, no. 5 (1919): 415–30.

———. "Le Philosophe Jamblique et son école." *Revue des Etudes Grecques* 32 (1919): 29–40.

———. *La Vie de l'empereur Julien*. Paris: Les Belles Lettres, 1930.

———. *Vie de Porphyre*. Hildesheim: Georg Olms, 1964.

Blume, H.D., and F. Mann. *Platonismus und Christentum: Festschrift für Heinrich Dörrie*. Jahrbuch für Antike und Christentum, Ergänzungsband 10. Münster: Aschendorff, 1983.

Blumenthal, H.J. "Did Iamblichus Write a Commentary on the *De Anima*?" *Hermes* 102, no. 4 (1974): 540–56.

———. "Neoplatonic Elements in the *De Anima* Commentaries." *Phronesis* 21, no. 1 (1976): 64–87.

———. *Plotinus' Psychology: His Doctrines of the Embodied Soul*. The Hague: Martinus Nijhoff, 1971.

———. "Plutarch's Exposition of the *De Anima* and the Psychology of Proclus." In *Entretiens sur l'antiquité classique*, vol. 21: *De Jamblique à Proclus*, 123–48. Geneva: Fondation Hardt, 1975.

———. "Some Platonist Readings of Aristotle." *Cambridge Philosophical Society Proceedings* 207 (1981): 1–16.

———. "Some Problems About the Body and Soul in Later Neoplatonism: Do They Follow a Pattern?" In *Platonismus und Christentum: Festschrift für Heinrich Dörrie*, eds. H.D. Blume and F. Mann, 75–85. Münster: Aschendorff, 1983.

Blumenthal, H.J., and E.G. Clark, eds. *The Divine Iamblichus: Philosopher and Man of Gods*. Bristol: Bristol Classical Press, 1993.

Blumenthal, H.J., and A.C. Lloyd. *Soul and the Structure of Being in Late Neoplatonism: Syrianius, Proclus, and Simplicius*. Liverpool: Liverpool University Press, 1982.

Blumenthal, H.C., and R.A. Markus, eds. *Neoplatonism and Christian Thought: Essays in Honour of A.H. Armstrong*. London: Variorum, 1981.

Boer, Charles, trans. *Marsilio Ficino: The Book of Life*. Irving, Tex.: Spring Publications, 1980.

Bouché-Leclercq, Auguste. *Astrologie grecque*. Brussels: Culture et Civilisation, 1963.

Boussier, F. and Carlos G. Steel. "Priscianus Lydus en de 'In de Anima' van Pseudo(?)-Simplicius." *Tijdsschrift voor Filosofie* 34 (1972): 761–822.

Brague, Rémi. *Le Restant: Supplément aux Commentaires du Ménon de Platon*. Paris: Les Belles Lettres, 1978.

Brandon, S. G. F. *Man and God in Art and Ritual*. New York: Scribner, 1975.

Brémond, A. "Un Texte de Proclus sur la prière et l'union divine." *Recherches de Science Religieuse* 19 (1929): 448–62.

Boyancé, Pierre. *Le Culte des Muses chez les Philosophes Grecs*. Paris: Editions E. de Boccard, 1972. (Originally published 1936)

———. "Théurgie et téléstique néoplatoniciennes." *Revue de l'Histoire des Religions* 147 (1955): 189–209.

Bréton, Stanislas. "Actualité du Néoplatonisme." *Revue des Théologiques et Philosophiques* (1973): 184–200.

———. "L'Homme et l'âme humaine dans les Oracles chaldaïques." *Diotima* 8(1980): 21–24.

———. *Philosophie et mathématique chez Proclus*. Paris: Beauchesne, 1969.

———. "Téléologie et ontogonie: Variations sur les 'Oracles chaldaïques.'" *Recherches de Science Religieuse* 66, no. 1 (1978): 5–26.

Brown, Peter. "Approaches to the Religious Crisis of the Third Century A.D." *English Historical Review* 83 (1968): 542–58. Reprinted in his *Religion and Society in the Age of St. Augustine*, 74–93. London: Faber and Faber, 1972.

———. *The Making of Late Antiquity*. Cambridge: Harvard University Press, 1978.

———. "The Philosopher and Society in Late Antiquity." In *The Center for Hermeneutical Studies in Hellenistic and Modern Culture*, 34:1–17. Edited by E. C. Hobbs and W. Wuellner. Berkeley: Graduate Theological Union, 1980.

———. *The World of Late Antiquity*. New York: Harcourt Brace Jovanovich, 1971.

Burkert, Walter. "Craft Versus Sect: The Problem of Orphics and Pythagoreans." *Jewish and Christian Self Definition*, edited by Ben Meyer and E. P. Sanders, 3:1–22, 183–89. Philadelphia: Fortress, 1982.

———. *Lore and Science in Ancient Pythagoreanism*. Translated by Edwin L. Minar Jr. Cambridge: Harvard University Press, 1972.

Cameron, Alan. "The Date of Iamblichus' Birth." *Hermes* 96 (1968): 374–76.

Charles, Annick. "L'Imagination, miroir de l'âme selon Proclus." In *Le Néo-platonisme*, 241–49. Paris: CNRS, 1971.

———. "La Raison et le divin chez Proclus." *Revue des Sciences Philosophiques et Théologiques* 53 (1969): 458–82.

Charles-Saget, Annick. *L'Architecture du divin: Mathématique et philosophie chez Plotin et Proclus*. Paris: Les Belles Lettres, 1982.

Chroust, Anton-Hermann. "Late Hellenistic Textbook Definitions of Philosophy." *Laval Théologique et Philosophique* 28 (1972): 15–25.

Chuvin, Pierre. *A Chronicle of the Last Pagans*. Translated by B.A. Archer. Cambridge: Harvard University Press, 1990.

Combès, Joseph. "*L'Anthropeion hen selon Damascius*." *Diotima* 8 (1980): 25–29.

————. "Damascius, lecteur du Parménide." *Archives de Philosophie* 38 (1975): 33–60.

————. "La Théologie aporétique de Damascius." In *Néoplatonisme: Mélanges offerts à Jean Trouillard*, 125–39. Paris: Les Cahiers de Fontenay, 1981.

————. "L'Un humain selon Damascius." *Revue des Sciences Philosophiques et Théologiques* 62 (1978): 161–65.

Corbin, Henry. *Avicenna and the Visionary Recital*. Translated by Willard Trask. Spring, Tex.: Spring Publications, 1980.

————. *Creative Imagination in the Sufism of Ibn Arabi*. Translated by Ralph Manheim. Princeton: Princeton University Press, 1969.

Cornford, Francis M. "Mysticism and Science in the Pythagorean Tradition." *Classical Quarterly* 16, no. 3 (1922): 137–50; 17, no. 1 (1923): 1–12.

Coulter, James. *The Literary Microcosm: Theories of Interpretation of the Later Neoplatonists*. Leiden: E.J. Brill, 1976.

Cremer, Friedrich W. *Die Chaldäischen Orakel und Jamblich de Mysteriis*. Meisenheim am Glan: Anton Hain, 1969.

Critchlow, Keith. "The Platonic Tradition on the Nature of Proportion." In *Lindisfarne Letter: Geometry and Architecture*, 11–32. Stockbridge, Mass.: Lindisfarne Press, 1980.

Cushman, Robert. *Therapeia: Plato's Conception of Philosophy*. Chapel Hill: University of North Carolina Press, 1958.

Daniélou, Jean. "Eunome l'Arien: L'exégèse néoplatonicienne du Cratyle." *Revue des Etudes Grecques*, 69 (1956): 412–32.

Derchain, Philippe. *Le Papyrus Salt 825* (B.M. 10051): *Rituel pour la conservation de la vie en Egypte*. Brussels: Paleis der Academien, 1965.

————. "Pseudo-Jamblique ou Abammon?" *Chronique d'Egypt* 38 (1963): 220–26.

des Places, Edouard. *Etudes platoniciennes*, 1929–79. Leiden: E.J. Brill, 1981.

————. "Les Oracles chaldaïques et Denys l'Aréopagite." In *Néoplatonisme: Mélanges Offerts à Jean Trouillard*, edited by Chantal Gillette, 291–95. Paris: Cahiers des Fonteray, 1981.

————. *Syngeneia: La Parenté de l'homme avec dieu d'Homère à la patris-tique*. Paris: Librairie C. Klincksieck, 1964.

de Vogel, C. J. "Problems Concerning Later Platonism I & II." *Mnemosyne* 4, nos. 2 and 3 (1949): 197–216, 299–318.

————. *Pythagoras and Early Pythagoreanism*. Assen: Van Gorcum, 1966.

————. "The *SŌMA-SĒMA* Formula: Its Function in Plato and Plotinus Compared to Christian Writers." In *Neoplatonism and Early Christian Thought*, 79–99. London: Variorum, 1981.

Devore, Nicholas. *Encyclopedia of Astrology*. New York: Philosophical Library, 1947.

Dihle, Albrecht. *The Theory of Will in Classical Antiquity*. Berkeley and Los Angeles: University of California Press, 1982.

Dillon, John. "The Descent of the Soul in Middle Platonic and Gnostic Theory." In *The Rediscovery of Gnosticism*, edited by Bentley Layton, 1:357–64. Leiden: E. J. Brill, 1980.

————. "Iamblichus and the Origen of the Doctrine of Henads." *Phronesis* 17, no. 2 (1972): 102–6.

————. "Iamblichus of Chalcis." In *Aufsteig und Niedergang der Römischen Welt*, Part II, 36. 2, 863–78. New York: de Gruyter, 1987.

————. *The Middle Platonists*. London: Duckworth, 1977.

————. "Speusippus in Iamblichus." *Phronesis* 29, no. 3 (1984): 325–32.

Dodds, E. R. *The Ancient Concept of Progress and Other Essays on Greek Literature and Belief*. Oxford: Clarendon Press, 1973.

————. *The Greeks and the Irrational*. Berkeley and Los Angeles: University of California Press, 1973.

————. "Iamblichus." *Oxford Classical Dictionary*. Oxford: Oxford University Press, 1970.

————. *Pagan and Christian in an Age of Anxiety*. New York: Norton, 1965.

————. "The Parmenides of Plato and the Origin of the Neoplatonic 'One.'" *Classical Quarterly* 22, nos. 3–4 (1928): 129–42.

————. "Tradition and Personal Achievement in the Philosophy of Plotinus." *Journal of Roman Studies* 2 (1960): 1–7.

Dornsieff, F. *Das Alphabet in Mystik und Magie*. 2 Auflage. Leipzig: B. G. Teubner, 1925.

Dörrie, H. "La Doctrine de l'âme dans le néoplatonisme de Plotin a Proclus." *Revue des Théologiques et Philosophiques* (1973): 116–34.

Duméry, Henry. "Le Néant d'être." *Etudes Philosophiques* 3 (1973): 315–27.

————. *The Problem of God in Philosophy of Religion*. Evanston: North-western University Press, 1964.

Dunn, Michael. "Iamblichus, Thrasyllus and the Reading Order of the Platonic Dialogues." In *The Significance of Neoplatonism,* edited by R.B. Harris, 59–80. Norfolk, Va.: International Society for Neoplatonic Studies, 1976.

Eitrem, S. "La Théurgie chez les néo-platoniciennes et dans les papyrus magiques." *Symbolae Osloenses* 31 (1942): 49–79.

Eliade, Mircea. *Yoga: Immortality and Freedom.* Translated by Willard Trask. Princeton: Princeton University Press, 1958; reprint 1969.

Festugière, A.-J. "Contemplation philosophique et art théurgique chez Proclus." *Studi di Storia Religiosa della Tarda Antichita* (1968): 7–18; reprint in A.-J. Festugière, *Etudes de Philosophie Grecque.* Paris: J. Vrin, 1971, 585–96.

———. *Etudes de philosophie grecque.* Paris: J. Vrin, 1971.

———. "La Pyramide hermètique." *Museum Helveticum* 6 (1949): 211–15.

———. *La Révélation d'Hérmès Trismégiste.* Vols. 1–4. Paris: Gabalda, 1950–54.

Finamore, John F. *Iamblichus and the Theory of the Vehicle of the Soul.* Chico, Calif.: Scholars Press, 1985.

Findlay, J.N. Plato: *The Written and Unwritten Doctrines.* New York: Humanities Press, 1974.

Fowden, Garth. *The Egyptian Hermes: A Historical Approach to the Late Pagan Mind.* New York: CambridgeUniversity Press, 1986.

———. "Late Antique Paganism Reasoned and Revealed." *Journal of Roman Studies* 71 (1981): 178–82.

———. "The Platonist Philosopher and His Circle in Late Antiquity." *Philosophia* 7 (1977): 359–83.

Friedländer, Paul. *Plato.* 3 vols. Translated by Hans Meyerhoff. New York: Bollingen Foundation; 1, 1958; 2, 1964; 3, 1968.

Gaiser, Konrad. *Platons Ungeschriebene Lehre.* Stuttgart: Ernst Klett, 1968.

Gersh, Stephen. *From Iamblichus to Eriugena: An Investigation of the Prehistory and Evolution of the Pseudo-Dionysian Tradition.* Leiden: E.J. Brill, 1978.

———. *KINĒSIS AKINĒTOS: A Study of Spiritual Motion in the Philosophy of Proclos.* Leiden: E. J. Brill, 1973.

Gilson, Etienne. *The Philosophy of St. Thomas Aquinas.* Translated by Edward Bullough. Edited by G.A. Erlington. New York: Dorset Press, 1948.

Griffiths, J.G. "Theurgy." Review of E. des Places, *Jamblique: Les Mystères d'Egypte.* Paris: Les Belles Lettres, 1966. Reprinted in *Classical Review,* n.s., 18 (1968): 52–55.

Guérard, Christian. "Le Danger du néant et la négation selon Proclus." *Revue Philosophique de Louvain* 83 (1985): 331–54.

———. "La Théologie négative dans l'apophatisme grec." *Revue des Sciences Philosophiques et Théologiques* 68 (1984): 183–200.

———. "La Théorie des Hénades et la mystique de Proclus." *Dionysius* (1982): 73–82.

Guthrie, W.K.C. *History of Greek Philosophy.* Vol. 6, *Aristotle: An Encounter.* New York: Cambridge University Press, 1981.

Haar, James. "Musica Mundana: Variations on a Pythagorean Theme." Ph.D. diss., Harvard University, 1960.

Hadot, Ilsetraut. *Le Problème du néoplatonisme alexandrin: Hiéroclès et Simplicius.* Paris: Etudes Augustiniennes, 1978.

Hadot, Pierre. "L'Etre et l'Etant dans le Néoplatonisme." *Revue de Théologie et de Philosophie* 2 (1973): 101–15.

———. "Exercices spirituels." In *Annuaire: Ecole Pratique des Hautes Etudes,* 63–70. Paris: Scolarité, 1976–77.

———. *Exercices spirituels et philosophie antique.* Paris: Etudes Augustiniennes, 1981.

———. "L'Homme 'plante céleste.'" *Etudes Philosophique* 16, no. 3 (1961): 79–83.

———. *Porphyre et Victorinus.* 2 vols. Paris: Etudes Augustiniennes, 1968.

———. "Théologie négative." *Encyclopedia Universalis* 15:1093–95. Paris, 1968.

Hankey, Wayne. "Aquinas' First Principle: Being or Unity?" *Dionysius* 4 (1980): 133–72.

Harris, R.B., ed. *The Significance of Neoplatonism.* Norfolk, Va.: International Society for Neoplatonic Studies, 1976.

Hathaway, Ronald. *Hierarchy and the Definition of Order in the Letters of Pseudo-Dionysius.* The Hague: Martinus Nijhoff, 1969.

———. "The Neoplatonist Interpretation of Plato: Remarks on its Decisive Characteristics." *Journal of the History of Philosophy* 7, no. 1 (1969): 19–26.

Hoffman, Philippe. "Jamblique exégète du Pythagoricien Archytas: Trois originalités d'une doctrine du temps." *Etudes Philosophique* 3 (1980): 307–23.

———. "Theurgie." *Pauly-Kroll-Mittelhaus,* vol. 6, part A, 258–70.

Hornung, Erik. *Conceptions of God in Ancient Egypt: The One and The Many.* Translated by John Baines. Ithaca: Cornell University Press, 1982.

Jambet, Christian. *La Logique des Orientaux: Henry Corbin et la science des formes.* Paris: Editions des Seuil, 1983.

Johnson, Sarah. *Hekate Soteira*. Atlanta, Ga.: Scholars Press, 1989.

Joly, Henri. "Platon égyptologue." *Revue Philosophique de la France et de L'Etranger*, no. 2 (1982): 255–66.

———. *Le Renversement Platonicien: Logos, épistémé, polis*. Paris: J. Vrin, 1974.

Kissling, Robert. "The *OCHĒMA-PNEUMA* of the Neoplatonists and the *de Insomniis* of Synesius of Cyrene." *American Journal of Philology* 43 (1922): 318–30.

Klein, Jacob. "About Plato's *Philebus*." *Interpretation: A Journal of Political Philosophy* 2, no. 3 (1971): 137–82.

Kramer, H. J. *Der Ursprung der Geistmetaphysik*. Amsterdam: P. Schippers, 1964.

Larsen, B. D. *Jamblique de Chalcis: Exégète et philosophe*. Aarhus: Universitetsforlaget, 1972.

———. "La Place de Jamblique dans la Philosophie antique tardive." In *Entretiens sur l'antiquité classique*, vol. 21: *De Jamblique à Proclus*, 1–30. Geneva: Fondation Hardt, 1975.

Lawlor, Robert. *Sacred Geometry*. London: Thames Hudson, Art and Imagination Series, 1982.

Leadbetter, L. W. "Aspects of the Philosophical Priesthood in Iamblichus' *De Mysteriis*." *Classical Bulletin* 47 (1971): 89–92.

Lewy, Hans. *Chaldean Oracles and Theurgy*. Edited by M. Tardieu. Paris: Etudes Augustiniennes, 1978.

Lloyd, A. C. *The Anatomy of Neoplatonism*. Oxford: Clarendon Press, 1990.

———. "The Later Neoplatonists." In *The Cambridge History of Later Greek and Early Medieval Philosophy*, edited by A. H. Armstrong, 269–325. Cambridge: Cambridge University Press, 1967.

———. "Neoplatonic Logic and Aristotelian Logic." *Phronesis* 1, nos. 1 and 2 (1956): 58–72, 146–59.

———. "Non-Discursive Thought: An Enigma of Greek Philosophy." *Proceedings of the Aristotelian Society* (1969–70): 261–74.

Lowry, J. M. P. *The Logical Principles of Proclus' STOICHEIŌSIS THEOLOGIKĒ as Systematic Ground of the Cosmos*. Amsterdam: Rodopi, 1980.

Mead, G. R. S. *The Doctrine of the Subtle Body in the Western Tradition*. Wheaton, Ill.: Theosophical Publishing House, 1967. (Originally published 1919)

Merlan, Philip. "Aristotle's Unmoved Movers." *Traditio* 4 (1946): 1–30.

———. *From Platonism to Neoplatonism*. 2d edition. The Hague: Martinus Nijhoff, 1960.

————. "Religion and Philosophy from Plato's *Phaedo* to the Chaldean Oracles." *Journal of the History of Philosophy* 1 (1963): 163–76.

Michel, P.H. *Les Nombres figurés dans l'arithmétique pythagoricienne.* Paris: Histoire des Sciences, 1958.

Miller, James. *Measures of Wisdom: The Cosmic Dance in Classical Antiquity.* Toronto: University of Toronto Press, 1986.

Nock, A. D. "Posidonius." *Journal of Roman Studies* 49 (1959): 1–15.

O'Brien, Denis. "Plotinus On Evil: A Study of Matter and the Soul in Plotinus' Conception of Human Evil." *Downside Review* 87, no. 286 (1986): 68–110.

O'Donnell, J. "The Demise of Paganism." *Traditio* 35 (1979): 45–88.

O'Meara, Dominic J. "New Fragments From Iamblichus' Collection of Pythagorean Doctrines." *American Journal of Philology* 102 (1981): 26–40.

————. *Pythagoras Revived: Mathematics and Philosophy in Late Antiquity.* Oxford: Clarendon Press, 1989.

————. *Structues hiérarchiques dans la pensée de Pseudo-Denys.* Leiden: E. J. Brill, 1975.

Pearson, Birger A. "Gnosticism as Platonism: With Special Reference to Marsanes (NHC 10, 1)" *Harvard Theological Review* 77, no. 1 (1984): 55–72.

————. "Theurgic Tendencies in Gnosticism and Iamblichus' Conception of Theurgy." In *Gnosticism and Neoplatonism*, edited by R.T. Wallis and Jay Bregman, 253–77. Norfolk, Va.: International Society for Neoplatonic Studies, 1992.

————. "The Tractate Marsanes (NHC X) and The Platonic Tradition." In *Gnosis: Festschrift für Hans Jonas*, edited by Barbara Aland, 373–84. Göttingen: Vandenhoeck and Ruprecht, 1978.

Pétrement, Simone. *Le Dualisme chez Platon: Les Gnostiques et les Manichéens.* Paris: Presses Universitaires de France, 1947.

Philip, J. A. "The Biographical Tradition—Pythagoras." *American Philological Association Transactions and Proceedings* (1959): 185–94.

————. *Pythagoras and Early Pythagoreanism.* Toronto: University of Toronto Press, 1966.

Préaux, Claire. "De la Grèce classique à l'Egypte hellénistique: Traduire ou ne pas traduire." *Chronique d'Egypte* 42 (1967): 369–83.

Rich, Audrey N.M. "The Platonic Ideas as the Thoughts of God." *Mnemosyne* 4, no. 7 (1954): 123–33.

Rist, John M. "Integration and the Undescended Soul in Plotinus." *American Journal of Philology* 88 (1967): 410–22.

―――. "Mysticism and Transcendence in Later Neoplatonism." *Hermes* 92, no. 2 (1964): 213–25.

―――. "Prohairesis: Proclus, Plotinus et alii." In *Entretiens sur l'antiquité classique*, vol. 21: *De Jamblique à Proclus*. Geneva: Fondation Hardt, 1975.

Robbins, Frank Egleston. "The Tradition of Greek Arithmology." *Classical Philology* 16, no. 2 (1921): 97–123.

Robin, Léon. *La Théorie platonicienne des idées et des nombres d'après Aristotle*. Hildesheim: Georg Olms, 1963. (Originally published 1908)

Rosán, Laurence J. *The Philosophy of Proclus: The Final Phase of Ancient Thought*. New York: Cosmos, 1949.

Rosen, Stanley. "The Role of Eros in Plato's Republic." *Review of Metaphysics* 18 (1965): 452–75.

Rougier, Louis. *La Religion Astrale des Pythagoriciennes*. Paris: Presses Universitaires de France, 1959.

Ruelle, C. E. "Alphabet vocalique des gnostiques." *Dictionnaire d'archéologie chrétienne et de liturgie*, 1:1268–88. Paris: Letouzey et Ane, 1907.

―――. "Le Chant des sept voyelles grecques." *Revue des Etudes Grecques* 2 (1889): 38–44.

Saffrey, H. D. "Abammon, pseudonyme de Jamblique." In *Philomathes: Studies and Essays in the Humanities in Memory of Philip Merlin*, 227–39. The Hague: Martinus Nijhoff, 1971.

―――. "La Dévotion de Proclus au Soleil." *Institut de Philosophie (et Science Morale) Annales*, 73–86. Brussels, 1984.

―――. "Les Néoplatoniciennes et les oracles chaldaïques." *Revue des Etudes Augustiniennes* 27 (1981): 209–25.

―――. "Quelques Aspects de la spiritualité des philosophes néoplatonicienes: De Jamblique à Proclus et Damascius." *Revue des Sciences Philosophiques et Théologiques* 68 (1984): 169–82.

―――. *Le PERI PHILOSOPHIAS d'Aristote et la théorie platonicienne des idées nombres*. Leiden: E. J. Brill, 1955.

―――. "The Piety and Prayers of Ordinary Men and Women in Late Antiquity." In *Classical Mediterranean Spirituality*, edited by A. H. Armstrong, 195–213. New York: Crossroad, 1986.

―――. "Plan des Livres I et II du *de Mysteriis* de Jamblique." In *Zetesis Album Amicorum*, edited by E. de Strycker, 281–95. Antwerp: De Nederlandsche Boekhandel, 1973.

Sambursky, S. *The Concept of Place in Late Neoplatonism*. Texts and Translation. Jerusalem: Israel Academy of Sciences and Humanities, 1982.

————. *The Concept of Time in Late Neoplatonism.* Texts and Translation. Jerusalem: Israel Academy of Sciences and Humanities, 1971.

————. *The Physical World of Late Antiquity.* New York: Basic Books, 1962.

————. "The Theory of Forms: A Problem and Four Neoplatonic Solutions." *Journal of the History of Philosophy* 4, no. 4 (1968): 327–39.

Sandmel, Samuel. *Philo of Alexandria.* New York: Oxford University Press, 1979.

Sauneron, Serge. *The Priests of Ancient Egypt.* Translated by Ann Morrissett. New York: Grove, 1960.

Scott, Walter, ed. and trans. *Hermetica: The Ancient Greek and Latin Writings Which Contain Religious or Philosophic Teachings Ascribed to Hermes Trismegistus,* vol. 1: *Texts and Translations;* vol. 2: *Notes on the Corpus Hermeticum;* vol. 3: *Notes on the Latin Asclepius and the Hermetic Excerpts of Stobaeus;* vol. 4: *Testimonia* (First ed., 1924–36; reprint, London: Dawsons, 1968; Boston: Shambhala, 1985).

Shaw, Gregory. "The Geometry of Grace: A Pythagorean Approach to Theurgy." *Incognita* 2, no. 1 (1991): 48–78. Reprinted in *The Divine Iamblichus: Philosopher and Man of Gods,* edited by H. J. Blumenthal and E. G. Clark, 116–37. London: Bristol Classical Press.

————. "Rituals of Unification in the Neoplatonism of Iamblichus." *Traditio* 41 (1985): 1–28.

————. "Theurgy as Demiurgy: Iamblichus' Solution to the Problem of Embodiment." *Dionysius* 12 (1988): 37–60.

Sheldon-Williams, I. P. "Henads and Angels: Proclus and the pseudo-Dionysius." *Studia Patristica,* 11:65–71. Berlin, 1972.

Sheppard, Anne D. R. "Proclus' Attitude to Theurgy." *Classical Quarterly* 32 (1982): 212–24.

————. *Studies on the 5th and 6th Essays of Proclus' Commentary on the Republic.* Göttingen: Vandenhoeck and Ruprecht, 1980.

Shorey, P. "Simplicius *de anima,* 146, 21." *Classical Philology* 17 (1922): 143–44.

Sicherl, Martin. *Die Handschriften, Ausgaben und Übersetzungen von Iamblichos de Mysteriis.* Berlin: Akademie-Verlag, 1957.

Smith, Andrew. *Porphyry's Place in the Neoplatonic Tradition: A Study in Post-Plotinian Neoplatonism.* The Hague: Martinus Nijhoff, 1974.

————. "Unconsciousness and Quasiconsciousness in Plotinus." *Phronesis* 23, no. 3 (1978): 292–301.

Smith, John H. *The Death of Classical Paganism.* London: Geoffrey Chapman, 1976.

Smith, Jonathan Z. *Map Is Not Territory.* Leiden: E. J. Brill, 1978.

—————. "Towards Interpreting Demonic Powers in Hellenistic and Roman Antiquity." In *Aufstieg und Niedergang der Römischen Welt,* part II. Principat 16.1. Berlin: de Gruyter, 1987, 425–39.

Steel, Carlos G. *The Changing Self: A Study on the Soul in Later Neoplatonism: Iamblichus, Damascius, and Priscianus.* Translated by E. Haasl. Brussels: Paleis der Academien, 1978.

Tannery, Paul. "Psellus sur les nombres." *Revue des Etudes Grecques* 5 (1892): 343–47.

Tarán, Leonardo. "Aristotle's Classification of Number in *Metaphysics* M 6, 1080a 15–37." *Greek, Roman, and Byzantine Studies* 19 (1979): 83–98.

—————. "The Creation Myth in Plato's *Timaeus.*" In *Essays in Ancient Greek Philosophy,* edited by John Auton, 3172–407. Albany: State University of New York Press, 1971.

—————. *Speusippus of Athens.* Leiden: E. J. Brill, 1981.

Tardieu, Michel. "Sabiens Coraniques et 'Sabiens' de Harran." *Journal Asiatique* 274 (1986): 1–44.

Tarrant, H. "Speusippus' Ontological Classification." *Phronesis* 19 (1974): 130–45.

Taylor, Thomas. *The Theoretic Arithmetic of the Pythagoreans.* London, 1816; York Beach, Maine: Samuel Weiser, 1983.

Thesleff, Holger. *An Introduction to the Pythagorean Writings of the Hellenistic Period.* Abo: Abo Akademi, 1961.

Thillet, Pierre. "Jamblique et les mystères d'Egypte." *Revue des Etudes Grecques* 81 (1968): 172–95.

Tigerstedt, E. N. *The Decline and Fall of the Neoplatonic Interpretation of Plato: An Outline and Some Observations.* Helsinki: Societas Scientiarum Tennica, 1974.

—————. *Interpreting Plato.* Stockholm: Almquist and Wiksell International, 1977.

Trouillard, Jean. "L'Activité onomastique selon Proclos." In *Entretiens sur l'antiquité classique,* vol. 21: *De Jamblique à Proclos,* 239–52. Geneva: Fondation Hardt, 1975.

—————. "Ame et esprit selon Proclus." *Revue des Etudes Augustiniennes* 1 (1959): 1–12.

—————. "Convergence des définitions de l'âme chez Proclus." *Revue des sciences philosophiques et théologiques* 45 (January 1961): 2–20.

—————. "Les Degrés du *poiein* chez Proclos." *Dionysius* 1 (1977): 69–84.

—————. "La Figure du choeur de danse dans l'oeuvre de Proclos." In *Permanence de la Philosophie,* 162–74. Neuchâtel: La Baconnière, 1977.

————. "Jamblique." *Encyclopedia Universalis*, 9:286–88. Paris, 1968.

————. "Le Lien de l'âme et du corps selon Proclos." *Diotima* 8 (1980): 128–33.

————."La médiation du verbe selon Plotin." *Revue Philosophique de la France et de l'Etranger* 146 (1956): 66–69.

————. *La Mystagogie de Proclos*. Paris: Les Belles Lettres, 1982.

————. "Le Néoplatonisme de Plotin à Damascios." *Histoire de la philosophie*. Encyclopédie de la Pléiade, vol. 1. Paris: Gallimard, 1969.

————. "Néoplatonisme et gnosticisme." In *Metaphysique et histoire de la philosophie* (Mélanges Brunner), 43–52. Neuchâtel: La Bacconière, 1981.

————. "Note sur *PROOUSIOS* et *PRONOIA* chez Proclus." *Revue des Etudes Grecques* 73 (1960): 80–87.

————. "La Notion de *DYNAMIS* chez Damascios." *Revue des Etudes Grecques* 85 (1972): 353–63.

————. *La Procession plotinienne*. Paris: Presses Universitaires de France, 1955.

————. "Proclos et la joie de quitter le ciel." *Diotima* 11 (1983): 182–92.

————. "La Puissance secrète du nombre chez Proclos." *Revue de Philosophie Ancienne* 1 (1983): 227–41.

————. *La Purification plotinienne*. Paris: Presses Universitaires de France, 1955.

————. "Reflexions sur *l'OCHĒMA* dans les 'Eléments de Théologie' de Proclus." *Revue des Etudes Grecques* 70 (1957): 102–7.

————. "Rencontre de néoplatonisme." *Revue de Théologie et de Philosophie* (1972): 1–14.

————. "Sacrements: La Théurgie païenne." *Encyclopedia Universalis*, 14:582–83. Paris, 1968.

————. "Le Sens des médiations proclusiennes." *Revue philosophiques de Louvain* 4(1957): 331–42.

————. "Sur un pluriel de Plotin et de Proclus." *Association Guillaume Budé* 4 (1958): 88–91.

————. "Le Symbolisme chez Proclos." *Dialogues d'Histoire Ancienne* 7 (1981): 297–308.

————. "Un Texte de Proclos sur la foi." In *La Croyance*, 149–60. Paris: Institut Catholique de Paris, 1982.

————. "Un (philosophies de l')." *Encyclopedia Universalis* 16:461–63. Paris, 1968–73.

————. *L'Un et l'âme selon Proclos*. Paris: Les Belles Lettres, 1972.

Van den Brock, R. "The Authentikos Logos: A New Document of Christian Platonism." *Vigiliae Christianae* 33 (1979): 260–86.

Wahshiya, Ibn. "The Long-Desired Knowledge of Secret Alphabets Revealed." In *La Magie arabe traditionnelle*, entitled by René Alleau, with introduction and notes by Sylvain Matton, 132–241. Paris: Retz, 1977.

Walker, D. P. *Spiritual and Demonic Magic from Ficino to Campanella.* London: Warburg Institute, University of London, 1958. Reprint, Liechtenstein, Klaus Reprint, 1976.

Wallis, R. T. *Neoplatonism.* London: Duckworth, 1972.

Westerink, L. G. *The Greek Commentaries on Plato's Phaedo,* Vol. 1: *Olympiodorus* (1976); Vol. 2: *Damascius* (1977). New York: North-Holland.

Whittaker, John. "The Historical Background of Proclus's Doctrine of the *AUTHUPOSTATA.*" In *Entretiens sur l'antiquité classique,* Vol. 21: *De Jamblique à Proclus,* 193–237. Geneva: Fondation Hardt, 1975.

———. "Neopythagoreanism and Negative Theology." *Symbolae Osloenses* 44 (1969): 109–25.

———. "Neopythagoreanism and the Transcendent Absolute." *Symbolae Osloensis* 48 (1973): 77–86.

Witt, R. E. "Platonism after Plotinus." *Diotima* 4 (1976): 87–97.

Zandee, J. *The Terminology of Plotinus and of Some Gnostic Writings, Mainly the Fourth Treatise of the Jung Codex.* Istanbul: Nederlands Historisch-archäologisch Instituut, 1961.

Zeller, Eduard. *Die Philosophie der Griechen.* 3 vols. Hildesheim: Georg Olms, 1963.

———. *Plato and the Older Academy.* Translated by S. F. Alleyne and A. Goodwin. New York: Russell and Russell, 1962.

Zintzen, Clemens. "Bemerkungen zum Aufstiegsweg der Seele in Jamblichs *De Mysteriis.*" In *Platonismus und Christentum: Festschrift für Heinrich Dörrie,* 312–28. Münster: Aschendorff, 198.

INDEX